Aline MacMahon

Aline MacMahon

Hollywood, the Blacklist, and the Birth of Method Acting

John Stangeland

UNIVERSITY PRESS OF KENTUCKY

Copyright © 2022 by The University Press of Kentucky

Scholarly publisher for the Commonwealth,
serving Bellarmine University, Berea College, Centre
College of Kentucky, Eastern Kentucky University,
The Filson Historical Society, Georgetown College,
Kentucky Historical Society, Kentucky State University,
Morehead State University, Murray State University,
Northern Kentucky University, Spalding University,
Transylvania University, University of Kentucky,
University of Louisville, University of Pikeville,
and Western Kentucky University.
All rights reserved.

Editorial and Sales Offices: The University Press of Kentucky
663 South Limestone Street, Lexington, Kentucky 40508-4008
www.kentuckypress.com

Cataloging-in-Publication data is available from the Library of Congress.

ISBN 978-0-8131-9606-0 (hardcover)
ISBN 978-0-8131-9607-7 (pdf)
ISBN 978-0-8131-9608-4 (epub)

This book is printed on acid-free paper meeting
the requirements of the American National Standard
for Permanence in Paper for Printed Library Materials.

Manufactured in the United States of America

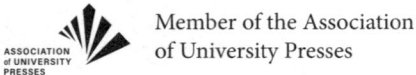

Member of the Association
of University Presses

To Christine, my partner in art, travel, food, film, and love.

CONTENTS

Introduction   1
1. Till the First Star Shook in the Air   6
2. Life Begins   28
3. Teach Me, and Set My Feet on the Way   50
4. The River of Stars is Rolling   65
5. No One Has Ever Known Her Alive   77
6. Once in a Lifetime   108
7. At Once They Circled Her Round   131
8. Reward Unlimited   147
9. Gold Digging   162
10. Seeds of Freedom   185
11. One Way Passage   211
12. The World Changes   231
13. We Fight It Round by Round   258
14. Ah, Wilderness   278
15. Set My Feet On the Way   297

Acknowledgments   309
Notes   311
Selected Bibliography   335
Index   337

INTRODUCTION

On New Year's Day, 1931, the *20th Century Limited* lumbered out of Grand Central Station, bound for Chicago. In the passenger car, hungover holiday revelers found their seats with difficulty and winced at the train's whistle as it passed out of Manhattan. At the far end of the car was a young woman with large, gloomy eyes, sitting alone, sobbing uncontrollably. Aline MacMahon should have been joyful that day; it was a new decade, and she was on the threshold of a great success, heading west to star in the Los Angeles production of the massive Broadway stage hit *Once in a Lifetime*. But even this amazing and long sought-after opportunity could not counterbalance the sad anticipation of an extended separation from her husband, the well-known architect and city planner Clarence Stein. While changing trains in Chicago, the tearful actress posted a letter to Clarence, back in New York. "To part," she began, "is to die a little."

Within months of arriving in California, Aline's enormous success as the cynical actress in *Once in a Lifetime* put stars in the eyes of Hollywood's power brokers. She had come to Los Angeles at the right time. The film industry was then only a few short years into its painful transition to sound pictures, and Hollywood was teeming with talent poached from the Broadway stages of New York. As the voiceless stars of silent film quietly faded away, they were replaced by a new generation of highly modern urban stylists. Along with her contemporaries James Cagney, Edward G. Robinson, Joan Blondell, and Ginger Rogers, Aline perfectly embodied this new fast-talking, street-smart creature of Depression-era America. By the autumn of 1931 Aline was on the nation's theater screens in Warner Brothers' gritty newspaper drama *Five Star Final* and being courted by every studio in the industry. It was the Warner Brothers who finally won the right to exploit her, acquiescing to Aline's stubborn insistence that her long-term contract contain a clause guaranteeing six months off every year to be in New York with her husband.

ALINE MACMAHON

Devoted to Clarence and keen to maintain a sense of proportion, she would periodically retreat to New York, to her marriage, family, and friends, to the real world outside the seductive, opaque chrysalis of Hollywood.

During Aline's decades commuting between Hollywood and New York, that first letter from Chicago soon grew to hundreds, then thousands, exchanged between the devoted couple. Their correspondence touched the trivial and the sublime—friends, politics, love, loneliness, money, work, travel, and art. When they were apart rarely a day went by when one didn't confide their thoughts to paper for the other to read. Over those years Aline and Clarence diligently saved and catalogued every scrap and sheet of paper in their decades-long correspondence as if they were love-struck teenagers. This massive personal archive includes Aline's private, heretofore unknown thoughts on the directors, writers, producers, and stars at the nervy heart of pre-Code Hollywood, and has never been seen by historians or film fans until uncovered and used in the preparation of this book. It is movie history in the moment.

Yet, even with the wealth of intimate and unseen details from those letters some might still ask, "Why Aline MacMahon"? In spite of quickly achieving above-the-title stardom, she is not particularly well known, even among fans of studio-era Hollywood, and no historian or critic has ever championed her as an important or transformative figure in the movies. Contemporary viewers know her primarily as the acerbic comedienne of *Gold Diggers of 1933* or *Once in a Lifetime*, but her time as a leading player was fleet, and the rest of her filmography has little that is familiar to mainstream film fans today. However, anyone who has read the life stories of enough movie stars knows that merely having a popular filmography does not make a satisfying book. That takes a life. And years of detective work into Aline MacMahon's life have revealed everything you could want in a biography: passionate romance, exotic travelogue, Victorian melodrama, political intrigue, and—above all—a subject who *is*, indeed, a transformative figure in movies and on the American stage.

The transformation began in the spring of 1923. At a mansion nestled among the rolling hills of Westchester County, New York, the twenty-four-year-old Aline MacMahon was taking part in a historic milestone. She was there as one of the first ten students anywhere in America to study the principles of Konstantin Stanislavski's Russian Method acting system, the revolutionary technique of emotional honesty and internal truth that would dominate stage and screen following World War II.

Introduction

History often tells us that after arriving in America the Method gestated in the New York acting schools of Lee Strasberg and Stella Adler for almost two decades before exploding into postwar public consciousness through the breakthrough success of Montgomery Clift in *Red River* (1948) and Marlon Brando's feral performance in *A Streetcar Named Desire* (1951). But that is not quite how it happened. Far earlier, that little workshop in upstate New York had already produced the true, invisible pioneer of the Method in America, Aline MacMahon. Of those onstage when Aline and her fellow students debuted the Method in the autumn of 1923, only she achieved mainstream success and fame on Broadway. And when Hollywood plucked Aline from the cast of *Once in a Lifetime* in the spring of 1931, she also became the first successful actor to bring this new voice to talking cinema. "I was in the first group to be exposed to what has become the Method," Aline said proudly, late in her six-decade career. "Out of that has developed everything that the Method actors are doing today." Stanislavski scholar Mel Gordon has called the Method's introduction to America "one of the most significant—if subterranean—cultural transmigrations in world history," and it all began with Aline MacMahon in a mansion at Pleasantville, New York, thirty miles north of Manhattan. Largely forgotten to history, the native pioneer of this migration launched her highly successful career a generation before Brando, over a decade before the Method-trained John Garfield, and years before even the Grande Dame of Method teachers, Madame Maria Ouspenskaya.

The beginning of this revolution is not difficult to see. From her first screen appearance as Edward G. Robinson's cynical secretary in *Five Star Final*, Aline MacMahon's modernity stands out as if plucked from the twenty-first century and placed among the magnificent declaration of the film acting of that earlier age. While the raw theatricality of Robinson's performance may be undeniably electric, it is Aline's understated simplicity that captures the modern eye. Unlike the dominant style of the era, Aline is playing the character, not emoting for the camera. With no knowledge of her Method training, critics and the public noticed the difference, and Aline was hailed as a new kind of actor for the screen: as unaffected and natural as the other performers were keenly manufactured. From the beginning, it was Aline's goal—nearly her obsession—to use the tenets of the Method in search of an emotionally honest, interior life. "I pass emotions through a filter not generally used by actresses," she once wrote. "I find the grounds to meet my characters and am able to move from one feel to another. It is real stuff—no tricks, simply expressed." When Aline MacMahon arrived on America's theater screens in 1931, it was truly the first look at something that moviegoers of the era could scarcely be expected to recognize—the future.

During her fifty-five years as a professional actress, Aline MacMahon was a welcome sight on stage, screen, and television, and rarely did she endure a bad review. "I have been seeing Aline MacMahon for more years than I'm going to be ungentlemanly enough to count," critic Walter Kerr once wrote. "Always she has pleased me, sometimes more, sometimes less, nevertheless always; she is an actress who in every dimension is wholly present, complete, and committed." This striving for total authenticity—a hallmark of her Method training—makes Aline's characterizations memorable regardless of their brevity, and reminds us that *good* acting is a remarkably human art. But make no mistake—although acting was an essential element of Aline MacMahon's self-image, it was not everything. Her life was too full and too diverse to be defined by mere work.

Outlined in these pages are the other dimly lit, barely known chapters of Aline MacMahon's remarkable story: A deep devotion to liberal politics that found her under long-term covert surveillance by the FBI and blacklisted during the anti-Communist witch hunt of the 1950s. The tragedy of mental collapse and a dark, *Cuckoo's Nest* hospitalization that stalled Aline's film career just as the intoxicating fruits of stardom were within reach. Old-world steamship voyages to China, Bali, Turkey, India, and Iran at a time when those destinations were still far-flung and rarely visited by polite Westerners. Intimate remembrances of Broadway royalty of the Roaring Twenties, including Aline's friends and coworkers in New York's clandestine LGBTQ subculture. Her encounters with great artists of the twentieth century, among them Eugene O'Neill, Thomas Wolfe, Aline Bernstein, E.E. Cummings, George Kaufman, Moss Hart, and Isamu Noguchi. And the long shadow of Aline's nationally renowned aunt Sophie Loeb, a childless social worker once called "America's greatest mother." All this, and the voluminous, daily diary of that amazing Hollywood era when the movies were momentarily known as "the talkies."

Shortly after Aline retired in 1975, she allowed an aspiring writer access to her personal archive—including the enormous, day-to-day chronicle of her early years in Hollywood that makes up the spine of this book. Although Aline herself was dubious of its value, the writer—the daughter of a close friend—saw great drama in her life. After some discussion, Aline was convinced to allow a literary agent to evaluate the archive for possible publication as a memoir. Within just a few days, however, a polite note from the agent appeared, saying that she did not believe there was a book to be gleaned

Introduction

from Aline's life story. It is likely that those letters—daunting in their number and scope—were not examined closely enough. If they had been, this book may have come to pass decades earlier. Fortunately, however, it has been *my* pleasure to decipher, sift, and triage the record of Aline MacMahon's life, and bring new focus on this seminal artist and woman of dignity and character.

As the past retreats, opportunities to be connected to it dwindle and history fades into fragments. Aline MacMahon's contribution to the evolution of American acting in the twentieth century has been splintered and lost. It is more than that of a mere practitioner; it is the midwife's hand. When she began performing as a child, the legitimate stage was mired deep in the throes of Victorian declamation and silent film was still the domain of uncouth pantomime. By the time of her final stage appearance alongside a promising newcomer, Meryl Streep, the modern naturalism that Aline helped birth in 1923 had grown to middle-aged adulthood. Follow the thread of Method acting in America back through Robert DeNiro and Marlon Brando to John Garfield and Maria Ouspenskaya and you will find Aline MacMahon holding the spool. She never sought credit for her part in the revolution, only the opportunity to use her talents to communicate honestly with an audience. This she did, paving the way for others. And that sounds something like a legacy.

1

TILL THE FIRST STAR SHOOK IN THE AIR

On a spring day in 1978, Aline MacMahon's mother, Jennie, was seated in the living room of the Spanish-style bungalow her famous daughter had purchased for her just off the Sunset Strip in Los Angeles. On the fireplace mantle was a letter from President Jimmy Carter, congratulating Jennie on having recently reached her hundredth birthday. Warmed by the California sun streaming through the windows at her back, Mrs. MacMahon—known affectionately as Jennie Mac—was being interviewed about her life and the acting career of her famous daughter. Still vigorous and mentally sharp at one hundred, Jennie Mac was also guileless in the pleasure she took from the attention placed on her by the reflected glow of Aline's fame. "As a child, I was stage struck and wanted to be an actress," Jennie began. "But in those days if you were an actress you were just *no good*. They weren't considered 'honest girls.' So I made up my mind that if I had a child and she had any talent, that I would let *her* be an actress." By the time Aline MacMahon was just three years old, her mother was—benignly, it must be added—grooming her for a life on stage and screen.

That afternoon, Mrs. MacMahon's memory drifted a hundred years into the past, across the Atlantic Ocean to a small town in Ukraine, Rovno, Guberniya, where she was born as Yachna Sosa Shimon in 1878.[1] Like the majority of Rovno's inhabitants, the Shimon family was Jewish, and Yachna's father, Samuel, was struggling to extract enough resources or money from the area to take care of five small children and bury a sixth that died at birth. With such hardship, Samuel Shimon resolved to follow the lead of so many other Russian Jews during the final years of the nineteenth century; he would set out for America and hope to make the money needed to bring the rest of the Shimon family to the Promised Land. Soon he was steaming across the

Aline's mother Jennie—known to all as Jennie Mac—was the primary catalyst for Aline's career. Not quite a stage mother, she taught her daughter to "speak pieces" as a young child and took her to perform at recitals as early as age six. Jennie Mac herself lived to the ripe old age of 106. Donated to NYPL by Aline MacMahon without copyright transfer.

Atlantic Ocean to New York City, where he disembarked and melded into the gray mass of slowly moving shadows spilling onto the streets of Manhattan.

"Mother never explained how or why it happened," Jennie allowed, but Samuel Shimon—freshly extruded from the Americanizing bureaucracy of Ellis Island as Sam Simon—found his way west, settling in the town of

McKeesport, Pennsylvania, fifteen miles from Pittsburgh. There, he took up work as a jeweler and clockmaker. "He was always working on these clocks," Jennie Mac recalled. "Clocks for different people from around the world. From Switzerland, from all different places, he was working on those timepieces."[2] Time was good to Sam Simon. In just two years he was able to bring his wife and five surviving children to America.

For rural Russians, a trip across the Atlantic seemed almost as much a journey through time as distance; in America, even humble McKeesport was centuries removed from Rovno's medieval poverty. By the time Jennie, along with her mother and Aline's future aunts and uncles Sophie, Abe, Israel, and Celia joined Sam, he had already established himself among the Jewish population of greater Pittsburgh. "There were quite a few Jewish families in McKeesport," Jennie recalled. Russia provided the second wave of Jews in McKeesport after the Hungarians had arrived there earlier in the decade. It was an opportune time for the Simon clan to settle in Allegheny County. With the coal-mining industry long established as an employer and steel production seeing exponential growth, McKeesport's population was steadily increasing. Although local anti-Semitism generally excluded Jews from mining and millwork, the need for trained craftsmen was booming. For the moment, it appeared that Sam Simon had made a good choice.

While Sam fixed jeweled movements and wound precision springs, there were not too many revolutions of the clock face before McKeesport saw him working behind the window of his own store. There, he sold jewelry purchased from local wholesalers and continued to repair the passage of time for his customers. Soon he was an established member of the professional guilds and associations that were so essential to the ethnic groups coming into America at that time. "My father belonged to several societies. And when they had meetings, my sister Sophie and I used to tell stories or sing there." This led to the sisters being pressed into service as extras for the road shows that came through McKeesport. "A lot of times the traveling companies didn't have children along," Jennie explained. "If a play came through town and they needed a child, they'd come to the Simon girls for it. I've been in *Uncle Tom's Cabin*—a lot of those plays." Here was the earliest origin of Jennie Mac's interest in the stage, and by extension, the eventual catalyst for Aline's entrance into a life of performance.

It was around 1890 that this pleasant story of immigrant success in midwestern America began to sour. According to family lore, Sam Simon was undone by his charitable nature. "He was very civic minded," Jennie said of her father's downfall. After his success in business, she said, "he wanted to do something for McKeesport, and he decided to build a natatorium." The term "natatorium"—a fancy Latin moniker for an indoor pool or bath facility—was known only slightly better to our nineteenth-century counterparts than it is today, which is to say hardly at all. The story of its failure is even more obscure. According to Aline, "[My grandfather Sam] had some big ideas about real estate, so he built this big natatorium. Well, alas, it failed and he lost everything."[3] Many reasons—or excuses—are given for Sam's real estate fiasco. The most popular version is that a fellow investor was to blame. "His partner absconded with all the money," Jennie said in 1978, repeating the tale she had been told by her mother almost ninety years earlier. However, after closely examining the Simon family oral history, there are enough inconsistencies that just one thing can be said with certainty: Sam had lost the family's only savings—his wife's dowry—on the venture. And—if you choose to believe it—he could not take the stress of the situation. "He had a nervous breakdown," Jennie recalled. Apparently Sam was so distraught that he was unable to continue work in the jewelry shop. According to Jennie Mac it was the family doctor that gave Sam the piece of advice that unraveled the very fabric of the Simon clan. "Father had friends who were going out to San Francisco, and the doctor said, 'Why don't you go with your friends to California? It will do you good to get away from all this.'" So, in 1891, behaving more like a man a half-step ahead of the law than a loving father, Sam Simon left his wife to navigate a crippling debt and raise five young children while he traveled 2,500 miles west for an indefinite time to take a dubious mental "cure." Only a few months later, Jennie and the other Simon children were dismayed by a new and unexpected change in their life. "My mother was pregnant with another child," Jennie said. "After that birth we were all supposed to go to California." But it was not to be—the vagaries of fate were not through with the Simon family. "My father died out there," Jennie said of the events that occurred the summer she turned thirteen. "And my mother suddenly had to raise six children with no income. So we all went to work."[4]

Jennie was forced to quit school and found employment in a butcher shop, handling the cash and merchandise that flew in baskets suspended from a lattice of wires above the heads of retail customers during those days. Jennie smiled at the memory, nearly ninety years past: "I sat way up high, with all those baskets going back and forth, with the money in them. How anybody would trust a girl thirteen years old for that, that's remarkable." In short order everyone was doing their part; Jennie's older brother Abe worked his

ALINE MACMAHON

Aline's hometown of McKeesport, Pennsylvania, circa 1905, just about the time her father William packed up the family and moved to Brooklyn.

way through school and was soon an attorney, while Israel worked in real estate. Jennie's older sister Sophie—then barely sixteen years old—was able to balance work with study and, following her graduation from high school, became the local elementary school teacher. "You didn't need a degree to teach in those days," Jennie explained.

Here, Fate—generally visible only in hindsight—can be seen pointing one of her long fingers. In Victorian-era America, there were no social or financial resources to improve the dire circumstances in which the Simons found themselves. Writing in 1920, Sophie reflected on the strength of her mother's resolve in shepherding her children through the crisis with no support system. "It was only through her Herculean effort," she said, "that each of us secured the proper foundation for self-reliance to face the future.[5] I must say that what little I am today I owe to the orthodoxy and teachings of my mother." This tragedy of the Simon children's early life inflicted a particularly deep wound on Sophie's psyche. Molded by these forces seeded in her youth, Sophie Simon developed into one of the great figures of social justice in the early twentieth century. Before she was out of her teens Sophie's life's course had been set—she would make effort to see that no family would go through what the Simon family was forced to endure. Soon, her byline was appearing in the McKeesport newspaper above a column championing causes of the underprivileged. In 1896 Sophie married Anselm Loeb, and following their divorce in 1910 she was offered a column in Joseph Pulitzer's prestigious New York *Evening World*. Moving to Manhattan, Sophie turned out widely read essays, articles, and books on the necessity of help for widowed mothers and orphans. Within a few short years Sophie Irene Loeb became internationally famous as a tireless champion of charitable causes for lost youth of the world, having helped to found the Child Welfare Committee of America. On her untimely death in 1929, the *New York Times* called her "America's Greatest Mother,"[6] and she was lionized as "the woman who had done more than any other person to bring home to the general public what child welfare really means."[7] If you live in New York and have taken advantage of the local civic centers, eaten a school lunch, received help from the state relief system or Widowed Mothers Fund, you have likely benefited from programs that Aline MacMahon's aunt Sophie helped bring into reality. Sophie was influential enough for New York to also memorialize her in stone and concrete. Amid the youthful chaos at Levin Playground in Central Park is an octagonal stone fountain dedicated to her memory carrying the inscription "Her Greatest Wealth Was Her Heart of Gold," and in Chinatown the Sophie Loeb Playground has been entertaining children in her name since 1933. Sam Simon's true, lasting legacy—a century of charity for orphaned children and single mothers—was the result of the psychological toll visited on his eldest daughter when he left his family.

Earlier, low in the paternal branches of Aline MacMahon's family tree was a man incessantly traveling the Midwest. In later years Aline loved to relate the history of her grandfather's early years as if she were reading a fable to a child. "In the mountains of Kentucky," she would begin, "there came every season a Jewish peddler with a pack on his back. The man who carried it was, they said in the mountains, a Frenchman because he had an accent and his name was Laveen. And he fell in love with a very tall Kentucky lady and they married." If her audience was made up solely of adults, Aline would then add, in her deadpan style, "Every time he came back on the tour there was *another* baby."[8] Eventually they numbered thirteen.

Among the girls born to the tall Kentucky woman was Aline's paternal grandmother, Rose Laveen, donor of her mellifluent middle name. When Rose eventually got engaged to John MacMahon—an Irishman—her father nearly disowned her. According to Jennie Mac, "He said he would only forgive her for marrying a shaygets [Yiddish slang for a non-Jew] if the first boy would be a Jew." As a Jewish woman in a mixed marriage, all Rose's children would clearly be ethnically Jewish, but they would also need to be circumcised, not something her Irish husband might necessarily accept in nineteenth-century America. Here is where Aline dropped the children's story. "When Rose had her first boy, she named him William for her favorite brother, and in order to identify him with that brother—and to appease her father—she had him circumcised." Aline's father, William MacMahon—the one and only circumcised MacMahon boy—had now entered the story.

William MacMahon eventually made his way to Pennsylvania as a telegraph operator, arranging dots and dashes for the McKeesport *Times* newspaper. In 1896—shortly before her marriage to Anselm Loeb—William became acquainted with the perspicacious Sophie Simon. As Aline tells the story, "My dad originally came to call on my Aunt Sophie—my mother's sister. He was interested in her because she was the brilliant one in the family." Brilliant, certainly, but not always timely. "When my father called on Sophie, my mother Jennie came to the door because Sophie was late, and they fell in love! It really happened—he walked up the steps, my mother opened the door and that was it!"[9] Time thus continued its mercurial influence on the Simon family.

William MacMahon and the eighteen-year-old Jennie would quickly find that things had not changed much from the previous generation; nineteenth-century prejudices were still deeply ingrained. "My grandmother was incensed at the idea of an Irishman taking out her Jewish child," Aline said. "She told my mother 'If you bring him into this house, I'll pour boiling water on his head!'" The forbidden love between a Jewish girl and an "Irish" boy—let's remember that William's mother was Jewish and he was circumcised—soon resulted in a long estrangement between Jennie and her mother.

After two years of courtship, when it was clear that regardless of William's Jewish heritage there would never be a blessing for the union from mother Simon, the couple eloped. "We ran away to get married," Jennie recalled. "We went to Youngstown, Ohio. It was a very, very hot day in July, and the reform rabbi was on vacation. But I wanted to make sure I was properly married because my mother never would have forgiven me." Now sharing, perhaps, too much information, Jennie continued: "Of course the only way they could tell a Jew was the circumcision, and when we were married my husband had to show that he was circumcised. I had to get a certificate

The unmistakable sleepy eyes of Aline MacMahon are already evident in this portrait with her father William and mother Jennie. At just three years old, Aline has the serene look of a cultured Tsarina. *New York Public Library, *T-Mss 1990.011.* Donated to NYPL by Aline MacMahon without copyright transfer.

from the *not* reform rabbi to show my mother that I was properly married in the orthodox way!" When husband and wife returned to McKeesport to announce their nuptial, mother Simon finally removed her embargo on Jennie's semi-interracial marriage. "When Granny found out that Jennie had married an Irishman who'd been circumcised," Aline said, "it was alright. And of course my father was utterly charming and became the favorite of the family!"[10]

The newly married William MacMahon harbored ambitions beyond mere telegraphy. A diligent, thoughtful man, Aline's father also worked as a stock broker and dreamed of making a career as a writer in New York. "He wanted to be an author," Jennie said. "He worked all day, then at nighttime he would write stories." William MacMahon was soon regularly sending pieces to New York magazines, including the popular and influential *Munsey's Magazine*, a powerhouse of Victorian-era publishing. "I heard that typewriter going with two fingers every night," Aline recalled decades later. "He was a very disciplined man."

"At the beginning we had no money. I bought a sewing machine and made my own clothes," Jennie remembered. "I wore the same dress for two years before I noticed I had made a mistake and only put half a pattern in front! But we had to start somewhere." On May 3, 1899, barely ten months after their wedding, Jennie and William MacMahon welcomed their one and only child, Aline Laveen MacMahon, to the family.

For a family that combined Irish-Catholic and Jewish traditions, the MacMahon household just after the turn of the century was quite cavalier concerning the concept of faith. "My father was very vague about religion," Aline said of her early home life. "And my mother became very vague about it after I was born, because she did not insist that I go to synagogue. I *did* keep the Jewish holidays as a child though, because it was very nice to get out of school!" During the Christian holidays, Aline also enjoyed the other side of the family coin. "Every Christmas," Jennie said, "the minute Aline was born, we had a Christmas tree, because Christmas was *so* beautiful in McKeesport and I envied the Christian children and their celebrations."[11] Although Aline generally identified as Jewish and maintained a lifelong interest in Jewish culture, these dual influences in her youth resulted in an amorphous relationship with religion. She never became affiliated with any church, and observed no traditions or dogma—Jewish or Christian—during her life. According to Aline, her father had an adage about her mixed heritage. "He said that because of those two halves that I 'ran with the hares and hunted with the hounds.'

By age seven Aline MacMahon was a well-known figure among the child elocutionists of New York City. Aline recalled her father telling her that "among the violinists I was a pretty good elocutionist and among elocutionists I was a fair fiddler." *New York Public Library, *T-Mss 1990.011.* Donated to NYPL by Aline MacMahon without copyright transfer.

I never knew who he meant to be the hares and who the hounds."[12] In the end it was still her maternal heritage that held a slight advantage. "I think everyone ought to be a little Jewish," she often said.

After finding some success selling short stories to *Munsey's Magazine*, William MacMahon decided that his aspirations as a writer would be more realistic if he lived in New York City. In 1902, Aline's father secured a job as an arbitrage broker with the New York Stock Exchange and moved the family to the Brooklyn neighborhood of Borough Park, just as a wave of Jewish immigrants began populating the area. "My parents chose a house in Borough Park because they thought it would be 'healthy' for me to live in the country," Aline said.[13] According to Jennie Mac it was here that she noticed something unique about Aline. "She was only three years old when I realized that she had a talent. We lived in one of those railroad flats, where you go through one room to another to another. One night we had a party and Aline had been put to bed. Just as the guests were about to leave I saw her get up and come through. She was singing, and said [imitating comments made by the partygoers], 'And she walked like this, and she walked like that.' Then, I realized that she had mimicking talent." Suddenly, Jennie MacMahon had a project: to create in Aline the actress she was never allowed to be. Although not *quite* the quintessential stage mother, Jenny Mac was positively the catalyst for Aline's career path. "I was delighted when I found that Aline liked to speak. From then on I taught her all the rhymes and pieces—everything that I could get."[14]

Later in life, Aline MacMahon looked back at Jennie's influence during her formative years not as a burden, but rather a bedrock foundation of her art. "Mother had trained me to learn all the pieces that she knew. *Learner's Elocution Book* was very popular at that time, so that was my early training. And when she started taking me by the hand and going around to different religious things and performing at their festivals, it was inevitable that I was going to be an actress. I was a show off."

In the era before television, radio, or even the serious spread of the motion picture, public speaking programs were ubiquitous as a low-cost evening's entertainment. A typical bill might consist of as many as fifteen or twenty recitations of various lengths, usually by children and young adults. Poems, short stories, monologues, and religious texts were interspersed with music, and the performers often used pantomime and dramatic gestures to enhance the emotional content of their readings. As a protégé of her self-trained mother, Aline had some modest success at these local gatherings. But it wasn't long before Aline had wrung everything possible out of the teachings she received at home. To ascend to the next stage of the career her mother had set out for her, it was clear that Aline would need professional training in elocution.

A curious relic of Western upper- and middle-class life, the elocution movement had its heyday from the early nineteenth century until World War I, during which time wealthy families—and middle-class, social-climbing families—sent their children to learn the art of public speaking. Proper elocution education included not only memorizing poems and stories, but all aspects of delivering successful public readings—recitation, articulation, inflection, accent, emphasis, voice, gesture, stance, and dress. By the time Aline was six, she was performing regularly around Brooklyn and Manhattan, and making handsome money for a girl just after the turn of the century. "They paid fifteen dollars for three pieces," she remembered with pride. "I went to all the churches, I went to every Strawberry Festival in Brooklyn and recited—religious ceremonies, everywhere." As Aline grew older and more accomplished, she often performed to musical accompaniment—a subgenre of the elocution movement, dominated by young women and girls—and eventually also performed her own music. "I played the violin, badly, but I played at concerts and recited the same night, and my father—who had a good sense of humor and kept me in my place—observed that among the violinists I was a pretty good elocutionist and among elocutionists I was a fair fiddler."[15]

As the result of William's success on the stock exchange, the MacMahon family's early years in Brooklyn were prosperous ones. "For about five years we were rich," Aline said. "But in the panic of 1907 my father lost a lot of money and his job." Through his part-time writing career, William MacMahon was fortunate to have made connections in Frank Munsey's publishing empire, which included the popular *Munsey's Weekly*, the seminal pulp fiction magazine *Argosy*, and as many as seventeen newspapers. From this freelance arrangement he was able to transition to an associate editor's job with *Munsey's*, where he stayed for decades. "After that we were just comfortable," Aline said with mock disappointment.

Before the new century even matured into its teens, Aline MacMahon had already been tramping the stages of New York and New Jersey for nearly six years, reciting prose and poetry, singing songs, and playing her violin. Upon this groundwork Aline was gradually gaining a modest local reputation for her precociousness and poise, and was simultaneously giving her

The twelve-year-old stage elocutionist Aline MacMahon, in the costume she donned for her reading of the lyrics to the popular story song "My Little Kickapoo." Donated to NYPL by Aline MacMahon without copyright transfer.

mother the opportunity to vicariously bathe in the reflected glow of her success. "She did what I wanted to do," Jennie admitted.[16] Here perhaps is where a granule of discontent crept into the mother–daughter relationship. Although Aline loved her mother, she perceived Jennie as the primary disciplinarian in the household, regularly setting her schedules and lessons, and receiving subconscious resentment for it. Meanwhile, Aline's father, content to love his daughter with no ulterior motives or agenda, forged the closer bond and became first in Aline's affections.

While Aline was raking in adult earnings by performing at church socials and festivals, she was also attending Borough Park's PS 103 grammar school on 14th Avenue. At the school she found a mentor in Miss Lillian Shaw, a teacher with a love of drama and the stage who organized local shows featuring her students. Many of these programs attracted as many as 500 people to the Borough Park Clubhouse, and contained a veritable blizzard of dramatic readings, dances, music, playlets, and blackouts—sometimes as many as forty individual pieces with nearly as many performers.

Aline's appearances on Miss Shaw's local programs were frequent and varied. Among them she sang the Indian-themed love song "My Little Kickapoo," recited the popular 1904 poem "Little Orphant Annie," performed a skirt dance, essayed a recitation of "You're Just the Boy for Me," and did a star turn as Miss Liberty in "My Dream of the U.S.A." In Flushing, Queens, she took five encores for her reading of "The Old Man and Jim," a poem about a farm boy going to war, expertly delivered by Aline in southern patois.[17] In 1909 she performed a series of songs and dances to an audience of 800 people at a benefit for the expansion of St. Jude's Church, and the following year sang "I'm Bringing Up a Family" at a charity event for the Henrietta Aid Society. At the famous Wanamaker's department store in Manhattan, Aline had a weekly Saturday afternoon engagement entertaining children while their parents shopped. And in an era of entrenched sexist attitudes that meant boys routinely dominated local contests, her reading of Alfred Noyes' "The River of Stars" made Aline the only girl in Brooklyn to win a prestigious gold medal in elocution.[18] After Aline became well known on Broadway, a grammar school classmate recalled the formative years of her old friend. "Aline MacMahon ... is merely following along a line of work which she began when she was a mere child some fifteen years ago. When I knew her at Borough Park School, she had a wonderful impersonating talent. I remember her crashing the gates at no less than six different Sunday school gatherings, impersonating absent members. Miss MacMahon simply can't help acting. It's part of her

Brooklyn Grammar School P.S. 103, where Aline found her first community of friends and teachers interested in the performing arts.

life."[19] In short, before she too was in her teens, Aline MacMahon was preparing for a life on stage and screen.

In early April 1911, less than a month before her twelfth birthday, Aline gave a reading for the International Art Society at New York's sumptuous Hotel Astor in Times Square. In it she recited a series of poems by the enormously popular writer James Whitcomb Riley, including "An Old Sweetheart of Mine," which recounted the tender story of an elderly man who comes across a photograph of an old flame:

> ... *The lamplight seems to glimmer with a flicker of surprise,*
> *As I turn it low, to rest me of the dazzle in my eyes,*
> *And light my pipe in silence, save a sigh that seems to yolk*
> *Its fate with my tobacco, and to vanish with the smoke* ...

From these seemingly innocuous lines a controversy was born, and a building block of the social conscience of the adult Aline MacMahon was unknowingly mortared into place.

The United States in 1911 was a largely conservative and primarily rural society. More than two-thirds of Americans still lived in the country and distrusted the character of those that resided in the big cities. Populist movements against sex education, alcohol, contraception, and general immorality were ubiquitous, well funded, and vocal. It was the era of America's first modern Evangelists: Billy Sunday, Henry Ward Beecher, and Carrie Nation, each of whom denounced iniquity and sin wherever—and in whatever infinitesimal amounts—they found it. Among these temperance crusaders and morality movements was a strong antitobacco lobby, which had recently helped secure a ban on the sale or distribution of cigarettes and cigars in thirteen states.

In New York the leading maven of the anti-tobacconists was Charles G. Pease—doctor, dentist, pathologist, and self-appointed killjoy of human pleasure. Besides tobacco, Mr. Pease also publicly railed against the perceived evils of alcohol, coffee, tea, vinegar, and ginger ale, as well as the consumption of meat, cocoa, chocolate, various condiments, and (seriously) lollipops. Most misguidedly, he advocated a complete, worldwide ban on women's corsets. Unfortunately, this puritanical rabble-rouser was sitting in the audience as a member of the International Arts Society when young Aline MacMahon had the temerity to quote Mr. Riley's poem containing a reference to tobacco.

Pease wasted no time in letting his outrage be known, raising a row that night at the Hotel Astor and later alerting New York's notoriously yellow press to the transgression. "In this poem," Mr. Pease indignantly told newspaper reporters after the event, "the opium of the West, tobacco, was mentioned four times, and presented in a voluptuous and seductive way not fit even for a fourth-rate concert hall exclusively for adults." In high dudgeon, Pease continued: "But when presented by a precocious child before children, some of very tender years, it constitutes a crime against the human family."[20] Apparently Mr. Pease was entirely unfamiliar with the concept of proportion.

While it was clear to most everyone that the eleven-year-old Aline MacMahon had done nothing wrong, much less committed a crime against humanity, the controversy quickly found column space in six separate New York newspapers. And although it would take eight years and a world war to make tobacco a mainstream habit among Americans, Charles Pease succeeded only in accomplishing the very opposite of his goal: he inadvertently made Aline the David in a very mismatched battle against his Goliath. The head of the International Art Society, Mrs. J. Christopher Marks, wasted no time speaking vigorously against the crusading doctor. "The poem of James Whitcomb Riley speaks for itself. It could arouse unfavorable comments from no one except such a man as Mr. Pease."

Aline's aunt Sophie Irene Loeb was a newspaper columnist and nationally famous crusader for the rights of single mothers and orphaned children. Aline's liberal social conscience began as a teenager when Sophie took her along on regular inspections of New York City's slums. *Library of Congress, LC-USZ62-116626*

Aline's parents—and the community—quickly rallied to her defense. When an outraged Pease threatened to resign from the society unless the reading was condemned, Mrs. Marks speedily accepted his offer. "Mr. Pease is a nuisance and we're glad to be rid of him," she enthused.[21] Sitting quietly in her teapot as the tempest whirled around her, the eleven-year-old elocutionist of more-or-less liberal parents learned a valuable lesson about the exercise of blind authority. It was one of Aline's first opportunities to see people—especially people she personally knew and admired—stand up for what was right. It was a lesson she did not forget.

By her final year of grammar school at Brooklyn's PS 103, the silhouette of Aline MacMahon's life was already taking shape. "I knew I was going to be an actress by then," she insisted. "It was inevitable, because my mother had trained me so well."[22] Aline was encouraged not only by her mother but also her grandmother, who by that time had softened the disdain she held for acting, as long as she deemed it socially acceptable. "When my grandmother came to visit us in New York, we always went to Second Avenue and saw Boris Thomashefsky." The Yiddish Theater was then nearly at the height of its influence in Manhattan, and in addition to Thomashefsky Aline saw all the stars of the era performing in the height of classical style. "I may be absurd, but I have a feeling that my emotions flow more freely because of my Jewish background," she once said, hesitantly. "I don't know."[23] All these experiences were conspiring to push Aline closer and closer to a career on stage.

Another of Aline's lifelong passions was also already taking hold in the spring of 1912. That season, Aline became one of the rotating student editor/writers of a half-page feature called the "Junior Daily Eagle" that appeared in the *Brooklyn Daily Eagle* newspaper. That spring she penned a column extolling the school's weekly program of stereopticon slides (a forerunner of the filmstrip), featuring photographs of far-flung foreign locations and cultures. "Among the most interesting scenes," she wrote, "are to be found descriptions of China, Switzerland, the United States and India."[24] Undoubtedly this is the seed from which the inveterate and adventurous world traveler of Aline's adult years sprang. For decades, she and her husband embraced a wanderlust that took them across the world in search of new sights and experiences. It certainly seems no accident that following her college graduation in 1920, Aline's first trip outside of America was to Switzerland, followed in 1930 by a long stay in India, and just six years later a five-month sojourn living in China and other points in the Far East. Those humble slides had a powerful influence in the days before the Internet, television, radio, color photography, or talking pictures.

In the summer of 1912, Aline was poised to move on to the next level of education. For an aspiring actress near the beginning of the twentieth century, there were few New York–area high schools better than Erasmus Hall in Brooklyn's Flatbush neighborhood, adjacent to Borough Park. Erasmus Hall's dedication to the arts extended back to 1786, when it was established as the

At the height of her elocution career, teenage Aline MacMahon was already a professional powerhouse, earning adult wages at recitals and readings across greater New York. Donated to NYPL by Aline MacMahon without copyright transfer.

first secondary school chartered by New York State. The original schoolhouse, constructed using donations from, among others, adversaries in a famously fatal duel, Alexander Hamilton and Aaron Burr, can still be seen today, nestled inside the quadrangle created by the buildings that expanded the school's footprint between 1904 and 1940. The day Aline arrived in the summer of 1912, she passed through the imposing, Tudor-inspired entrance hall on Flatbush Avenue and found what had been lacking in her creative life until then—a community. Before high school Aline's influences consisted primarily of Jennie Mac, her local elocution teacher, and the other adolescent performers who crossed paths on New York's Strawberry Festival circuit. Erasmus Hall, however, was positively brimming over with teachers and students who loved music, theater, and dance, and Aline was thrilled to make friends who shared her enthusiasm. Before Aline arrived, a tremendous array of artists and actors found similar creative energy there, including Clara Bow, Jane Cowl, Moe Howard, Mae West, and Norma Talmadge. And in the following decades the shadows of Mickey Spillane, Barbara Stanwyck, Eli Wallach, Jeff Chandler, Betty Comdon, Susan Hayward, Bernard Malamud, Neil Diamond, and Barbra Streisand also passed across the school's limestone facade.

Almost immediately Aline joined Erasmus Hall's long-standing drama club, the Garrick Dramatic Society, a group dedicated to putting on challenging productions that pushed the boundaries of typical high-school theatrics. During her years at the Flatbush school Aline appeared in Garrick programs as varied as Gilbert and Sullivan's operetta *Iolanthe* (which Aline and cast spent months planning), the Indian-themed drama *Strongheart*, and Winchell Smith's comedy farce *The Fortune Hunter*. At the same time, she was a charter member of the Junior International Arts Society (a spin-off of the progressive group that had so handily dispatched Mr. Charles Pease from their ranks following the imbroglio surrounding "An Old Sweetheart of Mine") and an editor on the monthly paper *The Erasmian*. Aline was so ubiquitous and enthusiastic that twenty years later a schoolmate writing a remembrance of his Erasmus years recalled her fondly: "Aline MacMahon—steeped in high school theatrics, getting the training that would later see her name emblazoned in the theatrical world."[25] The only others that remained in the author's memory of those days were boys of his acquaintance who he described with profound feeling and respect. All had died fighting in the Great War.

By her sophomore year in Erasmus Hall it was clear to her teachers that Aline MacMahon was that rare student—the one who was truly dedicated to art, not merely biding time until a husband, or children, or a more commonplace profession came along to push it aside. One of them, Jerome Schaeffer, was impressed enough to become a mentor to Aline, and in early 1914 suggested that she prepare for her professional debut. Although Aline had been making money with her readings for years, this would be her first stage appearance as a true professional actor. With her parents' approval, Mr. Schaeffer arranged a program to feature Aline's readings of selected scenes and poems with musical accompaniment. "When I was fifteen I gave a recital at the McAlpin Hotel," she remembered with some bemusement. "I was billed as 'The Entertaining Girl.'" The McAlpin, then just two years old, was at that moment the largest hotel in the world—and at twenty-five stories, one of the tallest buildings in New York. In its day it was a marvel of engineering and architecture, with a staff of 1,500 and rooms for 2,500 guests. It boasted all the amenities the hotel industry could imagine: restaurants, saunas, post office, gymnasium, Turkish baths, gender-specific floors, and soundproofed, darkened rooms for night-shift workers.

Amid such opulence, quality entertainment was also needed for the guests. On the evening of April 22, 1914, fourteen-year-old Aline MacMahon was that entertainment. "It was a terrible, snowy night," Aline recalled of the late-season blizzard that blanketed the city that spring.[26] Her program was wide ranging, including excerpts from Shakespeare ("All the World's a Stage" from *As You Like It* and two scenes from *Romeo and Juliet*), single-act monologues, and poetry readings. A few days later *Brooklyn Life* reported on her debut, calling the program "very finished," and pronouncing her Shakespeare readings "particularly good." If we can truly date the start of Aline's professional career from this program, she now has only sixty-one years to go before retirement.

While Aline was gathering the tools of her future profession, her aunt Sophie Loeb was becoming a major force in public policy and charity causes in New York. She was now nationally famous through her column in the New York *Evening World* and the political connections she had developed in the city. In Aline, Sophie saw an energy and drive similar to her own. Hoping to prod her niece toward a career in social causes and charity, Sophie soon began toting Aline with her on wellness calls and inspection tours of the slums of New York. "I saw life in the raw," Aline said of her travels with Sophie. "I saw the poverty and tragedy of immigrant families struggling for a toehold in their new country."[27] The sordid life of New York's underprivileged made a deep impression on Aline, but not in the exact manner that her aunt had hoped. The things Aline saw in the tenements and on the streets of

New York did indeed provide the framework of a social conscience that lingered through her life in the form of curiosity about issues of equity and Communist theory. But more importantly for Aline, they provided a deep wellspring of unique memories—sights, sounds, smells, behaviors, and emotions that would prove useful when she began the serious study of acting. After her introduction to the Russian Method school, she began to understand that those emotions from her youth could be called upon again and again to inform her characters on stage and screen.

As her senior year at Erasmus Hall waned, it was now time for the MacMahon family to consider Aline's educational future. Since the stock market downturn that crippled their finances, William MacMahon's job in the Munsey's publishing empire had solidified into a career. Although he was variously purported to be the New York correspondent for the *Chicago Tribune*, an editor with the *Associated Press*, and the Editor-in-Chief of Frank Munsey's flagship magazine, he appears actually to have had a low-level editorial position in the company. But William MacMahon was nothing if not a devoted and loving father to his only daughter. That season he resolved to place Aline in New York City's premiere college for women. Not he, nor Jennie Mac, Sophie, or even Aline could guess the series of professional and personal ripples that would expand out from her entrance into the halls of higher learning.

2

LIFE BEGINS

In the Upper West Side Manhattan neighborhood of Morningside Heights, a gently rising slope up Broadway gives way to a natural high point, known locally as the "Academic Acropolis" for the density of university buildings clustered there. Situated on the Acropolis between 116th and 120th street, and from Broadway to the Hudson River, Barnard College has stood since 1892.[1] By 1916 Barnard was already among the finest women-only universities in America, alongside six others known collectively as the "Seven Sisters." Although Aline and her mother were single-mindedly focused on a career in acting, Aline's father, William, and her aunt Sophie considered the stage an extremely mercurial profession. Barnard, they reasoned, would provide the well-rounded education needed if the stage did not cooperate. "You must get that piece of paper, in case anything happens," William MacMahon told his daughter. "You could always teach."[2] Pressured to satisfy everyone, Aline entered Barnard with a double major in English and psychology. What she really wanted, however, was a place in the school's respected dramatic society, known as "Wigs and Cues."

With the family home situated fifteen miles south in Brooklyn, William MacMahon resolved to make college life easy on his only child. "My parents originally chose the house in Borough Park because they thought it would be 'healthy' for me to live in the country," she recalled. "Then, when I went to Barnard they left Brooklyn and rented an apartment in Morningside Heights.[3] All my personal experience consisted of very determinedly wanting to do 'thus and so' and my father and mother making it possible by giving me plenty of security."[4]

As Aline MacMahon walked through the arched entrance of Barnard in the summer of 1916, World War I—then known as the European War, or the Great War—was just beginning its third year of the wholesale destruction of Europe. While the United States was still steadfastly neutral, a series of aggressive moves by the Germans in 1915 and '16—including the sinking of the ocean liner *Lusitania* and the deadly explosion by sabotage of two million pounds of munitions in New York harbor—were gradually driving the country toward a war footing. Many political and civilian elements of the population were on a preparedness drive, gathering goods for our European allies and mobilizing for a seemingly inevitable entry into the conflict. Meanwhile, as Aline neared voting age, New York's woman suffrage movement was anxiously awaiting the imminent passage of a state law to at last provide women legal enfranchisement at the ballot box. These two enormous issues of the day were omnipresent in American life, and at the progressive women's school in New York, they would soon become major elements of Aline's college years.

The modern image of New York in 1916 is that of a genteel, button-down environment in which women's skirts were long, men's hair was short, and propriety was a tightly binding force. In reality, America's largest city also had an unruly, kinetic wonderland of crime and vice percolating just beneath the surface. For Aline, a New Yorker through and through, this dual aspect of Manhattan life was familiar and navigable, but for the vast majority of Aline's incoming Barnard peers it was their first opportunity to personally experience the excitement and potential dangers lurking in a big city. And although Barnard—created in, and directed by precepts of, the Victorian era—professed a wish to "keep the social life of the college as free from rules and regulations as is consistent with safety and good breeding," it actually maintained just such a set of rules designed to *prevent* students from personally experiencing New York life. With the MacMahon family home now just two blocks from Barnard's campus, Aline was able to circumvent many of these restrictions; others were not so lucky. All students were on notice that they could not go out in the evening—for dinner, sightseeing or socializing—without a chaperone and the approval of their hall director. They were also warned in writing that "it is unsafe for girls to walk in Riverside or Morningside Parks," and "not to venture alone in small shops of which they have no knowledge."[5] Among the precious few approved safe havens were Barnard's libraries, residence halls, and dining areas—doubtless the least interesting locales to be found within the boundaries of Manhattan, the Bronx, Brooklyn, Queens, and Staten Island. Aline, meanwhile, had the run of what was then perhaps the most cosmopolitan city on Earth.

If Erasmus Hall had been Aline's first real opportunity to feel the excitement of a community of the arts, Barnard now provided the teeming energy of a city. From the moment she arrived, Aline threw herself into the school's creative life with abandon. She was fortunate to fall under the tutelage of

Aline (top right) took part in nearly every area of Barnard's creative life. In 1919 she was among the staff of Barnard's annual yearbook, the *Mortarboard*. Courtesy of Barnard College.

Minor Latham, a Mississippi southerner who came north to do graduate studies at Bryn Mawr and entered Barnard's faculty as an English professor in 1914. An expert in Elizabethan drama and medieval mystery plays, Latham was the guiding spirit of Wigs and Cues, and nicknamed her best students "Minnesingers" after the poetry-writing knights of medieval Germany. When Aline took her class in the summer of 1916, Latham saw genuine talent and dedication in the young girl from Pennsylvania. "I took Miss Latham's course in drama and got a great kick out of it," she said in 1933. "I was devoted to Miss Latham. I was one of her Minnesingers."[6] When Aline also joined Wigs and Cues that summer, Latham became the next important mentor shaping Aline's acting career, following Jennie Mac, Lillian Shaw, and Jerome Schaeffer.

Within months of her enrollment, Aline had already become a mainstay of the dramatic life of Barnard. In November she was elected the chairman of Barnard's famous "Greek Games," the annual Hellenic-themed contest between the freshman and sophomore classes. "The traditional Greek Games at Barnard

Life Begins

Aline is in the white toga and headdress as the Priestess in Barnard College's annual Greek Games contest between the freshman and sophomore classes, c. 1917. *Barnard College, BC15-23, Box 1*. Photograph by student, 1920, unpublished. Donated to Barnard University with no copyright transfer.

were my true introduction to the art of acting," Aline wrote in 1924. "These consisted of dramatic episodes with original staging, costuming and performing by the entire freshman and sophomore classes."[7] As chairman, Aline was responsible for the outline of the freshman program, including creation of the grand entrance motif (Prometheus returning with fire stolen from the Gods), and choosing "the God of freshman devotion" (Poseidon). The friendly rivalry, inaugurated in 1906, was scored by impartial judges, but with an infallibly predictable outcome. "It was a contest in which the sophomores usually came out ahead. But we had an enthusiastic class the year I was a freshman and we smashed custom by winning."[8] Aline's chairmanship of a freshman victory became lore at

Barnard, and this early responsibility made a lifelong impression on her. "It's awfully good to get a sense of being able to take hold of some problem and carry it through. I got that in my freshman year as chairman of the Greek Games," she said. "It was a perfectly marvelous aesthetic experience."[9] While preparing for the Games to be held in April, Aline also appeared in her first Wigs and Cues production, as Lawyer Hawkins in George Bernard Shaw's *Devil's Disciple*. Of her inaugural Barnard performance the school drama critic found it, rather meekly, "worthy of memorable mention."[10] After her debut, Aline was seen in nearly every production of Wigs and Cues at Barnard's Brinckerhoff Theatre. In *The Tail of the Dragon in Four Coils*, Aline was cast as Zena Serpentina, a not-at-all veiled parody of silent-era vamp Theda Bara, and in *David Garrick* she did a comedy turn as the drunken lout Squire Chivy. She was Beatrice in Barrie's *Rosalind* and Rose in *Trelawny of the Wells*, knew everything she should in *What Every Woman Knows*, found *The Way Out*, contemplated *Hearts Enduring*, and met *The Man Who Married a Dumb Wife*. In short, the Brinckerhoff stage became her home away from home.

In January 1917, Aline MacMahon's comfortable campus life—along with the fortunes and families of nearly everyone in America—was suddenly upended. That month, the US State Department intercepted a coded German telegram on its way to Mexican government officials. In it, the German government asked Mexico to join forces in war against the still-neutral United States, and promised a postwar repatriation of territories of the southwestern US formerly under Mexican rule. After successfully remaining neutral for over two years, President Woodrow Wilson severed diplomatic ties with the German government and readied to declare war. On February 6, 1917, Columbia University and its satellite schools were called to a general assembly where it was resolved to pledge all the university's resources to the government. Barnard quickly created the Committee on Women's War Work, and from the day war was declared on April 6, 1917, excepting Sundays, their office was open continuously until a month after the armistice of November 1918. Like many students, Aline was immediately subsumed in the war effort, volunteering at bond drives, helping organize the War Relief Council, and serving as the press chairman of the United War Work Drive.

As devastating as the Great War was to American life, it changed Aline's future in an entirely unexpected and positive way. During the summer of 1917, just as the first American doughboys were sailing to a deadly future on European battlefields, Aline accepted a summer position with the Hudson Guild Settlement House, a social services organization based in New York's

Chelsea neighborhood. There she was put under the supervision of Gertrude Stein, the erudite daughter of an upper-class New York family.[11] The two women quickly developed a friendship, and Gertrude soon decided that Aline was a potential companion for her older brother, Clarence, a successful architect who had graduated from the Ecole des Beaux Arts in Paris. There were reasons to think it might not be an ideal match. Clarence, a slender, bookish man of serious mind was seventeen years Aline's senior. Also, by this time Aline had blossomed into a tall, willowy young woman who probably could have successfully wrestled Clarence to the ground in a fair fight. But Gertrude saw in Aline's character the social crusader, the serious thinker, and the curious mind that she knew would appeal to her brother. It would be almost four years before Aline MacMahon finally met Clarence Stein, but the seeds had now been sown for a love affair that would last nearly five decades.

The war years were a whirlwind of activity for the young Aline MacMahon. At Barnard she was deeply involved in all areas of campus life, including editorial positions on the school's newspaper, the *Barnard Bulletin*, and its yearbook, *The Mortarboard*. On the weekends she continued her work at the Hudson Guild Settlement, and soon followed Gertrude Stein when she was put in charge of the Rehabilitation Bureau of the Department of Education. The bureau offered services to help reintegrate disabled men and women back into the workforce, and as wounded soldiers began returning from the war in Europe, these services were needed more than ever. During the summers Aline trudged to upstate New York, working as a camp counselor at Schroom Lake, putting on shows for Manhattanites trying to escape the summer heat. In her second year at Barnard Aline was elected president of the sophomore class, an honor that was again hers as a senior. All this was in addition to the normal student workload, and her deep dedication to the dramatic life of the school. When the war ended in November 1919, America—and Barnard—at last returned to some sense of normalcy.

By the time of her senior year, the critical community of Barnard had already pegged Aline MacMahon as a future Broadway star, and people outside the campus were also taking notice. Just before Christmas of 1919, Wigs and Cues mounted an elaborate production of J.M. Barrie's *What Every Woman Knows*, the story of Maggie (Aline), the plain young daughter of a well-to-do Scottish family whose parents fear will remain a spinster. When they discover that John Shand, a poor high-school student, has been sneaking into their house to read books from their large library, an agreement is made. The family will forgive his breaking and entering and fund his university education if, after graduation, John will marry their daughter. Even though he doesn't love Maggie, John accepts the pact, and Maggie secretly goes about helping his career thrive, exemplifying the play's title in the form of the (then) invisible power that women have in the success of their mates. "Aline MacMahon had charm for all," the *Barnard Bulletin* reported, "in addition to some histrionic ability of a high order. Barrie himself should be pleased with her interpretation. One wonders if Broadway may not find her out."[12] In this, the *Bulletin* reviewer's query was instantaneously prophetic. In the audience that night was James Light, the director of New York's popular and influential Provincetown Players theatrical troupe. In 1920 Provincetown was gathering in a remarkable assemblage of important new voices in the theater. One of its founders was John Reed, the Socialist activist and writer who was the subject of Warren Beatty's 1981 film *Reds*. Eugene O'Neill enjoyed his earliest success with the Provincetown Players, and was then preparing the box-office smash *Emperor Jones* for a November premiere. And acting in the company was a young Edna St. Vincent Millay, just three years from becoming the first woman to receive the Pulitzer Prize for poetry. Light was so impressed by Aline's sensitive performance that night, he immediately offered her a job with the Provincetown Company. Unfortunately, while she was deeply flattered, Aline's parents had already offered to pay her way on a tour of Europe after graduation. Believing, perhaps, that this might be her one real opportunity to explore the Continent without any responsibilities or cost, Aline reluctantly turned down Light's offer. Fortunately, it would not be the last time that members of the Provincetown Players would cross Aline's professional path.

Another distinguished suitor for Aline's services discovered her at nearly the same time. "When I was at Barnard," she recalled, "Walter Hampden offered me the opportunity to travel and work with his Shakespeare Company." In the 1920s, Hampden, now best remembered as Humphrey Bogart and William Holden's father in Billy Wilder's film *Sabrina*, was a highly respected actor and New York theater manager. If Aline had taken the offer, it almost certainly would have changed the course of her career, but it was not to be. "My mother wouldn't let me do it," Aline said, her disappointment ringing out nearly half a century later. "As a result I came to Shakespeare late in my career."[13]

In addition to her acting, Aline was also tasked with helping Minor Latham coach other performers, yet she still found time to write *and* direct her own play, *The Way Out*, in the spring of her senior year. It proved to be the most popular and provocative of a group of three pieces performed by the senior class in early 1920. "My great moment came at college when I wrote and acted in a one-act play. I was by this time the school's most veteran actress, having appeared in most everything given by Wigs and Cues. But it wasn't until I appeared in my own playlet that I received real recognition," she said, modestly underplaying her many previous successes.[14] "Aline MacMahon's play absorbed not only most of the interest of the audience," the Columbia critic wrote, "but also a great deal of the talent of Wigs and Cues. The performance was thoroughly satisfying."[15] Although no synopsis survives, the play was described as both "daring" and "gruesome" by the university press, and its ominous nature was alluded to in every review: "On 'The Way Out' rests much credit both as to play and acting. I would disbelieve it the work of a student—especially a woman—were not the author's name inscribed on the program, Mistress MacMahon. Although melodrama, I am not ashamed to say it impressed me much. In fact, I will probably sleep poorly on account of Ma Brockway, Mary and Nancy. I find it difficult to understand how Mistress Wallace could play in such an excellent manner a part so distinctly unpleasant. As for Mistress MacMahon, she need hardly have spoken, so expressive was her face of every emotion. I am hoping to see her at a playhouse downtown next year."[16] This obscure play of daring themes, mounted in a long-established bastion of Victorian ideals, was the first overt indication of Aline MacMahon as the rebel, a role she often wished to play, but in which she almost as often failed. From now through the 1950s, Aline will again and again find herself—by design or basic personal conviction—swimming with a controversial minority. Unfortunately, Aline's progressive, iconoclastic ideas would regularly find themselves at odds with an equally powerful sense of propriety and manners. Of this personal friction she once commented, "I was often running with the ball to a certain point, and then whatever was against it would set up obstacles. What shall I say? I guess that means I'm not a very serious protester."[17]

As Aline readied to graduate in the summer of 1920, she appeared in the final production of her university career, *Trelawny of the Wells*. She took the leading part of Rose Trelawny, a well-known actress who gives up her career for a man and finds that she is bored and angry at being consigned to a conventional domestic life. "Aline MacMahon made the most of her role. We were thrilled by her rebellion against a society that savored of the inquisition. With that act in our minds, it broke our hearts to see Rose reduced to a state of melancholia that admitted only the glistening tear and the weary smile. It is difficult to be lovelorn without being comic, but Miss MacMahon played

ALINE MACMAHON

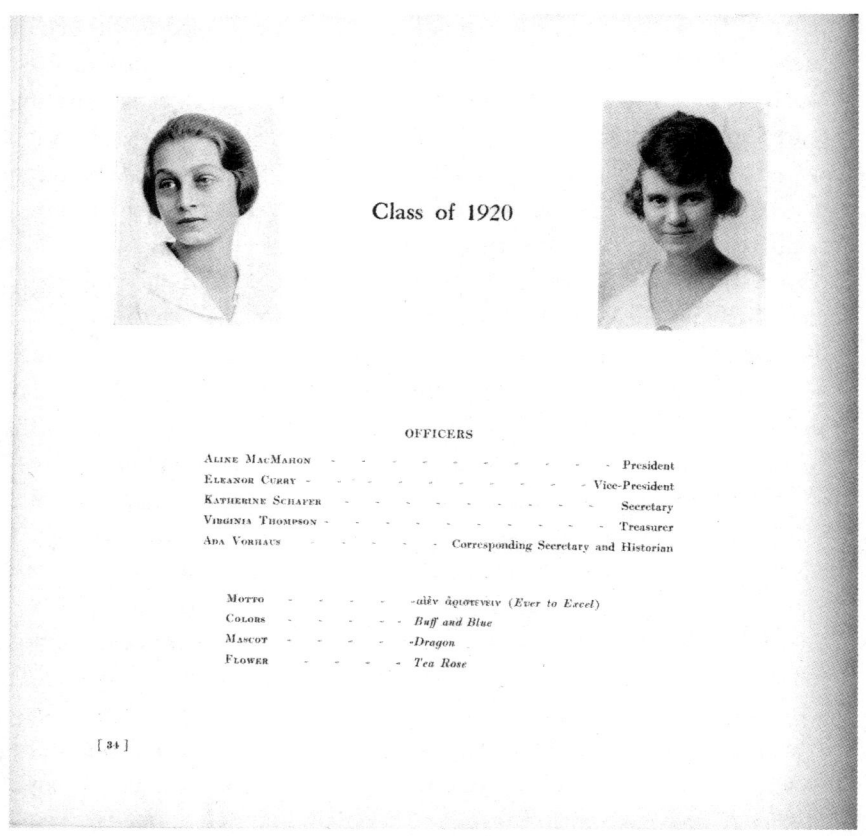

In 1920 Aline was elected President of Barnard's senior class. She was a favorite of the teaching staff, especially the school's drama teacher, Minor Latham. *Courtesy of Barnard College.*

the part in a manner that admits of no criticism."[18] Among the audience members touched by the depths of Rose Trelawny's despair that night was Rita Morgenthau, a wealthy Manhattan social worker who had created a series of acting clubs for inner-city girls and was an executive director of New York's important off-off-Broadway theater the Neighborhood Playhouse. Like James Light, Mrs. Morgenthau saw in Aline a talent that was undisguised by youth. Returning to her office at the Playhouse, she thought about the young actress who had made such a deep impression on her and resolved to ask her to join the company. In 1920, the preferred method of polite or professional communication was still the ages-old simplicity of the letter, so that night Ms. Mortgenthau wrote Aline with an invitation to become part of the

Playhouse. A few days later the envelope was in the pouch of a mailman servicing the MacMahon apartment on Morningside Drive. Here we see how history sometimes turns on unexpected and trivial moments; as the envelope made its way through the building it fell from the mailman's pouch and accidentally dropped into the gap between the elevator and the floor as if threading a needle. For over a year, Aline MacMahon's future would sit quietly among the jetsam at the bottom of the shaft, waiting to be found.[19]

At 11:00 A.M., June 2, 1920, Aline and the rest of her senior class gathered in Barnard's gymnasium to receive their diplomas and be symbolically released into the world. On hand to send the women on their way that morning was perhaps the most famous man in the world, General John "Black Jack" Pershing, Commander in Chief of the Allied Expeditionary Forces in Europe during the Great War. Himself receiving an honorary Doctor of Laws degree that day, Pershing was given a standing ovation when he began his speech by playfully commenting, "I'm proud to be graduating with such a good-looking set of girls."[20]

Thinking back on her higher education, Aline was undecided about precisely what those years meant to her. "I knew that someday I was going to be an actress," she said. "Barnard was a side step. I enjoyed it and my parents enjoyed it with me, but I don't quite know why I went to college." When asked why she thought of her higher education as a "side step," Aline was uncharacteristically expansive. "I don't know. Of course, college is not essential to a girl who is going on the stage. For some years after I graduated I thought it had been a waste of time, and I still feel that there is an atmosphere about it that is not good. We have such a short time in life to enjoy things in one's own vein, one's particular enthusiasm, and at college so many of us flounder about seeking them at a time when we should have discovered them. I sometimes wonder if it would not be better to go to college when one is thirty-five. Then you could compare the ideas you had worked out for yourself with those of other persons and know what you are talking about." Continuing, Aline gradually began to contemplate the more salutary aspects of her years in Barnard. "On the other hand, in my profession, all one's experiences help, and you cannot be exposed for four years to pleasant associations without having it do something to you. I liked my work. As I said, I was devoted to Miss Latham. I made a great many friends. And college did something else for me. It's awfully good to have a feeling of power and a sense of accomplishment. I got that in writing and acting in Wigs and Cues plays. It takes years before the world will let you have that much power, and so it's awfully nice to be able to have a taste of it when you are still young."[21] As years passed, Aline's memories of Barnard gradually warmed, like a sunrise in autumn. She frequently returned to the campus to give lectures and participate in career counseling, was a generous alumni donor, and attended every reunion without fail until she reached ninety and was unable to make the class of 1920's seventieth anniversary.

A snapshot of Aline's attitude toward the world at the moment she graduated was perhaps captured by a short article nestled in the March 31st edition of the *Barnard Bulletin*, entitled "On Which Side Are You?"

> Not long ago some questionnaires were issued to the class of 1920, asking for each student's stand on such questions as the breaking up of society into two great classes, capitalist and proletariat, the preservation of the family, the government policy with the Reds [Communists], the dissemination of birth control literature, the problem of divorce, universal military training, intervention in Mexico, and sedition bills. The results of this inquiry were as we expected. Barnard divides itself up into Radicals and Conservatives. The cleavage cuts across all ordinary distinctions. On the right side is the immense majority that hates every disturbance of the established order with an instinctive and profound hatred; on the left a minority of the restless and those who sympathize with the unrest. To the second class, the deportations, the sedition bills and the suspension of liberties seem evidence not of a desire to administer justice or protect rights, but of a nation wide hysterical nervous breakdown. The majority of the girls in Sociology were on the left wing. Whatever the reason, all are taking sides nowadays; Some because they are natural rebels, some because they have the imagination to put themselves in the rebel's place.

If Aline did not yet place herself among the rebels, she at least understood the rebellion. "I am one of the people who would prefer it to be a more equal world," she once said, voicing an idea that some conservatives would qualify as radical. "I don't like to see anybody hungry."[22] Between the deeply damaged soldiers she encountered at the Rehabilitation Bureau and her continuing visits to the inner city with Sophie, Aline found her Victorian ideals being slowly eroded, while she is increasingly intrigued by the emerging postwar radicalism. Little by little Aline is moving ever further to the left.

The 1920 graduating class of Barnard College. Aline MacMahon is in the second row from the bottom, behind the second woman to the right of the banner. *Courtesy of Barnard College.*

ALINE MACMAHON

Although she had refused James Light's invitation to be considered for the Provincetown Players, the summer of 1920 found a different opportunity at her doorstep. Through various connections to New York's upper-class donors, Aline's aunt Sophie had become acquainted with the successful Broadway producer/director Edgar Selwyn. Sophie—ever the instigator—arranged an introduction for Aline. After meeting with Selwyn, the producer agreed to hire her for a small, nonspeaking part in his upcoming production of *The Mirage*. Although Aline was not in the cast list (she appeared in a single scene as one of several craps-playing debutantes), the play, which opened on September 30, 1920, was her first professional appearance on Broadway. A big hit that lasted into March, *The Mirage* gave Aline her first taste of theatrical life in New York. Unfortunately, it was not a job that she appreciated. Legend tells that when Aline discovered that her dice-throwing character was "a lady of easy virtue," she had moral misgivings and quickly left the production. The story does not quite jibe, since only a few years later Aline would play both a prostitute and a lesbian to great acclaim in separate Broadway productions. Also, it seems unlikely that she would rush to take a small, meaningless part after she had so recently refused James Light's offer to join the prestigious Provincetown Players. Chances are the entire affair was forced on Aline as the result of Sophie's dogged insistence that she take advantage of the opportunity her aunt provided. Aline, who was often irked by Sophie's personal pressure to succeed, soon capitulated, then cleverly extricated herself through an ironclad—but false—morals clause.[23]

After her appearance in *The Mirage*, Aline MacMahon prepared for an extended overseas trip. It was an era when many American upper-middle-class families made effort to duplicate the centuries-old tradition of the European elite, who regularly sent their newly adult children to see the great sites of the Continent on what was called the "Grand Tour." For three months she traveled through England, Scotland, and Switzerland before ending in France. There, she reconnected with Gertrude Stein, who was also traveling the Continent with her sister Lillie. "I happened on them in Paris," Aline said, "and we all had supper at Sacre-Coeur." During the dinner, talk again turned to Gertrude's brother, Clarence, who had recently endured a costly romantic loss. "He had been in love with Gertrude's best friend, Lucille," Aline recalled, "but Lucille found another beau, and the sisters said, 'We have to find another girl for him.'" By now, however, Gertrude thought better of matching Clarence with Aline. "She said to me, 'You're not right. We have a boy for you, he'll be here next week—we've been travelling with him in Sicily, Ernest

The brilliant, bookish architect Clarence Stein fell for Aline MacMahon from nearly the moment they met. They married in 1928 and navigated forty-seven loving years as man and wife. Donated to Cornell University by Aline MacMahon without copyright.

Grunsfeldt.'" On paper, Grunsfeldt did indeed seem like a better match for Aline than Clarence; just two years older than her, he was a robust, driven man who also made his own mark in architecture, later designing Chicago's famous Adler Planetarium. "So Ernest turned up and I thought he was pretty good, actually, but I was headed back to America, and he was training at the Ecole des Beaux Arts."[24] Returning to the States in early 1921, Aline MacMahon did *not* immediately meet *or* fall in love with Clarence Stein. By this time the thirty-nine-year-old architect was embroiled in an "extended romantic interest" with a married woman, and not thinking about a new partner.[25] Their meeting would have to wait until 1922.

On her return from Europe, Aline was able to snag a berth in the Yorkville stock company of Blaney's Players, the venerable New York institution that counted half a dozen theaters and troupes across Manhattan and the other boroughs. Her first speaking part was as a ship passenger with a single line in play called *One Day: A Sequel to Three Weeks*. During the spring and summer of 1921 she tackled small roles, learning the ropes of the quickly changing productions common to the stock format. Meanwhile, another of the strange quirks of history was about to present itself.

One morning in July, just after the sun rose high enough to warm the Manhattan streets, a maintenance crew arrived to check, service, and clean the elevator and shaft of the MacMahon apartment building on Morningside Drive. Standing in the well a few feet below the ground floor, a workman found an unopened envelope at his feet. It was addressed to a recipient in the building, and he delivered it to the apartment. It had been sixteen months since Rita Morgenthau wrote this undelivered letter to Aline MacMahon, and with no response she likely assumed that the Barnard actress had decided against a professional career in the theater. The appearance of the letter was major news in the MacMahon house, and Aline was excited and curious about the opportunity. She quickly replied, and thus began a short correspondence with Mrs. Morgenthau on the subject of her auditioning for the Playhouse. But before the Upper West Side actress could arrange to travel to the out-of-the-way Lower East Side Neighborhood Playhouse, a fateful meeting took place. Aline herself described the episode as "sheer luck," a gift she believed was given her many times during her life and career, and marveled at its impact on her future. "Luck is travelling from a Greenwich Village party when I wouldn't stay all night, alone, on a Ninth Avenue trolley on a snowy night [in October] at three o'clock in the morning, and [Playhouse founder] Alice Lewisohn is on her way home from God knows why or what, a frail, exquisite, aristocratic, rich little woman, was on that Ninth Avenue trolley, and she said, 'I've been hearing about you from Rita Morgenthau and we're forming a new company, come on down to the Neighborhood Playhouse.'" The "new company" Alice was assembling was the culmination of the Playhouse's decision to hire, for the first time, professional actors instead of relying on gifted amateurs. Gratified by her memory of wistful Alice and her offer, Aline's enthusiasm was uncontrolled. "Oh, luck, luck, luck," she said in remembrance, "I think it's the biggest thing of all."[26]

It seems that Aline MacMahon was always seeking a creative community and continually finding it. Or perhaps those communities were always finding her. There is no doubt that the Neighborhood Playhouse became the touchstone of her early life. In it, she found a place of unconditional expression, a university course for her personal growth, and a window onto new horizons in art, culture, and society. There, she developed a surrogate family that gently challenged her Victorian ideals without outraging her sensibilities, and introduced her to the sub rosa world of alternate lifestyles that helped cement her liberal ideology. "It led to a life," she said. "That's where I met so many lovely people who influenced everything. That's just sheer luck."

The Neighborhood Playhouse was a product of the years that straddled the nineteenth and twentieth centuries, when New York developed an enormous slate of charitable organizations devoted to helping the immigrant poor. Largely financed by wealthy patrons, these charities offered after-school programs, tutoring, nursing, disease prevention, activities, and recreation for the impoverished residents of New York's poorest slums. In 1893 Miss Lillian Wald established the Henry Street Settlement on the Lower East Side with financing from a German immigrant, Jacob Schiff. There she and her volunteers became part of the fabric of the neighborhood, working across class lines to help the newly arrived residents from Europe and beyond. In 1913 Wald and a pair of other wealthy donors, sisters Alice and Irene Lewisohn, staged a weeklong street festival to honor the twentieth anniversary of the Settlement. The event was such an enormous success that Wald and her volunteers at the Settlement decided to create a theater program to service the culture-deprived residents of the area. Within just two years Lillian Wald was able to finance a brand-new building at 466 Grand Street to house what she dubbed the Neighborhood Playhouse. In spite of its inconvenient location and distance from Manhattan's theater district, the Playhouse quickly became a leading light in what was then known as the "Little Theatre" movement. Typified by small houses with permanent companies mounting unique and eccentric productions, the Little Theatre movement was in its heyday during the teens and 1920s. The two other main companies in New York allied with the movement were the Provincetown Players (of which James Light was a member), and the prestigious Theatre Guild, home of Alfred Lunt and Lynne Fontaine. Even sequestered on the Lower East Side, the Neighborhood Playhouse often found local residents seated alongside Park Avenue swells and Broadway power brokers. For over a decade it was one of the trendiest places to be seen in New York theater culture.[27]

The Neighborhood Playhouse was an organization run almost entirely by women, an inspiring environment for a recent Barnard graduate who was independent, socially conscious, and ambitious. When Aline arrived at the Playhouse in the late summer of 1921, she found there a group of women who became mentors and lifelong friends. There was producer and executive director Helen Arthur, twenty years Aline's senior, a whirlwind of activity topped by a shoulder-length crop of dark, curly hair who was nearly always seen dressed in men's clothes. Writer and director Agnes Morgan, round-faced and slight, was an amazingly clever and prolific satirist who created a simple sketch that single-handedly jump-started Aline's theatrical career. The Playhouse's primary financial benefactors, the aristocratic Alice and Irene Lewisohn, provided a historic professional opportunity for Aline MacMahon that simultaneously beget a once-in-a-lifetime revolution in the performing arts. Above all there was Aline Bernstein, the costume and set designer who was just then embarking on a legendary Broadway career. Bernstein is perhaps best remembered today for her torrid autumn-to-spring affair with the author Thomas Wolfe, but in 1921 she was working at the Neighborhood Playhouse, where she and Aline quickly became the closest of friends. From 1925—when Bernstein met Wolfe—Aline MacMahon was a confidant to one of the most closely examined liaisons in early twentieth-century American literature.

At the Playhouse, the still semi-sheltered Aline suddenly found herself within the heart of New York's subterranean lifestyle culture. Helen Arthur and Agnes Morgan were the creative power couple of the Neighborhood Playhouse—committed romantic partners dubbed by the Playhouse regulars as "the Morgan-Arthurs." Before she met Agnes, Helen had also been romantically involved with Lillian Wald, the originator of Henry Street. Wald herself was a liberal political firebrand who organized the isolationist American Union Against Militarism in 1915, and was accused of anti-American activities during the Communist Red Scare of the WWI era. In spite of their wealth and privilege, the Lewisohn sisters also held radical beliefs that closely followed Wald's. In correspondence with Wald, Alice Lewisohn once wrote:

"You must know that my love for the settlement [Henry Street], is not just for its own sake, for what it stands for, or for what you are accomplishing. But it is also for what you are working toward and helping bring about—Socialism. That is what Irene and I are living for."[28] These ideas, percolating in and around the Playhouse, would comprehensively wind their way through American intellectual circles in the decades after the Great War, and become the basis for Aline's own political education. Unfortunately, like Lillian Wald, a deepening dedication to progressive ideas will later result in damaging times for Aline and those around her.

Among the other Playhouse regulars who molded Aline's social conscience was an actor named Albert Carroll. Joining the Playhouse company at nearly the same moment as Aline,[29] Carroll was a strikingly handsome man with high cheekbones and a lithe figure who regularly performed on the Playhouse stage as a strikingly beautiful woman. His particular specialty was a facility for impressions of the elegant actresses and dancers of the day: Anna Pavlova, Beatrice Lilly, Laurette Taylor, and Irene Castle. Accepted by the public as a "female impersonator," today Carroll would of course be understood as transgender, or gender fluid, but in 1921 his true self could only be openly expressed on stage, and then as an "act." Albert Carroll and the other marginalized members of the Neighborhood Playhouse entrusted their secrets to the professional family that surrounded them, and in return found a community of unconditional acceptance.[30] For Aline, a young girl from a relatively conservative home, it was an eye-opening environment. In short order, however, she adopted this surrogate family, and was adopted by them in turn. By the 1921–22 season she was also on staff as the assistant to the Playhouse's press agent, Stella Hanau, and regularly pitched to help with preparations for new productions.[31] After she left the Playhouse for Broadway, Aline continued to work with Helen Arthur, taught in the Neighborhood Playhouse School, and touted the legacy of the Playhouse and its Little Theatre roots to all who would listen.

When Aline was hired for the Playhouse company they were preparing a production of Sir Granville-Barker's *The Madras House*. With themes of Victorianism versus modernity, women's equality, and the development of youth, *The Madras House* mirrored elements of Aline's own awakening. She was given the part of one of six sheltered daughters of a spartan, moral father who, through marriage, owns a colorful, upscale London couturier shop. The contrast between their dour home life and the vibrant, fashionable environment of the store can't help but inspire the dreams of the repressed girls. After her diabolically drab introduction in Act I, Aline reappeared in Act III as a butterfly of Flaming Youth—an image of the new, liberated woman of the Roaring Twenties. With sparkling dialogue and progressive ideas about women and morality, *The Madras House* was a major hit at the small theater on the Lower East Side. Critics were effusive in their praise, and continued to champion the Playhouse as one of the premiere companies in all of New York, regardless of size. After sixty-four performances, the Playhouse needed to close *The Madras House* to make room for their next offering, *The Green Ring*, already rehearsed and ready to play. But rather than close the still-popular *Madras House*, the Morgan-Arthurs elected instead to move it uptown to a bigger venue on Broadway. Unfortunately, its run at the National Theatre garnered only tepid audience response and quickly closed. Of this failure on Broadway—the Playhouse's second—Alice Lewisohn wrote a eulogy. "We watched 'The Madras House' give up its Broadway ghost," she said. "The bones and tattered relics were penitently and solemnly collected and removed to Grand Street as a sacred warning never again to stray from the native heath."[32] *The Madras House* was not seen again at *any* location in New York City for eighty-five years.

When *Madras* went uptown, Aline stayed behind to appear in *The Green Ring*. Imported from Russia and described as a "charming and wise little study of the relations of youth and age," the production was in itself unimportant to Aline's career. Its primary significance was in its numerous intertwined connections to the Moscow Art Theatre, a group that would soon indirectly prove to be the greatest influence on Aline MacMahon's development as an actress. Although *The Green Ring* opened and closed in April, soon after another milestone was marked in the life of Aline MacMahon.

Gertrude Stein had not quite forgotten her idea that Aline MacMahon might make a good match for her brother Clarence. When it became clear that his love of a married woman would not be returned, Gertrude resolved to at last arrange a meeting. In 1922 Clarence Stein was in the tenth year of a five-decade career that would make him a major name in American architecture and urban planning. Slightly built, with a high forehead topped by wavy hair and round wire glasses, he had a professorial aspect that belied a steel will. According to architect and friend Lewis Mumford, "His physical characteristics disguised his considerable talents for leadership. He could be tough, but was also modest and congenial, never inflexible or dogmatic."[33] After his return from studies at the Ecole des Beaux Arts in 1911, Clarence served as an officer in the Army Corps of Engineers, and the year before he met Aline he was a candidate for the US vice presidential nomination in New York State, under governor Al Smith's Independent Party ticket. As an architect he had already been involved in prestige projects such as the San Diego Exposition of 1915 and became the secretary of the City Planning Committee of New York. On July 10, 1921, Clarence was one of three principals who gathered at the Hudson Guild Estate House in upstate New York to plan the creation of the Appalachian Trail, an idea proposed and spearheaded by his friend, the well-known conservationist, Benton MacKaye.[34] Over his career he met senators, governors, and presidents, designed entire towns, held important positions in the War Department, championed the Greenbelt movement in the American suburb, and received accolades from around the globe for his visionary work in urban planning.

Ethnically Jewish, but raised in the quasi-religious philosophy of Ethical Culture, Clarence Stein was also a deeply thoughtful, moral man who was, like Aline, undergoing his own examination of American capitalism and class divide. Clarence's devotion to Ethical Culture—a movement based on the precepts of social reform, morality independent of religion, philanthropy, education, and supporting others in becoming more ethical beings—was ready-made for a woman who was also a deeply moral but essentially nonreligious person. Of their first meeting, little can be found, but it is clear that Aline was not immediately smitten with Clarence Stein. Although a strong platonic friendship eventually developed between the pair, it would still take years for the connection to blossom into love. At least for one of them. According to a friend's account, Clarence proposed marriage within months of their first meeting, but Aline—already a willful, reasoned woman bent on career success—said no, and continued to say no each time he asked, which apparently was relatively frequently.

For the 1921–22 Neighborhood Playhouse season, subscription ticket holders had been promised an exclusive production to take place following the final play of the year, but when *The Green Ring* closed, the staff of the Playhouse had not yet prepared anything to satisfy the subscriber base. Desperate, the directors hit upon the idea of expanding their private end-of-the-season party—which began as a lark for Alice Lewisohn's birthday, and consisted of an unruly, energetic satire of their previous plays—and inviting the subscribers. A far distant precursor to *Mad Magazine* and *Saturday Night Live*, the new show, dubbed the *Grand Street Follies*, offered mashups of earlier Playhouse productions and other Broadway fare. It had saved time, money, and several ulcers, and quickly became one of the hottest tickets in the New York theater. That first year Aline appeared in a parody of *The Madras House*, set in a brothel and renamed *The Mattress House*. In *The Royal Damn*

Fango, Albert Carroll was transformed into Irene Lewisohn as she appeared in the ballet *The Royal Fandango*. And in the lobby after the stage show, Aline and the other Playhouse regulars mingled with audience members in character as well-known producers, actors, and critics (including David Belasco, Laurette Taylor, and Alla Nazimova), who proceeded to mock the Playhouse and the entire Little Theatre movement itself. "The result was legendary," a biographer wrote, "and threatened to become the sole legacy of the Neighborhood Playhouse."[35] In spite of its enormous success, this was to be the last Neighborhood Playhouse production of any kind for over a year.

Just as Aline became an integral part of the Playhouse family, it momentarily dissolved. The 1921–22 season had been marginally successful, bringing in new, professional blood, taking artistic chances, and creating the wildly successful *Grand Street Follies*. But there were troubles within the family. A schism was developing within Grand Street, between the Lewisohns, who were in favor of amateur-based, neighborhood-oriented programs, and the Morgan-Arthurs, interested in a more ambitious, professional company. The success of the Playhouse had demanded that both factions think bigger, spend more money, and expand their horizons. Success beget ambition, and ambition played havoc with the bottom line. Something was going to have to give.

Their solution was novel, to say the least: the management of Grand Street decided to close the theater. "The cessation of public activity of the Neighborhood Playhouse for one year, it was declared yesterday," the *New York Times* reported, "is made necessary by the fact that the time will be required to develop the possibilities and potentialities of the organization. The intervening year will be devoted to 'the formation of a permanent company of players; further experimentation in lyric drama; finding new material; and an expansion of the workshop.'"[36] The Lewisohn's vowed that the time off would not be wasted. Over the following six months the sisters tramped (luxuriously, it must be added) through exotic locales in Egypt, India, Palestine, and Burma looking for unique new influences and ideas to bring to the Playhouse. On return, their tales of caravansaries, souks, dervishes, and their desert locales were so much catnip for Aline's increasing interest in exotic travel. In the meantime, however, it did her little good. She was—for a year, at least—out of a job.

Immediately, Aline returned to Edgar Selwyn, producer of *The Mirage*, to see if he had anything to offer her for the fall season. He cast her in a small part in *The Exciters*, a comedy starring Tallulah Bankhead, about a group of restless Smart Set types who resolve to wring maximum thrills from life regardless of the personal consequences. *The Exciters* filled up Aline's fall season, but was gone before the winter.[37]

After some months "resting," Aline was contacted by the Neighborhood Playhouse directors about a unique, exclusive actor's workshop that was in its earliest planning stages for the spring of 1923. Cloaked in mystery and secrecy, this all-expenses-paid retreat was offered to only a handful of Grand Street regulars, and would require Aline to spend four months living in upstate New York away from her still platonic but developing relationship with Clarence Stein. Fortunately, Aline's career ambitions were stronger than her friendship with the thirty-nine-year-old architect; the experiment upon which she was about to embark became the single most important event of her career, and contains the secret, hidden history of an incredible revolution on both stage and screen.

3

TEACH ME, AND SET MY FEET ON THE WAY

In the summer of 1923 Aline MacMahon found herself living in a picturesque mansion on the high outskirts of Pleasantville, New York, an hour north of Manhattan. Nestled anonymously among the lush, rolling hills of Westchester County, the mansion was ground zero of a coming revolution that would soon conquer the United States, and eventually the world.

This secret retreat was the site of the inaugural teaching class of the American Laboratory Theatre, comprising the first students anywhere outside of Russia to learn the modern tenets of acting set down by Konstantyn Stanislavski, the originator of the revolutionary system that became known worldwide as the Method. Famous as the founder of the influential Moscow Art Theatre, Stanislavski created and taught a series of exercises designed to develop a new style of acting for the stage. Before his techniques—which he called the System—germinated and took hold, stage and screen acting was primarily declarative, with emotions revealed largely through direct verbal and physical cues chosen by the director and mimicked by the actor. The Stanislavski method did away with this kind of direction in favor of unlocking the actor's ability to express complex thoughts and feelings by empathizing with the character's inner life. Russians, who had lived in the repressive eras of the Czars and the Communists, had an essential need to create and adopt this system. Both forms of government were paranoid and autocratic, and each saw public dissent and free speech as threats to their power. As a consequence, these governments regularly spied on, threatened, and punished their citizens on mere suspicion of having ideas contrary to the will of the state. This great collective fear of discovery created a deep ocean of secret inner thoughts and emotions in the Russian soul that were unknown to freely outspoken Americans. According to Stanislavski scholar Mel Gordon,

Teach Me, and Set My Feet on the Way

Konstantin Stanislavski's revolutionary Method acting technique began its transmigration from Russia to the United States at a makeshift school in Westchester County, New York, during the spring of 1923. Aline MacMahon was among the inaugural class of ten students to learn the system at a mansion nestled somewhere in this panorama of the Pocantico Hills, just outside Pleasantville. Photo circa 1910.

"Russians had to suppress their everyday private thinking, beliefs and impulses. Exposure of them, however, took place in the vocal chords and in minute muscular displays on the face and body. Stanislavski labeled this manifestation of subtext and used it as a Russian acting device."[1] For a public shrinking under the watchful eyes of the Czars and the Communists, acting was a fundamental survival tool.

Modern versions of the Method have metamorphosed far from Stanislavski's original teachings, but the core idea remains the same; the actor must find a truth within them—by experience, recall, observation, emotion—and use this personal connection in the role they play. Beyond the idea alone, Stanislavski's genius was in devising the drills to unlock these buried emotions, or to stimulate recall, which he called affective memory. After decades spent using Stanislavski's disciplines, Aline MacMahon offered this succinct summation: "The Moscow technique is how to dig out of your sub-conscious what you use to act. Stanislavski developed the remarkable technique of how to learn to do that easily." Critics and historians concur in her assessment. As early as 1922 his ideas were being acknowledged as something new in the performing arts. "Many will claim that the Moscow Art Theatre is not alone in its talent for simplicity and sincerity," one observer allowed, "yet to Stanislavski belongs the peculiar honor of having devised and introduced methods of performance which, until he did so, were unknown."[2] He was the first to have students imagine themselves as animals or inanimate objects such as a cup of tea or an empty inkwell. He invented elaborate situations for students to experience solely by recalling elements of their past, while in other drills he asked them to react to a stimulus (e.g., a gunshot or ghostly voices) as if they were various characters, such as a nun or a child. Although Stanislavski himself never taught outside Russia, by the 1930s a group of American devotees, including Stella Adler, Harold Clurman, and Lee Strasberg, were each teaching students their own reinterpreted version of his technique. As a result, during the decades that Hollywood stars like Gary Cooper, Spencer Tracy, and Bette Davis were perfecting the prewar American style, the Method was surreptitiously recruiting a new generation of actors to the Russian system, including Franchot Tone, Lee J. Cobb, and Rod Steiger. But in the summer of 1923 all this was far in the future, and a small workshop in Westchester County run by one of Stanislavski's original students was ever-so-quietly producing the first actor in America who would bring this new style to the stage and the talking film, Aline MacMahon.

The creator and Artistic Director of the American Laboratory Theatre was Richard Boleslavsky, a handsome man with a noble forehead and dark, swept-back hair, who arrived in New York from central Europe in the autumn of 1922. Beginning in 1906—just as the System was coming into being—he studied with Stanislavski in the Moscow Art Theatre (MAT), rising to become one of its most important members and a leader of the MAT's fabled First Studio. But by 1920 spies of the new Soviet state were already keeping watchful eyes on Boleslavsky, who had been a loyal Coronet in Russia's Imperial Army before the revolution. The surveillance frightened Boleslavsky enough to flee Russia for his native Poland, and then to continue on to Berlin. By 1922 he was living and working in London, where he soon accepted an offer to bring his vaudeville-style show the *Revue Russe* to Manhattan.

The timing of Boleslavsky's migration to America was serendipitous. Just months after he arrived, Stanislavski brought the MAT to the United States for the second of three rare and legendary tours.[3] When the MAT disembarked in New York City in January 1923, Boleslavsky was at the pier to greet his former teacher and mentor. Fluent in English and having established important New York theater connections, Boly (as his friends called him) quickly convinced Stanislavski to employ him as his aide-de-camp—the man capable of running his American touring company. Soon, Boly was procuring the necessary local talent, serving as liaison with theatrical agents, and eventually even substituting on stage for his weary master when the tour was extended into April.

The Moscow Art Theatre's six months in America proved wildly successful. Their productions of Russian and European classics, including Dostoevsky's *The Brothers Karamazov*, Gorky's *The Lower Depths*, and Ibsen's *An Enemy of the People* drew overflow crowds in spite of the fact that all were performed entirely in Russian.[4] Even in the notoriously cynical New York press the System was unanimously heralded as a revolution in stage acting, and Stanislavski as the eccentric genius of a new era in theater. "Never before had I seen whole performances so good, whole plays made to come true on stage by a group of actors," *Vanity Fair* reported,[5] and even the most hardened reviewers had to admit defeat. "As one who has never attended their performances out of disgust at bellicose Russian artism, we hereby eat dirt. It is impossible to convey the juicy, full ripe nature of the interpretive ability of these players."[6]

When Stanislavski and his company finally boarded an ocean liner returning to Moscow in June, Boleslavsky waved gaily from the pier as they slipped out of the harbor. In genuine danger of being imprisoned as an undesirable if he returned to Russia, Boly also found that being the sole remaining principal connected to the MAT had suddenly given him enormous artistic cachet. With Stanislavski and company gone, New York City's theater scene was momentarily at his feet.

Even before the MAT company sailed, Boleslavsky had set his sights on creating the theatrical company and school that he dubbed the American Laboratory Theatre. While the Lewisohn sisters were still touring exotic locales half a world away, the Morgan-Arthurs and other remnants of the Neighborhood Playhouse were excitedly watching the MAT's New York performances. "In our correspondence," Alice recalled, "we received an enthusiastic report of the Moscow Art Theatre productions, and a suggestion was made that an experiment might be tried with a group of Playhouse students. If these young actors were willing to study with Boleslavsky, and funds could be secured for such training, would we agree to the plan, and also to have a production of this experimental group open our next season?" From a Western Union office somewhere in the Middle East, Alice and Irene gave their response. "Cables were exchanged. If Boleslavsky's method reflected the type of realism more familiar in Russian literature than in our own, it might, if wisely handled, serve as a technical foundation. Our agreement was made. The die was cast."[7] In addition to the Lewisohns, Boleslavsky's other investor-partners were Dorothy Straight, a progressive, wealthy widow whose love of the stage led her to an interest in the Little Theatre movement, and Helen Arthur, who secured the use of a large country estate as a base for the summer of 1923. By spring, the Laboratory's first group of students had been chosen, including the twenty-four-year-old Aline MacMahon.

Of how she wound up living in that country mansion during the summer of 1923 Aline returned again to her belief in the power of chance. "I was very lucky in being taught by Boleslavsky. When the Moscow Art Theatre came here we were all overwhelmed with the magnificence of their performances and their productions. Mrs. Straight and the Lewisohns subsidized a small group of actors, six of us, to go off and live in Pleasantville with Boleslavsky, where he gave us the Moscow technique."[8] Thus, before Robert DeNiro, before Marlon Brando, before Kazan, Lee Strasberg, John Garfield, or even Maria Ouspenskaya, Aline MacMahon was *the* vanguard of Russian method acting in America. "I was the first," she said with genuine pride, "so to speak, in the first group to be exposed to what has become [the Method].[9] Out of this summer has developed everything that the Method actors are doing. Mr. Strasberg is a second generation of this teaching."[10]

If someone was paying close attention driving out of Pleasantville in the summer of 1923, they may have seen Aline MacMahon on an immaculately groomed roadside lawn, pretending to be a pearl emerging from its shell, or acting out the seasonal changes of the trees that surrounded their summer retreat. In a manufactured coincidence worthy of Dickens, this is exactly what the New York *Herald-Tribune* drama critic Percy Hammond encountered in mid-June when he claimed to have taken a wrong turn outside Pleasantville and "happened" upon Boleslavsky's school while seeking directions. "The result was that I discovered quite the most interesting adventure in the drama that has come to my notice in what is commonly known as many moons," he said, straining the credulity of even his widest-eyed readers. "As I approached, I saw Aline MacMahon and several other players well known to the New York stage; here was nothing less than the school of the American Laboratory Theatre." During his supposedly impromptu visit, Hammond

The enchanting eyes of Aline MacMahon are evident in a portrait taken while under contract to the Shubert Company, c. 1926. The arrangement was not creatively satisfying, and Aline had to feign a nervous breakdown to obtain her release. *Wisconsin Historical Society, White Studio, ID #149059.*

took measure of the earliest days of the first school of Russian acting in America. "I felt as though I had trespassed upon the secret maneuvers of creation," he said.[11]

At the estate Helen Arthur provided for his school, Boleslavsky had laid out a "severe regimen" in the fundamentals of acting in Stanislavski's system.

On the lawn of the great house, surrounded by the aspen, sycamore, beech, and hornbeam trees that dapple the summer landscape of Westchester County, Boly drilled his students with iron discipline from morning until night, Monday through Saturday. But this was more than a mere exercise in acting.[12] As expressed in American Laboratory Theatre literature, Boleslavsky's program description is positively metaphysical. "[The method consists of] discovering the 'tone' of the play that is the harmonious blending of the actors' spirits as expressed in sounds which constitute the music of speech. To evoke this harmony, the regisseur has to understand the psychological make-up of his group, namely the mental qualities of each actor, his emotional disposition, his comic or tragic potentialities, and the peculiarity of his relation to his fellow players. Then, we may arrive at the best results achievable through a harmony of their blended spirits."[13] Beyond this plumbing of personal psyche were exercises in stylized movement, vocal production, diction, relaxation, scene studies, costuming, and set design, as well as the more esoteric disciplines of Tempo-Rhythms (pace and cadence), Dalcroze *Eurhythmics* (the connection between music and performance), *Plastique* (the study of body motion), *Mimodrama* (mime), and Affective Memory (emotional recall). In the words of another visitor from the fourth estate, "It was rather like a military training camp with drama substituted for infantry drill regulations."[14] The study was so intense, precise, and eccentric that three of the original ten students quickly ran screaming from Pleasantville. But not Aline. "I took to it hard and I took to it seriously. I really felt that I had something important there. It gave me a new way of working; during that wonderful summer, Boleslavsky taught me how to concentrate."[15]

During his visit, Percy Hammond noticed that most of the students were relatively youthful—Aline was just twenty-four, and of the others, only a few had even reached thirty. When asked about the age of the players, Boleslavsky essentially chalked it up to an issue of control. "It was the director's intention to surround himself with actors not too steeped in the salesmanship traditions of Broadway," Hammond reported, "in order to be amenable to persuasion. His idea is to organize a theater with intelligent, sincere and progressive players who might be acquiescent to the Russian way of presenting drama."[16] Boleslavsky was in his own way the same kind of charismatic autocrat that Stanislavski had been when teaching his system in Moscow. Earlier in the year Boly had presented his thoughts on the new style in an issue of *Theatre Arts Magazine*, echoing the ideas his master had outlined in 1906: "In the Laboratory Theatre every detail must be considered afresh for each production. Old, tried forms and methods must never be relied upon. A new approach must always be sought."[17] And in America for the moment, this new approach was the exclusive domain of Richard Boleslavsky.

For Aline and her fellow students, their summer in the country was physically and emotionally grueling. Boleslavsky brooked no slack. According to him, "the actor's body is his instrument and must, in this ordered system, be made plastic to his art by hard discipline."[18] Not content merely with providing their schooling, Boly had also scheduled the first professional production to feature his students for October at the Neighborhood Playhouse. The debut of the Method used by Americans in the United States would also herald the reopening of the Playhouse after its yearlong sabbatical.

The intense study of the two plays chosen by Boleslavsky—George Bernard Shaw's *The Shewing Up of Blanco Posnet* and William Butler Yeats' *The Player Queen*—was new to American actors, who were used to the long-standing routine of the director analyzing the characters and spoon-feeding them his interpretation. "The two plays were pounded (or soaked) into the cast, and the parts of the plays analyzed and interpreted in terms of what they themselves knew and had felt," the *New York Times* reported. "That was done by reducing the character to what Mr. Boleslavsky calls the acting 'spine' of the part—the informing part. Boleslavsky does not tell the players what to do. He strives to evoke in them the state of mind of the real character."[19]

As the stage debut of the Method drew closer, few knew that it was in danger of being scuttled by its own engineers. Alice Lewisohn, in particular, was dubious of the quality of the performances—and the choice of material—for the reopening of the Playhouse. On return from her sabbatical in the east, Alice had seen what was being attempted at Pleasantville and was worried about its progress after such a short time. "I became aware that to break down the American inhibitions and to try to build up a quasi-Russian foundation would certainly be a process of years, if it could be accomplished at all. To open the Playhouse after a year of silence called for a production significant in material and quality. Both were lacking. The situation was crucial, even beyond the possibility of an opening that did not fulfill its promise."[20] The Lewisohns, becoming ever more polarized from the Morgan-Arthurs, now saw the Method as a potential threat to the stability of the Playhouse. "We were faced with the problem of whether or not to give this production the right of way in its obviously chrysalis state. In the end we reasoned, perhaps unwisely, that the one chance of restoring equilibrium was to see the experiment through." And so, the first American chapter of the Method was brought—reluctantly, by some—to the stage.

The first production of Western actors using Konstantyn Stanislavski's Russian "system" (later known as the *Method*) took place at New York's Neighborhood Playhouse in the autumn of 1923. The program featured Aline MacMahon as Decima, the false Monarch in William Butler Yeats' *The Player Queen*. Donated to Cornell University by Aline MacMahon without copyright.

The American Laboratory Theatre's debut on October 16 gathered a large and eclectic group at the Neighborhood Playhouse in Grand Street. In the lobby before the show a petite, chic-looking brunette wearing a monocle mingled with Broadway royalty such as Otto Kahn, Kenneth MacGowan, and George S. Kaufman, all curious about the christening of a new idea in the American stage.[21] The two plays garnered generally positive, if qualified, reviews. *The Player Queen*—the story of a monarch who secretly abdicates her throne and is replaced by a base impostor—was by far the better reviewed of the double bill, creating a sustained mood of eerie otherworldliness and described by the *New York Tribune* as "a fantastic, poetic and colorful farce." *Blanco Posnet* did not fare as well. Set in the American West, it concerns a horse thief who engages in a moral battle with a small town's minister and judge. It was *Blanco Posnet* more than *The Player Queen* that resulted in a raft of reviews calling the bill "mixed in more senses than one" and "a novel experiment," which may be read as polite code for "a noble failure."[22] However, even for those that found the Russian school no more effective than the decades-old declarative acting style of Broadway, there was still some equivocation in their criticism. "This is not quite fair," they allowed, "for Mr. Boleslavsky has had only three months to instill his philosophy into actors mostly habituated to the other way of doing things. Three months is a short time to work a revolution—even on the stage. Or perhaps especially on the stage." These were the exact reservations that Alice Lewisohn held about transplanting the Russian style to the West. She was visionary in thinking that if the Russian style were to spark a revolution it would be a long time gestating; the Method, in fact, took decades to truly shake off those long entrenched "American inhibitions."

Along with her astute understanding of the big picture, Alice Lewisohn also predicted a rare micro outcome hiding within the macro view directly in front of her. "Building up the Russian foundation *might* be affected in an individual case," she wrote, "just as occasionally one finds in the West an artist whose work indicates some institutional or inherited Eastern tendency." In this first class, the Method has already found its original, nonnative resonant voice. Aline MacMahon was the right woman at the right moment: young enough to be malleable to new input, thoroughly energized by seemingly limitless possibilities, and dedicated enough to stay the course. Immediately, in her debut incorporating the Method into her repertoire, Aline was singled out as the performer in which a difference in quality and sincerity was obvious. In *The Player Queen*, Aline is Decima, the harlot-impostor who replaces her errant Queen. Of her, the *New York Times* said, "The performance of the

Player Queen by Miss Aline MacMahon gave true evidence of understanding the hussy she played. Miss MacMahon seemed to have gotten into the skin of Yeats's wench; beautiful, ambitious, gutter-bred, thwarted, betrayed, sardonically tricked at the very last into the very Queenship she coveted. *The Player Queen* was really beautiful." One might wonder what personal experiences that the decorous Aline MacMahon was accessing that led her to capture the characterization of such a low woman. This of course, is the essence of Stanislavski's teaching: the ability to find those emotions to which we are all subject—anger, resentment, desire, envy—and bring them up in the service of understanding others.

For Aline, so steeped in elocution exercises and the rote acting techniques of the nineteenth century, her opportunity to study with Boleslavsky was an epiphany. "If you have something that you passionately believe in that helps you concentrate when you're acting, that's what counts. That's what I found in the Stanislavski Method."[23] Her time in the New York countryside changed everything. It had revealed a path to greater emotional truth, and she now began to think of herself as an artist instead of a mere actor. For the rest of her career, Aline MacMahon will rely on the ideas and exercises of the Method to find her emotional center. From here her desire for meatier, more important roles magnifies, and Broadway will soon oblige.

In her 1959 memoir about the Playhouse, *Leaves from a Theatre Scrapbook*, Alice Lewisohn summed up her feelings about the American Laboratory Theatre experiment and its first appearance on a western stage: "If a conclusion is to be drawn at a safe distance, this experiment can point to the dangers attending a new way or epoch in the growth of a group or individual, and the need to sacrifice the personal value for a widened outlook. Here it meant the conscious acceptance of an unsatisfactory, alien experiment in order to avert a schism in the group as in the values of production."[24]

Boleslavsky was far more prescient about what this fledgling effort could mean to the art of acting—and even more of its potential impact on the culture that it had invaded. Writing about the formation of a teaching laboratory before the Pleasantville experiment had even begun, he outlined the possibilities which might echo from it. "The creation of such a laboratory requires the consecration of its members to the work of the theatre. There is no place in this for people who wish to make a quick fortune. The group must be small. Some of the performances should not even be open to the public. But such a laboratory could push forward the theatrical art of the country twenty years. It could become a successful repertory theatre, ready in turn to cede its place to new labs—young, fresh and as enthusiastically searching for newer forms. Every theatre should point a way to the laboratory of the future."[25] Indeed, Boly's work with the Playhouse did exactly as he hoped—it spawned generations of performers and teachers who gradually integrated new ideas, thoughts, and techniques to the lexicon of the stage. When Alice Lewisohn wrote her dire summation of the Method experiment in 1959, she was primarily thinking of its effect on the Playhouse and not of Boleslavsky's nebulous future. She was, of course, terribly shortsighted. By then, the so-called unsatisfactory, alien experiment she helped birth had created nothing less than a revolution in the performing arts.

Following the double bill at the Neighborhood Playhouse, Boleslavsky planned a formal opening of the Lab Theatre for November 14. By then, none of the students who had attended Boly's school in the country remained with the company. Most, including Aline, simply took what they had learned and returned to the Neighborhood Playhouse, while the Lab moved to other quarters. In spite of its mixed results, the Boleslavsky experiment did result in positive change at the Playhouse. Out of the intense Russian boot camp came a new style of daily preparation. "Each day began early with technical work in voice and movement," Alice recalled, "followed by rehearsals, then more work on the current bill, and other specialized problems. Strenuous as it was, the actors thrived on it, and there had never been a better esprit de corps. Something electrical evolved out of that experience. This new impulse and sense of coordination had undoubtedly been stimulated by the experiment in Pleasantville."[26] By November the Playhouse regulars—other than Aline—had, to a greater or lesser degree, moved away from the Russian style and were preparing their next production, Percy MacKay's *This Fine-Pretty World*.

A naturalistic story of Kentucky coal miners, *This Fine-Pretty World* continued the repertory format of the Neighborhood Playhouse, with only thirty-three performances before the company quickly moved to another play with the same performers. Following her entrée into the Method style, repertory theater was the perfect format for Aline to put her new training to use. Here she could tackle complex roles one after another, exploring her own psyche and growth as an artist. Boleslavsky himself recognized this idea as a teaching tool. Writing in the opening night program of *The Player Queen* double bill he said, "Creating characters in two plays so diverse offers the actor a genuine opportunity for the development of his technique."[27] Over the years Aline became a champion of the repertory format, hoping that a national company could be created which would mount important plays that were unlikely to be seen anywhere else. *The Drama* magazine recognized the difficulty of quality plays to find an audience in their review of *This Fine-Pretty World*. "The play is conceded to be a valuable contribution to literature, but not so readily as an acting drama. We have been trained to look for 'punch,' for speed and clever lines, and [*World*] makes its points in slow humor, locale, and subtle language. Here, the repertory theater is needed. The public interested in this play is limited, therefore audiences outside New York will not be able to see it. As a repertory piece in large cities, it would afford many hundreds of people with a worthwhile evening in the theatre." Of the Playhouse's production came this final word, clearly describing the qualities that Aline had uncovered in her time with Boleslavsky: "Aline MacMahon's characterization of May Maggot, in its simplicity, naturalness, and native flavor, was an outstanding achievement."[28]

Unfortunately, the Neighborhood Playhouse, and the Little Theatre movement it sprung from, was already waning. Small off-Broadway companies were either giving in to the mainstream, or giving up the ghost. The relative failure of *This Fine-Pretty World* ("the audience response was negligible," Alice Lewisohn admitted) further polarized the schism between art and commerce solidifying within the Playhouse. The Morgan-Arthurs advocated to move the company uptown and emphasize commercial properties, while the Lewisohn sisters still held true to the original tenets of their charter: quality amateur productions of challenging plays, with only a nominal eye to profits. To paraphrase the author of *The Player Queen*, "the center could not hold." The company that had raised Aline from a pup was divided against itself. It had only four years to live.

Although it doesn't appear anywhere in her theatrical record, Aline was next in the Neighborhood Playhouse's obscure production of *An Arab Fantasia*. An outgrowth of the influences that the Lewisohn sisters absorbed during their travels abroad, it featured four scenes from Middle Eastern life set to music and dance: the Riverbank, the Desert, the City, and the Shrine. According to the prompt book for the production, it would "address the contemporary urban context, where the rapidity of motion, penetration of science beyond the human horizon, opening of gates to an invisible world and navigation through the seas of space, present a new concept and create another environment for the individual." Apparently more comprehensible on stage than in the program description, *An Arab Fantasia* was a major success for the Playhouse. As it ended, plans were already underway for the latest incarnation of the *Grand Street Follies*.

After an absence of one year, the *Follies* returned to the public schedule of the Playhouse. Along with everyone else in the production, Aline helped write sketches, sew costumes, and paint scenery. In 1924 however, the Follies had completed its maturation from private party, to subscription-only bonus show, to full-scale summer program. That season the show was so popular it lasted from May until November, packing in East Side—and migratory uptown audiences—for 172 performances. Among the sketches Aline played in the 1924 edition was "These Fine Pretty Depths, by Percy My Eye," and "Play the Queen," a parody of the Playhouse's own production of *The Player Queen*. In it, Aline reprised the role of Queen Decima, here being drawn into the ongoing political scandal of Teapot Dome, then splashed in tall headlines across every newspaper in America. The satire was so devastating to President Warren Harding's Republican administration that representatives of the Democratic Party offered a fortune for the players to repeat it at their New York City nominating convention. Not wanting to get their hands dirty with American politics, the Playhouse politely declined.[29]

While the 1924 *Follies* was a great success, it became much more for Aline MacMahon. It was there that Aline had her first true breakthrough performance with an imitation of the British music hall singer and actress Gertrude Lawrence. Lawrence, later known for creating the role of Anna in the original cast of *The King and I*, was riding high in the enormously successful *Charlot's Revue* on Broadway, which Aline had attended that summer. Aline's presentation of Agnes Morgan's dead-on parody of Lawrence's signature song, "Limehouse Blues" ("Well, Wouldn't You?"), drew a blizzard of press notices that quickly put her name on the lips of the Manhattan theater world. "Aline MacMahon was giving an imitation of Gertrude Lawrence that in its truthfulness was almost uncanny," the *New York Herald* reported.[30] Another notice, just six weeks after the *Follies* opened, said, "Aline MacMahon does many things in the Follies, but the thing that made her famous overnight was her impersonation of Gertrude Lawrence. We are sure you'll be amused at the likeness when you see it."[31] The playbill called her "inimitable," *Variety* noted that she was "a personality girl" who provided "a bright interlude," and the *Times* offered this: "[Aline MacMahon's] imitation came through with an efficiency and a humor of hearty gusto."[32] The hype was enhanced when Lawrence herself attended the revue in order to see what all the fuss was about. It was reported that she "squealed with unconcealed joy" at the sight, and made her way backstage to congratulate Aline on her performance. The 1924 edition of the *Follies* was so well received that New York critics, columnists, performers, and producers entreated the Playhouse to move the show closer to Broadway. "Everyone has been kind enough to suggest that," Aline said when confronted with the idea, "and you know that the producers have been offered any number of big theaters uptown. But they are going to finish what they have begun right here on Grand Street."[33] Before the summer was even a month old, Aline's new notoriety attracted her own uptown suitor— one who would test her loyalty to both the *Follies* and the Neighborhood Playhouse.

4

THE RIVER OF STARS IS ROLLING

During the summer of 1924 Aline MacMahon's star was sincerely on the rise. Between the coverage of Boleslavsky's Playhouse opening and her ersatz Gertrude Lawrence, Aline's notoriety was such that the *New York Herald* sent a reporter to interview her about the *Follies*. By now Aline had developed a healthy ego as it related to her talent and career, and when the writer asked if she "had ever appeared on Broadway," Aline responded with a slightly imperious pique that drew an apology in print. "Now, of course, we should not have put it that way," the *Herald* allowed, cleverly painting themselves as the culprit. "We might have known that anyone as brilliant as Miss MacMahon must be well known, even though we had missed her." After some other very kind words, the author ended the article on a cryptic note: "Next season something splendid is happening to Miss MacMahon. First, she said we might announce it, and then she asked us not to. So we won't."[1] When the article appeared in print a few days later, its headline revealed that the reporter's own ego had also been bruised: "Interviewing a Tenor Unawares is All Right," it said, "but it Isn't Possible With the Girl Who Looks Like Gerty Lawrence."

The secret that Aline wished momentarily to keep was that she had recently signed a contract with the Shubert Organization, then the most powerful theatrical syndicate in America, with nearly a thousand theaters under their control nationwide. With a keen eye for talent and money to burn, brothers Lee and J.J. Shubert regularly prowled the New York theater scene looking for quality performers to sign for their revues and legitimate productions. Having heard reports of "the bright and particular star" of the *Grand Street Follies*, Lee Shubert decided to find out for himself if the plaudits were deserved. A Shubert publicity department press release documented his visit for posterity. "One night, Lee went to the Neighborhood Playhouse to take a wee prospective peek at this fire that was causing such smoke. He found that the report of Miss MacMahon's excellence, far from being exaggerated, was overly mild—and before he left the theatre, he and Miss MacMahon had signed a contract."[2] It is indisputable that Lee Shubert visited Grand Street to see Aline MacMahon. As to the possibility of her signing a contract that night, trusting the accuracy of a Shubert press release is a fool's errand. Aline was not the least bit impulsive in these matters. She already felt great confidence in her value as a performer and could not be pressured into signing a contract without careful consideration and representation. Also, Lee Shubert's visit to Grand Street occurred no later than the beginning of June, and Aline did not affix her signature to the document until June 27th. Initially slated to take effect on September 1, Aline insisted that she could not begin working until the *Follies* closed in October.[3] By now the Playhouse had become her surrogate family. Aline Bernstein was her closest friend, Agnes Morgan and Helen Arthur were mentors and confidants who entrusted Aline with their deepest secret, and the Lewisohn sisters (among others) were responsible for her life-changing opportunity to study with Boleslavsky. She would not have countenanced leaving them in the lurch merely for money and a move uptown.

In discussions with Lee Shubert, Aline had made it known that although a musical comedy performance was largely responsible for his interest in signing her, she was actually seeking the kind of dramatic opportunities that distinguished her performance in *This Fine-Pretty World*. Highly enamored of Aline's talent, Lee Shubert professed to understand, and the contract called for her to appear primarily in "legitimate dramatic plays." When the *Follies* finally closed in October 1924, Aline's five-year contract began at a weekly salary of $250, almost five times the wages of an average American household during the 1920s. Even at this, Aline found herself apprehensive at the prospect of being tied to anything for so long. "The day I signed my contract I said to Lee, 'Five years? How do I know what I'll want to do in five years?'" Without missing a beat, Lee Shubert smiled and said, "Don't worry. Any time you want to get out of it you can have a nervous breakdown."[4] She signed. And with that Aline MacMahon became the property of the greatest force on the American stage.

The Shuberts wasted no time in disappointing their new charge. By December Aline was rehearsing for a Christmas Day opening of J.B. Harold Terry's London smash, *Collusion*. Another of the era's innumerable "comedies of error," *Collusion* gave Aline her first top billing in the theater, above even her male costar, Richard Bird. Set during World War I, the comedy begins when a newlywed wife accidentally wrecks most of her husband's home (with a hand grenade, mind you) while he is away serving at the front. Somehow from this, her husband-soldier infers that she is pregnant, and the ensuing errors are eventually made right when the wife is forced to disown her platonic friend, an interior decorator who is afraid of burglars and always wears a gardenia. (Conclusions could be, and were, stereotypically drawn.) After three disappointing nights in New Haven's Shubert Theatre, *Collusion* moved to New York—and, hoping to live down the out-of-town response, changed its title to *Tame Cats*. It opened at the Princess Theatre on December 29, and was closed by January 5. No contemporary reviews can be found anywhere, even within the Shubert Organization's archives. Apparently even a corporation can feel shame.

Collusion was nothing like what Aline hoped to receive from the Shuberts, and she made it known to the brothers. During early 1925 they offered a series of weak vehicles that Aline turned down, including *The Conqueror*, which dissolved into nothingness during January. With no appropriate vehicle sitting on the shelf, the Shuberts now insisted that Aline take part in a large-scale musical.[5] Signed primarily on the success of her Gertrude Lawrence song in the *Follies*, the brothers had inserted a clause in Aline's contract that explicitly called for her to appear in at least one "musical play" during the 1924–25 season. Of course, performing a single song parody is quite different than heading an entire musical ensemble, and Aline knew it. With great amusement and relief, she later recalled how she was excused from the assignment. "J.J. Shubert insisted that I could sing. He said, 'You can sing. You can sing,' and I said, 'No, I can't,' and he insisted, 'Yes, you can. Now—you come down tomorrow and we'll have the orchestra here and I want to hear you sing.'" Under a contract that called for her to sing, Aline did as she was told. "So I went down and he heard me sing. And he said, 'No, you're right.'"[6]

After a spring season of unsuccessful attempts to find a vehicle for their new star, the Shuberts were simultaneously receiving a series of polite but insistent notes from Aline reminding them that her salary was due whether they had work for her or not.[7] In spite of some singular successes that season—Rudolph Friml's opulent musical *The Vagabond King* and Al Jolson in *Big Boy*—1925 saw the Shuberts with a raft of other underperforming shows. Also confronted by mounting losses on Aline's contract, the brothers politely asked if she would be good enough to help them recoup some of their unused investment. "Inasmuch as they didn't have a serious drama for me and they still had to pay me, they asked whether I'd play the sketches and do the Gertrude Lawrence impersonation which I'd done in the *Follies*." With the suggestive subtitle "Paris Edition," *Artists and Models*, the Shubert's annual low burlesque of scantily clad dancers and racy comedians promised to be more Continental (read: scandalous) than ever before. Feeling guilty for remaining idle from the beginning of 1925, Aline agreed. "I'm doing my best in 'Artist's and Models,'" she told Lee Shubert. "Even though it's not my *ideal*, exactly."[8]

In spite of her misgivings about being diverted into comedy, the assignment was a memorable one. By now, her relationship with Clarence was turning more serious, and the whirl of romance and flush of Broadway success was intoxicating. "I got a great kick out of those years when Clarence was courting me," she said. "He would come to the Winter Garden stage door to pick me up at night. He liked that very much." In addition to her faux Lawrence, Aline was also performing small parts in four other skits, including "what we say and what we really think," and "what wives may look forward to in the near future." Thinking back on that summer, Aline was nearly joyous in the memory. "I played in all the knockabout sketches—all the bed sketches, and oh! that was great fun. At the time I thought it was somewhat infra dig [undignified], but I had a wonderful time!"[9]

That summer was memorable for another reason. Away from the singularly unique atmosphere of the Neighborhood Playhouse, and in a big Broadway revue with forty beautiful dancing girls for the first time, Aline was able to see the true, unvarnished vision of New York's backstage culture. It was something that again challenged her often-prudish opinions—in fact, her entire outlook on the racier aspects of stage life. "I had a good chance to see what I suppose is the classic gold-digger—the girl who takes a job in the chorus to get ahead by accepting expensive presents and sleeping with the guy, casually. But what interests me in life are the contrasts. What impressed me especially were the gold-diggers who called up their mothers on Sunday in Wisconsin and cried over the telephone; and the gold-digger who had a brother who wanted to be a doctor and was putting him through college. It was perfectly possible to have a guy who was buying you a fur coat and you could come and walk around in practically nothing on the stage, and yet be absolutely melted by the sound of the voice of a family member back on the farm. I was very surprised by that. I don't know why, but at that time I thought everything was neatly boxed—this is one kind of person, that's another." By the time Aline reached Hollywood, her Victorian-era attitudes had been eroded by the simple realities of life. "In the thirties Hollywood was an extraordinary show-shop for beauty, and therefore there was a good deal of gold-digging going on there, too. Naturally a great deal of that would go on where all the beautiful girls were, and where all the lively fellows were, and I don't know why it shouldn't."[10]

The River of Stars is Rolling

After signing with the Shubert Theatrical Company, Aline was assigned to their annual revue of music and sketches, *Artists and Models,* for 1925. In it Aline reprised her impersonation of Gertrude Lawrence, which had received great acclaim at the Neighborhood Playhouse. Aline is the front row, second from left. *Courtesy of The Shubert Archive.*

Artists and Models was an enormous success, lasting 412 performances and running well into the 1926 season. But when the production went on tour in June, Aline instead went on a vacation in Europe. "It was on that vacation that I decided that what I cared most about in the theatre was dramatic work, not revues or musicals."[11] In London and Paris she scouted the local theater scene and reported her thoughts to Lee Shubert. "I've seen 'Mon Cure Chez les Riches' and the 'Folies Bergere', as I thought them most likely for New York presentation," she wrote. "Won't you please have your secretary make me a list of London plays you are interested in, so that I will be up on the productions you're planning for the fall?" Ultimately, her attention was not entirely for the benefit of her employers. "Of course I have an eager eye trained for a grand role for myself," she admitted.[12] On her return to the States, the Shuberts offered her more of what she had done in the *Follies*, or a lead in *The Pearl of Great Price*, a melodrama that other actresses had already turned down. Reluctantly, she accepted the assignment. In late October *Pearl* premiered with Aline in Brooklyn, but when it opened on Broadway, she was nowhere to be seen. With her contract now up for renewal, Aline's proverbial "nervous breakdown" was imminent. "The first year of my contract has expired," she wrote J.J. Shubert, "and there should be some definite understanding between us in the very near future. It is rather difficult for me to write about business, but if the contract is to continue, it should be for the additional $100 from the end of the first year. Will you agree with me that we should know definitely what our business relations will be and how long they are to continue?"[13] Shortly after receiving this correspondence, the brothers summoned Aline for a face-to-face meeting and released her into the wild. "It was a friendly agreement," she recalled. "I talked my way out of it."[14] Considering the amount of money the brothers had lavished on her over the previous year with little in the way of return, Aline likely did not have to talk too eloquently. "The Shuberts were always very nice to me, and we parted ways only because I wanted to do dramatic plays."[15] Years later, Aline considered the fruits of her decision to leave lucrative employment with America's premiere theatrical company in favor of the tenuous possibility of artistic opportunities. "I learned to act in the five years which followed," she recalled with satisfaction. Now released from servitude, Aline soon scored the dramatic breakout of her career, and a milestone for the Method in America.

When Aline returned from her European vacation, she had first visited her parents, and then her distinguished beau, Clarence Stein. The couple's time apart appears to have intensified their burgeoning love affair, and their courtship soon became more serious. Aline was then living on Sixth Avenue at 27th Street with her friend and roommate, superstar model and actress Marion Morehouse, later the wife of poet E.E. Cummings.[16] Although we cannot know with certainty, it is likely that Clarence took the opportunity of their reunion to again propose to Aline. Enjoying her recent independence away from the MacMahon home, and with a stage career just beginning to proffer high dividends, Aline reiterated her polite refusal of 1925. "I was pretty ambitious," she admitted. "I said no for a long time."

Toward the end of 1926 Kenneth MacGowan, the managing director of The Actor's Theatre, was planning a revival of Eugene O'Neill's *Beyond the Horizon*. After a string of successful debuts during his long association with the Provincetown Players, O'Neill had become America's premiere playwright. To direct his production of *Horizon*, MacGowan hired Provincetown director James Light, the man who was so impressed by Aline's senior performances at

Barnard that he offered her an invitation to the company. Light's intimate knowledge of O'Neill and his work made him the natural choice for this new production of the play, which had its premiere in 1920. While discussing casting, the two men considered the critical role of Ruth Atkins, the young girl who is loved by two brothers, and who—through capriciousness and immaturity—ruins all three of their lives. Both Light and MacGowan were familiar with Aline, mainly through comedic roles; Light from the Barnard production of *What Every Woman Knows*, and MacGowan from the *Grand Street Follies* and *Artists and Models*. But unlike the Shuberts, who could see only Aline's comic face, each of them recognized untapped dramatic possibilities boiling beneath the surface. The men called her in for an audition.

Ruth Atkins is the catalyst on which *Beyond the Horizon* turns. In the country, two brothers living on a farm neighboring the Atkins are each in love with her. Robert, the dreamer, is about to embark on a sea voyage around the world, while Andrew plans to run the family farm and hopes to marry Ruth. But just before Robert is about to leave, he discovers that Ruth loves him and cancels his trip in order to marry her. Heartbroken that he is not Ruth's choice, Andrew leaves the farm, taking Robert's place on the voyage. In short order Ruth realizes that she has made a grave mistake in marrying Robert. As the farm sinks into poverty under Robert's inept management, Ruth becomes so frustrated that she announces that she never loved him, and instead loves his brother. By the time Andrew returns, his love for Ruth is dead and gone, and he tells his brother so. But later, as tuberculosis is about to claim Robert's life, Ruth privately tells Andrew that she still loves him, and had never loved Robert. Andrew is so horrified that he insists Ruth must tell his dying brother that she loves him—but it is too late. Robert is dead, and the survivors must now forever live with their guilt. Under the heightened drama of O'Neill's pen, *Horizon* plumbed powerful depths. Here was a story tailor made for Aline's Method training.

When she read for the part, MacGowan and Light knew immediately that Ruth Atkins lived behind Aline's half-closed, gloomy eyes. Where her deep streak of sadness and defeat came from only Aline could say, but here is where her talent for pathos was comprehensively revealed for the first time. Throughout her career, her most effective dramatic performances conjure these wan qualities—emotions of melancholy, regret, sympathy, or disappointment. In Ruth she would call on all of these.

"It was a great experience," Aline said of her time working in *Beyond the Horizon*. "Mr. O'Neill was there every day at rehearsals and he dealt with

Aline with Robert Keith in the 1926 production of Eugene O'Neill's *Beyond the Horizon*. Her performance was a sensation, prompting no less a critic than Noel Coward to call her "astonishing, moving and beautiful." Studio publicity material.

everything he wanted to deal with in that play." During the ten weeks of the production Aline forged a fast bond with the author, and had a firsthand look as he corrected and perfected his own writing. "He cut *Beyond the Horizon* to pieces," she recalled. "He was not prolix—he did not want a hundred thousand words in every paragraph. He was a theater man and he found a better form to say the things he wanted to say." For Aline, the opportunity to work closely with one of the great dramatists of the twentieth century embodied everything she had been hoping for as an artist, and confirmed her decision to leave the plebian hands of the Shubert brothers. "It was my first extraordinary experience [in the theater]. Mr. O'Neill was a very handsome, beautiful fellow—a great pleasure to be with."

When *Beyond the Horizon* premiered in December, Aline MacMahon immediately became the uncontested dramatic sensation of the New York theater world. "'Beyond the Horizon' is receiving something of a distinguished revival at the Mansfield Theatre," the *Brooklyn Daily Eagle* said. "Distinguished not for the fame of those who presented it, but because, chiefly, of the serpentine, Machiavellian acting of Miss Aline MacMahon. She it was who, largely, made the production a delight to see. As the young farm girl recklessly in love in the first act, as the disillusioned wife of an incompetent young farmer in the second, and in the third as a woman of less than thirty who, nevertheless, 'wouldn't know how it feels to love if I wanted to,' she brought a realism into this play that made it a play of life instead of imagination alone."[17] Again and again—without the general knowledge of Aline's Method training, critics observe the precise exemplars of its tenets that she exhibits. Of her, Alexander Woolcott said, "That girl, who in the *Grand Street Follies* gave such a fine travesty of Gertrude Lawrence at her most girlish, played a bitter, tragic role with extraordinary beauty, vitality and truth." According to the New York *American*, "Miss MacMahon, in her utterly discouraged helplessness, her mute recognition, her complete indifference to the future, gave a performance of tremendous significance and beauty." Meanwhile, the *New Yorker* had a further superlative: "Her performance tempted one to rank her immediately among the Olympians." Finally, no less a figure than Noel Coward, recounting for London readers what he had seen in New York, expressed his deep admiration. "The performance of a comparatively unknown young actress, Aline MacMahon, remained in my mind as something astonishing, moving and beautiful."[18] Nearly fifty years later, Coward's praise was still stuck—largely—in Aline's mind. "When Noel Coward went back to England," she recalled, "he said that the three great experiences of his trip were, one, me in *Beyond the Horizon*, and . . ." (here she smiled and paused for effect), ". . . two others that I have naturally forgotten."[19]

At the box office *Beyond the Horizon* was a modest success, lasting seventy-nine performances, but for Aline it was incalculable. She had received instant notoriety in Manhattan stage circles and well-known producers kept her busy for the rest of 1927. In March she appeared in *Spread Eagle*, the story of a wealthy industrialist who engineers a revolution in Mexico to protect his mining interests. Aline played a corporate bookkeeper who is held hostage and subsequently killed by the revolutionaries that her own employer has hired. The experience was not a pleasant one for her. "On *Spread Eagle* I worked with [producer] Jed Harris, a villain," she said. When asked why he was a villain, her answer was vague, but suffused with venom. "Well, he is a sadistic man—he was, at least in my book and I didn't like him."[20] Aline had good company in her opinion; Jed Harris was hated by everyone on Broadway. Laurence Olivier called him "the most loathsome man I'd ever met," and Katharine Hepburn paid $14,000 to be released from a contract simply to avoid ever having to see him again. The last word in personal animus toward Harris came from writer/director George S. Kaufman. "When I die I want to be cremated and have my ashes thrown in Jed Harris's face," he said.

On May 6, 1927, Clarence Stein left New York for an extended tour of Russia and Turkey. In spite of her burgeoning career opportunities Aline desperately wanted to share in the adventure with him, but in 1927 such an arrangement would not have been deemed proper. "I missed my chance because we weren't married," she said.[21] As a representative of Canadian interests in town planning, Clarence was researching new construction in Turkey and Russia's North Caucasus district. This sojourn in Russia changed much for the couple. First, it gave Clarence a firsthand look at the Soviet State in situ, clarifying and solidifying his positive thoughts—at least at the micro level—about Communism, something he would impart to Aline. Second, the time apart appears to have convinced Aline that her feelings for Clarence were deep-seated and genuine. "After he got back I decided to marry him," she said, perhaps simply to be certain that she would not miss out on any other exotic travel plans.

Shortly after *Spread Eagle* closed, Aline was contacted by her mentor Richard Boleslavsky about appearing in a series of charity performances of *A Midsummer Night's Dream* that he was directing to benefit the Actor's Fund. The opportunity to reunite with Boleslavsky was a welcome tonic for the months she spent under Jed Harris's yolk. In June Aline strode the stage as Titania, Queen of the Fairies, and soaked up the opportunity to perform Shakespeare under Boleslavsky's kind baton. The June performances were such a success that they were repeated in August and the coffers of the Actor's Fund swelled with gratitude.

In the summer of 1927 Aline MacMahon was twenty-eight years old. She was a beautiful, if offbeat-looking woman with a smooth, round face and a crown of hair of which a Gibson Girl would be proud. That season Aline auditioned for *Her First Affair*, a comedy about a Jazz-Age flapper, engaged to a milquetoast fellow, who is entranced by a book on the sexual liberation of women. When she encounters the extremely handsome and successful older author in person, the girl announces her intentions to seduce him (to the author's wife, no less) in an effort to facilitate her own liberation. Unconcerned, the wife steps aside and, after some ever-so-polite machinations, the girl returns to her comfy fiancée, and Victorian-era ethics are restored.

Among the producers of *Her First Affair*, there was never any chance that Aline MacMahon might play the girl. At twenty-eight, and with her proper manner, she already seemed too mature, too worldly, to play the callow voice of youth. "When I started out in the theatre," she observed, "there were only five categories of players: leading woman, leading man, ingenue, juvenile and old character player. If you were a young actress you were supposed to be an ingenue, and at that time ingenues were little and round. I was tall and thin, so I became a character actress."[22] *Her First Affair* seems to have been Aline's moment of becoming. She was cast as the author's wife and never quite looked back. Far from being disappointed, she saw her ability to take on character parts as a blessing for her type. "I was lucky because when I began to act, playwrights were beginning to write good character parts." Her Method training had resulted in the golden opportunity to have a career that included all types of roles, even those in which she portrayed women far beyond her years. In *Affair* she was again singled out, this time for a character that was as much as fifteen years her senior. The *Brooklyn Daily Eagle* found her so convincing that they felt she could replace Ethyl Barrymore, then nearly fifty (and playing a character closer to sixty), in her hit production of Somerset Maugham's *The Constant Wife*.

Her First Affair was just one of the era's innumerable stage and screen stories of the triumph of Victorian mores over the loose morals of the Jazz Age. It was not an unexpected response to the jarring cultural shift ushered in by World War I; the hegemony of America's Old World, rural paradigm was being contested, and the elderly, moneyed elite were frightened by the schism. But there was no holding back the change—by the end of the 1920s the city will have usurped the farm, sex will be permanently liberated from behind the parlor screen, and youth will have its sway. In many ways this inner war of American culture was also the inner war of Aline MacMahon. Even with her feet planted firmly among the Roaring Twenties loosening norms—the experimental arts, alternate lifestyles, and radical politics—

Aline was still that creature of propriety from her parents' age. Aline's internal struggle, like America's societal struggle—still raging to this day—would never be truly resolved.

As 1927 was ending, so was Aline's successful run in *Her First Affair*. That winter, an idea that had been hatched in Europe months earlier was now coalescing in Manhattan. It would result in Aline's appearance in the most talked-about stage production of 1928, and one of the most notorious stories of Broadway in the 1920s.

5

NO ONE HAS EVER KNOWN HER ALIVE

The payment of a single dollar was all it took to introduce a plague of sin and iniquity to New York City.

In the summer of 1927, Helen Arthur was on a working holiday in France with her partner Agnes Morgan.[1] Earlier that year Helen and other members of the now defunct Neighborhood Playhouse had formed the Actor-Managers Corporation and began producing plays in New York with the remnants of the Playhouse's resident company. Traveling on behalf of the new organization as its executive director, one of Helen Arthur's tasks was to peruse the Paris theater scene and determine what she might find for Actor-Managers to import to New York that hadn't been seen there before. In August, just as Aline was opening in *Her First Affair*, Helen happened upon a play appearing at the Theatre de l'Avenue, *Maya*, written by an obscure but respected author and poet, Simon Gantillon.[2] The production was enjoying a successful run in the French capital (eventually reaching 425 performances), and had also been mounted to popular acclaim in South America and half a dozen major European cities.[3]

Sitting in the audience that warm summer evening, Helen Arthur watched the story of Bella, a Marseilles prostitute whose sordid life is illuminated through her dealings with the clients she entertains during the course of a day. Nine men of disparate social class and nationality step through Bella's curtained door, each looking for something different from their encounter. In her, each finds a unique, essential aspect of womanhood that momentarily fulfills their shapeless desire; by turns she is mother, confidant, lover, companion, friend, confessor—the mercurial embodiment of a kaleidoscope of illusions known by the Hindus as "Maya." Helen Arthur was immediately swept away by the dignity, beauty, and power of *Maya*. "It is the

In 1927 the New York District Attorney's censorship of the Broadway drama *Maya* sparked a political firestorm. Aline received glowing reviews as Bella, the Marseilles prostitute who stirred up all the fuss. Studio publicity material.

most interesting and stimulating play I have encountered in several years," she wrote in 1928.[4] "It faces life without flinching." Before Helen Arthur had even left the Theatre de l'Avenue that night, she resolved to do two things—to bring the play to New York, and to have her friend Aline MacMahon play the gloomy, world-weary prostitute Bella.[5]

What Helen Arthur may not have fully considered at that moment was that while *Maya* was popular and respected in France, it was not the kind of entertainment likely to be accepted on the metropolitan stage in America. Between the wars, Continental Europe enjoyed a liberality in the arts far exceeding that of the United States, where movements toward modernity were still being hindered by remnants of the Victorian power structure. Even in 1927, the portrayal of prostitution and open sex in the theater would usually result in police herding a tangle of producers, actors, and managers into the dark box of a Black Mariah. Even in London—then somewhat more tolerant than the United States—two different productions of *Maya* were forced to side step the censorial wrath of Scotland Yard by presenting them in private performances on a subscription-only basis.[6] In New York it was far worse. Since 1922, the city's theatrical morals had been regularly submitted to, and judged by, a civilian Play Jury, a self-policing body created by Broadway producers to stave off then-imminent government censorship of the stage. Under the jury, when the suitability of any production was called into question, twelve citizens were impaneled from a pool of volunteers and, after viewing the offending play, they would vote to censor, continue, or close it. Despite the fact that during its five years in existence the Play Jury failed to shutter even a single production, its decisions—backed by an agreement with Actor's Equity obliging their members to withdraw from any offending play—were assumed to be legally binding. Until they were revealed not to be.

When the jury eventually condemned a sketch revue show called *The Bunk of 1926*, its backers simply refused to close it, or even change it. And when Actor's Equity requested that the cast honor their contracts and remove themselves from the play, producer Ramsey Wallace received a legal injunction against Equity and then threatened to sue individual members of the jury that had condemned *Bunk*. The case went to the New York Supreme Court, which found in favor of Wallace and his revue. In writing the majority decision, Justice George Mullan declared that there was "entirely too much meddling in public affairs by unofficial bodies" and called the jury system a "terrifying instrument" that could be as easily applied to the closing of a butcher shop as a theatrical performance.[7] With this ruling the Play Jury was shown to have all the bite of a scurvy sailor. When, a few months later, the toothless jury failed to condemn *The Captive*, a sincere drama concerning a socialite's lesbian affair, New York's highly conservative district attorney, Joab Banton, decided that he could no longer tolerate the arrogant machinations of Broadway producers in his city. Patiently waiting for the right moment to institutionalize his repressive agenda, Banton eventually saw an opening on the political horizon and took action. On February 5, 1927, while New York's popular liberal mayor Jimmy Walker was vacationing in Florida, the DA unilaterally disbanded the Play Jury system, and made himself the official censor of the New York stage.[8] Just four days later, Banton dispatched police wagons to three separate Broadway theaters, using his autonomous power to ceremoniously stop each performance and jail more than forty producers and actors, including Basil Rathbone and Helen Menken. The fates of the three raided productions were varied. *The Captive* was deemed immoral and closed following a long and costly court battle. *The Virgin Man*, a melodrama about the base temptations of a pious gentleman, endured a series of legal contretemps that closed the play but ultimately provided the offenders a mere slap on the wrist. Finally, in the most famous case of Banton's crusade, Mae West's long-running star vehicle *Sex* was closed, and the actress confined for ten days in the Woman's Workhouse on Welfare Island.[9] Instead of being ostracized, Miss West received enormous publicity and good will from the situation. "Give my regards to Broadway," an unapologetic West told reporters as she sashayed off to serve her sentence. Finding the outcome of his censorial efforts less than ideal, Banton began to rethink his tactics.

Joab Banton may have been a prude, but he was not a fool. In the wake of the Play Jury's ineffectiveness and his own public relations failures, the district attorney knew that criminal prosecution was not the tool with which to bring the stage to heel. He would need a bigger cudgel with which to bludgeon Broadway producers. He found it with the help of the New York State legislature. The law they passed on April 7, 1927—possibly the most expeditious whirlwind of civic outrage in state history—would censor the New York stage by intimidation for the following forty years. Known as the Wales Padlock Act, it moved away from criminal prosecution of producers and actors and instead attacked the theater owner's pocketbook. Under the new law, New York's commissioner of licenses was granted the power to revoke for one year the license of any theater presenting obscene or salacious material. Unlike other laws, Wales Padlock left no ambiguity for defendants or the courts to dwell on. "The production of any drama depicting or dealing with sex perversion or degeneracy is made illegal, and conviction may be based on only part of the play."[10] It is not difficult to imagine the chilling effect this had upon theater owners. Few would dare challenge the law in court where a ruling against them would mean the loss of twelve months revenue. Now that Banton had his club, he began looking for a head upon which to unleash it.

It was just at this moment that Helen Arthur resolved to bring a play about a prostitute and her tawdry clientele to the heart of America's theater industry. On August 23—just four months after the passage of Banton's censorship act—she tendered a single dollar to Bory Osso, Simon Gantillon's Paris agent, and secured the rights to produce *Maya* in the United States.[11] Whether or not Helen understood it, producing *Maya* in New York was like bringing a bomb-wielding anarchist to a Park Avenue gallery opening. The police would certainly be called, but you couldn't be sure that concerned citizens might not beat the Bolshevik interloper to within an inch of his life before they even arrived.

Returning from Paris in the fall, Helen wasted no time in preparing *Maya*'s introduction to conservative America. On November 4, the rights to the play were transferred to the Actor-Managers Corporation, and the young producers immediately set out to locate financing. Quickly, they found a financial angel in Gertrude Newell, a Broadway costume and set designer who had also produced (or at least bankrolled) a series of plays during the previous decade. Additional financing came from Sidney Ross, who had provided funds for Actor-Managers recently closed flop *If*, and was simultaneously involved in their latest production—another bust—*The Love Nest*. Mr. Ross's only caveat to investment was that his name be kept off the program bill, the first clear sign that anyone associated with *Maya* understood that there might be trouble ahead.

Meanwhile, Helen Arthur gave a detailed description of the play to Aline MacMahon, and asked her if she would be interested in taking the part of Bella. The timing was perfect. At the end of November, *Her First Affaire* was winding down after a very successful three-month run, leaving Aline at liberty just as Actor-Managers would need her. With the understanding that she needed to first read the translation, Aline tentatively came onboard.

Things began moving very quickly for *Maya* now. By contract, Actor-Managers had to present an English translation to author Simon Gantillion (and Aline) for approval no less than sixty days in advance of opening.[12] For this they chose the well-known Irish writer and critic Ernest Boyd (author of the 1925 biography of H.L. Mencken), and tasked him with having a draft ready by mid-December. While Boyd was working, Actor-Managers secured a booking agreement for a February debut at the Comedy Theater on 41st Street, owned by Aline's former employers, the Shubert brothers.[13]

Few people knew the pulse of the big city theatergoer better than brothers Lee and J.J. Shubert. Although they would not be the producers of the show, the Shuberts knew that *Maya*'s "immoral" subject matter could immediately provoke DA Banton to attempt to padlock it. But they also understood what we still know today: sex sells, and one can always count on the public's desire to see anything they're told they should avoid. With a clear grasp of this dichotomy of human nature, the Shubert's decided to do the only thing they could do under the circumstances: be represented on both sides of the fence. First, they inserted a clause in their contract with Actor-Managers allowing them to give a termination notice to the company if the play were deemed obscene. Then they also quietly purchased a significant percentage of the production.[14] "I understand that [Mr. Shubert] does not care to have his name used on the program," a disappointed Helen Arthur wrote after learning that their investment was to be kept secret.[15] The Shubert brothers knew better than to be associated directly with *Maya*, but they were perfectly willing to accept the profits that might come in her wake.

The Shubert company's disinterest in being publicly connected to *Maya*—except as landlords of the production—perhaps gave Helen her first glimmer of the potential dangers she was courting. Previously, she and her partners in Actor-Managers claimed to be so convinced of Gantillon's sincerity and of the beauty of the play, that there was no serious consideration of running afoul of New York's censorship law. "We felt that *Maya* did not come within the meaning of that law, as it was not indecent or salacious."[16] For now, they continued on their path, hoping that the artistic merits of the play would overcome the Victorian priggishness of New York City officials.

Ernest Boyd delivered his translation in late December, just as Aline was ending her three months in *Her First Affaire*. Helen quickly passed her leading lady a copy of the completed script, and the beauty and poetry of Gantillon's words impressed Aline immensely.[17] Here at last was a part that indulged her genuine desire for important, difficult work, and perfectly framed her gift for pathos. The character of Bella was something she had been waiting for almost since her first serious appearances on stage: a woman of character, but one who was also degraded and flawed. And although Aline knew that the play—and the role—would be controversial, her professional courage would not allow her to back down from a challenge. Her sense of moral fearlessness, handed down from her mother and aunt, was well formed. *Maya* would be a valuable opportunity for audiences to see that she was capable of so much more than her recent Shubert assignments had delivered. Here again was the twelve-year-old girl who forged an ethical resolve from unwarranted attacks on her character, still fighting on against Puritanical, small-town sensibilities. She agreed to be Bella.

After six years of courtship, Aline at last married Clarence Stein in 1928. "I was very ambitious. I didn't want to get married for a long time," she said. *Courtesy of The Shubert Archive.*

Aline reported for rehearsals on January 12, 1928.[18] After a few years away from her Neighborhood Playhouse compatriots, the production was like old-home week for her, as it featured many of the actors and artists she counted as friends from those heady days. Agnes Morgan, who oversaw Aline in the *Follies of 1924* and *The Madras House* was to direct, following the dissolution of Actor-Managers ill-fated maiden effort, *If*. The production designer was Aline's close friend Aline Bernstein (then in the dysfunctional center of her not-so-discreet liaison with author Thomas Wolfe), and the cast and crew featured a half dozen other faces so familiar from earlier years.

January 1928 was a time of change for Aline and Clarence. Since his return from Russia Clarence had been embroiled in writing his first serious outline of a project that would be his long-lasting legacy, the development of the planned community at Radburn, New Jersey. It was the logical extension of several earlier steps in his career, including the 1923 creation of Sunnyside Gardens in Queens, New York, and would call to bear all his skills and energy. Although Radburn would soon consume his career, his personal life was about to undergo a similar change. Although Aline had previously given loving refusals to Clarence's marriage proposals because of her theatrical ambitions, she was now well established on Broadway and knew that he understood and respected her independence. "I didn't want to get married for a long time," Aline recalled, "but after looking everybody over and deciding that nobody could come up to him in quality, I married him."[19] Or more precisely, Clarence married her. After his series of unsuccessful proposals, Aline knew that Clarence might be wary of another attempt. So, following a dinner with friends on a windy January night in New York, Aline MacMahon at last proposed marriage to Clarence Stein. His answer was "yes."

True to her powers of discernment, Aline had found a perfect partner for her love and her ambitions: throughout his life Clarence Stein took joy in her successes, commiserated in her setbacks, endured their periodic separations, and loved her unconditionally. They were so mutually respectful it is impossible to know for certain which of them found more pride in the other. Although outside forces would eventually intervene, for now the horizon was bright and infinitely wide.

While Aline considered her matrimonial future and Clarence waded into the architectural planning and manufacture of an entire new community, *Maya* coalesced behind the closed doors of the Comedy Theater. "I think the play is working out in very good shape," Helen Arthur told her investors after a few weeks of rehearsals. "It seems to be as interesting as the Paris production—and that is saying a great deal."[20] Unfortunately by early February it is clear that Actor-Managers and their backers have suddenly become more than a little worried about the possibility of legal action against *Maya*; the conviction that its honesty and poetry would protect it from prosecution by the Wales Padlock Act was quickly eroding. "We are not going to have any invitation dress rehearsal of any sort," Helen wrote to the Shuberts. "We think it would be a mistake to have the play discussed the day before we open."[21] Actor-Managers apparently did not want Joab Banton to be aware of the content of *Maya* before it appeared on stage opening night. The fear was serious enough for them to consider offering tickets to *Maya* on a subscription-only basis, hoping to end-around the censors as had been done in London. In a letter to Helen Arthur, the Actor-Managers attorney, Melville Cane, quietly disabused her of the idea: "I have been considering the matter [of subscription tickets] . . . but fear that this method will be of no assistance, as the law makes no distinction between public and private performances," he wrote."[22] As a postscript to his comments, Cane instead offered a canny political idea as a solution to their worries: "How about inviting the Mayor to the opening?" he asked. The next day Helen resolved to do just that. "It may be only an idle gesture," she said, "but we would be very glad if it turns out that he is free and cares to come."[23] The liberal but very politically minded James J. Walker was completely and utterly at liberty, and did not care to come.

Maya opened on Tuesday, February 21, 1928, and in spite of scant advance publicity, the house was full to overflowing.[24] As the curtain rises, we see Bella in her room, hair looped high on her head and eyes half-seen under heavy lids. She awaits the arrival of the fleet to Marseilles, and the trek of long-at-sea sailors to her "Port of Call." Then, in the words of the New York *Evening World*, "before the eyes of all who attend, there goes on freely, with every attention to detail, the day to day business of milady of the quarter, the shady queen of the peignoir, the slippers and the majestic comb."[25] What unfolds through those scenes is both trivial and profound. There is a Cockney coal shoveler who cries in Bella's arms at the vagaries of fate that destroyed his life, and an old man who is reminded by her of his childhood sweetheart, a symbol of youth now well and truly gone. When a new client suddenly recognizes Bella as a youngster he'd known years before, she angrily denies her true identity and sends him away. Another vignette reveals a deep-seated building block of Bella's damaged psyche when she is told that her daughter, given up long ago to adoption, has died. Heartbroken from a lifetime of trauma, Bella stares numbly, like a soldier hoping to be released from his pain. "She's probably better off," is all she can say. Later, talking with a neighborhood laundry girl of her daughter's age, she cynically admonishes the child to "save up your happiness now for later on," entirely certain that she won't. And when a good-hearted Norwegian peasant arrives carrying a doll he has bought for his sister back home, Bella's fragile construct of toughness turns in on her, and she feels something like love for the first time in years.

By all accounts—even those of the moralists—*Maya* was a sincere and compassionate effort to understand the forces that shape our lives, for good or ill.

Somebody, of course, was going to have to pay for it.

The next day, the reviews of New York's newspapers were divided into three tiers. There were those that praised the production as an artistic

THE NEW YORK MAGAZINE PROGRAM

COMEDY THEATRE

West 41st Street, between Broadway and Sixth Avenue
LEE and J. J. SHUBERT Proprietors.

FIRE NOTICE: Look around NOW and choose the nearest Exit to your seat. In case of fire, walk (not run) to THAT Exit. Do not try to beat your neighbor to the street.

JOHN J. DORMAN, Fire Commissioner.

WEEK BEGINNING MONDAY EVENING, FEBRUARY 27, 1928
Matinees Thursday and Saturday

THE ACTOR-MANAGERS, Inc.
(In association with GERTRUDE NEWELL)
present
Simon Gantillon's Play

MAYA

Translated by Ernest Boyd
Directed by Agnes Morgan
Setting and Costumes by Aline Bernstein

CHARACTERS
(In the order of their appearance)

PROLOGUE:
THE SAILOR......................................OTTO HULETT
THE GIRL..ALINE MacMAHON

THE PLAY:
BELLA...ALINE MacMAHON
CELESTE..HELEN TILDEN
PHONSINE......................................MARY ROBSON

PROGRAM CONTINUED ON SECOND PAGE FOLLOWING

The opening-night program of Maya did not need reprinting. Deemed indecent by the district attorney's office, the producers were ordered to close the show after only twelve days, or risk having their theatre forcibly shuttered for one year and their players thrown in jail.

triumph, those who derided it as dull and pretentious folderol, and a few who eschewed any theatrical judgment, instead reviewing its very existence as obscene. "There are things that it is impossible and undesirable to be explicit about in the pages of a great family newspaper," critic Leonard Hall wrote, "though they seem fit enough for the public stage, if only they are presented under the false face of poetic symbolism. There isn't enough beauty here to pay for *Maya's* beastliness. The theatre going public are better off without it." Countering Mr. Hall's haughty disdain, Alexander Woollcott stated flatly: "The experience enlarges the heart; you can say no more for any play than that," while the *New York Times'* Brooks Atkinson observed that author Simon Gantillon "looked through sordid material to universal values with a good deal of artistic integrity."[26] The arguments continued in the *Sun*, where Gilbert Gabriel declared that *Maya* "waded in monotony and stupidity," while the respected Burns Mantle called the production "drab and spiritless."[27]

In spite of these harsh words, there was one thing upon which Mr. Mantle and all the other critics pro or con could agree. "Miss MacMahon," he allowed, "is a striking figure as Bella, and plays with considerable power and sensitivity."[28] This was a refrain repeated in each review, regardless of the writer's level of enthusiasm, priggishness, or boredom. "Aline MacMahon catches all the preternatural patience of Bella in a splendid performance," Atkinson wrote in the *Times*. "Hers is notable character acting."[29] The *Journal* was similarly appreciative. "Miss MacMahon portrays Bella with much understanding and sympathy, imparting splendidly to the character its dual qualities of earth and mysticism. It is a fine piece of work."[30] Even Gilbert Gabriel admitted, "Miss MacMahon plays Bella with grateful restraint, with an edge of rare irony, with a complete recess from that self-pity which makes the rest of her fellow actors sound stertorous and oftentimes appalling."[31] The *World* declared Aline's acting "admirable in its clean, audacious reticence," and others variously dubbed her "excellent," "wonderful," "earnest" and "eloquent." Robert Lytell summed up the feelings of many critics when he stated simply, "Nobody else came within a mile of her."

With opening night come and gone, it was now only for Aline and her fellow troupers to wait and see what the public and, more importantly, the police thought. Alexander Woollcott perfectly encapsulated that sense of apprehension in his morning-after review with just two sentences: "*Maya* is so beautiful a play and at the Comedy they play it so well that it cannot fail. But, brought face to face with such a testing play, there is always a chance that New York will fail."[32]

Unknown to anyone in the company, the New York police were already scrutinizing *Maya*. The commissioner's office had gotten wind of the play's content and placed an officer in the opening night audience at the Comedy Theater. Although there had been "no legitimate complaint" from the public, the officer's report that night roused the ire of Police Commissioner Joseph Warren and District Attorney Banton, both of whom where itching for a noble victory over public indecency.[33] The following evening they dispatched James Sinnott, secretary to the commissioner, and assistant District Attorney James Wallace to see the show, where the two men anonymously purchased their tickets and sat in the last row of the orchestra. After the performance both men returned to the commissioner's office in a state of high dudgeon. Without a word of complaint from anyone in the city except these three men, Wallace declared the play obscene and advised Banton that it should definitely be closed on the basis that it would "corrupt the morals of youth."[34] The failure that Alexander Woollcott had warned of was at hand. Hereupon, a complex whirlwind of politics, journalism, bribery, broken promises, public debate, and good, old-fashioned American Puritanism exploded over the City of New York.

On Thursday, February 23, Helen Arthur was woken by a call from J.J. Shubert. It was an inopportune time for a theatrical upheaval in the Shubert agency. Both brothers were away from New York, J.J. on business, and Lee vacationing in Palm Springs. Over the long-distance line, J.J. gave Helen bad news: *Maya* was in grave danger, he said. The district attorney was threatening to close the show, and had demanded that Helen be at his office that afternoon at 3:30 to discuss the matter. After some legal consultation, Helen squared her shoulders and prepared for a fight.

Accompanied by a pair of lawyers from the Shubert organization, Helen made her way across town to the meeting with deep apprehension, but also a certain level of righteous pique. She genuinely admired Gantillon's play, and felt it neither salacious nor obscene. In fact, the very idea that *Maya* might be considered titillating was distasteful to her. "I do not like the kind of audience which comes when a play is being discussed as a little off-color," she insisted.[35] "I would rather close my theater than have that."[36] Unfortunately, the sincerity of Helen Arthur's ethics was irrelevant. A firestorm is not dampened by righteousness.

Helen had barely warmed her seat in the DA's office when the fate of *Maya* was put in front of her. Assistant District Attorney Wallace, attending alongside James Sinnott, immediately declared that the production must close within ten days, or the Comedy Theater would be padlocked and the cast of *Maya* arrested and thrown in jail. Helen was thunderstruck. Before she could even digest this turn of events, Wallace followed his icy threat by smugly insisting that he was being very nice about the entire affair in giving the company ten days notice before closing—something that was explicitly provided for in the Wales law itself, *not* gifted by Wallace's personal fiat. But Helen Arthur was not about to give in so easily. She had brought *Maya* to the States and put a great deal of time and effort into her story. She'd seen her friend Aline MacMahon essay one of the magnificent performances of the Broadway season, and sellout shows were piling up at the box office. "Mr. Wallace," she asked, trying to calm herself. "Did you find anything in the play salacious? Or did you think that the audience responded to it in a silly or frivolous way?" Wallace's terse response was designed to quash all further questions. "My objection is not to the treatment," he insisted. "My objection is to the simple fact that it is laid in a brothel and is about a prostitute." Helen tried again. "But it isn't about the act of prostitution. It's the writer's method of interpreting a phase of life—he chose a prostitute the same way a scientist chooses the amoeba when he wants to discuss certain kinds of growth." Wallace and Sinnott were not interested in what they considered semantic excuses. *Maya* must close immediately, they insisted. Flummoxed, Helen now tried another tack, asking if a rewrite might change their minds. The men were still resolute; no changes and no further discussion would sway them. "The Assistant District Attorney, the Secretary of the Police Department and I simply do not speak the same language," Helen said after the meeting.[37] "Mr. Wallace is not interested or influenced by the nature of the play, its motive, purpose or treatment. In other words, the opinion of one citizen as to the 'immorality' of a given play can operate to end its existence," was her frustrated conclusion.[38] Before Helen left the office, Wallace and Sinnott admonished her to keep their meeting a secret from the press. It was claimed by the DA's office that this was standard procedure to avoid curious New Yorkers flocking to a play that might be deemed obscene. They hoped, Sinnott said, that the play would simply close after ten days and quickly be forgotten. Of course this edict was designed not to protect New Yorkers against smut, but to allow the district attorney to get out in front of the public relations battle before Actor-Managers. Angry, but still accepting Sinnott's sincerity, Helen agreed to keep the meeting quiet.

James Sinnott's sincerity was entirely unworthy of Helen Arthur's trust. Hours before she had even arrived at his office, Sinnott had already arranged a leak to the New York *Morning Telegraph* concerning his department's interest in *Maya*.[39] In his version, "someone" complained to the New York police department that *Maya* was obscene, and the play was under review as a corrupter of youth. Here, Sinnott was clever. Although his aggrieved informant was, in fact, a police department plant, he could truthfully maintain that there had actually been an opening night complaint that led to scrutiny of *Maya*.

Shortly after Helen Arthur left the district attorney's office, James Murry, the Shubert's booking agent, arrived for his own "secret" meeting with Broadway's de facto censors. Wanting to leave no avenue open to *Maya*, the two men called Mr. Murry into their offices to impress upon him the danger the Shubert company was courting. They threatened Mr. Murry with the cold reality that the Comedy Theater would be immediately padlocked for an entire year if the Shubert organization allowed the play to continue there beyond March 3. Murry, fully aware of the power Sinnott and Wallace wielded through the Wales Padlock Act, immediately recognized the difficult position the Shuberts were in. Although their rental contract explicitly allowed them to dispossess Actor-Managers from the Comedy Theater, they also owned a financial stake in *Maya*. It seemed to Murry that there was no way out; they would either be forced to close *Maya* at a loss to both the lease on their theater and the royalties on their investment, or endure a costly legal battle. While Murry was still digesting the possibilities in his head, Wallace asked him what he expected the Shubert company to do about the closure of *Maya*. "I don't know," he said, downcast. With nothing left to discuss, Murry quickly left the meeting to confer by telephone with J.J. Shubert, and anxiously await Lee's hurried return from Palm Springs. Through blunt intimidation and economic blackmail, and without the realistic possibility of legal redress, *Maya* was already very nearly dead, just three days after opening.

Even with these inescapable legal edicts placed against Actor-Managers and its landlords, District Attorney Banton's henchmen were not finished. They were desperate to put the final stake in *Maya*'s heart. If Actor-Managers or the Shubert brothers had any idea of a legal challenge to the Wales Padlock Act, Wallace wanted to stave it off at the source. Wallace now called the Actor's Equity theatrical union to discuss the repercussions for the cast of *Maya* if it did not close. He reminded them of the boilerplate clause in their theatrical contracts calling for actors to refuse to perform in any production deemed obscene. If a union actor appeared in *Maya* anywhere beyond its imposed closing date, he said, they would be arrested and sent to prison. At this, Equity shuddered. They did not want to see their members pulled into a protracted legal battle similar to those of *The Captive* and *Sex* during the 1926–27 season, or to be party to a lawsuit like the one precipitated by *The Bunk of 1926*. But the union represented actors, *not* the district attorney, nor the New York public—none of whom had complained about *Maya* anyway. After a series of meetings, the Equity council threw the ball back to the DA's office. If the company of *Maya* wanted to continue in their efforts, Equity would not entreat them otherwise, and would not come in on the side of the censors of the New York stage.[40]

The capper to the crowded events of February 23 came late in the evening. Backstage at the Comedy Theater, Helen Arthur was still fuming over her daytime meeting with the powers that be in the District Attorney's office. The night's performance was a sellout, and Saturday's matinee sales looked to be the strongest of the run yet.[41] From the wings, Helen watched as Aline again mesmerized the audience with her soulful performance as Bella. At the stage door, a letter arrived by messenger from the Shubert company, addressed to Helen's attention. This was it, she knew—would they fight or give in? "Dear Miss Arthur," it began, "this is to officially advise you that your attraction "Maya" . . . has been publicly criticized as indecent, obscene, immoral and publicly offensive. We hereby give you notice that we reserve the right to terminate the run of said attraction after the performance on Saturday, February 25th or at any time immediately thereafter."[42]

This was a dagger to the heart of Helen Arthur. Joab Banton and his lap dogs Sinnott and Wallace had been busy. In just twenty-four hours they had viewed, judged, and executed *Maya*.

In spite of the DA's directive on secrecy, by the morning of Friday, February 24, New York's newspapers were wet with leaks concerning *Maya*. "Plays tinctured with vice will be officially slapped with the same mailed fist which so effectively closes night clubs that smell of liquor," the New York *News* reported. "'Maya' bids well to be the first."[43] While Helen Arthur and the Shuberts continued to honor Wallace's request for secrecy, the DA's office was like a dam with the Dutch Boy laughing as it crumbled. "There seems to be little doubt that 'Maya' will be closed tight at the end of [next week]," trumpeted *The Sun*. "It is understood that the Police Department is contemplating action to protect the city's morals."[44] Responding to incessant questions from the New York press, Banton's office admitted to holding a conference with Jules Murry, but did not want to "officially" say any more than that. When pressed about the circumstances behind the play's scrutiny, Banton himself personally contradicted his assistant DA's cover story and instead proceeded to accuse Actor-Managers of spreading the leaks in order to increase interest at the box office. "My office has received no legitimate complaint about *Maya*," he said. "And by that I mean no complaint without suspicion of a press agent."

At this Helen Arthur was furious. She had honored her word to Sinnott and Wallace to keep silent about their behind-the-scenes machinations, and now they had not only broken the pact, but also libeled her in the press. "I was bound by a promise to say nothing while the other side made whatever insinuations pleased them," she said after *Maya* had closed.[45] Her silence would not last much longer, but for now she continued to pretend ignorance of the situation; with the DA's admission that Jules Murry had been called in, he could speak to the press without reservation. When reporters descended on him, Murry was diplomatic. "'Maya' will run tonight," he said. "It has not been decided whether it will run next week." Through it all, Helen Arthur maintained a dignified cool. Continuing to tell reporters that she had received no official word of impending censorship of her *Maya*, Helen then added a knowing condemnation of men who had deceived her. "But I don't believe that anyone would really want to stop such a play, do you?" She asked.[46] No doubt the subtle jibe passed their moralistic eyes unnoticed.

By the time Friday's late editions hit the streets, *Maya* was a cause célèbre. The leaks from city hall now created the exact opposite effect of their stated intent. With three days of solid receipts in the Comedy Theater coffers, ticket seekers now deluged the box office, making most performances a complete sellout, many overflowing with standing-room patrons. From Park Avenue swells to Village bohemians, New Yorkers rallied against arbitrary censorship of the theater industry. "The 'Maya' audience is typically Greenwich Village," the *Morning Telegraph* said of the ticket boom at the Comedy Theater. "Long-haired men and short-haired women elbow each other to get to the box office with their greenbacks." A mad scramble was now on to see *Maya* before the New York police could shut her down for good.

Among those who visited the box office that weekend was a young man who was not looking for tickets, but instead presented himself and asked to see the treasurer. When the Actor-Managers treasurer came out to the lobby he was surprised by a brazen proposition. For two thousand dollars, the man promised, all of *Maya's* troubles with the law could be made to disappear.[47] The box-office treasurer immediately identified the shakedown as a bunco scam and sent the offender out of the theater. Just a few days later, the same man appeared again outside the backstage entrance to the Comedy Theater and stopped Aline MacMahon herself as she arrived for the day's performance. Taken aback, the actress listened warily as the man repeated his claim that in exchange for a cash payment he could remove any legal difficulties that the company was having with the DA's office. Aline had already seen many unique things in her career on Broadway during the Roaring Twenties, but this was something new. Clearly *Maya* was not your typical New York show.

Inside the theater, Aline warned Helen Arthur of the solicitation, and they quickly realized that this was the same man who talked to their treasurer a few days earlier. Now more than a little worried at having her star accosted outside the theater, Helen put the doorman on notice to watch out for suspicious characters hanging around the stage entrance. The man was not finished, however. The next day he again appeared at the box office, indignant that his offers of help had been ignored. "What kind of manager is running this show," he bellowed at the teller. "Doesn't she know it could be fixed?!"[48] Ultimately nothing came of the bribery scheme, but Helen Arthur eventually testified about it at a meeting of the Dramatist's Guild concerning the unsavory effect of censorship on the theater.

Meanwhile, the New York newspapers continued to splash the rumors of *Maya*'s imminent closing across their Arts pages. "'Maya' Will Wash Up or Off in 10 days," announced the *Sunday News*, while James Sinnott's print puppet the *Morning Telegraph* gleefully taunted: "Broadway's Long-Haired Boys Chant Swan Song of Paris Sex Play." Press coverage of the story now leapt outside of New York, with articles about *Maya* appearing in papers across the country. Even the *Washington Post* weighed in, proclaiming, "Producers have brought censorship on themselves. Until they stop producing the type of filth that has been present upon Broadway of late, it is to be hoped that [the Padlock Act] will be brought into play." As a result of the increased interest created by the press, scalpers were now routinely fetching eight to ten times the face price of three-dollar tickets to *Maya*. It is entirely possible that New York's resale ticket industry made more profit on *Maya*—with no financial risk—than Helen Arthur, the Shuberts, or anybody connected with the Actor-Managers Corporation.

On Saturday, February 25, *Maya*'s matinee performance was a sellout and hosted a further seventy standing-room patrons. In the newspapers, both the DA's office and Actor-Managers would still confirm nothing concrete about the situation, but behind the scenes the drama was already nearly over. For two days Helen Arthur, Aline MacMahon, and the cast and crew had been vaguely hoping that some miracle would save *Maya*. There was talk of negotiations to evade the censor by changing the play; petitions were circulated in high circles asking the mayor to spare the production,[49] and there was speculation that if it were closed, *Maya* might move to a new house elsewhere in New York. But none of this was to be. That evening Helen spoke to J.J. Shubert, who confirmed that his office had drafted a letter exercising their contractual right to terminate the rental agreement on the Comedy Theater on the last day that the police department would allow *Maya* to play. Disheartened, Helen immediately contacted her attorney to see if there was the possibility of a legal injunction against the closure. He looked over the contract and assured her that there wasn't. The Shuberts had protected themselves very well indeed.

Even then there seemed to be a dim light twinkling at the end of a very long tunnel. Lee Shubert was returning from Palm Springs on Monday and asked his brother to hold the letter until he had a chance to see the play. J.J. reminded him that $50,000—a year's rent at their theater—was at stake if they found themselves on the wrong side of a court case. Lee insisted that they had nothing to lose in waiting a few days, and Helen Arthur again dined luxuriously on crumbs of false hope.

During this time of uncertainty Aline was continuing her remarkable daily performances as Bella. In spite of preparations for her marriage to Clarence, the distractions of not knowing how long the production would continue—or even if she might suddenly be pulled off the stage and arrested—Aline's focus never wavered. Accolades continued in every review; *Brooklyn Life*, latecomers to the show said, "[T]he remarkably perspicacious and delicately subtle interpretation of this role by Aline MacMahon is the compelling attraction of this play." Indeed. But could it last?

At the end of a weekend-long string of sellouts for *Maya*, Lee Shubert returned to New York. Helen Arthur believed this to be her last chance for the play to survive. If Lee could be convinced of its beauty and sincerity, perhaps he would consider putting up a fight against the Wales Padlock Act. After all, the play was now enormously successful, and the Shubert company still secretly owned a significant piece of it.

On Monday night, Lee Shubert sat in his box at the Comedy Theater and watched *Maya*, nodding approvingly from time to time.[50] When it was over, he made his thoughts known to the press. "It's beautiful," he told the reporters who gathered around him. "It's very, very beautiful." When then asked if, in advance of official disapproval, he would have considered the play a challenge to public morals, he did not hesitate. "No," he said. "That play would not have seemed to me to be a moral risk, and what's more I don't think it's a moral risk now."[51] Although this was the exact reaction that Helen and Aline were hoping for, it all changed nothing. Lee Shubert was not about to risk $50,000 on this particular windmill. "Whatever we may think of the merits of a play, however," he resigned, "we have to follow the wishes of the public authorities in these matters."[52] Unless something remarkable changed, *Maya* was dead—at least at the Comedy Theater.

On Tuesday, February 28, Helen Arthur finally admitted direct knowledge of the problems between Actor-Managers and the district attorney's office to the press. When some vague talk emerged of negotiations between the Shuberts and the DA, false hope was again momentarily renewed, but this was merely the act of setting the date of burial. Although Helen had not yet officially been served with papers demanding the ouster of *Maya*, it was clear that the show would have to close by the end of the week.

The next afternoon, as Aline arrived backstage for the evening performance, she saw members of the company huddled around the Comedy Theater's bulletin board. Shouldering her way through the crowd she found the Shubert organization's final word on *Maya's* fate posted there:

> *This is to advise you that the District Attorney of the County of New York has advised us that he will not permit the attraction 'Maya' to be performed in the City of New York after March 3, 1928. You are fully aware of the fact that the District Attorney's office has indicated that no amount of revision will satisfy him.*

That day there was a rumbling of a possibility that some brave theater owner might be willing to take up the cause and move *Maya* to a new house. But Helen Arthur's attorney, Melville Cane, warned her that DA Banton had made it clear to him in a private conversation that the first performance of *Maya* anywhere else in the County of New York would be raided and all the principals would be jailed under the padlock law. Helen decided that the only way they could go on was if there was a unanimous agreement among the players to risk imprisonment. She called a meeting on the question for Thursday. In the interim, she resolved to contact District Attorney Joab Banton, whom she had never met—and who had never seen *Maya*—hoping that a direct plea might accomplish what had failed so comprehensively with Sinnott or Wallace—a change of heart.

"We have notified Mr. Wallace of our readiness to consider any reasonable changes," she wrote in her letter to Banton on Tuesday, "but Mr. Wallace declares that his objection lies with the subject matter. We believe that this decision is unwarranted, and bars from the theater an established work of art. In the interests of justice and fair play, we ask you to reconsider this decision." Desperate, Helen then offered to hold a private performance for the DA and anyone else involved in the suppression of *Maya*, or even to submit to the conclusion of a reconstituted version of the Play Jury.[53] Sadly, Helen Arthur held the world's most meager understanding of big city politics. The DA ignored her letter, and made it crystal clear to Wallace that Miss Arthur should be locked up if *Maya* passed its on sale date.

On Wednesday, February 29, the management of the Neighborhood Playhouse's fellow "Little Theatre" comrades, the Provincetown Players, sent a message to Actor-Managers, offering their theater should Helen and her troupe wish to challenge Wales Padlock in court. Since Wallace had personally assured Helen that any company performing *Maya* anywhere within his jurisdiction would be arrested, this would undoubtedly provide a legal test case for censorship in New York. Helen was touched by the courage of her friendly rivals, but advised them to seek legal counsel on the matter before anyone committed to anything. In the meantime, a secret ballot among the cast and crew concerning the fate of *Maya* was scheduled for the next afternoon.

Aline arrived at the theater on Thursday uncertain of what would happen. On one hand she believed completely in the righteousness of the cause *Maya* embodied. On another she was also a creature of dignity and propriety. Although Aline often yearned to be the iconoclast, her upbringing and an innate sense of decorum often rebelled against her own rebellion. She was not entirely comfortable with the idea of being the center of a moral firestorm within the city. There was also another factor to consider. Her fiancée was a well-known and highly respected architect, regularly seeking jobs and patronage for his services from New York's conservative elite. During the previous three years, Clarence was one of the primary architects of the recently completed Temple Emanu-El, housing one of the largest Jewish congregations in the city. It would not do for Clarence to have to explain to his wealthy and sometimes deeply pious clients why his wife was in jail for cavorting on stage as a prostitute. Adding to the pressure was the couple's upcoming nuptials, already planned for late March. It would be a memorable wedding day indeed if the bride were unavailable as the result of confinement to the Women's Workhouse on Welfare Island. Confronted by what appeared to be an insoluble problem, Aline was unsure of how to proceed. Capitulate, or fight?

On the afternoon of March 1, the question of continuing *Maya* in New York City was decided in a secret ballot. Seven of the twenty-seven cast and crew members voted against moving *Maya* to the Provincetown Players stage or anywhere else in the city.[54] Aline MacMahon was one of the dissenters. Late in her life Aline recalled the moment. "I had a chance to defy the world. I could have fought for it. The producers begged me to go to court on it," she said, in vague disappointment of her choice. "But it was my shrewd, perhaps mistaken judgement that you couldn't fight it, and I told Helen that we couldn't fight it."[55] In the evening of that same day however, Helen Arthur presented her company with one more last ditch option—an option that she thought might circumvent Aline's misgivings. At Helen's request, Lee Shubert had looked into the possibility of securing out-of-town bookings, and found potential offers in both Baltimore and Washington, DC. After weeks of fighting against the arbitrary censors of New York, the continuation of *Maya* had become almost an obsession with Helen Arthur. Now, at a hastily called evening conference, Helen tried to convince her company to take the play on the road.[56] Another vote was in order.

It was here that the battle between Aline's public conscience and her social propriety was settled. At the evening meeting Aline asked to personally address the company and stated plainly that she thought it would be "humiliating" to travel from state to state in a suppressed play. As the discussion between the leading lady and her fellow cast members continued, Helen Arthur contemplated Aline's feelings and gradually she began to understand the value of her friend's objections. After all she had done to save *Maya*, Helen at last gave in. "On second thought," the *New York Post* reported, "Miss Arthur agreed [with Aline's misgivings] and *she* convinced the others."[57]

As predicted, New York City had failed *Maya*.

"Censorship of the theatre now exists in the City of New York," Helen Arthur boldly declared in Actor-Managers first open statement on the entire farrago. "The opinion of one citizen [Assistant DA Wallace] as to the 'immorality' of a given play can end its existence. This is what has happened in this present instance." On Friday, over 600 actors and actresses descended on the Comedy Theater for a hastily arranged industry-only matinee performance of *Maya*. Afterward, more than half the audience remained to hear Helen tell the story she had refused to give the press. She implored them to stand up against censorship, and revealed plans to organize a committee to work for the repeal of the Wales Padlock Act, "which is so drastically worded and which places this enormous censorship power in the hands of a single individual." She was passionate and persuasive. And the Wales Padlock Act stayed on the books for another forty years.

ALINE MACMAHON

Aline and her classmates from Barnard College at an informal reunion, circa 1930. Aline made many lifelong friends at Barnard and attended every decennial reunion of the class of 1920 until 1990, when she was too ill to attend. *Courtesy of Barnard College.*

On Saturday, March 3, 1928, Aline MacMahon walked off the stage for the final time as Bella. *Maya* did not return to New York until it appeared without incident at the Theatre de Lys in 1953. It lasted a grand total of six performances. Like the Hayes Code, which censored Hollywood films beginning in 1934, the Wales Padlock Act provided a drag on artistic and social development on Broadway for decades to come. Eventually it was simply the changing tastes of the public that provided the key for the padlock. By the 1950s there were two new generations of liberalized thought to contend with, and its power gradually winnowed away.

Aline did not have much time to grieve the death of *Maya*. She was already preparing for her wedding, as well as a honeymoon, both to take place in less than a month. After three years of serious courtship, a union was about to be cemented that would last nearly fifty years. On March 27, the twenty-eight-year-old Aline and forty-five-year-old Clarence made their way to lower Manhattan, near the foot of the Brooklyn Bridge, and presented themselves at city hall for marriage by Judge Peter Schmuck (yes, Schmuck). The civil ceremony was likely a calculated financial choice; the Steins almost certainly preferred to have money for their honeymoon trip than waste it on an extravagant wedding. The Steins' wedding day was so modest that the couple had to visit Clarence's parents to give them the news. Mother Stein was delighted, and told her new daughter-in-law the raw, unvarnished truth about her son. "He is the apple of our eye. He has never given us one moment of unhappiness," she said. "You may find that he is a little too neat."[58] In early April the newlyweds boarded the recently launched luxury ocean liner *Europa* on only its sophomore voyage from New York to Bremerhaven in Germany. Thanks to the *Europa*'s modern design and superior engineering, the Steins disembarked on the Continent in less than five days. Shortly after, they were on their way to England, where they stayed until returning home on the *S.S. Olympic* during May.

After a summer and fall moving in and outfitting the couple's new apartment on West 59th Street, Aline was ready to return to work. Late in the year she secured the lead in *Daylight Saving*, a light comedy / fantasy about an elderly woman of (gasp!) sixty who undergoes a radical rejuvenation treatment to restore her youth. The theme of discontentment with middle age was somewhat prevalent on stage and page at the time, with people over fifty often portrayed as feeble and embarrassingly obsessed with recapturing their youth. As Mrs. Merriam, Aline goes from elderly crone to youthful beauty between acts one and two. By act three she has met her former lover of years past—a frail, wizened old man of sixty (gasp again). The shock of his appearance quickly drains away her new youth. Learning the folly of her choice, she dutifully returns to the comfort of her cozy armchair, apparently to live out her days saving up enough energy to retrieve a cup of tea from the sideboard. Although Aline was duly lauded in the press ("Aline MacMahon does the youthful old woman to perfection. She gives you a rare specimen of her ability when before your eyes she ages gradually"),[59] *Daylight Saving* was, itself, feeble. After a series of dismal performances in Albany, it was retitled *Indian Summer* and mooted to open in New York, "probably" the week of January 21. It "positively" was never seen again.

What *Daylight Saving* did give us was another early example of Aline's unwitting drift into middle-aged character parts before she had even turned thirty. For a character performer, this is a godsend—the opportunity to play roles of nearly any age opens up a wealth of possibilities for which most actors would not even bother to audition. On film we will eventually see Aline tackle roles like the middle-aged spinster of *Kind Lady* (1935) using the techniques she honed on stage as a twenty-something performer.

Late in 1928 Aline received word that her aunt, the world-famous social crusader Sophie Loeb, had been diagnosed with cancer and had only a short time to live. Although Jennie Mac and Sophie had remained close, Sophie's insistence on directing Aline's life choices was long a source of friction. "Frankly, Aline didn't like Sophie very well, because she was a driver," Jennie Mac said. "I mean she insisted on Aline getting ahead, doing so-and-so and so-and-so, and she didn't like being pushed." From her youngest days Aline had been gently prodded by Jennie Mac's ambitions, and she often resented Sophie's expectations being added to them. But it was clear that in Aline, Sophie saw much of the unique talent and ambition that drove her. What she may have missed in Aline was the same kind of independence and strong will that rebelled against any decisions that weren't hers.

Sophie spent two months slowly wasting away in New York's Memorial hospital while the family rallied around her. In spite of the coolness between Aline and Sophie, it was here that the niece observed the best of her aunt. "Sophie did the one generous thing of her life," Aline recalled. "She wouldn't let mother nurse her that last winter. She said, 'I wanted her very much, but I couldn't let her. She's too softhearted and I didn't want to make her unhappy.'"[60] Sophie Loeb died on January 18, 1929, at the age of fifty-three. In spite of their rocky relationship, Aline respected her aunt's dedication, compassion and indefatigable energy, and those of all progressive women of that era. "I think Sophie's generation will never be equaled. No generation will get the same thrill out of discovering the world. They were the *real* career girls. We are already too accustomed to women's achievements—we've had the thrill of succeeding, but not the kick out of the revolt."[61] Aline's own social conscience, including her benign flirtation with Communism, was no doubt an outgrowth of the inequities she saw while visiting the tenements and slums of New York with Sophie during her school years. Aline may never have quite warmed up to her famous aunt, but whenever she spoke of her, it was with genuine admiration and respect.

Aline's next recorded professional opportunity did not come until the summer of 1929. Before the era of air conditioning, most of Broadway's theaters were routinely closed from July to September in order to dodge the sweltering temperatures that annually killed box-office returns across the city. Among those "summer stock" venues luxuriating in the cool(ish) ocean breezes of the Northeast was the Berkshire Playhouse in Stockbridge, Massachusetts. Begun in 1928 with an investment of just $20,000, the theater was then in only the second season of a run that still continues today as the third

This Memorial fountain was erected in honor of Aline's aunt Sophie Loeb in New York's Central Park after her untimely death at the age of fifty-three. Author Collection.

oldest regional theater in the United States. In June Aline became a member of the sophomore troupe beginning their eight-week season in July. The playbill at Stockbridge that summer featured Edna Ferber and George Kaufman's *The Royal Family*, as well as Bernard Shaw's *You Never Can Tell* and *Fanny's First Play*. Aline herself debuted in the Massachusetts company on July 22 in *Thunder in the Air*.[62] By then Aline's reputation in Manhattan theater circles was well established, and the local press took notice. "Miss MacMahon's splendid work in *Beyond the Horizon* and *Maya*, and her reputation as the actress of the New York intelligentsia make her appearance in Stockbridge a welcome event."[63] *Thunder*, a British import in its first appearance stateside after nine months on the London stage, affected a Shakespearean fantasy, where the son of a wealthy family dies and is later returned to life, teaching his venal relatives a lesson in the process. American audiences were less interested in the living dead than Londoners; when *Thunder* made it to Broadway in November it lasted just sixteen performances. Aline and her Berkshire compatriots were fortuitously absent.

More important to Aline than the Berkshire Playhouse's second season was the beginning of her long-lasting friendship with the company's director, Cowles Strickland. Although inadvertent, it was Strickland's last-minute agreement for Aline to return to Massachusetts the following summer that would prove a major turning point in her career.

After a season in the sticks, Aline returned to a New York that was then at the dizzying zenith of the Roaring Twenties. In early September the stock market was at an all-time high, ladies' skirts were marching steadily upward, and summer temperatures had climbed well into the nineties. Every day, Manhattan residents were watching the Chrysler Building and Radio City Music Hall rise floor by floor into the sky. Only the old Waldorf-Astoria was shrinking, being demolished to make way for a still greater peak of American ingenuity, the Empire State Building. At this moment, perhaps, the Steins were at an apex of their own—newly wed, financially sound, and each well respected within their profession. From the distance of history, however, we can see a shadow approaching with the speed of an eclipse. The Depression is only moments away.

By late September 1929, it was already clear to prudent investors that something was dreadfully wrong on the American stock exchange. After years of bull markets, prices on the exchange were sagging and confidence was ebbing. Either through ignorance or fear, Wall Street brokers put on a brave face, but during October a series of steep downturns in the market did not rebound as they had in the recent past. Again and again stocks dropped to obscene new lows, and brokers hoped the bottom had been reached only for prices to retreat again the following day. The enormous losses of Black Tuesday (October 29, 1929) culminated the greatest economic disaster the world has ever known; the Great Depression was underway. And America had still not touched bottom.

Unlike most Americans, the Steins were relatively insulated from this financial free fall. Although their expenditures in travel and entertaining were somewhat extravagant, both had stable, lucrative careers and were generally modest spenders in other areas of their lives. "I dislike spending money without some good reason for it," Aline once told a reporter. "It seems so unintelligent."[64] Moreover, the couple had not indulged in the margin-buying speculation of the stock market that gripped the country for the previous five years. With a portfolio of paid-up blue-chip stocks including General Electric, General Motors, and International Harvester, they felt confident that their resources would outlast the crisis, where these stalwart giants of American commerce would regain their proper value.

Unfortunately, the stock market crash will eventually affect Aline MacMahon and her husband in ways more complex than mere personal finance. Already interested in social justice issues, the Depression intensifies the couple's unease over disparities in class and income in America. Since the end of World War I, Communism had been lurking in the gray spaces of American life. The stock market crash now provides a catalyst that allows the Communists to comprehensively question the very foundations of Democracy in America. In the early years of the 1930s, Aline and her husband gradually migrate from the progressive policies of mainstream reformers like the Democratic New York governor Al Smith toward the more radical change promised by the Socialists and free thinkers.

Just weeks after Wall Street collapsed, Aline accepted an offer from James Light to appear in his upcoming production with the Provincetown Players. Light was the man who had offered Aline a job after seeing her perform in her senior class at Barnard, and had provided her first true dramatic role in his production of O'Neill's *Beyond the Horizon*. "Jimmy called me up and said, 'I've got an awfully interesting play with two very good women's parts. Will you see which one you'd like to play?'"[65] With the Depression beginning to entrench itself in the social order, Aline and Clarence understood that no matter how well situated they were to ride out the crisis, no one could know exactly how long it might last. Aline quickly agreed to taking the lead in Provincetown's production of Thomas Dickinson's *Winter Bound*, a controversial script concerning two women who sequester themselves on a Connecticut farm in order to prove they can live without men. Dickinson, an unpaid adviser to the management of the Neighborhood Playhouse before the informal arrangement was ended in 1924, had observed the company's exclusively distaff management hierarchy, and the same-sex relationships between Helen Arthur, Agnes Morgan, and Lillian Wald, up close. With characters who desire a retreat to an exclusively feminine domain, *Winter Bound* appears to be an outgrowth of Dickinson's thoughts about the women of the Playhouse.

ALINE MACMAHON

If Aline MacMahon was not fearless, she was at least intrepid. *Winter Bound*'s barely disguised lesbian theme seemed designed to again enrage James Sinnott and his one-man censorship board. After the hurricane of controversy surrounding *Maya*, it would have been understandable if she had wanted to avoid potential exposure to similar consequences again. But Aline claimed that the material—and the opportunity to work with James Light again—was the deciding factor in her choice. In truth, it may have been the simple fear of being unemployed that most motivated her.

The story of *Winter Bound* concerns a "masculine" female artist, Tony Ambler (Aline), who retreats to her Connecticut farm with her more feminine friend Emily "to prove that women can make a go of it without the interference of men."[66] Tony is, apparently, in love with Emily, and wordlessly hoping that the time together will give her an opportunity to see that love returned. Momentarily, a romantic spark is indeed kindled between the women, until Tony's plans are scuttled by the arrival of Chet, a local farmer who woos Emily away from her affections. When Emily announces her intention to marry Chet, Tony is devastated. In a rage she destroys her work-in-progress, a sculpture that was a symbol of her man-free utopia. Meanwhile, during this emotional travail, a naive young handyman has fallen hopelessly in love with Tony, who, of course, can never return his affections. Deeply hurt by Emily's rejection of her love, Tony cruelly dispatches the handyman, whose only transgression was that he cared for her unconditionally. In her loveless solitude, Tony soon learns that the boy has committed suicide, distraught in his conviction that the woman he adored simply did not believe in love. Here Tony is left, nearly mad with grief at the boy's misunderstanding of the reasons for her actions.

If interpreted as Dickinson's reaction to his experience with the Neighborhood Playhouse, *Winter Bound* is at least an indictment of its matriarchal hierarchy, and at most a condemnation of the lifestyles of its founding members. This was an idea to which the director of *Winter Bound* adhered. "James Light said he always thought that Dickinson had fallen in love with a lesbian," Aline recalled, "and this was his way of getting even."[67] The collapse of Tony's relationship and the destruction of her art can also be read as Dickinson's angry metaphor on the downfall of the Playhouse as the result of the women's rejection of his offer of help and council—or even the rebuff of romantic intentions toward one of its members.

The subtext of homosexuality in *Winter Bound* fooled no one except those who did not want to see it, which included, strangely, its lead actress.

Decades later, in response to an interviewer's somewhat condescending question, Aline said: "Of course I knew what a lesbian was in 1929, but I never thought of the character as being one. The friendship between the two women was very clearly the usual, normal and platonic female relationship."[68] It seems strange that even forty years on Aline would miss the river of subtext in *Winter Bound* (there is a scene where Emily waits expectantly in Tony's bed for her). Aline's reading of the characters also clearly contradicts her knowledge of James Light's thoughts about Dickinson's intentions. Perhaps it is just sheer propriety that kept her from explicitly discussing homosexuality in public. When Aline was first taken into the confidence of her gay friends in the 1920s, it was widely understood that the information was personal and confidential. Even by the 1970s, when America's attitude toward LGBTQ people had softened, most were still protective of a secret that could cost them their livelihood and more. Aline's reticence to discuss it was simply a continuation of the decades of discretion she had long practiced. Additionally, Aline's rejection of the idea of Tony being gay may have been an acting choice. The Method would require Aline to attempt to tap into personal emotions and thoughts that would lead her to a clearer understanding of Tony Ambler. As understanding and supportive as Aline was of her gay friends, she was still largely driven by a veneer of Victorian dignity. Thus, it was perhaps easier to ignore the obvious and sidestep the difficult work of examining something with which she was uncomfortable.

Most critics openly reviewed *Winter Bound* on the basis of the author's apparent intentions, in spite of his character's insistence that there were no such ideas present. "Mr. Dickinson went out of his way to emphasize that Tony's love for Emily was pure and holy," the *Brooklyn Daily Eagle* observed, "But by this time the play had moved so far that only one construction could be placed upon this affection."[69] *Brooklyn Life*, on the other hand, reviewed *Winter Bound* as a simple drama, implying only obliquely at any hint of the underlying connections between the women. Still, the reviews were extremely kind, especially to Aline: "Aline MacMahon gave a performance that made decidedly stronger the unwritten lines of the play. Hers was a hard and unsympathetic role. Still, she created a character that is one of the outstanding figures of the present season. From an acting standpoint her Tony Ambler was perfect."[70] Aline herself later singled it out as among her favorite characters.

Winter Bound was not a success, at least on the surface. It lasted only thirty-nine performances, closing on December 13. Considering the outright hysteria connected with *Maya*, and the previous uproar over the lesbian-themed *The*

Captive, it seems impossible that the New York District Attorney's office did not notice *Winter Bound*. Although there is no documentation to confirm it, there is a possibility that New York's one-man censor, Joab Banton, scuttled the show. While it did not work with *Maya*, Banton's insistence on secrecy had previously resulted in other Broadway productions being closed by the Wales Padlock Act without public knowledge of it. The producers of those shows simply discontinued the play under the pretense of poor box office and remained mum on the matter. It wasn't until six months after *The Matrimonial Bed* was hastily closed in October 1927 that it was revealed to be a victim of the law.[71] *Winter Bound* may have met the same fate.

When *Winter Bound* died it took with it both the Provincetown Players and the Garrick Theatre. The economic crisis already had Provincetown teetering on insolvency, and the failure (or suppression) of *Winter Bound* precipitated their demise after fourteen years of commercial and financial success. The obituary was brief. "The death of the Provincetown Playhouse is the first major fatality in the arts traceable directly to the Wall Street crash."[72] The venerable old Garrick, also in deep fiscal trouble, shuttered its doors and was demolished in 1932. Here, the Depression was reaching directly into Aline's life to remind her that very few people were completely immune to the collapse of normal order in the United States.

Notwithstanding the sinking economy, Aline and Clarence could not resist planning their next sojourn across the ocean, this time to the exotic and time-warped Asian subcontinent of India. It is entirely likely that their interest in India was piqued through the continuing press coverage of Mahatma Gandhi's nonviolent struggle against the British Empire's colonial rule over the country. At this time, the couple was gingerly exploring Socialist ideas, class and income inequality foremost among them. India had been struggling with these ideas on a grand scale, with Socialists taking an early lead in backing the liberation movement. In 1930, India was the epicenter of the struggle against the rule of wealth over poverty.

The trip lasted for four months, from January to April 1930, a season that would lead to great change in India. The month before the Stein's arrival, India's Congress designated January 26, 1930 to be their Independence Day, and pledged to practice civil disobedience until they received complete severance from the British Empire. In March, Gandhi undertook his famous fourteen-day Salt March to protest taxes on the manufacture and sale of sea salt. For sixteen weeks the Stein's were adjacent to one of the great ideological battles of the twentieth century: Empire versus self-determination.

The irony of wealthy American travelers trekking through India at the very time when both nations were enduring ghoulish economic inequality may not have occurred to the Steins. However, the simple recognition of the disparity did create in the couple a desire to do what they could to help. During the coming years they would work diligently for liberal political causes, and contribute regularly to charities for unemployed actors and draftsmen. With Clarence's friends in the building trade, he had a hand in creating housing opportunities for low-income families, and although they began the decade as liberal Democrats, the Steins continue to drift gradually toward a Socialist ideology that speaks out about the inequities of capitalism. For now they prepared to return to an America that was itself gradually moving deeper into depression. Of their own relative prosperity, Clarence declared they might one day enjoy it, "if we can forget the boys who are sleeping over in the park and waiting for a nickel to get coffee, and the 2,500 unemployed draftsmen, and the actor's lunch place that is having a hard time surviving. Life is complicated . . ."

6

ONCE IN A LIFETIME

In late April, just as Aline and Clarence were sailing their leisurely way across the Atlantic back to America, two writers were sequestered in an Upper East Side Manhattan brownstone working on a play that was proving to be something less than cooperative.

One was George S. Kaufman, the celebrated theatrical script doctor and charter member of the legendary group of New York City writers known as the Algonquin Round Table. The other was a star-struck Jewish boy from Brooklyn making his first mad dash into a legendary Broadway career, Moss Hart. Their stubborn antagonist was *Once in a Lifetime*, Hart's embryonic farce about Hollywood's recent, painful transition from silent to sound film. By the time Aline and Clarence docked in New York harbor at the beginning of May, the men felt they had wrestled *Lifetime's* nettlesome third act into submission and were now scouring lists of New York actors to call in for auditions.[1]

After just a few days back in her familiar bed, Aline was contacted by producer Sam Harris's office about coming into the Music Box Theater to audition for *Once in a Lifetime*. "Moss Hart had seen me at the Neighborhood Playhouse," Aline recalled decades later, "and he gave me my first chance at 'Once in a Lifetime.'[2] I was very nervous about doing it, because it was so different than anything I had attempted at that point. But when Moss and Mr. Kaufman urged me, I agreed to try."[3] Hart wanted Aline to read for the central role in the play, a cynical, quick-witted vaudeville actress who travels west with a pair of second-rate actors to masquerade as experts in voice culture for Hollywood's dispossessed silent stars. Aline needn't have worried. The part fit her perfectly: both she and May Daniels were clever, savvy New Yorkers, creatures of the stage, and veterans of childhood elocution lessons and the public speaking circuit. May Daniels also had other dimensions that would pull on all the varied talents Aline had developed during her years on stage, being alternately comic, sensitive, bawdy, and morose.

The following day Aline made her way to the Music Box Theater, and in front of Kaufman, Hart, and Sam Harris, proved her affinity for the role. The producer quickly handed her the lead in a production set to begin try-outs in Atlantic City just three weeks later. With a sprawling cast of almost fifty speaking parts, six elaborate sets, and a fortune in costuming, Sam Harris did not want to spend time—or more precisely, money—dawdling. "Almost before I was aware of it, or would have dreamed it possible," Moss Hart said, "the play was cast and I was walking toward the Music Box for the first rehearsal."[4] Aline had not even been home from India for a full week.

If she had been granted the opportunity at that moment to look just a few months into the future, Aline would have been bitterly disappointed by what was awaiting her. But a glimpse at the future does not always tell the whole truth. Although the proverbial crystal ball would have revealed that Aline would not be in *Once in a Lifetime* when it debuted on Broadway, it could not have shown the series of events that rippled out from her short association with it. Misfortune would soon rear its capricious head, but Aline MacMahon's life and career were about to be changed in ways that she could then scarcely imagine.

Rehearsals began on May 7 with George Kaufman himself directing, and the first out-of-town try-out scheduled for Atlantic City just nineteen days later. That first afternoon the actors, seated onstage in a semicircle facing the authors and their producer, proceeded with the maiden run-through of *Once in a Lifetime*. Moss Hart painfully recalled that by the end of the initial reading the play had ground down to what he called "a slow death rattle." "It sounded terrible," Hart said queasily when it was over. "So plain *awful*." What the first-time playwright was experiencing was a simple rule of the theater world. "It always sounds terrible at a first reading," Sam Harris's aide-de-camp Max Siegel reassured him. "By the third act they'll forget themselves and even act it a bit. You watch."[5] The cast responded according to theatrical tradition and Hart's freshman fears were momentarily assuaged.

Starting that very afternoon George Kaufman began coolly grooming and cajoling his actors in the intricacies of the play. As was his style, he would periodically take Aline or another cast member aside and whisper quiet advice to them, looking for the perfect balance of cynicism and charm. Most often he allowed them to devise their own interpretations, making himself available for support and council when they were uncertain. For the first and only time in his long and varied career, Kaufman was also acting in *Once in a Lifetime*, as an acerbic New York playwright who has been financially seduced to travel west and write for Hollywood. It is presumed that director Kaufman—a noted wit with an acid tongue—did not need to whisper to actor Kaufman about the proper way to play the part.

After only eight days, the company performed a read-through for Sam Harris, complete with stage blocking, entrances, and exits. The producer, whose money was daily being spent extravagantly, watched intently and left the theater without saying a word. Aline and the rest of the company were mortified by his response until Max Siegel called them together and professed that this was good news. "You'll seldom hear him give praise," he said. "You'll only hear what he doesn't like." For the next ten days Harris said nothing, and the best was assumed.

Almost as soon as Broadway was established as America's premiere stage venue, producers were evaluating the strength of their shows by testing them in front of paying audiences outside Manhattan. Here they could decide if the script needed work, a character should be recast, or the sets should be struck and rebuilt. In extreme circumstances—like a third act that simply refused to cooperate—it could also mean cutting your losses and throwing the entire production on the ash heap. On the morning of Saturday, May 24, Aline and the company of *Once in a Lifetime* made their way to Pennsylvania Station and boarded a train for New Jersey to endure their own trial by fire.

In 1930 Atlantic City was a bustling resort town and *the* top tryout spot on the East Coast for New York–bound stage productions. Every day the famous boardwalk was a kaleidoscope of form and color as vacationers, tourists, and residents strolled the promenade that divides the city's opulent hotels from the incessant waves of the Atlantic Ocean. Yet, even as the city seduced with her picturesque charms, a knife was always hidden behind her back. Over the years Atlantic City audiences revealed heretofore-unseen defects in plays that had killed the dreams of thousands of Broadway hopefuls.

After three days of final preparations, Aline MacMahon stepped out on the stage of the Apollo Theater on May 26 for the maiden appearance of *Once in a Lifetime* in front of a paying audience. For an act and a half, the audience laughed with the abandon of inebriation. The play was momentarily a sensation. Then, from the middle of the second act, *Once in a Lifetime* gradually deflated, until by the finish the audience exited the theater disappointed for reasons they did not fully understand. Neither quite did Kaufman or Hart. The script they had brought to heel in May was once again fighting back. "Some basic human element was missing in 'Once in a Lifetime,'" Hart vaguely concluded. He and Kaufman—as well as producer Sam Harris and a discern-

Aline was the sole survivor of the Los Angeles stage company of *Once in a Lifetime* to make it into Universal's 1932 film version. With her were a raft of top-drawer comics and comediennes of the era, including Jack Oakie and Zasu Pitts. Studio publicity material.

ing cast—all knew there was something amiss. Harris, normally a weeklong resident of Atlantic City if the preview was going well, hurried out of town the same night. In the morning, the writers received a note from him in their hotel box with those three little words that every playwright yearns to hear: "It needs work."[6]

On the surface, the next morning's reviews did not seem as bad as the looks on the faces of the first-night audience as they left the Apollo. Most were complimentary, singling out Aline as "superb" and calling her the brightest spot in a solid entrant for Broadway's summer sweepstakes. But underneath the accolades was one recurring theme: the show needed work and Kaufman would save it. "There is a little revising to be done, of course," *Variety* allowed, "and the need of smoother performance which is sure to follow."[7] It was only George S. Kaufman's reputation as a theatrical miracle worker that convinced New York's hard-nosed critics that this amusing but half-baked show would be perfect by the time it made it to Broadway. "We all got very good reviews," Aline remembered later, "but everyone thought the *play* was weak."[8] The pressure was on; Sam Harris was not one to waste time and money on a potential flop no matter who had written it. "You can't pinch pennies in show business," Harris once said, "but the great secret is to know when to cut your losses."[9] Kaufman and Hart now had just two weeks before a scheduled Broadway opening to discover what the trouble was and fix it or the entire endeavor would be doomed.[10]

The professional temperament of Aline MacMahon was heavily taxed over the following fortnight. Every day came new and radical changes to the script of *Once in a Lifetime*, but Aline did not complain. After decades of experience on stage she had developed an iron will and dedication to work. Whatever Kaufman and Hart threw at her she committed to memory in the afternoon and performed at night until it was invariably changed the very next day. One evening the script was chopped to the bone; the next night cuts had been restored and new material added. Scenes were broken apart and glued together like shards of a mirror. *Once in a Lifetime* was fighting hard against its writers in an effort to be merely an amusing failure. Through it all, Aline leaned heavily on her Method training. The core of May Daniels's character dwelled none too deeply within Aline's own experience, and the Stanislavski system which taught her to use that personal connection now gave her an anchor that would follow May Daniels no matter where Kaufman and Hart took her.

On June 2 the company moved to Brooklyn's Brighton Beach Theater for another week of shows. It was here that the play would truly be made or broken. Brooklyn was where the Broadway elite came to eye the competition before it opened in Manhattan, and they were not as disposed to uneducated kindness as were the tourists in a simple resort town. The critics in Brooklyn were in truth sharper edged than the stiletto of Atlantic City. In proof Hart observed, speaking of the reaction of Brooklyn's opening night crowd, "Their silence had the breathless, hushed quality of a death watch."[11] Things were looking down.

Again, critics appeared amused and complimentary, and again they perceived that something was desperately wrong. "'Once in a Lifetime' regales its audience with more laughter than any local audience has been privileged to since 'Strictly Dishonorable,'" the *Brooklyn Daily Eagle* pronounced. "But Mr. Kaufman, unless he is less shrewd a dramatist than the past has proved him, hasn't nearly finished the work he can find to do upon it." Then, after astutely observing Kaufman's need to shore up poor timing, rewrite weak scenes, stiffen a limp second act, and compose a worthwhile third act, the *Eagle*'s reviewer politely noted, "once those chores are done, 'Once in a Lifetime' will cease to be labored and become a Broadway hit."[12] With an entire week available to Kaufman for these trivial changes, the reviewers may have expected him to also defeat Lex Luthor, save Lois Lane, and still provide a scoop for Perry White at the *Daily Planet*.

The second night's performance in Brooklyn was worse still than the opening. Throughout the week audiences thinned out and nothing seemed to subdue the unruly third act. Although still vague, the writers understood that the trouble was in the relationship between the three main characters at the end of their Hollywood sojourn. The writers continued their futile efforts, but by the end of the week a dismal feeling had draped over the company. After the last performance in Brighton Beach, Moss Hart drifted backstage, fearful of the fate of his first opportunity at Broadway success. Kaufman gave him the bad news that had already been decided by Sam Harris. There would be no Broadway opening. "I haven't anything more to offer to this play," Kaufman told the fledgling writer. "I've gone dry on it, or maybe I've lost my taste for it. Sam will make a very generous arrangement on the scenery and costumes with any other producer that wants to do it."[13] Hart knew that if Sam Harris had given up on his play after spending a fortune to stage it, no other Broadway producer would be eager to take it on. Superman had failed. *Once in a Lifetime* was dead, and with it, a plum role for Aline MacMahon.

Aline was devastated by the turn of events that killed *Once in a Lifetime*. During the course of the rehearsals and try-outs, she had become close to the young Moss Hart, and those days of rehearsal and performance began a lifelong friendship between the two. She was hurt not only for the loss of a magnificent part, but also the failure of her friend. But Aline had now been around Broadway for nearly a decade and knew the vicissitudes of a life on the stage. It was not time to lament. It was time to look for work.

The dissolution of *Once in a Lifetime* also caught Aline completely off guard. In 1930, expecting to open on Broadway in a play cowritten by, directed by, and starring George S. Kaufman was a certainty to be placed neatly between death and taxes, and she had made no contingency plans. Also, *Lifetime* had been a special animal: a play by a major producer and director to begin during the teeth of New York's summer heat. Unlike the previous year, Aline's dedication to *Lifetime* left her without an out-of-town company just as they were rapidly filling their quota of actors to begin performances later that month.

Aline wasted no time. Just days after *Once in a Lifetime* died, she contacted Cowles Strickland to see if he had a slot available for her in the Berkshire Playhouse company that she had performed with in Massachusetts during the previous season. She couldn't know it then, but Strickland's last-minute agreement to take Aline into the company was perhaps *the* turning point of her career. On June 16 the company's season was announced with Aline as the featured player, along with Donald Meek (the world's most aptly named actor), Leo G. Carroll (Mr. Waverly of *The Man from U.N.C.L.E.*), and Zita Johann (Boris Karloff's reincarnated lover in *The Mummy*). Following rehearsals, her contract called for eight weeks of service beginning June 30.[14] Her summer was now locked up.

Meanwhile, Moss Hart had performed the hardest task of his young career; he had somehow convinced a tired and skeptical George Kaufman that he had cracked the third act puzzle of *Once in a Lifetime* and that they should begin again. Only days after it had died—and likely before Aline had signed on with the Berkshire company—Hart bluffed his way back into Kaufman's home and explained the new finale to his erstwhile writing partner. "We can go into rehearsals by August," Kaufman told a surprised Hart when he finished the pitch. "How soon can you move in here?"[15] Astonishingly, *Once in a Lifetime* was suddenly revived and would soon be the biggest hit of Broadway's fall season. Unfortunately, Aline MacMahon was completely oblivious of its rebirth, and contractually barred from having anything to do with it.

As *Once in a Lifetime* had been limping through its final performances in Brooklyn, George Kaufman's most recent success, *June Moon*—also produced by Sam Harris—closed after eight profitable months at the Broadhurst Theater. Its star, Jean Dixon, had received plaudits for her comedic timing and effervescent personality, and both Harris and Kaufman credited her with a good part of the success of the production. In July the writers and their producer were confident enough in their labors to begin recasting *Lifetime* with the actors that were then available to them. With Aline now engaged in Massachusetts and Jean Dixon at liberty in Manhattan, Sam Harris did the only thing he could do under the circumstances. He cast Ms. Dixon as the lead in the reincarnated production of *Once in a Lifetime*. "It broke my heart," Aline said, thinking back on the disappointment. "Suddenly the whole thing fell apart."[16] On returning to New York at the end of her Berkshire summer she would have to perform the thankless task of graciousness in watching a role she had created become a smash hit for the actress that replaced her. In spite of her low-key, forgiving nature, it was one of Aline's most difficult performances.

The summer in Stockbridge was unremarkable. There were parts in *The Admirable Crichton*, *Juno and the Paycock*, and *The Torchbearers*, among others. Aline also had her first performance as the nurse in *Romeo and Juliet*, a role that she was to repeat periodically during her career. Barely out of her twenties, Aline was playing a woman perhaps twice her age, as she had also done less than a year earlier in the mercifully forgotten *Daylight Saving*. Aline's ability to project wise maturity would quickly become a central element of her on-screen persona once she reached Hollywood. This appearance of experience and worldliness distinguished Aline from her early contemporaries, and allowed her to take on rich, complex character parts at a young age. It was another product of Aline's Russian training, perhaps channeling the feelings of physical inadequacy that came from Jennie Mac's long-standing negativity about her daughter's looks. "I never thought Aline was beautiful," Jennie said in 1978. "When she was young only pretty girls got the acting jobs. Aline achieved everything *without* good looks."[17] Sadly, even at the age of one hundred Jennie Mac could never temper her personal observations to spare Aline's feelings.

As the new decade trudged on through a worsening economy, the Method too, was struggling for stability. Of its small band of American devotees in 1930, only Aline MacMahon had achieved significant critical and professional Broadway success. After the Method's US debut in 1923, the Neighborhood Playhouse severed ties with Richard Boleslavsky and he was forced to move the American Laboratory Theatre first to a run-down Manhattan apartment, then to a condemned mansion on the city's East Side. When, late that year,

Konstantyn Stanislavski and the Moscow Art Theatre returned to the United States for a second tour, Boleslavsky reconnected with the troupe, which included an actress who would become a major figure in the spread of the Method, Maria Ouspenskaya.[18] Film fans remember Madame Ouspenskaya as the witchy Gypsy fortuneteller of 1941's *The Wolf Man* and for her Academy Award–nominated roles in *Dodsworth* and *Love Affair*, but in 1923 she was considered only a minor talent within the MAT. When the Moscow Art left America in the spring of 1924, Madame elected to remain behind and soon took up an offer to teach in the acting school of American Laboratory Theatre.[19]

During the mid-twenties the Lab constantly struggled to attract financial backing, and Boleslavsky was often forced to accept well-paying directing assignments to keep it from insolvency. These money troubles found the school regularly evading angry landlords by moving around Manhattan; in two years the Lab went from its dilapidated mansion, to Greenwich Village, then to the Upper West Side, and back to the Lower East Side. With Boleslavsky often absent, it was more and more left to Madame Ouspenskaya to operate the teaching classes. Soon she had infused the Lab with her peculiar brand of highly influential lessons, including a scene where students were told to create a character that lived in a remote fishing village. After a few minutes of improvisation, Madame's assistant would announce that a boat containing dozens of the village's fishermen had capsized and all were dead. Then, with no direction, Madame Ouspenskaya would force the actors to continue the scene for perhaps as long as thirty minutes. Gradually they grew frustrated at being obliged to behave in character and invent things to do or say. Only then did Madame remind them that in the real world people do not stop behaving—they simply exist.

Even with these techniques, the student productions of the American Laboratory Theatre during the 1920s were often dismissed by New York critics as amateurish or not fully realized, and its few financial successes could never quite reconcile the balance sheets. But the foundations of future Method structures were slowly emerging. Lee Strasberg, Stella Adler, and Harold Clurman all attended classes with Boleslavsky and Ouspenskaya during the late twenties. In the years ahead they would emerge as the new generation of teachers of the Method, and soon create an important and influential company in New York.

By the time Wall Street collapsed in the autumn of 1929 the Lab was already in its own private Depression and had still produced no performing students of popular note. Regularly away from the school on commercial assignments, Boleslavsky was eventually forced to resign under pressure from his board of directors, which is perhaps exactly what he wanted. Soon he was in Hollywood, where he achieved some success as a director for Metro-Goldwyn-Mayer. Only a year later—just as Aline was traveling to Stockbridge for her summer at the Berkshire Playhouse in June 1930, the Depression also destroyed the American Laboratory Theatre. Without Boleslavsky's charisma and drive, Madame Ouspenskaya and the Lab's board could not entice new blood or money. Or more simply, there was no blood or money to be had. The Lab was forced to close its doors. Thus, at the start of the 1930s, the sole teaching school of the Method was gone, and the Russian technique was momentarily without a champion in America. Except, of course, for Aline MacMahon.

When Aline returned to New York following her engagement in Stockbridge, she and Clarence decided it was time to find a permanent home for themselves. Since their wedding, they had been living in Clarence's apartment in the Dalhousie building, on the southern border of Central Park. Anxious to have a new home, but not wanting to lose their view, they fortuitously located a beautiful 12th-floor penthouse apartment at 1 W. 64th street with a magnificent, never-to-be obstructed eastern panorama of Central Park. It likely came to their attention as a result of Clarence's membership in the Ethical Culture Society, whose headquarters were—and are—immediately across 64th street on Central Park West. Although appearing extravagant (especially for Communist-curious artists in the midst of a worsening depression), the rental of the apartment was one of the savviest investments the Steins ever made. Decked out in exotic Asian motifs of magnificent green and blue, it boasted a balcony jutting out over Central Park West from which morning coffee could be taken with the sunrise. As a meeting place for Clarence's important clients and organizations, it was invaluable. For entertaining it was unparalleled. And in the long run, it would prove remarkably inexpensive; the building eventually became rent controlled, giving the couple an amazingly low-cost and beloved home for over sixty years.

While Aline had been whiling away her summer in Massachusetts, the newly revised *Once in a Lifetime* was coalescing into a hit that would run on Broadway for over a year. Shortly after it opened in September, Sid Grauman, the legendary West Coast theatrical producer whose name has become immortal through Grauman's Chinese Theater, saw the box office numbers of *Lifetime*'s New York run. Unlike some other California producers, Sid Grauman was unafraid of mounting a play that mercilessly lampooned the Hollywood

In 1930 the Steins moved into the penthouse of 1 West 64th Street, with a never-to-be-obstructed eastern panorama of Central Park. Later rent controlled, it remained Aline's East Coast home for sixty-one years. Author Collection.

elite as brainless dunderheads right under their noses. In the early fall of 1930, he contacted Sam Harris about bringing a road production to his Mayan Theater in the heart of Los Angeles. "Unfortunately, I didn't open [on Broadway] in 'Once in a Lifetime,'" Aline said of the series of events that changed her life in 1930. "But as a result I was available when Sid Grauman wanted to do it for the picture colony. So he asked me to go out there to do that part." Aline MacMahon's bad luck was about to pay off.

It is entirely unlikely that Sid Grauman knew anything about Aline MacMahon or her connection to *Once in a Lifetime*, but Sam Harris did. When Grauman licensed *Lifetime* for its West Coast premiere, a deal was struck for Moss Hart to go west as its director, and to also take on the role of Lawrence Vail, which George Kaufman had played in the New York company. By the end of December the other details were hastily worked out, and Grauman insisted that Hart and company begin for Los Angeles immediately. On New Year's Eve, 1930, the phone rang in the Stein's new penthouse apartment. It was Sam Harris's aide-de-camp Max Siegel with an offer—even a friendly demand—that Aline sign on to the road company of *Once in a Lifetime*. Siegel, who had loved Aline in the previews of *Lifetime*, also insisted that she must leave for Los Angeles the next day. It being New Year's Eve, Aline thought Max may have begun his alcoholic celebrations a trifle early. "Max," she said, "call me up tomorrow when you're sober and know what you're talking about."[20] Although Max Siegel may have indeed been drunk, his offer was sincere. One way or the other, 1931 would begin with a life-altering decision.

Aline was delighted to be offered the opportunity to go on the road with *Once in a Lifetime*, but she also had a husband to consider. Although her relationship with Clarence was mutually supportive, progressive, and equal, this was still 1930, a time when the average man made the rules in his home. With Max Siegel's offer in hand and just half a day to decide, Aline sat down with her husband to discuss it.[21] As he had always done, Clarence encouraged her to take advantage of her artistic opportunities. For the era, he was a remarkably liberal man as it related to the role of women in marriage. He considered Aline a true equal, and took great pride in her accomplishments. It would hurt him for her to be away, but it would have hurt him more if Aline had again missed her chance at the part that had so painfully eluded her. The next day a messenger arrived with a boilerplate contract from Sam Harris. "At the request of Sid Grauman I have been asked to help cast several of the principal roles in 'Once in a Lifetime.' I have recommended you for the role of May Daniels at a salary of four hundred dollars a week. It is hereby distinctly understood that I am not contractually a party to your employment, but that Sid Grauman is the manager and you will enter into a contract with him upon your arrival on the coast. If this is understood and agreed, kindly sign this letter."[22] So, on New Year's Day 1931, Aline signed the agreement, packed her bags, and stepped aboard the *20th Century Limited*, bound for Hollywood.[23] Almost immediately Clarence confided to a friend, "Aline promises me she will try to get back by the middle of April. In the meantime, naturally I am very lonely."[24] The gloom that Clarence felt at their separation would not be his last, and would grow deeper as her first West Coast sojourn became a regular ritual that would be repeated for years to come.

Clarence was not alone in his sadness. While changing trains in Chicago Aline posted a letter written en route, back to her man in New York. "To part is to die a little," she wrote in her old-world-romantic way. "Who would have thought that getting my heart's desire would dissolve me in sobs as far as Harmon?[25] I look on the blue snow and grey hills and say, 'If *he* was here they'd be purple and pink.'"[26] This was the first of thousands of coast-to-coast missives exchanged between these devoted lovers over the following decades. On hotel stationary, onionskin, or scrap paper, long and short, intimate and informational, they rarely passed more than forty-eight hours without confiding their thoughts to the page. "I miss you even more on Sunday," Clarence responded, "but I don't know how to express it. Your grand letter from Chicago was so full of all the things I can't put into words; I love you says so little."[27]

Since the debut of *Once in a Lifetime* on Broadway, Moss Hart and George Kaufman had been tinkering with Aline's alter ego May Daniels. Over the life of the play they wrought significant changes to May's persona, making her much more sympathetic (and perhaps a micron less cynical), while crafting a subtle romantic angle with one of her partners in the voice business. This was one of the third-act changes—the "human element" they were searching for—that helped save *Once in a Lifetime*. Aline knew little of this when she sat down to reacquaint herself with the play while headed cross-country. After reading the reconstituted script she could barely contain her enthusiasm. "I read the part again—and Darling, it is a *stunner*," she wrote to Clarence. "Now listen," she continued, asking a question to which she already knew the answer, "should I play it impassively—almost monotone—making the points, of course—which is Jean Dixon's style—or shall I bring all the variety of light and color to the part I can? I lean to the latter, keeping it in character, of course. With the way [Moss has] rewritten it there's so *much* to do with it—the love stuff and the warm note toward the boob [Jerry] has

Once in a Lifetime

been played up wonderfully. I'm ecstatic over it."[28] A few days later Clarence weighed in. "You ask me to advise you how to play your part—*ME!*" he said, incredulous. Then, he told his wife exactly what she wanted to hear. "Play it your way! Give it all the variety you have—to hell with Jean Dixon's way. Don't forget you know more about acting than all of them put together!"[29]

After four long days on the rails, Aline stepped off the Atchison, Topeka and Santa Fe *Chief* in Los Angeles, dropped her bags at the Biltmore Hotel, and again rode the sinuous wave of a new, exciting opportunity. Even as she was consumed with costume fittings, rehearsals, contracts, social engagements, and grief at her separation from Clarence, her proximity to Hollywood almost immediately gave rise to persistent daydreams about the possibility of breaking into films. Sid Grauman helped stoke her fantasies by name dropping the executives and bigwigs he knew at the Metro-Goldwyn-Mayer, Warner Brothers, and Paramount studios. Everywhere Aline went she was introduced to powerful movie people, and those adjacent to powerful movie people. It was the beginning of an idea that she could not entirely believe would be hers. "Except by a miracle," she told Clarence, with heartbreaking self-assessment, "I would never do for the talkies—I'm too tall and not beautiful." Then, as if to reassure him of her devotion by dimming the stars in her own eyes, she added, "And it's out of the question anyway—unless I work in New York."[30] In closing she inadvertently emphasized how much the idea of a life on film meant to her by comparing it to the most important thing she could think of. "*You're* my talking picture," she insisted.

After two weeks of rehearsals, *Once in a Lifetime* was ready to begin a week of preview performances in Santa Barbara. As she had experienced rarely before—perhaps only in *Beyond the Horizon* and *Maya*—Aline recognized that she was a part of something that was stretching her talent to its fullest. "I'm doing it my way," she said, "and everyone likes it a lot. It's collaboration again—not just playing a part. I think I'm going to be grand—I've really got a grip on it, and hope to make it a real living picture—lots of depth and several dimensions—at least five. But dearest—it is *so good* to act. It seems to fill my heart with something more than air. I'm enjoying it enormously." This is one of the rare professional moments that Aline lived for—and she began to realize that such roles were potentially more plentiful, varied, and lucrative in film than anything Broadway could offer. The lure of Hollywood had well and truly begun its influence on Aline MacMahon.

Just before the preview of *Lifetime* opened, Moss Hart came down with flu severe enough to keep him off the stage for the entire run in Santa Barbara.

Director Robert Sinclair—also Hart's understudy—substituted for him. "We're damn lucky to have him to do it," Aline said. During the engagement a large number of Hollywood stars motored up to watch a group of impudent New York stage actors lampoon their livelihood. The stars mere presence—as well as their surprisingly positive reaction to the deadly satire—contributed to a highly successful run that sent an audible buzz through the film community.

Following the Santa Barbara performance of Friday, January 23, the wish of a young girl who started acting just as cinema was coming into adolescence began to coalesce into reality. Backstage after the show, a handsome young man from San Francisco cut his way through the crowd to speak to Aline. Warner Brothers director Mervyn LeRoy was then basking in the success of his violent and highly influential crime film *Little Caesar*, which had premiered in New York to a box office flood only two weeks earlier. The dapper, up-and-coming LeRoy was so impressed with Aline's performance that he made her a promise: "He came around after the show and said that he would give me the first good picture job that came his way." Here, after only a few weeks in the capital of world film, was the opportunity she had grown to crave so deeply. In spite of the incredible excitement and desire she felt ("I was *so flattered* in getting Mr. LeRoy's kind interest"),[31] the next day Aline wrote a deeply conflicted letter that downplayed the possibilities of a picture career—and a long separation—to her lovesick husband. "Now don't become apprehensive," she counseled, enumerating the reasons for him to remain calm. "1) I wouldn't stay so far away from you for any really long time. 2) I'm too tall. 3) He won't call. 4) The tests will be lousy." Aline MacMahon—a pragmatist with a healthy professional ego—almost certainly did not believe any of these things. At the same time, she was deeply devoted to her husband, and had an innate understanding of Clarence's sometimes-fragile emotional makeup. She desperately wanted the opportunity to bring her art to the screen—but she also wanted to protect her mate, and enjoy the life they had made together.

By late January, *Once in a Lifetime*—a play about the foolishness and vapidity of Hollywood—was about to have its gala Los Angeles premiere in front of the notoriously humorless elite of the film industry. "No one has the faintest idea how it's going to be received," Aline told the *Los Angeles Times* just before the first performance. "There's no way of telling. We're prepared for the worst because things have been going so well," she said with a wink. "The tryout in Santa Barbara went beautifully—those charming people laughed their tiaras off—wonderful notices in all the papers!" But on the

West Coast, Santa Barbara is to Los Angeles as Brooklyn is to Broadway. In LA, *Lifetime* would be submitted to the microscopic scrutiny of the executives and power brokers that controlled everything in the industry—even the opinions of the people on their payrolls. Suddenly skeptical of all the unvarnished enthusiasm, Aline turned baleful at the prospects for Los Angeles. "It looks ominous," she said.

The day before *Once in a Lifetime*'s Los Angeles premiere, Aline's mock premonition of doom seemed momentarily to be justified. At the dress rehearsal author Moss Hart decided that he had recovered from the flu enough to attempt the performance, and took the stage with a voice that was barely a whisper. Almost immediately Hart knew he had made a grave mistake and had to stop the play and have the curtain lowered. Co-Director Bob Sinclair again stepped in for the third act, *and* would have to do the same at the gala premiere the next night. "Can you imagine a worse break?" Aline wrote. "I'm so sad for Moss. His heart was absolutely set on doing it." Also, that afternoon Sid Grauman's seventy-seven-year-old mother was nearly killed in an auto accident that fractured her leg in two places. "Now the audience will be full of apprehension," Aline playfully lamented, "and of course the entire first night's audience are all bosom friends of Sid Grauman's mother!"[32]

Tuesday, January 28, saw a true Hollywood extravaganza at the Mayan Theater. Sid Grauman had decided to treat the opening night of *Once in a Lifetime* as if it was a Cecil B. DeMille spectacle or a Douglas Fairbanks blockbuster and, ever the trouper, went on with the show. Police lined South Hill Street as arc lights swept the night sky, while film stars and industry notables were escorted from their glittering automobiles through hordes of excited movie fans to the theater. In the ornate lobby of the Mayan were wax figures of Clara Bow and Dolores Del Rio standing on a replica of Stage Four of Glogauer Studios, the fictional setting where Aline and her cohorts scammed the elite of Hollywood. Opposite, a band played hot jazz among explosions of lilies, orchids, and roses. Advance word had sent opening night tickets to premium prices. Grauman was able to charge main floor prices for balcony seats after he announced that Marion Davis would be sitting there as his guest of honor. So many of the attending starlets were draped in fur that Mary Astor was nearly barred as an impostor for wearing a modest satin coat. Occupying the premium seats were the executives and producers of the studios: Jack Warner, Louis Mayer, Daryl Zanuck, and so on. Sequestered safely at the back of the house, meanwhile, was the wretched refuse of the Hollywood dream machine: screenwriters, dialogue coaches, and New York playwrights. The sheer density of film industry power brokers was such that one critic wrote, with a mischievous tinge of hope, that if a bomb had exploded at the Mayan Theater that night "whole dynasties would have been wiped out."[33] His hope—however insincere—was unfounded. There would be no bomb for *Once in a Lifetime*.

When Aline finally walked out on the stage in front of the assembled hordes of Hollywood for the first time, something strange happened. It was revealed that the film industry could laugh at itself. "By the time the curtain came down on the first scene it was clear that those out front were not only taking it, but liking it," a bemused *New York Times* reporter noted. "Under what were probably as trying a set of psychological circumstances as ever presented themselves to a company of actors on an opening night," he continued, "the cast of 'Once in a Lifetime' gave a smooth and satisfying performance."[34] The next morning, the *Los Angeles Times* offered a stellar review and noticed one member of the company above all. "The cast are all capable performers, with Miss MacMahon standing out in a feelingful, thoroughly warming portrayal of the patient May Danials."[35]

Backstage after the premiere, Aline's dressing room was host to an impromptu reception for the company and assorted audience members. "What good sports they were!" she enthused, still flush with the thrill of the evening's success. "It could have been ghastly—but it was probably more fun than any performance of the show has ever been!"[36] Thinking back on that evening years later, Aline chose to forget any trepidation she may have had about the possibility of failure. "What a wonderful entrée it was for an actress," she said with a sparkle. "Everybody had come to see themselves satirized, and therefore I had an extraordinary opportunity to show my stuff."[37]

Once in a Lifetime became an enormous hit in its Los Angeles run. "They laugh so and we've been SRO for two days now," Aline reported to her husband early in February. Clarence was truly thrilled at Aline's achievement, but the possibility of enduring a long separation was already deepening his loneliness and apprehension. In New York he was relying on friends to assuage his gloom, but he could not hide it either from them or Aline. In writing to congratulate her on the opening night success he quickly betrayed his deeper feelings: "But remember, it is to be only a *short* success," he said.[38] This must have been a tiny dagger to the heart of both the actress and the wife. Aline knew that she was the instigator of their separation, and the friction that she felt between the joy of her art and the love of her husband was becoming difficult for both of them. "My beloved, oh my darling—I am so concerned about you," she counseled, again trying to ameliorate his fears. "Don't get too lonely or I'll throw the whole thing up and come home." Then, trying to console him and express her own desires at the same time, she wrote, "I miss you cruelly, but it's different for me. For one thing, I'm working—and oh!—the intoxication of it." At the end of her letter, she too was perhaps unconsciously hurtful to her sorrowful mate. "Don't be blue," she said, "I couldn't enjoy all of this if you are."[39]

While Aline MacMahon the wife was making effort to keep her sense of self, Hollywood was doing its best to seduce Aline MacMahon the actress. During March she was sincerely trying to arrange a trip to Europe with Clarence that would follow the close of *Lifetime* in early April. It was to coincide with Clarence's appearance at a town planning conference in Berlin, and Aline was regularly reassessing their departure date (and location) based on *Lifetime's* daily box office. ("It looks like a long run—how long, no one knows.")[40] But underneath her enthusiasm about the trip there was plenty of equivocation. Sid Grauman had already booked the show for a San Francisco engagement that would start on April 7 and last at least into early May. "I hate to bring up the possibility of leaving the show in advance," Aline said. "But they ought to have loads of time to find someone. Now, if—this is just thinking in pen and ink—if I leave the show on April 25th [in order to sail from New York on the ocean liner *Europa*] they'll be in Frisco, and it will be hard to get someone there. They'd probably rather not pay my fare to Frisco, too—they'd rather replace me on April 5th when we close in L.A. That means I'd lose three weeks salary [at $400 per week]—or the $900 I could save before the end of April." In her roundabout way, Aline was placing polite leverage on the case for postponing the European trip by some weeks and going to San Francisco with the company. She would rather give up time spent touring Europe before going to Berlin than miss the dream opportunity that Mervyn LeRoy had placed so boldly in front of her. "If they are to replace me before they open in Frisco, the girl should have two weeks of rehearsals here," she said. Then, cleverly flinging the ball off her playing field, she added, "What do you advise?"[41]

While there is no question that Aline loved her husband dearly, she was nearly defenseless in the face of the film colony's enormous powers of seduction. After just a few weeks, Hollywood was already on second base. "I'm afraid I'm getting awfully impressed by the talkies," she admitted, and for good reasons. On a sojourn to Paramount studios with her friend from New York, writer Arthur Kober, she visited the set of *Up Pops the Devil*. "The

ALINE MACMAHON

The myth that Aline MacMahon was "not attractive" is dispelled in this Warner Brothers publicity photo shot by Irving Lippman, c. 1933. At her best she displayed the kind of exotic beauty that later captivated fans of Anjelica Huston or Cher. *Wisconsin Historical Society, Irving Lippman, ID #149060.*

director, Eddie Sutherland said he'd like to use me in a picture and will get in touch with me next week," she reported. Unfortunately, her exclusive run-of-the-play contract with *Once in a Lifetime* meant she was unable to accept Sutherland's offer. Later, accompanying Moss Hart on a trip to Metro-Goldwyn-Mayer, she watched Joan Crawford shoot takes for *Laughing Sinners*, and chatted with Ramon Novarro and Helen Chandler on the set of *Daybreak*. "[Miss Chandler] said she'd much rather be in the theatre," Aline observed, "but I notice she's staying in the talkies."[42] Later that week Sid Grauman told Aline that MGM had also inquired if she was available for a part in an upcoming film. "Not during the run of the play," he replied, firmly. On the Warner Brothers sound stages she met Walter Huston (one of her favorite actors), Dudley Digges (then shooting the first film version of the *Maltese Falcon*), and John Barrymore. And at Universal she reported seeing a flock of "great ones." "And they had all seen *me*," she said, surprised. "It was *very* interesting." Hollywood, naturally, was placing in her path everything that would make Aline MacMahon's head turn.

All through the Los Angeles engagement of *Once in a Lifetime*, Aline waited to hear from Mervyn LeRoy, who had managed to end-around Sid Grauman by speaking directly to her. She tried not to dwell on his promise, well aware of what she called "the vicissitudes of the stage," but for the increasingly star-struck actress it was a losing battle. "I'd really like Mervyn LeRoy to keep his promise and call me for a test," she lamented when the director failed to phone. Aline now understood a central tenet of Hollywood life: it doesn't pay to get too excited about anything until a contract is signed, and sometimes not even then. In this case, however, LeRoy was as good as his word. "Mr. LeRoy called me today and said he found a part in 'Five Star Final,' the part of Eddy Robinson's secretary," she enthused. Just a few days after her conversation with LeRoy, Hollywood formally summoned Aline MacMahon. It was March 20, 1931. "Warner Brothers sent for me yesterday," she warned Clarence. "Mind you, it's a 500 to one shot that I won't do it, but just in case I went to the studio to discuss it. There's no doubt I could find work here—it's a gold mine—but I'll do no 'prospecting' and only stay if they offer me a swell part and a swell salary. I'll know more next week."⁴³

On Monday, March 30, Aline MacMahon reported to the Warner Brothers studio for a screen test. At thirty-two she had played in every type of venue in front of every kind of audience. From ice-cold church basements to the opulent theaters of New York society, she had spent all her energy preparing for what came next. But film was still an unknown quantity. "On Sunday I had to prepare for the test," she wrote. "Monday was *really* exciting. I arrived at 1:00—was made up very carefully by their crack make-up men, then shot the two scenes I'd prepared. I didn't leave until 5:30. It was all strange and exciting." Once again, however, Jennie Mac's voice reverberated carelessly in Aline's ears. "But of course I barely slept all day Tuesday worrying about myself—convinced that I'm too *fat*—too *tall*—wore the wrong clothes, and so on." But the die had been cast—it was now too late for anything but second guesses. And third, and fourth.

Things were happening so quickly now that it was impossible for the United States Post Office keep up with events. Aline's worried missive about the schedules for *Once in a Lifetime*, their European trip, and a potential contract with Warner Brothers didn't receive a reply until after the test was finished. By that time Clarence, who was often disinterested in taking the bull by the horns in his marriage, finally picked up the ball that Aline had thrown in his court a few weeks earlier. "I'm glad the test is over," he said, "but I think you are foolish not to stay a little longer. You should go to San Francisco [with *Lifetime*]—I am well taken care of here." Then—without pique—Clarence referenced an example of Aline's strength that pointed up the futility of having even been offered the ball in the first place. "But what is the use of telling you what to do? [Clarence's friend] Henry Klaber said you were the perfect boss the evening their auto got bogged down and you came down the hill, ready to take command."[44] In Clarence's mind perhaps, the ball never truly left Aline's hands.

The day after the test, Aline's insecurities were at war with her anticipation. "I was supposed to call LeRoy at 10:30 Wednesday morning, but I couldn't stand the strain and called instead at 5:45 on Tuesday, but he was out." LeRoy had already taken a keen liking to Aline, and when he was told that she had called, he decided not to prolong her agony into Wednesday. Making his way backstage at the Tuesday evening performance of *Once in a Lifetime*, he rendered his verdict. "The test was fine," he said, grinning enthusiastically. "You won't know yourself!" The young director then added the critical piece of information that would make or break a career in those early days of sound film. "And your voice is *wonderful*," he said. With Mervyn LeRoy's endorsement, the following morning Aline went to discuss her first motion picture contract with Warner Brothers casting director Rufus LeMaire, the same man who had recently discovered and signed Warren William to the studio. Aline knew and disliked LeMaire from her days under contract to the Shubert Company in New York, calling him "as mean an S.O.B. as you can imagine." With this long-standing animus, there was immediate friction in the negotiations. Aline had then been on the Broadway stage for over a decade and knew well her value. In their discussion she disclosed that her weekly *Lifetime* salary was $450, and LeMaire quickly offered her $500. "My New York salary is $750," she pointed out. "I took a cut to come here." LeMaire wondered what she wanted. Aline would not sell herself short. In her record of the meeting she recalled, "I laughed and gurgled, '*$1500.*'" When LeMaire raised the studio's offer to $750, Aline curtly responded, "No. Twice that." Incredulous at this upstart first-timer, LeMaire told her that the conversation was over. Instead of giving in, Aline quickly stood up to leave. At this, an angry LeMaire gave her a parting shot worthy of the script in a Warners' gangster picture. "You are out like a lamp," he said. "You burn me up!"[45]

On April 2, with contract negotiations now in limbo, Mervyn LeRoy invited Aline to the studio to see her test reel. It was her first look at the next forty years of her life. The letter she wrote to Clarence that day crackled with the energy of a person on the moment of realizing their dreams. "Angel, my one," she began, "today I saw me—and Darling!—I'm swell! I look and sound not a bit like an actress, but like a very nice person—unaffected—intelligent—pleasant—nice to look at. The camera flatters me outrageously!" Here however, even the objective proof of the moving picture was not enough to convince Aline that she was actually beautiful. "In fact, I appear the way I like to *think* I look. If only to have seen myself, the trip has been a colossal success—a sort of milestone," she allowed, before then retreating to a dissection of her art. "I say—well, if I've done this these first ten years—whittled any emotions down so that they come clean and crystalline—developed poise without *pose* (that's the hardest), then I'm pleased with me. How full life feels to me just because I've been outside looking on at myself—and because the camera is flattering. I'm *so* well pleased!" Still, even in this state of euphoria, Aline was dubious of Warner Brothers interest. "I probably won't play the part," she continued. "They're sending for Betty Compson, Kay Johnson and Dorothy Burgess—all 'names' who work for $1500 a week, and they won't pay me more than $750—so, goodbye for now, talkies! But someday I'll have a good time with them—they interest me colossally as a form—a means of expression—and I'm not unconscious of their vast rewards."

Once in a Lifetime finally closed in Los Angeles on April 5 with Warner Brothers stonewalling Aline by testing other actresses. In order to be available for a possible breakthrough with the studio, Aline had arranged to travel with the company to San Francisco and star in the first week's performances. If Warners did not use her she would then head east to reunite with Clarence and catch a steamship to Europe. The couple had now been separated more than four months and both were heartsick of it. "It's been a happy engagement, even though my love is so far away from me," Aline said. On the company's second day in Frisco, Rufus LeMaire's office called with a new offer of $850. Aline's desire to return to Clarence—and her antipathy toward LeMaire—made it easy to refuse the offer. "I said okay for *$1000*," she reported that night, "and they said 'Goodbye, Darling!' I'm just as well pleased," Aline said with resignation. "I want to go home. I want to go home."[46]

But Dorothy was not transported to Kansas. Only hours later Warner Brothers called again and reiterated that they wanted her in the picture, but that $850 had to be their final offer. At last, Aline relented. The seduction was complete. Oz had won. After all her anticipation and enthusiasm about the creative allure of film, Aline's reaction was unexpected, even to her. Scrawled beneath the letterhead of the El Cortez Hotel was the soul of an artist fighting the devotion of a lover. "It's awful—awful," she lamented to Clarence. "What can I say? It looks like a good chance to try the talkies. But it's awful. I'm sick. I'm so sorry. I love you."[47]

Within days the homesick actress received a performer's contract for the part in *Five Star Final*. "So I left *Once in a Lifetime* in San Francisco and went back to Hollywood to play it," she recalled. "This was the curious chance that started me doing dry comedy in Hollywood."[48] In New York, Clarence glowed with her success, but continued to lament his misfortune at her absence. "I was just thinking forward, twenty-five years from now," he playfully wrote. "As I look out on New York, there on the thousandth floor of the Metro-Goldwyn-Mayer building is Louis B. Mayer himself, announcing that after twenty-five years, Aline MacMahon, *in person*, is returning to her home town. And there you land in your private plane. I still know you; you look just like your pictures." The husband of the new movie actress Aline MacMahon closed his imploring, revealing fantasy with a simple postscript: "I love you so."[49]

Thus, Jean Dixon—still playing May Daniels to great acclaim on Broadway—won the battle and lost the war. Aline's loss of an outstanding lead in one of the great hits of the 1930–31 New York stage season instead started her on a forty-five-year career in film and television, while Miss Dixon managed just a handful of minor Hollywood credits over the next seven years. Dixon herself was only too aware of the opportunity she had missed; early in January, just as the *Lifetime* road company was heading to California, Dixon had confided to friends that she "would give anything to be in the opening at Los Angeles."[50] This is how history works. It often takes the long run.

7

AT ONCE THEY CIRCLED HER ROUND

Five Star Final is the story of a jaded big-city newspaper editor named Randall (Edward G. Robinson) who is bullied by his publisher into revisiting a decades-old murder story in an effort to boost circulation. In his cynical zeal, Randall reveals the identity of the murderess who has since served her time and is then living incognito in the city with her husband, and a daughter who is unaware of the mother's previous life as the notorious Nancy Voorhees. The series of events that follow this cruel revelation—family dissolution, a double suicide, and attempted murder—are shocking enough to place the film among the grimmest pictures of Hollywood's barely regulated pre-Code era, then near the beginning of its long-lasting carnival of indecency.

The core of *Five Star Final* is Randall's transformation from sardonic muckraker to rehabilitated (if still sardonic) human being. Nudging him along in the process is his loyal and secretly love-struck secretary Miss Taylor (Aline). Throughout the film, Taylor watches Randall's thinning morals with such increasing disdain that Randall exhorts her as his "visible conscience." And it is this conscience that is largely responsible for his return to humanity. When the *Gazette*'s story has begun to topple the lives of Nancy Voorhees' entire family, Randall feels a twinge of regret burrowing through the dulling effect of bourbon. "You don't like this mess, do you?" he asks the secretary, half-hoping she won't answer. "I'm not paid for opinions," Taylor says, behind sleepy eyes. Then, after some silent consideration, she narrows her gaze further and disdainfully adds: "I think you can always get people interested in the crucifixion of a woman."

After events have later spun nearly out of control, Taylor confronts Randall about his pursuit of the Voorhees story, emboldened by her own efforts to medicate with liquor. "You're letting this rag seduce you with a lot of money!

Can't you see what this might do to her family?" she says, her voice cracking with heartbreak. "You ought to be ashamed of yourself." In this single scene, Aline imparts remarkable depth to the simple secretary. In her hands Miss Taylor's emotional turmoil is more than just innate compassion; it is born of personal shame and guilt—she can't ignore her own part in this entirely preventable destruction of human lives. And the one certainty of her heart—her love for Randall—is being tested. She wants him to be the man she has idealized through the years and is terrified that her image of him has been a mere projection. This character dynamic—a woman who not only fails to attract her man, but also to save him from himself—is a dual type that will recur in Aline's later films.

Watching Aline MacMahon in *Five Star Final*, one can instantly recognize the gap between her performance and the other supporting players in the film. In 1931, screen acting was entering a new phase. As the production of talking pictures was codified, a new kind of actor and personality was coming into popular consciousness. This style, which was to become the dominant form for nearly twenty years, was primarily declarative. The subtext of thought and interior life that had necessarily developed in the best of silent film was—unfortunately—deemed redundant in a cinema where characters could now simply say what they felt. And in the Depression era, audiences were looking away from the old-world construct of America after the Great War; the conformists, the swells, the go-getters—these types no longer seemed relevant in a society fraying at the edges. To survive, men—and women—now needed to be tough more than thoughtful. Thus, two generations of actors followed a template that came from the post-WWI New York stage to the new Hollywood of talking pictures. From the advent of sound film until after World War II, actors (as well as writers and directors) were generally more dedicated to explicating the story than in plumbing nuances of human psychology. Story and action drove character, not the other way around. James Cagney once described the attitude of his generation of performers with admirable brevity: "Learn your lines, plant your feet, look the other actor in the eye, say the words, and mean them." Spencer Tracy, another polished practitioner of this era's style, was even more cavalier: "Come to work, know your lines and don't bump into the other actors," he said. Before the end of the war, you would be hard pressed to hear a Hollywood actor describe his job as anything other than work—and sometimes not even honest work, at that. After the war came the era of actors and actresses who publicly declared themselves artists and found it more important to know what the character hid than what they showed. Even as this interwar style was first solidifying its hold on screen acting, Aline MacMahon was working against its grain. Following her entrée to the Russian Method, she was continually refining and honing the techniques of what she considered her true art. "I pass emotions through a filter not generally used by actresses," she said shortly after arriving in Hollywood. "I find the grounds to meet my characters and am able to move from one feel to another. It is real stuff—no tricks, simply expressed. I don't know if I'll ever make real art, but I have *so much* to say in acting. I feel so far from the norm."

Marlon Brando, who studied the Method with Stella Adler and did more to popularize the Stanislavski system than any other actor, believed that the prewar performance style had long outlived itself by the time he exploded into the national consciousness in 1951. "In the thirties and forties you had a particular kind of acting," he said. "You knew who you were going to get when you went to the movies. Gary Cooper, Bogart, Clark Gable; crunchy fruit loops—they were just like breakfast cereals. That kind of acting became absurd. I wanted to change motion pictures to something nearer the truth."[1]

Like everyone else in the world, Marlon Brando was unaware that Aline MacMahon had predated him in this desire by twenty years. Although there were others using the technique scattered throughout the mid-1930s and 1940s, *she* was the first of cinema's Russian naturalists. The only person with a potential challenge to Aline's primacy as the first proponent of the Method in talking film is the Russian émigré Olga Baclanova. In America as a member of the Moscow Art Theatre during their second tour in 1923–24, Baclanova elected to stay behind when the troupe returned to the Soviet Union. She soon achieved some success in American silent films, but when talkies arrived late in the decade, Olga's Russian accent immediately threw her career into decline. Her only noteworthy appearance in the sound era was Tod Browning's infamous horror/revenge film *Freaks* (1932), which was so controversial that it was immediately withdrawn from circulation and largely unseen for more than three decades. Now, if this were the full story of Baclanova's training and career, she might well be counted as the first—albeit minor—proponent of Konstantyn Stanislavski's Method on film. But there is a little-known fact that disqualifies her for the honor: She never *actually* studied acting with Stanislavski.

Olga Baclanova was a fine actress, trained at Russia's prestigious Cherniavsky Institute. But it wasn't until much later that she was accepted directly into the company of the Moscow Art Theatre without having received any instruction in the Method. Because of this, her success with the MAT was a subject of deep resentment among the other actors in the company. As a primary member of the studio from the very birth of Stanislavski's system, Aline's friend and teacher Richard Boleslavsky related a firsthand account of Baclanova's entrée into the MAT to her. "Boly told us that Stanislavski gave a number of leading parts to this brilliant young actress who turned up [Baclanova], and the rest of the company were furious because she had never studied the Stanislavski Method," Aline related. "Well, Boly was delegated to go to Stanislavski and protest, and he did—he told him what an outrage it was. And Stanislavski looked at Boly and he said, 'But she can *act*.'" Here, Aline laughed heartily. "So, this is a great story that everybody forgets."[2] Whatever Baclanova may have had brought to the Hollywood screen—silent or sound—it did not come from Stanislavski, and it was not the Method.

From Aline's limited scenes in her first movie, we can see the nascent beginnings of this long-off postwar style ever so quietly emerging on screen. In contrast to the brusque directness of Ona Munson, or even the magnificently raw declaration of Edward G. Robinson, she brings a different set of tools to bear. Aline is playing the character, not pitching to the audience, and in this way she invites attention by not inviting it. On the relentless Warner Brothers assembly line, there was so little time for any artistic indulgences that the actors were often left to fend for themselves. "I'd pick up the script and write in, a la Stanislavski, what I was going to do in the scene," Aline said of her technique. "I had the advantage of a director who was so busy with so many other details that when the camera started, he was delighted that I knew what I was going to do. Nobody else did."[3] In each of her scenes in *Five Star* Aline devises a small piece of business for Miss Taylor; in one it is a dull fixation on her fountain pen, in another, the compulsive breaking of matchsticks. Far from being mere scene-stealing tools, these behaviors are subtle cues that help magnify Taylor's disconnection or anxiety. She presents as a real person, not the creation of a screenwriter—not a construction designed to impart mere information and surface emotion to a story. Her emotions seem real because Aline is doing what no other actor of the era is doing—dredging her own past to connect with the feelings of the character. And she is discovering that film might be the medium wherein this technique could work best. "It's taken the whole picture to figure out what to do," she confided near the end of the shoot, "but really, the movies are my oyster. I'm enough of a technician not to depend on an audience. I always act from inside myself and try to give the audience as much as they need to get the idea or emotion—so you see, I'm just right for the movies."[4] Here, as nothing before in talking cinema, is the birth of the style of acting that came from Russia to eventually conquer the silver screen through Monty Clift, James Dean, and Brando himself.

On its release *Five Star Final* was hailed as a raw, earthy drama, powerful in its honesty. "'Five Star Final' was crackling through the projectors of Warner's Western Theater last night," *Los Angeles Times* critic Phil Scheuer wrote. "It started like other pictures and, gradually gaining momentum, rolled out like a juggernaut of emotion over the packed theater."[5] It was rewarded with an Oscar nomination for Best Picture of 1931, while Robinson was hailed for his forceful performance. And critics and audiences immediately noticed Aline MacMahon, tucked away neatly near the end of the credits. "Aline MacMahon, one of the stage's grand actresses does a bored but honest secretarial job with finesse," was a typical observation. The *Los Angeles Times* declared, "[MacMahon] brings a wealth of understanding to her brief role," and the *Hollywood News* called her a "shining light."[6] In nearly every review she is singled out for praise, thus beginning a quiet and dignified love affair with audiences of the day.

In the middle of April, as Aline was deep in her work on *Five Star Final*, Clarence's mother Rose died unexpectedly.[7] Having his wife away at such an emotional time was difficult for Clarence, and it contributed to his growing depression. Mother and daughter-in-law were quite close, but with a new career beginning, and a minimum of three full days to make the cross-country trip to New York, there was nothing for Aline to do but continue working. She called the day Rose passed "the hardest of my life," and showed it in her letter to Clarence. "Here I am at the moment I might help you a little, so far away. How can I make it up to you?" she wondered.[8] In response, Clarence consoled himself. "Sometimes it is just so hard," he said. "Now there is only you."[9]

Following *Five Star's* wrap, Warner Brothers offered Aline MacMahon a long-term contract with the studio. It was just the wrong time to consider a permanent, or even a semi-permanent, move to the West Coast. In addition to Rose's death and Aline's simple desire to return home, there was still the matter of the trip to attend the exhibition of Clarence's work at the international town planning conference in Berlin. There was a suggestion by Aline that they now piggyback London, Paris, and Vienna on the end of the conference, but at this Clarence attempted to draw a line in the sand. Even with Aline's recent windfall in Hollywood, he insisted that they "limit [their] extravagance," since the travel-crazy couple had gone deeper into debt during their trip to India, among other indulgences. Still, they somehow eventually found themselves in London and Paris—as well as Hamburg, Frankfurt, Heidelberg, and Stuttgart—with nary another peep from Mr. Stein.

On May 1, 1931, with Aline just about to hop an eastbound train from Los Angeles to New York, the Empire State Building opened in Manhattan with much fanfare. From ground breaking to completion, construction had taken only 410 days—just over fourteen months—and thereafter it held the title as the World's Tallest Skyscraper for forty-two years. As one of New York City's most prominent architects, Clarence attended the opening gala and was treated to a special visit to what he derisively termed "the so-called 102nd floor, up in the so-called mooring mast."[10] The noted architect's disdain for the skyscrapers of New York was already well known. Only six months earlier he had given a lecture on the perils of tall buildings, predicting that New York and other big cities would eventually be "economically destroyed" by the need to maintain them. Naturally, the man who championed the Green Belt movement expected the skyscrapers to one day be replaced by verdant, open spaces. His prophecies about New York, like his hopes for the Communist movement, proved to be—shall we say—less than sage.

When *Five Star* wrapped in early May, Aline headed home at last. Although she found that she loved California and picture work, Aline craved a return to normalcy, however temporary. "All my activity [in Hollywood] has been ego-centric," she said. "I'm just a little tired of Aline MacMahon. Here's to Mrs. Clarence Stein!"

Less than a week after Aline disembarked in New York she and Clarence were on their way to Europe. The woman was, if nothing else, a trouper. Something forever seemed to be running just ahead of Aline MacMahon, and she could always be counted on to gather speed to catch it. As the Steins steamed for Germany, pieces of a dangerous and foreboding puzzle were quietly shifting into place on the Continent. From his stateroom on the *Europa*, Clarence wrote of his expectations for the trip with naive hopefulness. "We want to see the New World that is being created in Germany," he said sincerely.[11] Just a few weeks after the Steins ended their stay in Berlin and set sail back to New York, Adolph Hitler's National Socialists became the majority party in Germany. A New World was indeed, just beginning.

Upon return from Europe in July, Aline was once again called upon to gather her wits and step into the slipstream of a quickly moving opportunity. Before there was even a chance to get properly reacquainted with friends and family, the telephone rang at the Stein's penthouse with an offer. Since starting rehearsals in George Kaufman's *June Moon* in August 1929 and moving directly to the Broadway production of *Once in a Lifetime*, Jean Dixon had managed less than one month off in two years of performances. Sam Harris wanted to know if Aline would consider returning to her role as May Daniels in the Broadway production of *Lifetime* while Jean Dixon took a long-deserved vacation. By August, Aline was at last on Broadway in the role she created, although New York's brutal summer heat wave made the three-week engagement less satisfying than it might have otherwise been.

In September 1931—before *Five Star Final* had even reached America's theater screens—Aline was called in to read for the premiere production of Eugene O'Neill's *Mourning Becomes Electra* to be presented by New York's most prestigious company, the Theatre Guild. It was the exact kind of work she had been seeking from the beginning of her career, and felt she had lately been diverted away from. "I was determined to be a very serious actress," she explained. "I had done Shaw and Yeats and all that range, and I wanted to get back to that."[12] Sadly, Aline would again miss an important production for reasons beyond her control. "Just when they were casting it, they cast me for the girl [Electra / Lavinia]," she recalled with more than a hint of sadness and regret. "And about a week before the first rehearsal, my father died of a heart attack." William Marcus MacMahon, writer, editor, husband—and the father whom Aline adored so that she once described him as 'perfect'—was just fifty-five years old. Aline continued into rehearsals, but soon found life and art edging uncomfortably close together. "The play is about a girl and her father, really. That's what the whole thing is about," she said. In rehearsals, director Phil Moeller made an effort to pull on this familial connection, perhaps at an inopportune moment. According to Aline, after a period of regular readings, "Phil Moeller started stopping me on every line. Then he pointed out 'My God, but you are *Electra*—you've got to make the line *'I'll write to my father'* as portentous as any Greek tragedy!' It was a very strange feeling, rehearsing after that experience." She admitted, dejectedly, "I tried to do what he wanted, only I guess I couldn't." For Aline, here was an unexpected schism between the prewar Victorian acting tradition and her dedication to the emerging art of the Method in America. Phil Moeller—whom Aline loved ("a grand human being," she called him)—was a director of the old school, who wanted his players to do the part exactly as he dictated. Of course in the Method it is primarily the *actor* who decides the emotional direction for the character, and Aline's Russian training made her fully dedicated to that idea. When Moeller insisted he wanted an Electra "in Wagnerian fashion"

Aline simply decided that he was quite wrong in his choice of manner.[13] "Apparently—even though I try—I can't play it any way except my own," she lamented. "It's a fierce limitation, but perhaps it'll work out all right." In this case it did not work out all right. After a few days, the director politely informed Aline that he couldn't accept what she was giving him and would have to find someone else. "I'm desolate to lose the chance, but I would have done it magnificently—not their way, but in my own way I would have found things to do that aren't often done on stage."[14] Aline and the company parted with mutual respect. "Phil Moeller let me out and got Alice Brady to do it. And she was grand in it."[15] Reflecting on the experience in the days shortly following her ouster, Aline was introspective. "I've felt tremendously let down," was her initial response. Then, digging deeper, she seemed to confront the willfulness of her own ego. "I've thought a lot about being fired from *Electra*. It seems so stupid—I had and have everything for it, yet I felt as if it would happen from the first. I almost willed it to happen. Am I growing vulnerable in my advanced years—so fearful people won't think me good that I hurry to say I don't care before they have a chance to show what they think?" Finally she resolved, "I intend to argue it out in me and know. Still, it goes under experience—only whether it's disintegrating or constructive, I don't know."

The Broadway premiere of *Mourning Becomes Electra* was a tremendous critical and box-office success that ran through the following March. After the dust settled, Clarence offered his loving consolation in a telegram from where he was working in Kansas City. "Bet you get bigger and better part in four plays with director who has sense enough to let you run them all," he wrote. "As for me, you are the whole show. I adore you."[16]

The death of her father was a serious but subterranean trauma to Aline MacMahon. It appears to have been largely responsible for her removal from *Mourning Becomes Electra*, something of which Aline was only dimly aware in the moment. In a larger sense it created a long-term imbalance in her relationship with her mother, who had always secretly been second in Aline's unspoken affections. With William gone, Aline now felt obliged to see to Jennie Mac's needs, and when strong-willed Jennie moved west to be near independent Aline, sparks sometimes flew from the resulting crackle of stone against iron. It was years before Aline began to understand the origin of this loving friction. "With all the tact and understanding on both our parts I constantly hurt her," Aline said of her mother. "Of course it is my fault, but I cannot help it. With all Jennie's perfection of heart and character there is a devil in me that keeps saying 'you want to be free of that silver cord'! Also, in my darkest moments I fear that I *want* to hurt her. I suppose it goes back to my love for my Dad and inevitably Jenny was my rival. She'd be willing to let me have everything my way if she thought she was first in my heart, but she is only first in my responsibilities. I fear it is an insoluble problem—a delayed adolescent problem. I suppose a psychiatrist would have a field day with me," she concluded.[17]

By the fall Aline had finished mourning her father and *Electra*. Except for her three weeks substituting for Jean Dixon she had now been off the Broadway stage for over a year and was itching to get back to work. In November, the opportunity to return to the stage was provided by her old friends at the Actor-Managers Company. The play was *If Love Were All*, about a young couple, each with ostensibly happy middle-aged parents, who discover that his mother (Aline) and her father (Hugh Buckler) are having an affair. The production skirted the lean edge of controversy by offering a story in which (a) the cheating parents are unrepentant in their love, and (b) their partners know about and approve of the affair, which both surprises and hurts the children. "Such a delicately poised play must be, above all, wisely cast and intelligently written, if it is to escape censure," Burns Mantle said. "In this instance these needs have been attended to. The adult lovers are beautifully realized by Aline MacMahon and Hugh Buckler."[18]

In the audience on opening night was another man who was deeply impressed by Aline's performance. Ed Sullivan, then a little-known dramatic critic, was reviewing *If Love Were All* for the New York *Evening World*. "In reviewing the play, one performer in it caught and riveted my attention," he wrote in 1935. "This was Aline MacMahon. That same night I tried to persuade Harry Cohn [president of Columbia Pictures] to sign her immediately." It is unlikely that Columbia would have had any more luck signing Aline to a long-term contract than Warner Brothers did, but she would never have to make the choice. According to Sullivan, "Cohn himself never saw her, but instead detailed someone from the New York office to look her over." Tests were made by the talent scouts at their local studio. In the end, Sullivan said, "Columbia rejected her because she wouldn't screen properly."[19] Film audiences must thank God for such myopia—the thought of Aline MacMahon appearing as an extra in a Three Stooges short is too horrible to contemplate.

A few weeks after *If Love Were All* closed its eleven-night run, Aline was asked to join the cast of a new and prestigious production starring Blanche Yurka. Interestingly, this was the Sophocles telling of *Electra*, the source Eugene O'Neill drew on for his updated version from which Aline had been let go.

Although the venerable Yurka was twelve years older than Aline, she was playing the title role, with Aline tapped to play her mother, Clytemnestra. Here was more of the meaty drama that Aline had been seeking since her earliest days on the stage at Barnard, and a potential salve to the still-healing wound of *Mourning Becomes Electra*. But a call was about to come from an important friend in Hollywood that would present a challenging decision for Aline's career.

The friend was Mervyn LeRoy, with an offer of a part in his upcoming film *The Heart of New York*, based on the stage comedy *Mendel, Inc.*, a hit on New York's Yiddish theater circuit. Although Aline had just begun rehearsals for *Electra*, she decided that she would give notice and return to Hollywood and repay LeRoy's courtesies.[20] This was, perhaps, not an ideal artistic choice— *Mendel* was a small part in a forgettable picture—but it was a career- and relationship-building mile marker. Trading a short-term run in a respected Greek drama (*Electra* was slated for only a week of performances) to capture the confidence of a top-flight director at a major studio was something that made long-term sense. Aline's return to Hollywood for *Heart* did indeed solidify a warm personal and professional relationship with LeRoy, with the pair teaming on five pictures during their tenure together at Warner Brothers.

In *Heart*, Aline is the encouraging neighbor of Mendel, an amateur Jewish inventor who lives in a tenement on the city's Lower East Side. When Mendel creates an automatic dishwashing machine, its wealth-generating royalties cause strife in the family until the final reel, wherein order is restored and everything turns out movie perfect. It was a Warner Brothers assembly-line trifle, but it gave Aline her first chance to play comedy on screen, and would lead to another opportunity that she would not have enjoyed had she stayed in New York. Even so, she took her sophomore opportunity on film seriously. "I'm going to study hard—I intend to be more than a few jumps ahead of the production staff and try to wrangle a decent characterization out of it, somehow."[21] When *Heart* opened in theaters a few months later, Aline was again noticed by the critics; the picture not so much.[22]

While *The Heart of New York* was shooting in early January, the studio was simultaneously preparing *The Mouthpiece*, a fictionalized biopic of New York's flamboyant criminal defense attorney William Fallon, to begin shooting just after the New Year. Following the October release of *Five Star Final* Aline had received uniform critical praise, and the daily rushes from *Heart* were putting Warner Brothers line producers on notice that a new talent, equally adept at drama and comedy, was in the building. The studio again pressed Aline for a long-term contract, an offer that she continued to resist, knowing that a permanent move to California was not in the cards for Clarence or his New York architectural firm. Instead, with Aline scheduled to finish *Heart* on January 23, Warners tendered a freelance offer for her to move directly to *The Mouthpiece* upon completion of her current project. After consulting with Clarence, it was decided she would remain in Hollywood and take part in what became one of the studio's biggest successes of 1932.

The Mouthpiece is best remembered as the picture that made Warren William a star. It is the story of assistant district attorney Vincent Day, who, after the execution of an innocent boy he had convicted of murder, resigns his job in disgust and reinvents himself as the defender of the criminal filth of New York City. As Day, William commands the screen using the same forceful, declarative style as his contemporaries James Cagney and Eddy Robinson. And again Aline delivers a short but memorable performance that is miles away from the other members of the supporting cast. In the film Aline plays Hickey, Vince Day's cynical secretary who is also (again) secretly in love with her boss. Although she enjoyed the extravagant Depression-era money ($850 a week when the average American's *annual* salary of $1400 could support a solid middle-class lifestyle), Aline was already unhappy about the roles that Warner Brothers was assigning her. In addition to being irked at essentially repeating her misanthropic secretary from *Five Star Final*, she was dubious about the production in general. "The script is mediocre," she said. "The director is second rate," she added. "And the leading man is a ham," she concluded.[23] "But who knows—they may fool me."

Like Miss Taylor in *Five Star Final*, Hickey can see that there is an honest man buried in Vince Day, concealed under a deep layer of guilt and protected by cynicism and bluster. She makes effort along the way to maneuver him toward the straight and narrow, but her labor is like a rowboat trying to tow the *Titanic* around submerged icebergs. Futile. When Day resolves to seduce his underage stenographer Celia (Sydney Fox), Hickey tries to warn him off his course. "There's two reasons to keep her away from you," she says, askance. "She's jail bait and she's dumb." Later, when she browbeats Day about his interest in Celia ("that girl you did so much for and never got anything from"), Hickey is so cynical that even the hard-boiled lawyer shudders. "I'd hate to be the guy that shares a bed with you, sweetheart. Those are some *cold feet*." But for all her world-weary misanthropy, Hickey's intellect and tough-as-teak honesty is a source of enormous sex appeal. In Aline's hands she is more than just a bitter matron—this is a woman to trust and admire. When her boss disappears on a bender just as he is needed to save an innocent man's life, Hickey hunts him down in a seedy flophouse and roughly nurses him back to health. She is simultaneously tender and tough—a woman of the Depression if ever there was one. Unfortunately, Vince Day can see nothing except his own shortcomings; deep down, his apparent indifference to Hickey stems from the nascent idea that she is too good for him. As he punishes himself for past career transgressions he must also punish himself—and, unfortunately her—in love. When Day at last heeds Hickey's advice—or at least comes to understand it—his redemption arrives too late for either of them.

In *The Mouthpiece*, audiences and critics primarily thrilled to Warren William's commanding performance as the conflicted attorney—this was, after all, the role that began his ascent as "The King of the pre-Code." But there were also many people both behind the cameras and in front of the screen who took note of the woman from New York. "The hit of the whole picture is Aline MacMahon," the *Hollywood Filmgraph* proclaimed. "Here is a girl with a personality that just panics her audiences." Meanwhile, Mordaunt Hall called her "strikingly good," the *New York Times* dubbed her "splendid," and Norbert Lusk devoted a paragraph heading and special mention to her. Aline's own review after seeing the picture on release showed that the studio did "fool her" just a bit. "I saw 'the Mouthpiece,'" she said. "It has certain swell qualities. It is a picture full of incident, and there's a sort of richness it gets from that, but it's uneven in interest. I'm all right, but I honestly can't see what they're so impressed about in my work." Then, still listening to the voice of Jennie Mac reverberating in her head, she added, "Mostly I think I'm only average interesting, and several shots of me are pretty homely."[24] The best—and most succinct—appraisal came from Mae Tinee, one of the pseudonymous reviewers at the *Chicago Tribune*: "Laurels go to Aline MacMahon," Mae enthused. "She's immense!"[25]

With only three small parts under her belt, American movie audiences are already feeling a personal connection with Aline MacMahon. For men she is not the glamour girl or the ice-queen they may fantasize about but could never have, but rather appears to be a woman they might encounter in everyday life; attractive but approachable, intelligent and down to earth. For them she projects the image of someone *real* and honest. For many women, she mirrors their own personal struggles and desires—they see in her a kindred spirit, a fellow traveler. From the very beginning of her life in film, Aline commented on the amount of letters she received from working women—secretaries, nurses, and clerks—looking for advice on career and family. Clearly these are entreaties that are hard to imagine making their way to the mailbox of Greta Garbo. "I answer their letters," she said, sympathetically, "but I don't offer advice. I don't know *what* I might do if I were in the shoes of the girls who have those inter-office problems."²⁶ Aline was already becoming the audience's image of the average Depression-era American woman as they saw her: unpretentious, caring, self-sufficient, with the wisdom of experience and possessed of a great and secret depth.

Now again, after the enormous success of *The Mouthpiece* Warner Brothers renewed their interest in signing Aline to a long-term contract. Now again, she refused. As a happily married woman, a Broadway star, and a dyed-in-the-wool New Yorker, Aline was in no hurry to make a choice that would drastically change her life. "I was interested in being free to be at home and be Mrs. Stein part of the time, and—you know, just have another life besides whatever my acting period was."²⁷ Freelance movie offers were now coming her way, allowing her time to be with Clarence between projects, and her salary was expanding faster than contract players who were often locked into meager compensation packages that were agreed to while they were still little-known commodities. "It isn't that I don't think contracts have an advantage—they have," she admitted. "The studio plays up a contract player more than it does a freelancer, and rightly. But there is something comforting about reading a script and saying 'yes or 'no' to a role. Until I feel that I have something that I could stand featuring, I'd rather play the freelance field."²⁸ To the power brokers in Hollywood, Aline's lack of interest was heretical. Their utter inability to comprehend why anyone would fail to exchange their soul for what they were offering vexed them to no end. As a result they quickly decided that Aline MacMahon simply did not want to be a movie star, and told everyone who would listen that it was so, including writers who quickly filled page after page of fan magazines with manufactured declarations of Aline's disinterest in stardom. "That's nonsense," Aline said of her supposed disdain of Hollywood's siren song. "It's a lot of hooey. Of course I wanted to be a star, I wanted to be the starriest star that you could imagine for every reason." When asked what those reasons were, her answer was typically honest and spare. "You get all the money and all the gravy," she said.²⁹ So, yes, Aline MacMahon wanted to be a movie star. But circumstances would soon reveal to her that there were things she held in far higher regard. Within just a few years Hollywood's influence will become a distant second in Aline's hierarchy, and her orbit will move inexorably away from the star she wished to be.

By the spring of 1932 studio orphan Aline MacMahon had been more or less adopted by Warner Brothers. In April she took another freelance contract from the studio for a part in the trivial soaper *Weekend Marriage*, alongside Loretta Young and Norman Foster. Aside from some archaic ideas about domestic life (even for 1932), the film has a few rich moments. One is a gently comic scene between Aline and Roscoe Karns that is a marvel to watch, with those two seasoned performers showing effortless chemistry at work. In another, Aline expertly counsels Loretta Young on how to convince her beau to propose marriage. Even here, playing a second lead in a forgettable program feature, critics notice that Aline is doing something very different than her contemporaries. "Aline MacMahon is an unusually bright spot . . . and her appearances are all too seldom. Miss MacMahon is one of the most disarmingly natural performers we have ever watched, and at the same time she has a talent for building definite characterization out of the material given her."[30] The *Chicago Tribune* added this: "Aline MacMahon—ah, THERE is an actress!—sets her teeth firmly in the role of the sister and makes a deep impression."[31] With the Method still almost entirely unknown outside eastern theatrical circles, Aline's unique style is apparent even from those who know nothing of her training. Placed next to performers of the old school her aura is visible and unmistakable. After a short break following the wrap of *Weekend Marriage* in mid-April, Aline went directly to a somewhat more interesting Warner's freelance assignment, again alongside Loretta Young.

A look at the inner workings of a big-city maternity hospital, *Life Begins* features a litany of pre-Code transgressions, each revealed through the stories of an ensemble of expectant mothers. There's a murderess (Young) about to give birth before being sent to the penitentiary, a cynical alcoholic (Glenda Farrell) interested in selling her unborn twins at $75 each, and at least two women who are expecting, unmarried, and unrepentant. Strangely, none of these ladies appear to actually *be* pregnant, since the entire ward of soon-to-be mothers have apparently been shot by the Warner Brothers camera crew to *disguise* the fact that they're with child. They all seem to simply be waiting for the stork to arrive. Aline plays the head nurse, Miss Bowers, a kindly figure doling out sage advice and tough love to the ladies of the ward. It is a solid, well-rendered part, but the film gets most of its pre-Code juice from Glenda Farrell's mean-spirited disdain for anything related to freshly produced humans. In the end however, Glenda does an about-face, learns to love her twins, and accepts them as part of her apparently fatherless family. In this there is disappointment. It would have been much more memorable if the censors had allowed her to take the $150.

At Once They Circled Her Round

Aline's allure for audiences and critics is made crystal clear from the *Hollywood Reporter's* review of *Life Begins*. "Dominating the film is the head nurse, wise in the ways of human nature, resourceful in dealing with every mood and emergency and superbly played by Aline MacMahon, who manages also to be the confidential friend of every one in the audience—a grand woman, a grand actress."[32] Although Aline was mostly indifferent to her own work in the picture, *Life Begins* brought up a subject that was lurking quietly along the fringes of the Stein's marriage. Buried deep in a letter dashed off during the filming, Aline casually broached a subject that she and Clarence often left unspoken. "Quite a day at the studio," she began. "We used a real baby today, and a darling she was, too." Then, Mrs. Clarence Stein momentarily flashed what amounted to a subliminal message. "I really need a baby," she wrote, before immediately rushing to the next subject. Passing by as quickly as it did, the idea appears to have retreated to the gray, mute spaces in the Stein's marriage where it usually hid.

During the spring of 1932 the Depression was worse still than in 1931. On the East Coast, Clarence's architectural firm was having difficulties securing enough work to keep from laying off employees, contributing to a general gloom that was enhanced by the months he and Aline had been apart. Aline had implored him to come to the West Coast while the shop was idle so that they could spend time together before she started work on *Life Begins*. Warner Brothers had raised her salary to $950 a week for the film, and she was now carrying the lion's share of the responsibility for their semi-extravagant lifestyle, which now included a rented house in Brentwood, as well as maids, cooks, expensive meals, and exotic travel for each of them. "One of us is all in the red," he admitted, "and doesn't know when he will earn more." In an effort to shore up his sagging business, Clarence elected to delay his trip to Los Angeles and meet with a local developer about investing in large-scale housing, his specialty, but failed to let his wife in on the decision. On the West Coast, Aline was expecting a telegram announcing when her husband would step off the *Chief* and into her arms. The miscommunication caused a rare dust-up between the two. "I just took for granted that I would go if I possibly could and thought you would understand. And when a cold voice came over the telephone I just didn't understand," Clarence said. "Isn't it strange how you can be so inconsiderate without even knowing it?"[33] The incident did not result in any permanent trouble in the marriage, but neither did it result in any extra work for Clarence's firm.

By this time it was clear that if Aline wished to stay in Hollywood, she could work full time and have her pick of second leads and featured roles at the various studios. Demand was so great that columnist Hubbard Keavy opined, "Aline MacMahon seems to have been made for a niche that was unfilled until she happened along."[34] She was offered the part eventually taken by Verree Teasdale in the pre-Code classic *Skyscraper Souls*, as the mistress who kills Warren William and jumps off the 105th floor of the Dwight Building.[35] MGM director Clarence Brown sent out feelers for her to costar in the Joan Crawford vehicle *Letty Lynton*. Warners wanted her for the Joe E. Brown comedy *The Tenderfoot*, and a streak of agents were now stalking her with a dizzying array of possibilities at other studios. In the meantime, Universal Pictures had purchased the film rights to *Once in a Lifetime*, and even before she had started shooting *The Mouthpiece*, the studio was considering Aline to reprise her role as May Daniels. Also, Warner Brothers again suggested that she sign a long-term contract with the studio. But by now Aline's feelings about Hollywood were already deeply conflicted. She was acutely aware that the continuing seduction that had allowed Hollywood to reach second base now had them rounding third, and was unhappy about it. When Aline ran into Universal producer Carl Laemmle Jr. and told him of her interest in appearing in the film version of *Once in a Lifetime*, she felt cheapened. "I wanted to get away from him and all the awful sensations of ambition and the desire to succeed that such an encounter arouses in me. Seriously," she said, "I dislike intensely the excitement I cannot help feeling when I meet any powerful person in whose hands my future may be brightened. And I hope— I expect—to work hard against the sort of jag—emotional and base—that I find myself left with."[36] Additionally, the industry itself represented two disparate sides for her. "I must act to live," she wrote, "and here is a medium so intimate, so capable of variations—and the *vast* rewards! Leaving it all would be like walking away from a stream you've just found gold in." Fortunately, after just a year in the film capital, Aline MacMahon also had a deadly eye for the obverse: "I've the feeling this is all pretty juvenile—puerile stuff to sell the immature. The bosses at Warner Brothers are so shockingly tasteless—they outrage one's sense of decency!" The stage star that longed for O'Neill and Wilde could not overlook the baseness of her employers, no matter the lavish Depression-era salaries they were paying her. "Phooey!" she said. "If I work for gangster showmen I must not go on dreaming of fine productions."[37] What a game!"[38]

8

REWARD UNLIMITED

All through the early months of 1932 Universal stalled their decisions on who to cast and when to start *Once in a Lifetime*. During the shooting of *Life Begins* rumors swirled that Mervyn LeRoy would be loaned out to direct, and it was understood that he would schedule the project so that Aline could accompany him. Warner Brothers quickly scotched the idea of loaning one of their premiere directors for a project that would mock their industry, and things suddenly turned opaque. Aline soon learned that Universal's interest in her was waning ("It appears that the young Laemmle will not give me my part"),[1] and she quickly accepted another single-picture contract with Warners, hoping that if *Lifetime* became a reality, she would be done in time to fit it into her schedule. Unfortunately, near the end of *Life Begins*, Aline received the news she had been dreading. Helen Broderick (mother of Broderick Crawford) would take the role of May Daniels in *Once in a Lifetime* for Universal. A letter written to Clarence that day captured Aline's deep hurt and frustration; after relaying the bad news she wrote, simply, "To hell with it."

When *Life Begins* wrapped, Aline's next assignment found her on location aboard a rusty old ship in San Pedro harbor. *One Way Passage* is the story of a murderer (William Powell) being extradited from Hong Kong to the United States who falls in love with a terminally ill socialite (Kay Francis) during the sea voyage. Aline plays a career confidence woman masquerading as Bettina La Countess de Barrilehaus ("Barrelhouse Betty"), who is dodging her own morals charge while falling for the cop (Warren Hymer) who is escorting Powell to the gallows. The film gave Aline her best part yet in Hollywood, featuring a character that embodied both of her emerging film personae—the hardboiled, wisecracking dame and her earthy, sentimental counterpart. Rather than simply observing the machinations of the rest of the cast, here Aline is able to take a real hand in the story, making effort to help extricate

Powell from his unjust fate. Although the film belongs to Powell and Francis, it is clear that Warners was at last placing greater emphasis on Aline's appearance and presentation in anticipation of things to come. "[Casting director] Rufus LeMaire said they are considering doing a picture for me," she related. "If I go on getting good parts and good notices they'll undoubtedly star me."[2] The studio's image experts still seem entirely unclear as to how to sell her looks, but when they at last let Aline's long hair fall to her waist for the first time, she evokes the exotic sensuality of Morticia Addams. Warner Brothers never will truly discover how to exploit her beauty, but they have now fallen deeply in love with her talent.

In spite of the bedraggled condition of the forty-two-year-old sloop *Calawaii*, Aline called the location shoot on *One Way Passage* "the most fun yet" in Hollywood. After filming ended on the second night, with the ship anchored eighteen miles out in the Pacific, Aline was confronted in her cabin by director Tay Garnett and costars Frank McHugh and Warren Hymer. "They swooped down upon me and dragged me to the card room where there is a piano," she reported to Clarence. "And they staged the grandest show I've ever seen! Everyone was a little drunk except me, but the show was a marvel!" When McHugh discovered that Aline was born in McKeesport, just a bend of the Monongahela River away from his family residence in Homestead, Pennsylvania, he took up an old song he'd learned while tramping the Midwest with his show-business parents:

> *I'll return to the city that was built*
> *Among the hills*
> *Where the smoke is always flowing from*
> *Those old rolling mills*
> *And the boats in the river as they're*
> *Passing to and fro*
> *Down where the Allegheny*
> *And the Monongahela flow.*

Aline was touched by the moment, something—like her characters—she did not always want to show. "I'm not ruled by emotions," she once said, "but I'm very sentimental along with it. I can cry at the damndest nonsense you've ever heard."[3] McHugh's performance cast her back to her own youth, and she gave a recitation of the poem "On a School Day" for the crowd. The room of inebriates quieted, and soon all returned to their cabins, and sleep.

All during the location shooting of *One Way Passage* Universal had been working diligently to find anyone *other* than Aline to sign for *Once in a Lifetime*. After Helen Broderick fell out, the studio even considered an old rival: "Jean Dixon was being considered, but her test was fierce—they lit her very, very poorly," Aline reported, "and her voice did flip flops on the microphone." Yet another hidden episode of movie history had played out, and Aline's dream job was once again on the table. "There is only one MacMahon," she crowed in triumph.⁴

While the *Passage* company was still in San Pedro, Universal sent a representative to Burbank to ask Jack Warner if he would expedite Aline's shooting schedule in order for her to start *Once in a Lifetime* as soon as possible. He would not. Being sequestered on location and unable to take part in the discussion ate at Aline. "I'm so concerned over the Universal / Warner mix up—it's maddening to be so far away. I'm so afraid I'll lose the part," she said, proprietarily adding, "and the fact is, it is *my part!*"⁵ In the meantime there were more current troubles. "I saw four days rushes," she told Clarence of her work on *Passage*, "and I'm not so good. Except for one scene, all the rest are poor—I'm badly lit, and having the director drunk for four days did not improve things." Here again, in spite of the enormous confidence she had in her talent, Aline demonstrates insecurities about being viewed as inadequate, just as she had when released from *Mourning Becomes Electra*. "I'm really concerned. I think I'm very negative in it and will be thought to have failed. Oh, dear I need to be reassured about my work! I must get a good part to top it."⁶ In the end she was only vaguely conciliatory. "It may carry because it's a melodrama," she allowed, "but I doubt it."⁷ Of course, Aline was overcautious in her appraisal; on release critics loved her performance, the box office sang, and Robert Lord's original story was nominated for an Oscar.

All through the spring Aline had been begging Clarence to consider a trip to Japan, and after finishing *One Way Passage* she wanted nothing more (other than playing May Daniels just one more time) than to slip out of Los Angeles harbor toward the Orient with her husband. On June 7, Universal scuttled the couple's vacation when they at last signed a contract with Aline for the lead in *Once in a Lifetime*. For a Hollywood neophyte, Aline had played her cards perfectly. Having signed a contract with Warner Brothers would have made her unavailable to take part in Universal's production of *Lifetime*. Even if Warners had allowed her to be loaned out, she would have been legally entitled to only the weekly salary she received from her home studio, not the greatly inflated wages they would have extorted from Carl

Laemmle for her services. In bookkeeping jargon this extra money was labeled a "carrying charge" and went not to the actor, but straight into the loaning studio's coffers. As a freelancer Aline had no such worries—the decision was hers and the money was hers. And at $1,500 a week, that money was nearly double her recent wages at Warners.

The same day that Aline signed with Universal, she collected her last payment from Warners on *One Way Passage*. In June 1932 no one—not even well-heeled, childless artists—could forget the cloud of economic calamity hanging over nearly the entire civilized world. Over the last few years, the Depression had metastasized throughout the American body, growing stronger, while simultaneously weakening every system it touched. From the distance of history we know that 1932 was the nadir of the crisis, but at that moment it appeared as though the elevator had not yet reached the basement. In New York, business at Clarence's firm was on the wane, necessitating layoffs that deepened his disillusionment with the political system that he believed had failed them. Among Eastern intellectuals radical politics were increasing in popularity—at this time it was estimated that one in three guests at any literary party in New York held a sympathetic view of Communism.[8] For those who were still of means, helping displaced workers was an essential element of liberal ideology, a position that placed them squarely within Communist doctrine. For months Clarence had been chairing a committee to raise money for unemployed draftsmen, and he was dubious of the prospects of a turnaround. "You movie folks don't seem to even know that there is a depression," he told Aline. "But just you wait until Warners stock completely goes under and then where will you be?" Although Clarence was likely exaggerating somewhat for effect, Aline was well aware of the heights from which she could fall, and told him so. "It must be transitory, this sunny haven, all this gold showering on one, and dreading the end of the good luck." Fearful, she took extraordinary measures to protect her advantages. "I had my salary given to me in gold," she reported. "I put it in a safety box in the bank vaults, so we have money against the bank holidays, insolvency, or the collapse of the United States."[9] Even in Hollywood, the capital of fame and money, there was no certainty that life as it had been known would continue unabated.

Once in a Lifetime is a film ripe for reclamation. Although somewhat stage bound, it is one of the funniest and most acerbic pictures of the early sound era. Set at the very moment when silent pictures were poised to talk, the film closely follows the original stage story about a trio of hand-to-mouth vaudevillians—Aline (the brains), Jack Oakie (the boob), and Russell Hopton (the light bulb)—who recognize a once-in-a-lifetime opportunity in the industry's transition to sound. With silent stars being discarded like so many mah-jongg tiles, the group sells their stage act to fund a confidence game worthy of Charles Ponzi: they will head west and pass themselves off as masters of elocution, promising to save the studios from ruin by teaching people (well, actors) to talk. With a deeply cynical attitude and an acid-laden script ("That's the way we do it here," the studio head says. "No time wasted on *thinking!*"), *Lifetime* takes Hollywood to task for all its sins: mindlessness, pretension, opportunism, mendacity, self-importance, shallowness, venality, greed—this book is too short to list them all. Somehow, though, Kaufman and Hart managed to deflate the industry without fully condemning it, and therein lies the film's charm; it derides the movies without belittling the audiences that adore them.

When Aline arrived at Universal studios to begin shooting *Lifetime*, she found a production in disarray. Other than May Daniels, none of the central roles had yet been signed—in essence, the film was being built around her. With no cast available on her first day, Aline was instead asked to do tests with the final two candidates for the role of George, May's doltish partner in the voice business. The choice was between Jack Oakie, the magnificent oaf of many early sound comedies, and a youthful Andy Devine. Aline thought both were fine, but preferred Oakie, having appeared with him in *Artists and Models* on Broadway seven years earlier. "I'd love to have him do it," she said. "He's lots and lots of fun and we really need him!" Unfortunately, after an all-night bender resulted in Oakie missing his scheduled test, Devine was cast. Then, before a foot of film had been exposed on the first day of shooting, Universal reversed themselves, fired Devine, and hired the freshly sobered-up Oakie. Equally mercurial was Sydney Fox, who halted production by demanding to be released from her contract just as filming was about to start. Her character, a hick actress trying to break into the movies—and only a slightly poorer actor than Fox herself—provided a wide target for the script's jokes about the level of "talent" in Hollywood. ("What's a four-letter word for actor?" the script asks. "Dope," Aline replies.) Fox thought she herself was being lampooned, and after she "raised a terrible fuss," on the first day of shooting, the producers agreed to let her go—until they realized that her wardrobe had already been tailored and none of it would fit her replacement, June Clyde. Upon this revelation, studio lawyers suddenly discovered that Fox's contract was unbreakable. After just a few weeks of shooting, Aline had developed a well-informed opinion of

Ms. Fox. "She's probably the most obnoxious little one I've ever known," she said. "It's amazing how anyone can be 100% disliked around a studio."[10]

On the Universal lot there were also ongoing problems with the schedule, the script, the sets, and the dailies. With all these troubles, Aline was rethinking her attitude toward her primary sponsor in filmland. "Warner Brothers is nothing like this!" she said.[11] Fortunately Universal cleaned up its act, and Aline was soon thrilled to find herself working amid a wonderful group of experienced character players and comedians. They included Louise Fazenda, a former member of Mack Sennett's bathing beauties, and Zasu Pitts, the odd-featured comedienne who crafted the kind of memorable eccentric-character career that was only possible in studio-era Hollywood. Aline loved to watch accomplished performers, and she never stinted in her praise when she saw them. When Fazenda came on the set, Aline saw her immediately make the part of a pretentious Hollywood columnist her own. "Louise really did a marvelous tour-de-force—she caught the mood, the accent, the every reflection of the part! In three hours she did what it took the other actresses three weeks to do—I was dumbfounded!" Her enthusiasm over the cast was impossible to contain. "It's a riot on the set," she continued. "Jack Oakie and Fazenda, and Jobyna Howland and Zasu Pitts—all the old war horses of the profession. Ah, there *are* compensations of being successful in pitchers!"[12]

More than anyone, it was Zasu Pitts to whom Aline was regularly compared when she first landed in Hollywood. For Aline—who loved Pitts as a comedienne but fancied herself a serious actress who also happened to be adept in comedy—the comparison seemed inarticulate. "I don't like it even one bit," she said, trying to explain her displeasure. "I don't want people to think of me in any one kind of role. I know I'm no beauty. But I'd like to promote tears as well as laughs."[13] In *Lifetime*, Aline was able to do exactly that—but the tears were from laughter.

Although the waif-like (or, more properly, "wood-like") Fox is billed as the female lead in *Once in a Lifetime*, make no mistake—it is Aline MacMahon's picture. Fox was on her second consecutive assignment opposite Aline, having also played the underage object of Warren William's affections in *The Mouthpiece*. Although attractive and photogenic, Fox was the most rudimentary of performers, completely dedicated to the kind of elocution-style declaration that Aline had abandoned a decade earlier. In order to sidestep the shame of being perfect for the role of a hack actress just as she was, Fox overplayed the ineptitude of her character to the nth degree. As one critic noted, it was entirely unnecessary for her to exaggerate. "Sydney Fox would have contributed a charming interpretation to *Once in a Lifetime* if she had just gone right on being Sydney Fox."

Aline made the most of her appearance in *Once in a Lifetime*. With her long experience in the play and a character tailor-made for her, it is no wonder that she is singled out in nearly every review. The *Brooklyn Daily Eagle* declared, "The outstanding performance of the film is that of Aline MacMahon," while her biggest booster, the *Chicago Tribune*, said, "Aline MacMahon delivers one handsome performance. She's established her right to be classed with Marie Dressler, Edna May Oliver and the other grand girls who make laughter a necessity and a pleasure." Everyone seemed to notice that Hollywood had at last given her a part "made to her measure," and *Variety* summed it up best: "The part of the ex-vaudevillian who hopes that life isn't as futile as it seems, lives and breathes Miss MacMahon's own screen personality. It's the best role she's had—the most sympathetically costumed and artfully photographed."[14] Even a small-town theater owner whose *Lifetime* box-office receipts were so bad that he called it "a pain in the neck" and insisted he only wanted a film that bad "once in a lifetime" couldn't knock everything about it. "The one good spot in the picture was the fine acting of Aline MacMahon," he said. "That girl is some actress!"[15]

Lifetime was a box-office success, and Aline was grateful to have been part of it. For history now, the role of May Daniels would always be hers. And her performance in the film gave her a greater profile among studio executives and the public. Aline hoped the newly won prestige would allow her the chance to be the serious "Actress"—or, as she once put it—"a George Arliss in skirts." But even in the Golden Age of Hollywood, when stars were manufactured with tool-and-die precision, it was the public who ultimately decided what they wanted and how they wanted it. As it turned out, audiences preferred her to be the character type that *Once in a Lifetime* inadvertently solidified—the hard-boiled, bitingly cynical comedienne who hid a depth of character under her tough exterior. She may have been one of the great interpreters of O'Neill and Shaw, but it was the droll, acerbic wit that moved the turnstiles.

All during the summer of 1932, the thoughts of children that were placed in Aline's mind during the filming of *Life Begins* would not retreat. She was now thirty-three and could not shake the idea that time was slipping away. Moreover, Clarence had turned fifty during the spring, signaling a potential medical and lifestyle complication if the couple decided to conceive in the normal manner. "Clarence," she wrote, "[W]e must think seriously of adopting children. If I'm really going to make money at my work, I will need to share it. Not the money," she explained, "but the extra dividends it brings."[16] Clarence was not in the least bit encouraging to her desire; in response, he told Aline the story of a friend who brought her son along on a recent visit to New York. "[The boy] is full of life," he began. "*So* full that he gets a little on the nerves of his mother. Be warned before it is too late."[17] On another occasion, visiting friends who had an infant boy and girl, Clarence seemed simultaneously conciliatory and disdainful about the idea of a family. "They were lovely kids, particularly the boy. I almost think I could stand one like that around the place. But how could you be sure it would be like that? They don't come guaranteed."[18] For Aline's part, she seemed willing, even eager, to try. "Indeed you would like a little boy like theirs, and I wouldn't be the least bit ascared to take one on. I believe it would make life richer and the world gayer to have a new live creature with us."[19]

Also during *Once in a Lifetime* Aline was thinking harder about becoming a contract player at Warner Brothers. She craved more time to be with Clarence, but the pressure to take quality freelance opportunities when they presented themselves limited her ability to be away from Los Angeles for extended periods. Also, with the Depression sapping work at Clarence's architectural firm, she was now the primary breadwinner in the family. Fortunately, Aline had raised her stock immeasurably with recent assignments, and now commanded a salary—and a respect—that she couldn't have dreamed of when arriving in Hollywood just eighteen months earlier. She had also grown to like the Warner Brothers family—executives notwithstanding—and felt at home there. Among the agents that had recently been circling Aline's ship was Richard Orsatti, one of a trio of brothers running the high-powered Orsatti Talent Agency, whose clients included Edward G. Robinson, Frank Capra, Betty Grable, and George Stevens. Of all the sharks in the water, it was the Orsatti's who convinced Aline to let them negotiate with Warner Brothers on her behalf. "There were three Orsatti brothers, and they were exceedingly nice men," Aline recalled. "I liked them a lot. It was a very friendly kind of business, an awful lot of it done among friends. A lot of good parts came along because Frank Orsatti could make wonderful spaghetti and someone came over for dinner."[20] Never one for the self-promotion that Hollywood requires of its stars, Aline was now quite content to have the brothers relieve her of the duty. She did not give the boys an easy job, however.

When Aline considered what she wanted out of a studio contract, it came down to balance. "I was interested in being free to be at home and just have another life besides whatever my career was. I told Warners that if they could work out conditions that would make it possible to be home half of the year, I would consider being on their contact list." When the Warner execs told Aline to write her own contract as she wanted it, she did. "My final contract conditions were these: that I would do two pictures in the summer and two pictures in the winter, in three months each and be free for three months in the spring and fall."[21] For an artist without a strong history of box-office draw, the process of crafting Aline's nearly unprecedented contract showed just how much the studio wanted her talent on their roster. The Orsatti brothers began talks with Warner Brothers as early as May 1932, and the final contract was not executed until September 9. In between was an odyssey of negotiations, revisions, changes, and difficulties that taxed the patience of the Warners legal department. In particular, attorney Roy Lewis was irked at the unique nature of the arrangement, and tried to talk Warner Brothers chief counsel Roy Obringer out of enacting it. "I am very much perturbed over a contract of this type, as it may lead to endless trouble," he said.[22] "The mere keeping track of dates will be an extremely tricky and extensive task—it is very complex."[23] Obringer agreed with Lewis, but understood that they were only foot soldiers under Jack Warner's command. "Personally I think that this contract is unworkable," Obringer complained, "but nevertheless it is desired that such a contract be entered into."[24] In later correspondence Lewis jokes that he is working on "the 335th amendment" of Aline's contract. This may not have been far from the truth, since even on the day the final document was signed changes were still made and initialed by Aline and Jack Warner. This included a clause, pasted into the original document at the eleventh hour:

> It is further agreed that Producer will exert every reasonable effort to assign Artist to a variety of parts and will endeavor to build up the Artist along the same general line as has been adopted by the Artist in the past, the character of such parts being known to the parties hereto as best adapted to the ability of the Artist.

In the end, Warners was remarkably understanding and generous to Aline MacMahon. She received a contract unlike any offered to a newcomer at the studio, and began her tenure at a salary of $40,000 a year for just six-month's work at a time when $1,200 could support a solid middle-class lifestyle. If she stayed with the studio for five years, her graduated annual increases would top out at $125,000, making her one of the highest paid actresses in their stable. In spite of these concessions, there was still hesitation on Aline's part. "I am surrendering my most priceless advantage and privilege—that of saying 'I do not wish to play that part.' Ah well, we will see!"

ALINE MACMAHON

Unfortunately, Aline's unique contract came with unintended, hidden consequences that she and the Orsatti Bothers did *not* foresee. In the studio era, production schedules were regularly generated by a near assembly-line process of acquisition, research, script, casting, pre-production, shooting, editing, and distribution. At Warner Brothers in particular, this process was like a rapidly moving conveyor belt, with new productions stacked up behind current ones, waiting for their turn on the sound stage. The system needed to keep studio readers, writers, directors, producers, designers, cameramen, set dressers, technicians, and actors working in order to maximize return on their extremely high Depression-era salaries. No moving part should ever be idle. "There could be very little advance planning under those circumstances," Aline explained. "In a measure, those of us who were under contract had to catch the next vehicle that came along, as if you were catching the next trolley. But my contract called for planning, because they could only use me for three month periods." What Aline eventually discovered was that it was impossible for the studio to stall projects while waiting for her semiannual hiatus periods to pass; the factory conveyor stopped for nothing. "They found it very onerous, because when you run a big studio you really don't want to bother with a single actress who has to work on a certain date," she allowed. "I can understand it perfectly, but I wasn't very sympathetic with it, because I was thinking about me."[25] Warner Brothers, too, may not have understood the fallout from their contractual agreement; although they were very interested in promoting their new star, the studio would find that targeted opportunities to groom her career were limited.

For the moment, however, Aline MacMahon was pleased—as *Lifetime* was ending her contract with Warners was about to be signed, and her enthusiasm for work in Hollywood was near its height. "For me the studio life, the variety in the work, the respect of the directors, the tender services of the cameramen, the admiration of the other actors—oh, Lord, I could weep for joy. To be functioning—to be integrated, to be alive in the world!"[26] It is clear from Aline's private thoughts that she craves attention and appreciation—but more than mere ego, she is energized by the opportunity to operate at the fullest level of her capabilities, something she achieves far more in film than on stage. From the moment she arrived in Hollywood, Aline was one of the rare actors who had migrated from stage to screen and was willing to voice the heinous secret that all others falsely denied. "Working in pictures is better than the stage," she blasphemed. "The stage is grand, of course. But stage parts are few and far between. I've been lucky—since I arrived in Hollywood I've played seven roles and they have all been different. I was in the theatre for ten years and I didn't get as much variety. I might enjoy the theatre as much if it had that kind of variety.[27] It sounds like a publicity phrase, but the screen has other advantages over the stage. It is much more intimate. The tiniest emotion can be caught by the camera—emotion that slips by a stage audience unless it is greatly exaggerated."[28] For an actress devoted to subtlety, there is no doubt that the camera lens was a great friend. "In movies you have to be simpler—more direct," she concluded. "I like that better."

Throughout 1932 the Depression was continuing to push the nation to the left. Communism was gaining converts across the economic spectrum, but most successfully among urban intellectuals. In New York Clarence's friends were a closely-knit group of progressive radicals, including conservationist Benton MacKaye and Socialist architect Raymond Unwin, while Aline was slowly discovering like-minded people within the Hollywood community. The summer that year was also awash with other distractions for the Steins. The Los Angeles Olympics began in July, with Babe Didrikson winning two gold medals, and Paavo Nurmi suspended for alleged violations of amateur rules. In Manhattan, popular liberal Democratic mayor Jimmy Walker was investigated for corruption and forced to resign. And Technocracy—a social movement dedicated to replacing politicians and civic leaders with science-based experts—momentarily became a cause célèbre among progressives—including the Steins. Within six months its juice had run out, and America returned to its one true love, old-fashioned political quackery.

Aline's last picture before her new Warner Brothers contract kicked in was *Silver Dollar*, a fictionalized version of the life of the nineteenth-century "Silver King" of Colorado, Horace Tabor. Warners wanted Aline for the part of Tabor's first wife, Augusta (renamed Sarah Martin for the film), but felt it unwise to wait out her interminable contract negotiations. In June they signed her to a final freelance contract, and she immediately began researching her part, another manifestation of the then-novel art of the Method. "I've had a grand time reading the Tabor biography, and want to get more information on Augusta," she told Clarence, who was preparing a trip west to visit her. "I have an idea we could go to Central City [Colorado]—I want to see Leadville, which is nearby, and the locale for 'Silver Dollar.'"[29]

The film follows Sarah and Yates Martin (Edward G. Robinson) through the operatic travails of a small-town farmer and storekeeper who makes it to the governor's mansion and eventually returns to poverty. Although Aline was reported to have spent time in a maternity hospital for her role in *Life Begins*, this was the first time she had the opportunity to truly dig into researching the real-life subject of her portrayal. Aline read the personal papers of the Tabors, scouted libraries, and visited areas where Augusta had lived and worked. She was even able to procure a copy of Augusta's personal diary. "Got Augusta's own diary today," she wrote. "It's fine character stuff—the true idiom of her voice is revelatory!"[30] During her research Aline developed a tremendous sympathy for Augusta Tabor, who stood by her husband in the early, lean years and was cast aside and divorced when his stake in a local silver mine made him a millionaire. As Sarah, Aline ages through the decades of dedication, success, and heartbreak, reminding audiences of her wise maturity in character parts. Here, she continues the wan sadness of many of her other characters, one who stoically endures her travails and soldiers through. In spite of Aline's sporadic appearances in the film—from which she regularly disappears—she made the most of her scenes. "Aline MacMahon at last comes into her own in the movies," the *New York Sun* critic John Cohen commented. "She is really quite a superb actress, and it is hoped that she will not let the talkies misuse her unquestioned gifts."[31] Well, whatever their other faults, even critics have a right to hope.

Aline regularly placed *Silver Dollar* among her favorite roles, but the production was not entirely a happy one. She was again working with Edward G. Robinson, with whom she had occasionally socialized, but also considered a bit of a ham. The gulf between their respective styles was enormous, and Aline was particularly irked when Robinson—now one of the top stars in all of Hollywood—took it upon himself to teach her about acting. "Eddy Robinson is getting a little annoying, trying to direct my readings," Aline frostily reported. "The truth is I will be amenable to a degree, but beyond that I'll say him nay in no uncertain manner!" For an actress who took her craft as seriously—and personally—as she did, it was a high insult.

During the production of *Silver Dollar*, Aline was still dwelling on the contract sitting unfinished in the Warner Brothers legal department. In discussing it with Clarence she first took one side, then the other in deciding whether she should bind herself to the studio. While Aline was in a positive mood about signing with Warners, she found herself having dinner with her costar, Eddy Robinson. Quite naturally, Aline sought Robinson's counsel about the decision, and the story of *his* contract woes moved the needle yet again. "Eddy Robinson told me, 'Never mind what's in your contract—I have everything in the world in mine and they've got me in an awful fix. I'm going to have to bring it up before the Motion Picture Academy."[32] More and more I think I ought not to sign until I am to be starred," she said. "I am entirely fatalistic about it." Later, during a party at the house of the recently arrived producer of *Beyond the Horizon*, Kenneth MacGowan, she talked with Dudley Digges and Roland Young about her decision. "[Digges and Young] were pretty discouraging about the contract I described. They assure me a studio can find four bad parts a year for *anybody*—and Warners the worst of the bunch, they said." Yet, in spite of all the misgivings of famous contractees, Aline's positivity reasserted itself. "All I can see is the six months in New York, and the four movies in Hollywood to keep me from losing my mind. I recall too vividly the seven idle months before I came out here. And look at Jean Dixon—no job since 'Once in a Lifetime' closed last November."[33] After calculating all the angles—as she often did—Aline reluctantly signed. "I like the picture work," she concluded.

On November 8, 1932, just as the nation's morale seemed to be touching bottom, Democrat Franklin Roosevelt was elected president of the United States. Roosevelt's plans for dealing with the economic crisis with government assistance and social programs were catnip to middle-class workers and left-wing urban elites, and the American Communists soon aligned themselves with the new president. At this time, both Aline and Clarence were Roosevelt backers, and it is likely that both voted for him in the 1932 cycle. Clarence, in particular, was impressed when he met then New York governor Roosevelt in March for a one-on-one meeting to discuss a Regional Planning Authority for housing. "I had a long talk with the governor and I think he is a great guy, or a good actor, or both," he told Aline, with tongue only partially in his cheek. Clarence was lobbying him to impose tighter government regulation and control of housing, a typically left-leaning approach. Looking over Clarence's materials, Roosevelt was guarded. "Some people would call it Communism," he said, taking a long pause, "but the heads of our big industries would understand."[34] For now, Roosevelt had the Communists—and the Steins'—votes. Before long the Steins will migrate further to the left.

In November Aline reported for her first film under contract to Warner Brothers. Her assignment to *The Life of Jimmy Dolan* was not an entirely hopeful one. After reading the script, she pronounced the film "a weak imitation of 'Winner Takes All,' with Douglas Fairbanks Jr. doing a weak imitation of Cagney." Worse still, the script's stage direction for her character, Miss Moore, had not been scrubbed before it was delivered to her. "Enter Auntie Moore," it said, "an elderly woman—(Aline MacMahon type)." Annoyed at the insult, the not-in-the-least-bit-elderly Aline took an immediate dislike to director Archie Mayo, who she described as "an obnoxious vulgarian." They argued incessantly

Caricature of Aline by Salvador Baguez to publicize *The Life of Jimmy Dolan*. The film also featured Loretta Young and Douglas Fairbanks Jr. Studio publicity material.

about the part to the point where Aline fantasized, "I hope that they dislike me and replace me with a nice elderly actress who fits the part." Warners did not release her, but neither did they pair her with Mayo again.

Aptly described by one critic as "for audiences wanting offerings that will steer clear of subtlety and do not tax their mental powers," *Jimmy Dolan* offers very little for Aline to do. She plays a Scottish matron who runs a health farm for invalid children with Loretta Young. ("Loretta is furious because she has to play in it," Aline reported.) The unwitting women take in a local drifter (Douglas Fairbanks Jr.) who just happens to be the reigning light heavyweight boxing champion on the lam from a manslaughter charge. In short order Fairbanks falls in love (with Young, of course), and risks his freedom by returning to the ring to win enough money to save the orphanage. Although there is little for her to do, Aline has some priceless reactions at ringside during the climactic fight sequence, but according to her even these were spoiled in the editing room. After Clarence gave his opinion that she had "overworked," the scene, Aline responded: "You're right! It wouldn't have appeared that way if they had kept everything in. I actually graded the reactions up to a pitch—a climax—then they cut out four or five steps in that growth. They used practically nothing but the last round reactions." While *Jimmy Dolan* is not subtle, it is another of those quick-moving Warners programmers that satisfies because of sincerity, craft, and a cast that has the endearing familiarity of the faces so often seen in classic Hollywood.[35]

As Aline is beginning the most productive and financially rewarding period of her career, she is simultaneously grappling with what her success and wealth means in a world of depression and want. Clarence had recently received a new commission for public housing, and expressed a sad disappointment about the limited opportunity it would provide for an unemployed workforce numbering in the thousands. "There is only enough money to employ about seventy-five draftsmen at $15 a week," he said. "Seventy-five out of *two thousand*! Those seventy-five are probably only getting enough for food for their family—and any day they may be told that someone else will have to take their place."[36] Aline's response betrayed a deep conflict with the joy she felt from her creative freedom. "I think and I feel more and more about the social implications of life," she said. "Why is it all so sad, this life? Schopenhauer said, 'we spend our entire life in fear of pain, and when we are not hurt we think we are happy.' If you find out what it's all about," she asked of her husband, "won't you tell me?"

9

GOLD DIGGING

Following *The Life of Jimmy Dolan*, rumors swirled around the Warner Brothers lot about the next film under Aline's new contract. Her reaction to the possibility of appearing in *The Keyhole* reminds us that there was just a wisp of a diva lurking in Aline MacMahon. "A lovely rumor today," she wrote to Clarence. "I'm to be in *Kay Francis*' next picture, which takes place on a *boat*, and I'm a passenger who plays *Frank McHugh* for a sucker!" she said, clearly unhappy about *The Keyhole*'s similarities to *One Way Passage*. "And it is with Michael Curtiz—the *worst director* on the lot! He's a violent fool who keeps everyone on the set until the small hours of the morning, and *never made* a good picture."[1] In early 1933, Aline's coarse assessment of Michael Curtiz was only partially accurate. Although Curtiz would soon be responsible for a raft of Hollywood's best-remembered films, his star was only then coming into sharp focus. His reputation as an imperious, ruthless taskmaster, on the other hand, was already well established. Stories of deaths on the set of Curtiz' *Noah's Ark*, and the contentious battles with Bette Davis on 1932's *Cabin in the Cotton* had made Aline wary of ever stepping in front of his camera. And while the iron-willed Davis may have drawn strength from sparring with Curtiz (they worked together five other times), Aline's still-lingering Victorian sensibilities would not allow her to endure the kind of brusque treatment to which even Warners' biggest stars were subjected. The studio apparently understood this potential for disaster, and in their five-year overlap at Warners, Aline never shared a soundstage with Michael Curtiz.

Aline's comments about Curtiz shed nearly as much light on her *own* imperious streak as they do his. Her susceptibility to pique—justified or not—went back at least to her Neighborhood Playhouse days, and the *Times* reporter who had the temerity to question her acting bona fides. This involuntary exercise of ego rarely emerged outside the context of her work, but when she found herself in its grip she was quick to quell it. In this case, mortified by her angry—but private—outburst about Curtiz, Aline immediately upbraided herself. "I am a discontented baby," she wrote. "Pay no attention to me! A fat, profitable contract that leaves me free half the year and I yowl all the time! What did I *think* I was getting?"[2] But Aline sometimes found her ego a difficult opponent, regularly vacillating between outrage and conciliation. The very next day she sent a personal letter about *The Keyhole* to producer Darryl Zanuck, with whom she had generally enjoyed a mutually respectful relationship. "I certainly do not intend to play ["Dorothy" in *The Keyhole*]," she wrote. "A gold digger on a boat to Havana—as ugly a role as I ever saw! With every human effort on my part, I would still be terribly miscast as 'Dot.'"

Still, after the letter was in Zanuck's hands, she immediately regained composure and found herself embarrassed by such haughty behavior. "I don't want to be a spoiled child who won't play if she can't have all the marbles. I want to be grown up and responsible about it. It's only a couple weeks of unhappiness." Then, when she learned that her entreaties had failed to change Zanuck's mind, the venom flowed again:

Dear Mr. Zanuck—
What I can't seem to convince you of is that I know what I can and can't do. I told you I could make something of [Jimmy Dolan's] "Auntie," and though she's scarcely the answer to an actresses prayer, I made something of her. Believe me, "Dot" is not for me. There is an honest, sympathetic, believable quality about me which is out of place in a character like that. It was right for "One Way Passage," but it is wrong for "The Keyhole." Why waste me on a character for which I have no common ground?[3]

Relating the entire story to Clarence, Aline summed up her feelings with a bastardized Spanish phrase that she adopted while on the coast. "Ay mi!" she lamented."[4]

Darryl Zanuck did eventually assign Aline MacMahon to play a gold digger in her next picture, but it was not in *The Keyhole*. Realizing that Aline's tiny part in the film would only require one week's work, the producer thought better of wasting the final month of her quarter on / quarter off contract on it. Fortunately for Aline, her studio champion Mervyn LeRoy was then casting a musical comedy designed to capitalize on the success of Warners' recent blockbuster, *42nd Street*. More than perhaps any other film, *Gold*

Diggers of 1933 cemented Aline MacMahon's image in the public eye, and husbanded her memory for future generations.

Before *42nd Street* had even left the editing room, Warner Brothers was confident it would be a major hit that might also prove to be a trendsetter, and dispatched their scenario hounds and in-house pettifoggers to ferret out another musical-ready property whose rights they already held. The studio research mice returned with Avery Hopwood's play *The Gold Diggers*, a major hit on Broadway during the 1919–1920 season, which Warners had already filmed successfully in both 1923 and 1929. (Never let it be said that the brothers failed to squeeze every pulpy drop out of their contracts.) After a series of minor legal contretemps, the studio's shysters proved clear title, and *The Gold Diggers* was assigned to a series of writers for updating.

Soon after the release of the musical-comedy confection of 1929's *Gold Diggers of Broadway*, America had tumbled from frothy optimism to cynical hopelessness almost overnight. And although the economic crisis was infiltrating almost every area of American life—including studio balance sheets—it was rarely depicted in any comprehensive way by Hollywood films of the era.[5] Not so however, at Warner Brothers—they were the studio of the workingman; while MGM was selling high gloss fantasy, the brothers didn't even bother to clean the dirt from under their fingernails. A long list of early 1930s Warners features including *I Am a Fugitive from a Chain Gang, Under Eighteen, Heroes for Sale*, and *Employee's Entrance* were set in, and concerned with, the Depression. In this crucible, the 1933 edition of *Gold Diggers* would play quite differently than its predecessors.

On stage, *The Gold Diggers* was a straight comedy concerned with the machinations of three chorus girls trying to capture wealthy husbands from the wings of a popular Broadway show. With the advent of sound, Warners' 1929 remake, *Gold Diggers of Broadway*, became a musical comedy, adding songs and stage numbers. For the 1933 version it was decided to push the romantic-comedy elements to the back half of the picture, and use the early scenes to frame a series of elaborate Busby Berkeley musical set pieces within the backstory of the chorines. Here, the Gold Diggers are the acid-tongued Trixie (Aline), simple-minded Polly (Ruby Keeler), and around the block more than a few times Carol (Joan Blondell). The first scenes of the film instantly set *Gold Diggers of 1933*—known in development as *Highlife*—in the desperate heart of the Depression, with the girls flat broke and living together in a no-bedroom apartment in order to keep the big bad wolf from the door. ("If there was a wolf, we'd eat it," Carol says.) After some fitful starts, they are

Gold Digging

Joan Blondell snaps a candid photo of Aline with actor Guy Kibbee on the Warner Brothers backlot between shots on *Gold Diggers of 1933*. Aline and Kibbee appeared in eleven films together. "He was a darling to work with," she said. Unknown photographer, candid, unpublished.

able to hook onto a new show with producer Barney Hopkins (played with ferocious irascibility by Ned Sparks) who, when asked what the show is about, bellows: "It's all about the *Depression!* Men marching in the rain. Jobs! JOBS! The Big Parade—the Big Parade of *tears!*" (To which the girls reply, "Well, we won't have to rehearse that.") When comedienne Trixie wonders what *she'll* do in such a dour show, Barney might just as well be a Warner Brothers producer describing Aline's role in the film. "Plenty," he says. "You'll be the gay side, the hard-boiled side—the cynical and funny side to the Depression. I'll make 'em laugh at you starvin' to death. It'll be the funniest thing you ever did." (At this Aline retorts, "Didja ever see me ride a pony?") Eventually, *Gold Diggers of 1933* joins up with the remnants of Hopwood's play when wealthy blue bloods Warren William and Guy Kibbee show up to scuttle a budding romance between William's kid brother (Dick Powell) and Ruby Keeler's Polly. From this we're treated to the best comic scenes in *Gold Diggers*, as Trixie and Carol set about to chisel some cash out of those deep, upper-crust pockets.

ALINE MACMAHON

Strangely, far from being interpreted as a welcome change in fortunes, Aline's switch from *The Keyhole* to *Gold Diggers of 1933* instead rekindled deep feelings of professional inadequacy that she had hoped were long gone.

> We read the first script of "Gold Diggers of 1933," and my worst fears were realized—a duller, more talky and static script I never saw. It is curiously over-written for a Warner Brothers property and the audience will be a reel ahead of us all the time.
> My part is overwhelmingly large in point of lines and importance to the plot—but it's very mediocre stuff—a musical comedy comedienne, former show girl. Mervyn seemed disgusted about it. As for me, I left with the idea that I was wrong for the part and expecting to be notified tomorrow that they'd release me and put Ruth Donnelly in my place. I can always name half a dozen actresses who suit my role better than I. I was amazed to find all the old nerves come back and the general feeling that I was wrong for the part at the reading. It seems apparent that even two years of so-called success will leave me just where I was when I go back to the theatre—over eager, over anxious to be good—over convinced I'm not the type. I'm afraid I'm having an attack of what psychologists would call "The Will to Fail."

No matter how long she worked, no matter the confidence in her art, Aline could still never quite escape the seed of inadequacy that was instilled by Jennie Mac's assessment of her looks. Moreover, beyond even simple creative anxiety, Aline seemed to understand that her fears were perhaps the product of something deeper and more esoteric:

> Clarence, I don't want to be the slave to necessity if I can help it. I hope we will neither of us ever have to take a job we don't like, or be forced to be amenable to someone we prefer to avoid. Now I see what my Dad must have battled all those years. He used to say, "Nothing makes me rich!" and he must have been writhing against the necessity of doing a job he disliked. I suppose that's why he quit so entirely those last two years.[6]

It is just possible that these thoughts about personal control touched on Aline's subconscious feelings about the responsibilities of having children.

For a young girl, seeing her father become "a slave to necessity" by doing a job he hated for the sake of his wife and child could instill a sense that those institutions stifle creativity and create obligations that inhibit free choice. Aline had generally done as she pleased in her career and private life, having no children to interfere in her decisions and a mate who gave her uncommon latitude for the time. Even the concessions Aline made to her marriage were mostly voluntary, not imposed, and thus tolerable. And in spite of her continuing entreaties to Clarence about the possibility of adopting children, it never appeared to be a *true* priority for either of them. Deep down, Aline knew that motherhood would be a job requiring the kind of sacrifice to necessity that she expressly feared. During the filming of *Gold Diggers*, she once again brought the subject up to Clarence, and spelled out just what modest level of engagement she expected to provide if they adopted. "For myself, if I go on working, I know I can take a family in my stride," she said. "Of course I will be free of them—I would have a nurse maid."[7] This was not a woman likely to give up art—or self-determination—for children.

Although she was rarely satisfied with her roles at Warners, when Aline was at last presented with the final draft of the *Gold Diggers* script, her disappointment turned toward optimism. "The new version of 'Highlife' arrived yesterday, and it is 100% better," she said. "I'm much encouraged."[8] Moreover, with just a few days of shooting under her belt, Aline's personal confidence also rebounded, along with her enthusiasm. "They finished the first musical sequence yesterday, and now we go back to the story. This is a cinch to do—such light, inconsequential stuff, hard boiled and fast moving." Playing Trixie reminded her of the summer of 1925, and the sheer, exuberant fun of performing in *Artists and Models* on Broadway. "I really enjoy low comedy. I expect to be taking what we used to call pratfalls at the Winter Garden any minute now![9] I wonder if I'll be good in it, but it is a real adventure to try it. God knows it is a tough job—still, I'm ready for a tough job." All through February Aline grew more and more positive about *Gold Diggers*. "All goes well here—today we are commencing to shoot the part where I'm the show girl acting the part to gold-dig Kibbee, and it's such fun to play it! I'm all done up and Mervyn seems delighted."[10]

There is little doubt that Aline's warm relationship with Mervyn LeRoy was absolutely essential to the crafting of her timeless comic performance as Trixie. "The picture looks fair," Aline reported, tentatively, "but Mervyn is determined to make me more animated." Under any other director Aline would likely have balked at being asked to exaggerate, but her trust in LeRoy gave her the confidence to play the gold-digging scenes as broadly as he liked. "I've followed Mervyn's direction as faithfully as I could. I feel he has a better sense of farce than I do. I suppose a little over acting is permissible in a musical comedy comic," she allowed.[11] "It *has* been wonderful to have a chance to do such silly stuff!" History has proven LeRoy correct—Aline's scenes with Guy Kibbee sparkle with personal chemistry, something audiences and Warner Brothers producers noticed immediately. And at Warners that meant only one thing—the teaming would be repeated again very soon.

Even as *Gold Diggers* was approaching the end of shooting, the Depression was nearing a desperate tipping point. A week before Franklin Roosevelt was to be sworn in, the American economy was teetering on the edge of collapse. A bank holiday—a federally mandated temporary closure of all financial institutions—was proposed to forestall the enormous rash of failures that recently saw uninsured depositors' savings evaporate into thin air. Once the banks were taken off line, there would be no cash available to the public, and no transactions at all with any financial institution anywhere in the world. Just two days after Roosevelt took the oath of office on March 4, banks across the nation closed with a promise that they would reopen four days later. No one believed it. "William Randolph Hearst said the banks will stay closed for a *month*," Aline reported to Clarence.

Alarmingly, all the worries that had prompted Aline to take her salary in gold, to purchase paid-up blue-chip stocks, and to counsel her husband on financial matters now appeared startlingly prescient. "You have no appreciable bank balances, have you?" she asked Clarence. "I expect Warner Brothers to fold up in good earnest, and if so we will be in a very poor spot. If the same thing happens in N.Y. you'd better have some cash or gold on hand," she curtly advised her sometimes absent-minded husband. "As my pillar of strength you are expected to check on everything and see whither we are bound. If the banks stay closed—if the Warner Brothers fold up and you have nothing—then I would surmise that my pillar of strength is an *ostrich* with his *head* in the sand."[12] Even with their own financial worries, the Steins were still helping friends and family with an intricate series of loans and gifts ranging from $50 to $500 each. When Clarence's close friend Benton MacKaye needed a life-saving operation he was unable to afford, the Steins footed the bill.[13] And when the banks closed and checks could not be redeemed, Aline exhorted Clarence to send her old friends Agnes Morgan and Helen Arthur $100 in cash to replace the bank draft she had wired them. "They are desperately hard up," she advised.[14]

It is no wonder that Aline was worried about the solvency of Warner Brothers and in fact, the entire economy of the United States. On the same day the bank holiday went into effect, representatives of the major studios were deep in conference with the directors of the Academy of Motion Picture Arts and Sciences about measures to forestall potential bankruptcies. When the banks failed to reopen on March 8 as promised, the studios announced the frightening results of the AMPAS negotiations. Aline reported, "Today, Warner Brothers called a mass meeting in a most summary, almost *brutal* fashion. They demanded a 50% reduction on salaries to run a period of *eight weeks*. It will reduce my gross income by $5,000."[15] This agreement, endorsed by AMPAS, was not exclusive to Warner Brothers. It was visited upon every employee at every studio, including all of Hollywood's biggest stars. In mid-March, a salary waiver form was circulated throughout the industry, and one was placed in front of Aline for her signature. Her long-standing fear that the vein of gold she had been mining would run out seemed at last to be coming true. "Clarence," she wrote, "I signed [the waiver] the day Jack Warner told me the studio would close unless there were 100% of them signed. Harold Stern [Aline's lawyer] gave me the devil for being stampeded."[16] As a postscript, Aline absolved herself of foolhardiness by stressing compassion. "Having had my share of the honey pot," she said, "the least I can do is help them out now."[17]

Then, during a week that was already brimming with fear and uncertainty, all the tension and anxiety within the country seemed to coalesce into a physical manifestation of America's financial woes. On the evening of March 10, 1933, the mythological Gods of Homer woke from a long sleep and resolved to punish Hollywood for indulging in the wrong kind of idolatry. They sent an earthquake. "I was in the Brown Derby when the first shake came," Aline recorded the next day. "The lights dimmed, the restaurant rocked—someone said 'earthquake!' and we started running for the street." In a tight circle around the epicenter in Long Beach nearly 120 people were killed, the majority as a result of Aline's exact response—rushing out of buildings and being struck by falling debris. The 6.4-magnitude quake also caused fifty million dollars in property damage and became long-lasting lore among the Hollywood community. When it was over Aline still had her sense of humor intact. "My dinner is probably still sitting at the Derby!" she lamented.

Even after such vigorous physical and economic agitation, neither the Depression nor the earthquake could break Hollywood's will. California quickly got to work clearing the streets, and Roosevelt's bank holiday achieved its goal. Businesses and individuals weathered the closures through thrift and trust. Retail stores extended credit, churches called a moratorium on passing collection plates, and the manufacturers of Pebco toothpaste devised a promotional scheme for everyone to keep their smiles bright without paying out a cent. On March 13, banks reopened and the crisis was averted. With that, the reduction waivers were eventually phased out and the back salaries were (grudgingly) paid. It was also said that someone saw a rainbow, but those reports were unconfirmed.

All through the filming of *Gold Diggers of 1933*, Aline continued her routine of watching the dailies and rough scene-assemblies in the Warners projection room. "I saw *all* the rushes," she recalled of her Warners years. "I was always interested in how it came out, according to what I was planning to do and what I saw when I saw it."[18] Once again she realized that perhaps she had been too harsh in her early condemnation of the material. "The picture looks *grand*," she said, validating LeRoy's stylistic choices. "It's the very best work I've done—so light, so gay and free—I think the audience will like me in it better than anything to date."[19] They did—and so did the critics. *Gold Diggers* was a massive hit for the studio, nearly eclipsing the box office of *42nd Street*, and its success drew Aline ever closer to achieving star billing at Warner Brothers.

With Aline's semiannual hiatus period scheduled to start on April 1, the studio decided to squeeze a third picture out of her before she left for New York. *Heroes for Sale*—known in the script stage as *Breadline*—was another of Warner Brothers social comment films, this one an exposé of the plight of WWI veterans enduring hard times during the Depression. With its echoes of left-leaning politics and dark themes, *Heroes for Sale* should have appealed to Aline, but being a student of these ideas—and not always an astute judge of scripts in the raw—she found it all quite shallow. "'Breadline' is a sad failure of a script. I honestly believe the studio is only eleven years old when it comes to things economic. And they attempt to cover Communism and Technocracy and a few other such easy problems in the story. It is *pathetic*."[20]

The Warner Brothers archives contain a rare chronicle of the development of *Heroes for Sale*, from germ of an idea to finished screenplay. The story was hatched while Warner Brothers contract player Richard Barthelmess was waiting for his next assignment at the studio. At that time, Darryl Zanuck had no story in development for him, and was anxious to avoid paying Barthelmess' handsome salary while he remained idle. So, having long experience as a screenwriter, Zanuck himself hatched an idea from the current headlines: the story of a WWI vet who winds up in the Bonus Army, which was at that very moment protesting on the streets of Washington DC.[21] The next day Zanuck turned this one-sentence springboard over to screenwriters Robert Lord and Wilson Mizner to see what they could do with it.[22] As the result of a plagiarism suit threatened against Warner Brothers in November of 1933, the studio legal department asked Lord to record his recollections about writing the screenplay in case the troubles wound up in court:

> Mr. Mizner and I started working on this little germ of an idea and developed it into a little story outline. This outline was submitted to Mr. Zanuck. The three of us had long conferences on it—we developed it, changed it, molded it into some semblance of the story we used in the picture. After some weeks of work Mr. Mizner and I finished a first draft continuity which was submitted to Mr. Zanuck. As usual, this continuity was discussed, changed, molded and switched around to improve it. During this process, Mr. William Wellman, the director, sat in on conferences and contributed several story points. We then wrote a new script embodying all of the changes decided on by Mr. Zanuck, Mr. Wellman, Mr. Mizner and myself.[23]

In closing, Lord wrote: "I understand that [the complainant] alleges that we stole a story of his called 'Breadline.' I never saw his story and did not know until today that a story entitled 'Breadline' was ever submitted to this company." Now, Robert Lord may be telling the absolute truth about his ignorance of the situation. But the simple fact is that in its early stages, *Heroes for Sale* had the working title of "Breadline," something that was not widely known—if at all—by the general public. Whether this was merely a wild coincidence or not, the complaining author appeared to be a crackpot, with his letters to the studio written, literally, in crayon. The Warners legal team gathered and took action. The trouble vanished.

Putting aside Aline's usual gloomy outlook for the "pathetic" script, *Heroes for Sale* had, as Aline would say, "compensations." The project was her only opportunity to work with William Wellman, a sadly neglected workhorse of the Warner Brothers directing stable. Shooting at an unprecedented clip, even for Warners (he made five films in 1931, six in 1932, and seven in 1933), Wellman nonetheless maintained consistent quality, having recently completed the timeless gangster epic *The Public Enemy*, a successful adaptation of Edna Ferber's novel *So Big*, and Barbara Stanwyck's pre-Code classic *Night Nurse*.[24]

ALINE MACMAHON

On March 21 Aline stepped onto the set of *Heroes for Sale* to find that Wellman was quite unlike the other directors she had worked with. The first day under Wellman's direction turned Aline's head, perhaps in more ways than one. "The director is a miracle of ease and expedition," she reported to Clarence. "We move so quickly, so easily—[Wellman] has decided the night before exactly what he wants, his camera and his actions. He tells us in simple words what to do and generally lets the first take stand. It's a revelation—always provided the picture is good. I don't know enough of his past work to judge—his direction so far appears to be lively but conventional, with all the *stencils* of feeling." Before she encountered Wellman—as well as after—she had found most directors more interested in keeping a schedule than in true creative work. "Mervyn LeRoy said he never read the scenes ahead that he was going to do, because he didn't want to spoil 'the inspiration of the moment.' He and Alfred Green and Woody Van Dyke and a whole lot of others shot off the cuff, every day, according to what occurred to them. They weren't planning directors, generally speaking—but it wasn't a period when you were praised for doing it, so maybe they did it in the secrecy of their homes and pretended they were making it up as they went along."[25] Aline's admiration for Wellman, however, also strayed beyond the mere professional. "He's a much more picturesque *person* than a director," she said. "He looks like a satyr—a beautiful head, a great shock of hair and craggy features. What a fascinating chap—he was an ace flyer in the war and four times married—the set reverberates with his high spirits."

During her early years in Hollywood there is no innuendo or gossip to suggest that Aline ever strayed from the path of marital fidelity. Her deeply infused Victorian streak—and her true love and respect for Clarence—would not countenance such venality. In the abstract, however, it does appear that the button-down Aline MacMahon *could* be excited by a masculine contrast to Clarence's cerebral calm. War hero, roustabout, Casanova; Wellman must have positively glowed in comparison to the sedate, intellectual men who had surrounded Aline most of her life. "This business is so wonderfully entertaining!" she concluded.

Typically, Aline was too harsh in her judgment of *Heroes for Sale*. Wellman's sturdy direction supports Lord and Mizner's sprawling, pre-Code script. Tom (Richard Barthelmess) is a soldier who is gravely wounded while covering up the battlefield cowardice of his friend. After the war, treatment for his injuries turns him into a morphine addict, while the coward has meanwhile parlayed his false heroics into a comfortable life. After Tom is cured of his addiction, he moves into a tenement house and meets Mary (Aline), who promptly falls in love with him. With Aline now Warners' inarguable Queen of unrequited love, there is, of course, no hope for Mary. But she must try. After months living near Tom and being treated like a sister, Mary dresses up in an effort to show him that she is a woman after all. ("Trying to look pretty, huh?" an elderly tenant asks. "No," Aline replies, "just tryin' to look less like the family.") That night, instead of a chance at love Mary finds Tom in the arms of her friend Ruth (Loretta Young). With the help of Wellman's pictorial calm, the scene is emotionally devastating. Shot from her back, Mary opens the door to Tom's flat and finds the pair in each other's arms; even from behind, Aline's body language tells a vivid tale of disappointment and hurt, then quick composure. Only when Tom and Ruth leave does Wellman allow her to turn to the camera for a heartbreaking close-up. It is a study of subtlety from director and actor, and a moment of pure sadness that shrinks the heart.

Unfortunately, Aline's dramatic opportunities are few, as she periodically disappears from the story while we follow Tom's travails. And, with little to strongly engage her, Aline was undergoing yet another of the crises of confidence that regularly plagued her. "It seems to me I'm losing concentration—a power—a particularly personal quality I had. I've been trying to lighten my touch, to loosen up. The awful truth is that I am *less sure* of myself now than when I started pictures."[26] Certainly, the scripts that Warners was providing Aline—material she once described as "piffling"—do not have the kinds of characters that tax her abilities the way *Maya* or *Beyond the Horizon* did. Her fear of losing focus is an indication that no matter how much effort she put into these roles, they did not have enough depth to bring the best out of her. Aline MacMahon always felt the most alive when she was operating on the outskirts of her capabilities, riding the sometimes fearful excitement of succeeding or failing on a great dare of the unknown. But Warner Brothers' attitude concerning their star roster was just the opposite—they wanted to *avoid* challenges—to protect their valuable assets and to repeat easy success. This friction between Aline's excitement of risk and the studio's *fear* of it will eventually become an insoluble problem. For now, Aline seems to be developing a conscious resentment at being forced to play it safe, and in her own weakness in having a price that made that safety palatable. "I have a suspicion that complaining because you get $1250 a week is preferable to waiting for a better job to come out of the blue," she said. "Or is it?"[27]

The public was somewhere between lukewarm and indifferent to *Heroes for Sale*. Even Warners' blue-collar Depression audiences were wary of a picture where a heroic WWI veteran descends into drug addiction, has his mother die while he is in rehab, watches an angry mob kill his wife, and is then railroaded into prison, leaving his infant child to grow up without him. It was heady stuff for an era of incredible political, social, and economic turmoil, and critics were unsure of what to make of it—except for the writer in the *Hollywood Reporter*. "Preying upon every maudlin sentiment that human beings have to be ashamed of, Warner Brothers' 'Heroes for Sale' takes the prize as the vaguest, most tiresome, pointless and discouraging picture made in a long time," he said. "There is probably no audience in any part of the country which could swallow this film with any sort of enjoyment."[28]

On March 24, just as the finish line for *Heroes for Sale* was approaching, Aline MacMahon was informed that she was needed for retakes on *Gold Diggers of 1933*. In the studio era this request was a relatively common occurrence. Pictures were routinely sent to the editing room the moment they were processed, and a rough-cut would be quickly produced for Jack Warner and his various producers to view. Following this screening, suggestions were offered for editing (this, for example, is where it was decided that Joan Blondell's famous "Forgotten Man" number would be moved to the finale of *Gold Diggers of 1933*), and final details on the film were firmed up. Periodically, Jack Warner or his producers would discover that the director had missed something, or saw an opportunity to improve what was already in the can. With all the actors under contract and stages often still intact, it was a simple matter to reassemble the principals for a few hours and correct the error. It was so common, in fact, that a clause concerning availability for retakes was built into every contract.

When Darryl Zanuck saw the first cut of *Gold Diggers*, he decided that it needed something that only Aline could deliver. During the gold-digging sequence of the story, Warren William winds up passed out drunk in Carol and Trixie's apartment. The girls quickly decide to have him sleep it off in Carol's bed, convinced that in the morning the stiff-upper-lip Warren will be so mortified by his (imagined) immorality that they will be able to blackmail him into allowing Polly to marry his kid brother. As the scene was shot and assembled, we see the girls carry him off the couch, then cross-fade to Warren in bed, with Aline gleefully tossing his clothes—and some skimpy lingerie—around the room. It was here that Zanuck felt they had missed an opportunity, and Aline felt something like outrage. As she told Clarence, "Zanuck has decided we are missing a real belly laugh—the scene where I *take off Warren William's trousers!*"[29] Even in 1933—and especially in the pre-Code era—

disrobing a man down to his comically large boxer shorts was relatively tame stuff, but to Aline it was an affront to her dignity, and a clarion call to battle. Raising a terrible row, she refused to shoot the scene, and that very evening Warner Brothers froze her salary and sent the legal department into action. With sly politeness the corporate shysters feigned astonishment, claiming they were "reluctant to believe that you will not render your services."[30] Then came the knives, threatening unspeakable calamity unless she complied.

It is sometimes difficult to reconcile Aline's Victorian propriety with her progressive ideology. It appears to boil down to her personal image—she could tolerate, even take pride in, her dramatic stage roles as a prostitute or a lesbian (highly controversial in the 1920s) and dabble in fringe politics, but to be compromised for what she considered a cheap laugh was too much. "In 'Gold Diggers,'" she said, "at Mervyn [LeRoy]'s special request, and being unwilling to be obstructive, and above all—prudish—I did do a scene where I was in a bathtub. I did play a scene in my combination [lingerie]. I did, most decisively, and in full view of the camera, pinch Ginger Rogers in the behind. I feel that all these compromises with my taste are sufficient proof," she offered, "that I am not exaggeratedly a blue-stocking." Now, with all due respect to Aline, these examples—and the use of eighteenth-century slang to describe what she professes *not* to be—seem to make the opposite case. Which is exactly what her lawyer told her. "Harold Stern assures me it is inconsistent to refuse to do that scene if I did the other questionable compromises, and no jury would be sympathetic. I say—all right—let them sue! I will not even defend the suit. I have lost completely any notion I may have had that Warner Brothers look upon me as a special kind of person for whom only certain roles, situations or lines are appropriate. They are on such a toboggan of vulgarity and sex that I am genuinely apprehensive. If necessary I can go through bankruptcy—this is the time to take a stand." Aline's anger—which rarely overcame her—ran riot when her dignity or personal control was threatened. It was the trap of necessity that she so hated, and this outrage struck a raw nerve. "I'm very concerned," she told Clarence. "I only want power on the most dignified terms—and I most decidedly distrust Warner Brothers. I might add that all this dangerous inclination is of recent development. It is the result of a new system of contracting 'players' there. They have what they call 'stock' girls—about twelve young ladies whom they pay $50 a week—and who constitute a harem for the executives and supervisors. It's the least of my personal concern, of course, but you see what devious ways one can be influenced by being under contract to bastards. Whew!!!"[31]

On the morning of Wednesday, March 29, Warren William and a skeleton crew were on a soundstage at Warner Brothers, ready to shoot the retakes on *Gold Giggers of 1933*. Aline, also on the lot that morning, was directed by executives to appear on the set and perform. When she reiterated her refusal to take part, an evening conference was hastily called at the Burbank studio. Aline's record of the meeting was short, but it reminds us that she was no babe in the woods when it came to negotiation: "One of their attacks," she said, "was 'Well, the other actors don't object to the scene—do you think you are so much better than them?' The answer of course, was 'no—only I know where my next meal is coming from and they probably don't.'" Aline had observed that even in Hollywood, the stars who seemed untouchable could still be slaves to the same trap her father had endured. "I have *no* responsibilities," she explained in a letter, "and all the other actors hereabouts seem to be supporting extended families. It would be intolerable if I didn't feel free to refuse to do what is not to my taste. You see why I want to hang on to our [stock and dividend] income—it is the only freedom I can act upon."[32] This was Aline's unique leverage over the seductive power of money—her willingness to walk away.

The Wednesday night meeting ended with Aline insisting she would be returning to New York, as planned, on Saturday, without shooting the new scenes. "Well, it *can* be done," she said once the conference was over. "One *can* say no. Of course the *penalty* is yet to be imposed. But I am in a far better position now than I was two years ago, so I am not too concerned."

On Thursday, with Aline firmly ensconced at her home in Brentwood, the studio inexplicably again called Warren William back to the set to complete the retakes. There, he found an Aline MacMahon look-alike, willing—even eager—to remove his trousers. William climbed into bed and dutifully played dead. The ersatz MacMahon did her best to disrobe him in an amusing way. Quickly, the footage was processed and sent to the projection room. When it was screened, there were no laughs, just a ghastly silence. Now thoroughly stymied, Warners again exhorted Aline to appear and do the retakes or be sued.[33] With a railway ticket in her hand and bile in her heart, she again refused. Immediately, the wheels—and the teeth—of the Warner Brothers legal department began to grind.

Before Aline had even boarded her eastbound train Saturday evening, she found herself the defendant in a lawsuit filed by Warner Brothers in the Superior Court of Los Angeles. Throughout the troubles, Aline had hoped to keep the entire affair private. "I haven't told *anyone* about it," she said. "Any national publicity about doing a scene that is questionable will mix me up in the public's mind. It is clear that a suit on the subject would be very damaging to me no matter what the verdict." Unfortunately, within days of the filing, trade magazines and wire services had distributed the story across the country. "Aline MacMahon East as Warners Sue," was the *Hollywood Reporter* headline. "Warner Brothers filed suit Saturday against Aline MacMahon for $2157, claiming that amount as damages incurred when she failed to appear for recording a scene last Wednesday."[34] Whether as a misprint or mistake, other sources reported the amount of the suit first as $25,000, and then $27,500—astronomical figures that must have momentarily startled Aline and her lawyer. The Warners accountants themselves calculated the cost of the useless retakes at only $2,757, and would have found it quite impossible to recoup ten times that amount in court.

As Aline and Harold Stern probed her contract for loopholes, they found a clause that first gave them a bit of hope. "The company agrees that it will not require the artist to render her services in any two photoplays at the same time," it stated. Aline, of course, had still been working on *Heroes for Sale* when asked to return to *Gold Diggers*. But Warner Brothers had been in the business of contracts far longer than Aline, or even Harold Stern. "Excepting, however," it continued, "services of the artist may be required in the making of retakes, added scenes and / or changes in connection with any preceding photoplay in which she has appeared during the time she is working in a succeeding photoplay."[35] The experts had covered themselves quite well. With no legal grounds to keep Warners at bay, Aline resigned herself to losing the suit, and perhaps also her contract renewal, as a result of her stance. Here, her distrust of Warners may have hardened into a cynicism that kept her from seeing the big picture. During her service at the studio Aline's star was distinctly on the rise. Even with her fragmented working schedule, various line producers had spoken of future projects where Aline's name would appear above the title. All of Hollywood, in fact, was aware of the studio's faith in her, as evidenced by this blurb in the *Hollywood Reporter* about the Warners suit: "The court action of Warners against a contract featured player who was being groomed for starring spots is decidedly unusual in the industry." While Aline wondered if the studio would let her option lapse, Zanuck himself was unequivocal about where she was headed in 1933. "When I asked the studio if I could do a play in the spring, they said 'no,'" Aline reported. "Mr. Zanuck is planning to feature me and feared that a failure in the theatre would be bad for my prestige." Warner Brothers had already invested handsomely in Aline MacMahon, and would not let her go out of simple spite. "Since a studio seldom sues an actor," a syndicated columnist wrote, "it is believed that Warners brought their suit against Miss MacMahon only as an example to others who might consider disobedience."³⁶ The problem was settled quietly; Aline was not obliged to do the scene, and the final cut of *Gold Diggers* simply does without it. In punishment Aline was obligated to provide a few extra days of service to make up for the financial liability, and Warners paid the money they had withheld from her salary.

Although Aline's sense of personal propriety was sincere, it is a shame that Daryl Zanuck's idea did not make it to the screen. It is simply impossible to believe that the sight of Aline MacMahon attempting to remove the trousers of a comatose Warren William could be anything other than high art. Its absence from *Gold Diggers of 1933* is an unforgivable loss to the history of film comedy.

After two months in New York City as Mrs. Clarence Stein, Aline MacMahon headed back to Los Angeles. By the time she boarded her westbound train on June 10, *Gold Diggers of 1933* had already made its way to theaters and her legal troubles were in the rear-view mirror. En route she was happy to find Helen Broderick (Edward Everett Horton's wife in *Top Hat*) also on the *20th Century Limited*. "I introduced myself to her and we have been having a wonderful time discussing the perils—and pitfalls—and pathos of being a character actress," she wrote. Soon, Warner Brothers would add another chapter to the discussion.

While Aline was on the East Coast, Darryl Zanuck had resigned from his position as Warner Brothers head of production in protest of the studio's temporary refusal to reinstate full salaries following the bank moratorium.³⁷ The news of Zanuck's absence was a grave disappointment to Aline; she had grown to appreciate his instincts and honesty during their association. "I wasn't really type-cast under him; Zanuck was a very colorful and hard-hitting producer and was really interested in a variety of kinds of parts, as long as the play had a beginning, middle and an end, and was about people getting very famous and then getting into the dregs of life. You know, villains with hearts of gold. As long as they were colorful and hard-hitting, he didn't care whether you were one type or another."³⁸ Along with Mervyn LeRoy, Zanuck was one of Aline's primary benefactors within Warner Brothers, and she worried that his remove would leave a void in advocacy for her at the studio.

When Aline returned to the lot, she found that the enormous box-office and critical response to *Gold Diggers of 1933* (as well as *42nd Street*) had encouraged Warners to strike again with a musical comedy. In an effort to duplicate their recent success, Aline was assigned to the next of their pre-Code musical classics, *Footlight Parade*. Warner Brothers wanted to quickly recreate her popular teaming with Guy Kibbee, the portly comedy relief of *Gold Diggers* and so many other Warners properties of the era. She would have taken the part of Kibbee's unfaithful wife Harriet, but again Aline was wary of the role. "My part would be a silly, hard, obnoxious woman who likes young boys [Harriet is having an affair with Dick Powell]," she said. "I would appear *in three scenes*—I counted the lines—*26 lines* in my part." In spite of the fact that the studio was willing to pay a special rate of $8,000 for just four days' work, Aline refused the role. "But it's an all-star cast!" producer Robert Lord insisted. At this, Aline was unmoved. "Oh, I couldn't *do* it!! The character is the kind of which all the other characters say 'Thank heaven that old fool Mrs. Gould is gone.'"[39] The studio substituted Ruth Donnelly—at a significant cost saving—and proceeded without looking back.

Aline's one regret in sidestepping *Footlight Parade* was missing her only opportunity to appear with James Cagney, another man whose masculine energy appealed to her. "Cagney is the best of them all," she recorded shortly after seeing him in 1932's *Winner Take All*. "Always one hundred percent the role he plays and does such legitimate emotional work. Warner Brothers are crazy not to pay him anything he may ask. He's so wonderful and unique."[40] Aline's appreciation of Cagney's particular gifts as an actor, predicated on a foundation so unlike her own, reinforced a personal philosophy of hers: that it is not about *how* you get to an emotional place, but that you are honest once you arrive. "I don't think it matters what you believe in," she said of developing an actor's technique. "You can believe in Strasberg if you like, you can believe in Ouspenskaya, you can believe in any of them. As long as you believe hard enough to concentrate when you're acting, that's what really counts."[41] In the end, Aline's decision to refuse *Footlight Parade* was likely a cogent one. Her appearance would have offered her no real opportunity except to disappoint an audience who had grown to appreciate her as a sympathetic, likable figure. In January 1934 Aline recorded her thoughts about the picture, which, like so many, looked far different once it was assembled for an audience. "Saw 'Footlight Parade' last night," she said. "It was swell—so very cleverly played. Joan Blondell is a first rate comedienne, I think—and I do enjoy Cagney." [Sigh.]

Being at liberty meant that Aline had returned to the West Coast weeks early for nothing; her next film, the Paul Muni vehicle *The World Changes* (then known as *America Kneels*), would not begin for another month. In order not to waste her time away from Clarence, and since the Orsatti brothers were constantly fielding offers from other studios for her services, Aline asked Warners executives if she might fill that time by accepting a loan-out. "They said 'no,'" she reported. "They're building me up and want me to be associated in the public mind with nothing but Warners pictures." This affirmation went a long way to healing the wounds from the *Gold Diggers* debacle, and shortly after she had a surprising meeting with Warners' new head of production, Hal Wallis.

From nearly the beginning of her contract, Aline had regularly suggested properties to the studio that she believed would be proper vehicles for her, sometimes personally buying options on them. "I'm always looking for parts," she told a Brooklyn reporter. "I read dozens of books and see all the plays in New York. When I find something interesting to me I wire the studios. Sometimes I hear from them, sometimes I don't."[42] Later, she reflected on the problem of convincing the studio to do those literary properties. "I was getting my own material at my own expense, and urging them to do classics and fighting like the devil with everybody there. I learned that they knew what I was talking about, but Jack Warner himself said, 'Yes, we know what you mean, but we don't think there's a nickel in it.'"[43] But during her first meeting with the studio's new production head she was pleasantly surprised by something unexpected and exciting. "The book I suggested was sitting on Wallis' desk!" Aline enthused. "I honestly believe that if I present them a program of exploitation for me they will be inclined to accept it."[44] She was only partially right—the studio was amenable to making her a star, but not in her having a guiding hand in it.

The synopsis of *The World Changes* is most easily told in Aline's own words: "I read the script of 'America Kneels' today. What the [hell] it is all about I couldn't *possibly* tell you.[45] My part is at the beginning and the end of the picture—at the start I have a baby [Muni], then I see him playing with his little girl friend. Then he is restless to go to the city—Chicago. I drop out of the picture through the body of the film, but come in again as the great-grandmother of *ninety*. All the stuff between is Paul Muni being all ages, having a mad wife, and being ruined, etc., etc. Lord it is poor stuff. The picture says *nothing*." Aline may have—again—disdained the script, but Warner Brothers was continuing to show confidence in her. In spite of her relatively slim role on *World Changes* she was billed second only to Muni, and in front of Mary Astor, who was accorded more screen time and greater dramatic opportunities as Muni's wife, a luminous Gilded Age Gibson Girl who descends into madness and death. Although Astor had been a true star in the silent era, her career had somewhat dimmed by this time, and she would have to wait much longer than Aline for new headlining opportunities. It wasn't until 1941's *The Great Lie* and *The Maltese Falcon* that she would return to the first rank of film actresses. In 1936 however, turnabout became fair play. When Aline turned down the role of Edith Cortright in William Wyler's masterful *Dodsworth*, Astor was prevailed upon to take over the part. "They offered me the part in *Dodsworth*," Aline recalled, chagrined. "And I said, 'But after the Depression, nobody's interested. This is a different era—we've passed that 'rich man and the woman he's interested in.' I couldn't have been wronger!"[46] For Aline, it is a shame that *Dodsworth* does not appear in her filmography—she would have been wonderful in it—but for movie history, it is just as well. Astor's portrayal is so warm, honest, and tender that it is difficult to imagine anyone surpassing it.

Like much of the Warners' product of the era, *The World Changes* is largely about class divide. Generally appealing to the blue-collar audience they saw as their bread and butter, Warners product rarely aggrandized status or fetishized wealth. In any schism between lower class and upper class, their pictures sided with the simple, moral values of the common man. When Muni leaves his pioneer home and moves east he is seen to be abandoning his people, and the children he raises within this environment are portrayed as shallow, entitled poseurs. The screenwriter, Edward Chodorov, was a member of the Communist Party and likely relished the idea of turning Sheridan Gibney's story into a condemnation of the moneyed interests of Wall Street. Whether Chodorov and Aline were acquainted at this time is unknown, but it is certainly the period in which she is continuing to struggle with her political identity. "I am a Communist if Communism means a chance for everyone to justify himself *to* himself," she wrote in 1933. "To really help the disinherited you must feel that you are a tool, not a creature—but I fear that our ambition keeps our social conscience in check. Maybe a real revolution will fall upon us in about five years." Perhaps not quite yet decided on which horse to ride, she is meeting and exchanging ideas on the state of the world with liberal thinkers, and looking closely at the course.

Ultimately, the success or failure of *The World Changes* was built not so much on its story as on the mythology of Paul Muni. Touted as the Promethean talent of the era, he had arrived at Warner Brothers from Broadway, via the Yiddish theater that Aline had often attended with her grandmother. Muni was renowned for his ability to disappear into a role—and to play any age or ethnicity—sometimes through acting, sometimes through the makeup tricks and legerdemain he had learned on Manhattan's East Village stages.

World Changes was designed to showcase this ability to progress through various stages of life, and as a consequence Warner Brothers wanted the actress who played his mother to do the same; Aline's character aged from nineteen to ninety only because of the studio's desire to capitalize on Muni's mutability. This required Aline to undergo a long series of makeup tests to see if she could age convincingly on screen (she did), and which Aline endured so that she could "make a noise as of studio activity" while she was waiting for her starting date. The rest of her free time was spent at the LA library researching western lore and devouring Elizabeth Ellet's definitive 1852 book on the era, *Pioneer Women of the West*. "I have a pretty complete picture of those people now," she wrote, "and what a wealth of incident to play into a picture!"[47] Before Muni had even appeared on the studio call sheet Aline was on location shooting the film's early sequences, with Mervyn LeRoy once more behind the camera. It was a rugged week. Having learned to chop wood on location of *The Life of Jimmy Dolan*, LeRoy again put an ax in her hands and set her to work outside the little cabin that was built as her homestead. Aline's use of the ax is impressive, but her hands were not those of a pioneer woman—in two days she had acquired five blisters. Working on the covered wagon she received half a dozen splinters, her knees were scraped and aching from seventeen takes of her collapsing in childbirth, and wearing heavy period dress in the California's blazing July heat was a beastly job. "I love all this, though!" she said. "The hot sun and the steady breeze, and picnic lunches, and oh!—the good feel of a hot bath at the end of a day."[48] Whatever misgivings she had about the artistic elements of her job, Aline MacMahon did not mind the hard work of filmmaking. In that sense she was a trouper.

On return from location shooting, Aline began work with Muni on the Warners lot. She was immediately impressed. "Muni has great personal charm," she reported. "And his wife [Bella] who sits on the set all the while, is lovely—so simple and friendly. She's a great favorite." Muni, a true professional, helped make the shoot easy for Aline. One of their few face-to-face sequences comes near the end of the film, and captures the reunion of mother and son after forty years apart. In a scene of spare, understated sincerity, two great actors simply look wordlessly in each other's eyes and provide a heartbreaking moment of familial love buried deep under Scandinavian reserve. In the end it was Aline, far more than the widely respected Muni, who received acting plaudits from the critics. "Aline MacMahon is admirable," Mourdant Hall said, seeing perfectly where the true story of *World Changes* lay: "More might have been done with this lovely woman, as her appearance makes a story within a story."[49]

The most important thing that came out of *The World Changes* was the final word on Aline's ill-formed and ambiguous thoughts about children. After a baby was brought onto set to play Muni as an infant (the one age even Muni couldn't manage), Aline returned home to Brentwood where her mother and friends were temporarily boarding. Not even able to sleep in her own bed, and woken early by her guests, she took to her patio and put her thoughts to paper. "Now, I wouldn't mention this to you Clarence, except that I'm interested in the moral of the tale," she began. "I'm fairly convinced that I have waited too long to adopt children. I am too jealous of my privacy—not unselfish where others are concerned, but . . ."

Here her letter paused for an implied deep breath.

"As always, you were probably right about not having a family," she continued. "I would not have the patience or interest in them that I ought." Then, as was her way, Aline minimized what was perhaps the most painful admission of her life. "'Tis a pity," she said.[50]

Aline MacMahon and Clarence Stein never did start a family. After Clarence passed away in 1975 and Aline was very much alone in their New York apartment, she had time to reflect on what they missed. "I regret it very, very much," she said. "It was a choice, in a measure, but really it was just life, life. We married late, and I had a very moving around career, in the west half of the year. Neither one of us decided anything, life just happened that way." Aline's contribution to the situation was a manifestation of the same schism between love and art that she had confronted in her marriage. She knew that it was essential to work as hard at parenting as she had to become a great performer, and in this endeavor was not prepared to draw from one to feed the other. "I was too absorbed in my career and what I wanted to do," she admitted, "and I'm not sure Clarence thought I would be the ideal mother. You really do have to be a very dedicated parent. I had an ideal mother and an ideal grandmother, and it would be bad to be anything less, I think. I don't know—you can call it anything you want," she said, dismissing any deeper interpretation. "But that's how it developed. That's wha' happ'n."[51]

In August Warner Brothers decided to take up the annual option on Aline's contract, much to her vacillating dismay. She had been constantly assessing and reassessing her prospects for continued employment at Warners, first gratified by her (now) $63,000 annual salary, the next mortified by the cheap material she was forced to endure. That month she wriggled out of another attempt to reteam her with Guy Kibbee, this time in a kind of ersatz *Gold Diggers* called *Havana Widows*, wherein two chorus girls invade Cuba to dig gold from vacationing millionaires. "'Havana Widows' is 'low down,'" she complained. "It will make money and they'll laugh—in the way the Keystone Cops make them laugh—but it is not for me. I'd hate being featured in a sleazy version of 'Gold Diggers' just because the audience laughs when I vamp Guy Kibbee."[52] With her regular misgivings about poor scripts and miscasting, the likelihood of future battles with studio brass vexed her. "But," she admitted, "I know that it is just possible that I will not find parts at any *other* studio to my liking." Stuck between appreciating her opportunities and hating her options, Aline was in danger of becoming the Hamlet of Brentwood. "If—IF—all the ifs!'" was her refrain.

She couldn't know it then, but after retreating to New York for the autumn, Aline MacMahon would return to Hollywood to find that the long promised "if" had at last become "when."

10

SEEDS OF FREEDOM

As early as February—before *Gold Diggers of 1933* had even finished shooting—the publicity push that Warner Brothers had long promised for Aline whispered into print with a tiny blurb in the *Hollywood Reporter*. "Warner execs have decided to give Aline MacMahon an intensive build up as a featured comedienne during the coming year, and her first part in the campaign will be in 'Heroes for Sale.' Decision for the buildup was made after circuit theaters reported public reaction to her in several recent pictures had hit a high level."[1] Strangely, even as the publicity department slowly stoked the machinery of ballyhoo, Warner Brothers was still unsure of what they were selling. Was it the sardonic comedienne? Or the working woman's wan, long-suffering avatar? Or was it the female Arliss—the high-minded actress with a capital "A"? Of course it was the presence of all of these qualities, and more, that stumped the producers and publicists. Studios understood how to exploit dedicated comediennes like Zasu Pitts or Ruth Donnelly; they were never destined to be stars, just players, so they were kept in their particular box. "Actresses" generally played character parts; they didn't anchor pictures on their own. And true stars? Well, they might act too, but they must be beautiful, or glamorous, or sexy—and if Warner Brothers believed a single thing about Aline MacMahon, it was that she fit none of those descriptions. During Aline's four-year tenure at Warner Brothers—her only years in Hollywood under an exclusive contract with a publicity department dedicated to creating and honing her image—a steady stream of interviews and articles were generated in newspapers and fan magazines across the country. Besides the mundane if unique facts of her life (husband a famous architect, unusual Hollywood contract, university education) there was just one recurring theme to nearly every story: Aline MacMahon's complete and utter lack of sex appeal.

It seems incomprehensible, even cruel to modern ears, but this was the refrain that Aline's own studio advocates crafted for her. Even Warners' in-house pressbooks—providing ready-made stories designed to promote their films—followed this strange sales pitch. A headline in the exhibitors book for *One Way Passage*, for example, bluntly announced "Aline MacMahon Doesn't Want Beauty," which was essentially a declaration that she had none. Another pressbook featured a manufactured story supposedly "written" by Aline herself, under the banner "Aline MacMahon Prefers Homely Roles Over Heroic." In it, "Aline" tells the story of a cub reporter that interviewed her on the set. "What they want me to ask you," the boy says to her, sheepishly, "is—well, doesn't it take a lot of courage?" "Courage?" Aline asks. "I mean for you to appear—er—well, rather plain and unattractive on screen?"[2] Instead of being irked, the print Aline brushes off the boy's impertinent comment. "I'm not offended at questions like that," she says, tacitly admitting that she has no sex appeal and no sense of style.

Stories in the fan press were no better. The author of a 1932 *Modern Screen* profile (the kind of article that was regularly vetted and cleared by the studio) casually writes, "Aline, as she frankly admits, is no star, and neither is she a flaming new aurora on the sex horizon." And when the same author mentions that it was difficult to arrange a meeting with her, Aline's response was, "Why should I be picked for interviews anyhow? I'm no 'It' Girl." In the pages of *Silver Screen* magazine she was quoted as saying, "I have no beauty secrets—don't I look it?"[3] Elsewhere, this astonishing example of bad taste was on display: "Now take a look at that unmistakable MacMahon screen walk," the writer says. "There's no hint of a seductive, slithery slink in the decisive assurance of her almost mannish swagger, is there? She's *no one's* idea of a hotcha girl."[4] Critic Phil Scribe said she was "not a sexy type," and author Faith Baldwin declared Aline to be "among the girls who are not beautiful in the accepted sense, not born with sex appeal." The *Morning Telegraph* observed "she really isn't the most beautiful of movie stars," and nearly every other writer claimed she "had no hint of glamour." And when *Screenland* ran an article titled "Personality or Beauty—Which Have You?" it was Aline MacMahon who they consulted as an expert on "personality," to reassure those readers who—supposedly like Aline—were not "beautiful," that they still had a modicum of personal value. In the article, Aline posed a question. "Now, who has been adjudged the most popular woman in pictures?" Aline asked. "Marie Dressler!" Aline answered. Dressler, an important character star at MGM, was a large, raw-boned, rough-hewn matron type, then hovering around sixty-five years of age. "Would you call her beautiful? Would you?" Aline again asks. "Of course you would—beauty of personality! She's beautiful from within—everyone

"SIDE STREETS" with ALINE MAC MAHON – A First National & Vitaphone Picture

Studio producers and directors never saw Aline MacMahon's potential for glamour, but Warner Brothers' ace still photographers certainly did. The cat is a studio prop—she never owned one a day in her life. Studio publicity material.

who loves beauty of the soul loves her! Beauty, like everything else, is comparative," Aline again answers. Then the author—having had "Aline" establish that Dressler is not *physically* beautiful—proceeds to make an insulting comparison between the two. "If, some day, when Marie Dressler should wish to retire," she opined, "I should say that Aline MacMahon would be my candidate for the tremendous responsibility of replacing her." Aline, then just thirty-three, did not have to wait long; Dressler died suddenly only a year later. Hollywood never did quite find a replacement.

It is hard to imagine the woman who was so concerned with the propriety of her image would allow these casual insults to pass without notice or comment. Of modern stars widely considered to be beautiful and sexy, Aline had a look and presence similar to both Anjelica Huston and Cher. But as we have seen, the sad truth is that even at this stage of her career, Aline MacMahon did not believe physical looks to be among her chief assets. It was a manufactured fallacy built on decades of subtle undermining by her mother. "I never thought Aline was beautiful," Jennie Mac often said. "She had a beautiful carriage and a very nice manner and all that. But she just *wasn't* a beautiful girl."[5] This message—and Aline's own innate honesty—caused her to endure and even validate the myth that she was unattractive, and in the zeitgeist of the moment it became an uncontested truth.

While Aline was on hiatus in New York, *The World Changes* had been assembled and previewed in Los Angeles. The audience comment cards collected that night reconfirmed what Warners executives were already hearing from fans and exhibitors: that Aline MacMahon should be starring in a film of her own. Fortunately, the studio had a project that they believed could scarcely disappoint her. In New York during September Aline had attended the opening of *Heat Lightning*, written and staged by George Abbott, the legendary Broadway writer-director under whom Aline appeared in *Spread Eagle* during 1927.[6] Aline was intrigued by the dour story of two sisters who own a remote filling station in the southwest, and the next morning she wired Warner Brothers to suggest that the play might be a good vehicle for her. Beyond the dark characters and setting, there was a more esoteric reason for Aline to believe that *Lightning* might strike. Jean Dixon—the woman who had secured the role of May Daniels in the Broadway production of *Once in a Lifetime*—also played the lead in *Heat Lightning*. Aline, believer in luck that she was, always felt that Jean Dixon had been the charm that led to her entry into Hollywood. Here she saw a second opportunity to take over for Dixon in the film version of a Broadway play, this time one that would make her a star.

Sadly, for the next two months nothing emanated from the West Coast but static. However, when Aline finally disembarked in Los Angeles that December, she discovered a rare secret about Warner Brothers that few people knew: the studio sometimes listened. Warners had, indeed, purchased the rights to *Heat Lightning* and were now proposing it as her first starring vehicle. "You can imagine my surprise when I heard that I was to star, and that I would do 'Heat Lightning!'"[7]

When Warners decided to give Aline MacMahon a leading role in the second year of her contract, they were now *obliged* to make her a star, and keep her name above the title as long as she was continuously employed at the studio. Aline's original agreement, signed in the fall of 1932, mandated that in the *third* year of her option—if taken up—she must be the star in any films where she appeared. "It is understood, however," the contract stipulated, "that at any time Producer may, if it so desires, accord Artist star billing, but if such star billing be accorded during a period wherein such star billing would not be required hereunder, nevertheless, thereafter and in all subsequent pictures Artist shall be accorded star billing."[8] There was now no legal ground on which Warner Brothers could backtrack. In essence, they had officially decided to make Aline MacMahon a movie star.

It was mid-November when Mervyn LeRoy and the cast and crew of *Heat Lightning* set out for location shooting at Victorville, California, ninety miles northeast of Los Angeles. The temperatures in LA for that week were the hottest on record, and a trip to the Mojave Desert, with its cold nights and pleasant mornings was actually a welcome relief from the twenty-four-hour oppression of the city. The company encamped at a comfortable, if modest, ranch near the shooting site ("the cottonwood trees are the palest yellow and bronze, and the countryside is burnt a tawny beige with just the slightest tinges of autumnal green"),[9] and settled in for work. During the day Aline wore high, thick stockings for fear of red ants and scorpions roaming the grounds, and the moonlit desert nights were so frosty that she was obliged to don woolen underwear and have her fireplace ablaze in the early morning. "But I love it dearly!" she reported enthusiastically.

Unfortunately, on *Heat Lightning* Aline found herself for the first time at odds with her mentor and friend Mervyn LeRoy. It started—to her disappointment—when LeRoy refused to let her ride the horses that roamed the ranch's vast corral for fear that an injury would delay the production. Soon, Aline noticed other signs of friction. "The picture moves pleasantly, though Mervyn is very nervous, and sometimes short tempered. He's really being very nice to me, but so far he has refused every notion I've suggested."[10] From the beginning of their relationship, Aline found a champion in LeRoy, someone who respected her abilities and sought her contribution in the creative process, but now he was being uncharacteristically inflexible. One afternoon, *Heat Lightning's* assistant director told Aline confidentially that it had recently become increasingly difficult to get LeRoy to accept outside input, except through subterfuge. "The only way he'll take a suggestion," she wrote, "is if he thinks the idea is his own. The truth is that Mervyn is a lot more unsure of himself than I had thought, and it makes him fearful of taking anybody else's ideas. If only he weren't so on guard, lest I prove some point of superiority! I've decided he is afraid that I think he is a lowbrow and is determined to keep his position of authority. I'd like to win back his confidence, but it's okay—I'll do what I can secretly. I can be good anyway."

Aline's slight estrangement from LeRoy on *Heat Lightning* appears to have origins that were neither interpersonal nor creative. After being loaned out to direct *Tugboat Annie* (1933) at MGM, LeRoy was in the midst of a run of poorly performing films that would not end until 1936's *Anthony Adverse*.[11] After the nearly back-to-back blockbusters *I Am a Fugitive From a Chain Gang* and *Gold Diggers of 1933*, the failures of *The World Changes* and a second Muni vehicle, *Hi, Nellie!*, may have prompted him to tighten his control of the process. More immediately, 1933 had been a year of great turmoil in his personal life, with a divorce from his first wife and the dissolution of a serious liaison with Ginger Rogers. While on location for *Heat Lightning* LeRoy was also planning a January wedding to his second wife, Doris Warner, no less than the daughter of one of his studio's namesakes, Harry Warner. The couple had booked an around-the-world honeymoon on the ocean liner *Empress of Britain* to begin January 3, and LeRoy was acutely aware of the need to finish shooting with enough time to prepare for the 128-day trip and be in New York in time for the scheduled sailing. Creative changes in the middle of a location shoot could result in lost time, and LeRoy did not want to stress himself or his bride (and the boss's daughter) with the possibility of missing their ride. In spite of these tensions, Aline's deep affection for LeRoy eventually gave way to understanding. "I think he's a little awed by his coming marriage with an heiress—the daughter of the boss, etc., and is very much on edge. Still, one can't be with him as much as I have been and not be awfully fond of him. He is a very generous and sweet fellow, and whatever else is going on, the ledger balances very decidedly in his favor."[12]

When *Heat Lightning* finished at Warners' Burbank studios in early December—nine days ahead of schedule due to Leroy's impending nuptials—Aline contemplated the fruits of her first starring role in Hollywood. "I hope the picture won't look hurried. I don't think it has suffered by the speed at which we went. Its sins of omission are mine and Mervyn's. Mine because I was lazy in working out the emotional line I meant to pursue—Mervyn's because I see so clearly his limitations now that I've worked with him on a melodrama that should have been a director's feast. Still, from all angles it was a splendid break to have him for this picture. Oh, there are a few things I'd like to have a second chance at, but everything considered I think the job is a decent one."[13] Unfortunately, Aline MacMahon and Mervyn LeRoy would never work together again. In just a few years the man who discovered her would leave Warner Brothers to become head of production for rival MGM, and a mutually respectful and engaging friendship would dwindle away to nothing more than a series of fond memories.[14] When LeRoy passed away in 1987, among his possessions was a photograph of Aline MacMahon, with her personal inscription: "To my dear Svengali," it said.

Largely forgotten for decades, *Heat Lightning* is undergoing a much-deserved reevaluation both for its undeniable pre-Code pedigree and as a deliciously tawdry proto film noir. Set in the broiling heart of the Mojave Desert, sisters Olga (Aline) and Myra (Ann Dvorak) sweat out a meager living operating a second-rate service station and motor lodge. Olga is a bitter recluse, ashamed of an indecent past and hiding as far away from it as geography can allow. Much to her dismay, Myra is coming of age and flirting with the same kind of dissolute lifestyle from which Olga is in retreat. To Myra, who wants to explore the excitement of her mounting desires but is barred from doing so by her sister's edicts, Olga's world appears a frigid one. The pain and disillusion of Olga's previous life has caused her to swear off not just men but femininity itself, reinventing herself as a sexless—or more precisely—masculine figure. Dressed in overalls, with a bandanna hiding her magnificent cascade of hair, she pumps the gas and repairs the cars that pause on the road between nothingness and what lies beyond. But Myra has read the signs wrong: Olga is not dead inside; rather, she is desperately fearful of the dangerous passions that still haunt her, barely contained beneath furious self-denial—fearful too, of the irresistible pull of those same passions on her young sister.

In its bleakness, its pall of loneliness and despair—even impending doom—*Heat Lightning* is burned with the brand of film noir. Like Billy Wilder's *Ace in the Hole*, the harsh light of the desert setting merely adds to its effectiveness, providing a bright light cast on things that are generally best left in the dark. When Olga's old lover George (Preston Foster)—that one man from her past who held her in thrall, physically and emotionally—unwittingly turns up at the station after years apart, her fragile sense of control is put at war with a desire to surrender to his lure. And George is thrilled to find

Olga—not out of love, or nostalgia—but because he is on the lam from a robbery and murder rap, and expects to manipulate her to his advantage.

George is a progenitor of what we now call the *homme fatale*, and the evidence of his psychosexual hold on Olga is apparent whenever they are alone together. The moment she first catches sight of him outside the station is a wordless book; LeRoy has Olga walk directly at his stationary camera until she suddenly recognizes George after many years removed from his abuse and domination. At the moment of realization Olga betrays all her feelings in an instant—hurt, shame, excitement, and desire—it is a textbook example of Aline's method technique in a single shot. When the former lovers eventually find themselves alone, George reaches out to her and Olga physically shrinks from his touch, as if avoiding someone diseased, or leprous. But later, when he roughly admonishes Olga for hiding her beauty, she cannot resist the impulse to surreptitiously caress him. The moment is so subtle that it can easily be missed, as Aline slowly inches her hand up to his shoulder and fingers the cloth of his coat. After years of burying her sexuality, Olga can again see herself—however flawed—as a woman. That night sex, violence, and fear coalesce in a brutally dark finale. Olga's femininity, coaxed into the open, is soon a prisoner to George's magnetism. As a result, Myra is left without her sister's guidance, and is raped by a boy at the local dance. When she returns, traumatized, Myra discovers that Olga has been with George and is furious at her sister's hypocrisy. If Olga had been there to counsel her, Myra unreasons, her virtue could not have been so rudely taken. And Olga accepts the punishment—she believes it is *her* weaknesses that have despoiled Myra.

The denouement of this psychodrama is one of the great sequences of Aline MacMahon's years at Warner Brothers. Finding George breaking into the station's safe, Olga overhears him tell his crony Jeff (Lyle Talbot) that his seduction was designed merely to get her out of the way. Unseen, Olga leaves, then returns with a pistol retrieved from her room and levels it at George. Here, Aline is all interior—quiet and motionless, binding Olga's emotions under steely resolve—but those feelings register plainly nonetheless. It is a moment of strange quiescence, and the precise opposite of what most studio-era actresses (and directors) would do with such a potentially operatic sequence. Now, after years of running from her past, Olga has the opportunity to literally kill it. She shoots George, then allows Jeff to escape ahead of the law. Unexpectedly, her grief is profound—perhaps more for the death of her sexual self than for George. By the time guests show up hunting for the cause of the shots, Olga is numb. With George hidden behind the bar she sends them away. "I just killed a big rat," she says. And when the sheriff arrives the next morning, it is clear that Olga will pay no price for the murder except a psychic one. As she replaces her bandanna and returns to work, there is little doubt that Olga will forever be the haunted woman running from an inescapable past.

The debut of *Heat Lightning* during the spring of 1934 was inopportune. With its illicit sexual relationships and unpunished violence, it helped stoke the long-gestating puritan outrage at film content that would soon result in decades of enforced censorship. On July 1 stricter production guidelines were adopted, and *Heat Lightning* suddenly became part of what is now known as the pre-Code era. It would be more than a decade before postwar ennui and nuclear angst ushered in the bleak worldview and dark characters of film noir that registered positively with the public. For now though, the critics found *Heat Lightning* too coarse, too dour to praise. Not so, however, its star. "Aline MacMahon, whose brilliant character portrayals have brightened many an otherwise commonplace picture, emerges now as a star in 'Heat Lightning,'" the *Brooklyn Daily Eagle* wrote. "Miss MacMahon bears her new honors gracefully, and it is mainly her splendid performance which lifts this offering into a higher class photoplay. She proves once more that she is one of Hollywood's outstanding actresses. Undoubtedly she deserves her new rank of star."[15] Nearly every critic echoed the idea that Aline was the only thing that truly distinguished *Heat Lightning*. "Without one ingredient this would be another so-so film. Thanks to Aline MacMahon it is well worth seeing," one said, while according to another, "Although 'Heat Lightning' fails in many respects to equal the excellence of Aline MacMahon's performance, it manages to be an absorbing drama."[16] Ultimately, it was The *New Movie Magazine* that encapsulated the general drift of public sentiment: "The rest of the cast is satisfactory, but 'Heat Lightning' is Aline MacMahon's picture. She deserves more."[17] In 1934 it may have been seen that way, but modern audiences appreciate this story of repressed sexuality and carnal sin more than their pre-Code counterparts.

While Aline was shooting *Heat Lightning* in the late autumn of 1933, two things of note were happening in New York City. Since the start of the Depression, the ever-weakening housing market had threatened to plunge Clarence's architectural firm into bankruptcy. Now, he was at last on the threshold of securing a major commission from Franklin Roosevelt's Public Works Administration housing program. With New York City working on a plan of slum clearance and rebuilding—an idea Clarence decried because it displaced low-income families and provided them no help with relocation—he had been lobbying instead for a new middle-income community to be built on vacant land above 178th Street in the Bronx. He called it Hillside Homes, and it required every bit of the Herculean will Clarence possessed to realize it. With design then proceeding on a mere $15,000 retainer, it was entirely uncertain that Hillside would be fully funded, and in late 1933 Clarence was waist deep in political wrangling to obtain the capital that would keep his business solvent (not to mention lessening Aline's responsibility as the primary breadwinner in the Stein family). While Clarence worried that the project would fall through, Aline calmed his fears. "Patience, love," she counseled, "the time is near—near—near . . ."[18] When approval at last arrived in late November, Clarence was woken from months of despair about the general downward tilt of American life. Throughout the Depression, he had grown cynical about the erosion of ethics in what he thought of as a once-great society, and the approval of Hillside was an antidote to the general gloom that pervaded his thoughts. "I am as certain as you are," Aline wrote, "this world *is* a good one—people *are* capable of high ideals, and the balance still shows a good profit on the side of the angels." Then, dwelling again on the great friction the Steins felt between their privilege and social inequity, she continued: "Only think what sheltered lives we lead, when we have grown so old without having met cruelty or ruthlessness. I believe it is the daily fare of lots of people. We are pampered, and we daren't be cynical—there's no excuse for it."[19]

Meanwhile, Aline's mother was embarking on a project that went as far back in her memory as she could recall. After William MacMahon died in 1931, Jennie Mac had spent most of her time on the West Coast with Aline, who did not think it a good idea for her mother to be idle when she was still relatively young at fifty-five. "Mother," Aline told her, "you have to learn, to find something to do now. You have to keep busy. What do you want to do?" At this, Jennie Mac returned to the idea that had been in her blood since childhood. "Well, what I want to do, I'm too old to do. I want to be an actress," she said. Aline balked at the idea that age was a roadblock, and when mother and daughter returned to New York in the late summer of 1933, she installed Jennie Mac at the Barbizon-Plaza hotel, just around the corner from the American Academy of Dramatic Arts, where she soon took up studies. Unfortunately, the schooling did not result in a new career for the little girl who played bits on stage before the turn of the century in McKeesport, PA—but with a little help from her friends, she did, momentarily, experience the life of a working actress. "Moss Hart called me up one day," Jennie recalled with fondness. "And he said, 'how's the actress coming along?'" Mr. Hart adored Mrs. MacMahon, and the following year he gave her a small part in his new play with George Kaufman, a kind of American *Cavalcade* called *Merrily We Roll Along*. Lovingly billed as "Jennie Mac," she took 155 bows before the production closed in 1935. When, after the opening, a long article in *Variety* recounted the heartwarming story of Jennie's new career path, Aline was beside herself with joy. "I am so amused, touched and thrilled about her," she said triumphantly. In Hollywood Jennie also appeared in two films directed by her nephew (and Aline's cousin), the director Sylvan Simon. And in 1942, Aline and Jennie Mac were able to appear together on film for the only time, under Simon's direction in the Mary Roberts Rinehart pastiche, *Tish*.

Aline's next production—a domestic drama initially called *Fur Coats*—seemed to indicate that her home studio was still groping to find a formula they could exploit and which would speak to her growing fan base. Since Warner Brothers was then practically a factory operation, it would have been natural for them to assign her to droll comedies again and again, featuring the cynical persona on which audiences had already voiced their approval. But behind the scenes Aline was continually agitating for dramatic roles, and Warners executives knew that her talent was at least on a par with the up-and-coming queen of the lot, Bette Davis. With *Heat Lightning*, and now the newly christened *Side Streets*, the studio would test the waters to see if they could bring in the kind of impactful box office that Davis was gradually gathering.[20]

Side Streets leans heavily on the intersection between drama, melodrama, and soap opera. The script is largely responsible for the soap opera, Alfred Green's direction for the melodrama, and Aline for the legitimate drama. Aline plays Bertha, a spinster (another alternate title was *A Woman in Her Thirties*) who owns a successful fur shop in San Francisco. She meets Tim (Paul Kelly), a rootless cad who sees that he can take advantage of Bertha's lack of experience and quickly wins her over with his superficial charm. In due course they are married, and if there had been a good-looking bridesmaid in the wedding party, Tim probably would have been unfaithful during the ceremony. In short order there is an affair, a baby (Bertha's), a baby's funeral, a second baby (*not* Bertha's), a breakup, a secret adoption, a reconciliation, and an appropriately sudsy conclusion. As expected, the heart of *Side Streets* is Bertha, a woman who sees the world as it often is—ugly and cold—but who cannot resist her own impulses toward decency and compassion. It is a role crafted, if crudely, for Aline, featuring those sad, defeated emotions that she so easily conjured. Many of Aline's finest moments in the film involve

When Warner Brothers elevated Aline to star status in 1934, they momentarily made a serious effort to promote her. Sadly, they never quite found the key to properly exploit her talents. Studio publicity material.

silent sequences—one in which she packs away her dead child's clothes, another where she discovers Tim's infidelities—and these interludes remind us of her ability to wordlessly communicate complex thoughts. Unfortunately these opportunities are limited, and while Aline is excellent in what she does, the material does not challenge her range.

During the shooting of *Side Streets* Aline was typically divided about its prospects for success. In speaking to Albert Warner—the Warner brother in charge of the studio's sales department—she expressed her confidence in the film. "I suggested they hold *Heat Lightning*, as it is not a star builder," she wrote, "and *Side Streets* I hope, is. Albert agreed that *Heat Lightning* is only an average picture. I agree it is no world-beater, but it has a certain character and would do nicely as a follow up to *Side Streets*." Albert Warner listened politely to Aline's suggestion and ignored it. When she later repeated it to Jack Warner, he too ignored it.[21] The Warner Brothers theater chain needed summer product and they had no intention of delaying *Heat Lightning* for any reason. Near the end of production, Aline's attitude toward the film suddenly veered 180 degrees. "I'm bored with Bertha," she said. "I'm not interested in her any longer. The whole end of the picture—what she does [reconciling with a serial cheating husband] and how she plays it are so banal and bathetic! It looks particularly hopeless at the moment—even if I do click, it will be in tripe. I need novel material to put me over."

Unfortunately, *Side Streets* was *not* novel material, and did not put Aline over. On release the box office was a bust, barely making the studio's money back. Perhaps with Kay Francis or Loretta Young in the lead *Side Streets* might have sold more tickets, but the audience for Aline's pictures was a different animal—they wanted either the wry comedienne or the high-class actress in something better than a program melodrama. They were divided against themselves—and Warners. "'Side Streets' is one of those wearying examples of writing down to what the studio believes to be the intelligence of certain cinema audiences," Mordaunt Hall wrote,[22] and most critics agreed. "Aline MacMahon does all possible with her thankless role," one noted, while another made no effort to conceal his disdain: "To Aline MacMahon falls the unpleasant task of bringing sympathy to the cloyingly repellant character of Bertha."[23] *Side Streets* was a reasonably well made diversion, but not much more. As to Aline, she was again her cynical self. "Farewell fond dreams of Shaw and Shakespeare!" she said.[24]

That winter season, Aline was continuing to receive a stream of out of town guests who were constantly coming and going from her Brentwood cottage. Always an energetic, friendly host, she received much pleasure from touring friends through the Warners studio complex, taking them for meals at the famous Brown Derby, to live concerts at the Hollywood Bowl, or indulging the Los Angeles theater scene. In February, she and a friend attended a touring performance of the great Katherine Cornell in Shaw's *Candida*, and in the company was a young actor making his American debut who caught Aline's practiced eye. Even playing against Cornell and Basil Rathbone, Aline immediately recognized his ability. "There was a splendid young actor in the company—Orson Welles. He's touched with genius," she wrote. "He will be another Charles Laughton."[25] Within a few short years Aline will be working within Welles own theater company on the kind of serious literary properties she so craved, but the situation will ultimately prove to be less than satisfactory.

Katherine Cornell was among the finest actresses of the era, and was known for having the kind of wide-ranging, serious career to which Aline aspired. Seeing Cornell set Aline to thinking about acting, and the differences in style that were so obvious to her as the spearhead of the America's movement toward naturalism with the Method. "Katherine Cornell gave a lovely performance," she began. "I liked her so much. She doesn't touch home base the way I do—but there is form in what she does, and visual beauty. I constantly sacrifice the latter—to prove that what I'm doing is *true*—is *life*. But there is another theatre," she continued, "one that gives us dreams of another

"SIDE STREETS" with ALINE MAC MAHON ~ A First National & Vitaphone Picture

At the height of Aline's career as a star at Warner Brothers, the studio struggled to find proper vehicles for her. *Side Streets* (1934), the story of a single woman navigating the consequences of a poor romantic choice did not help her popularity. Studio publicity material.

being—out of time with our 1934 life, but in a beautiful tradition. I wonder if I'll ever set foot on that path? If I should it would be a rare treat—and coming to it through years of truth instead of years of simulated truth might be a treat for the audience too."[26] In spite of numerous offers, Katherine Cornell never allowed herself to be co-opted by Hollywood, appearing in only one film, a personal cameo in *Stage Door Canteen*. One wonders what might have been if Aline had remained on stage in New York, and sought the higher opportunities potentially available to her after successes like *Beyond the Horizon*. Her regular observations about the paucity of quality work available onstage (potentially no different than on film) and her recollections of unwanted periods of unemployment indicate that she preferred to work than be idle, regardless of the work itself. In the end, the point is moot—although Aline made certain to keep at least one foot on the stable ground outside of Hollywood, she had allowed herself to be seduced while Miss Cornell remained chaste.

Aline's social life *outside* her family, visitors, and a few close friends continued to be scarce. She rarely attended premieres, and her close circle consisted largely of remnants of the New York theater scene from which she had sprung and who were now making a living, or attempting to make a living, in Hollywood: Kenneth MacGowan, Mary Boland, and Gregory Ratoff, among others. She was also maintaining a very close friendship with Moss Hart, who came and went from Hollywood in the early 1930s as a script doctor and dialogue man. When George Kaufman accompanied Hart to Los Angeles in February 1934, Aline broke her homebody streak and attended a dinner thrown in Kaufman's honor. "I had a wonderful time—there was such funny conversation," Aline recorded. "Kaufman and Hart feeling apparently their responsibility as leaders of satirical wit. Even Herman Mankiewicz [co-screenwriter of *Dinner at Eight* and *Citizen Kane*] was a wallflower! I suppose it is the fact that I go out about once in three months that made it such a gay evening for me—going out so rarely, people are especially cordial to me."[27]

It appears that the eventual box-office failure of Aline's first two starring features forced a reassessment in the treatment of her image at Warner Brothers. Each had failed to prove a market for the kind of downbeat drama Aline preferred, and the sales department likely touted research confirming that audiences liked their $1,800-a-week star best as the wry comedienne with the heart of gold. "Having elevated Aline MacMahon to leading roles, Warner Brothers seems to be having trouble finding stories for her," the *Daily Mirror* observed. Studio producers also still wanted to recreate the positive chemistry from her teaming with Guy Kibbee in *Gold Diggers of 1933*, something Aline had dodged on *Footlight Parade* and *Havana Widows* out of fear of comedy typecasting. Now, after a grand total of two attempts to create a dramatic star, the studio suddenly remembered that it was also a factory, and that their employee had a built-in persona that audiences appreciated. Whatever good

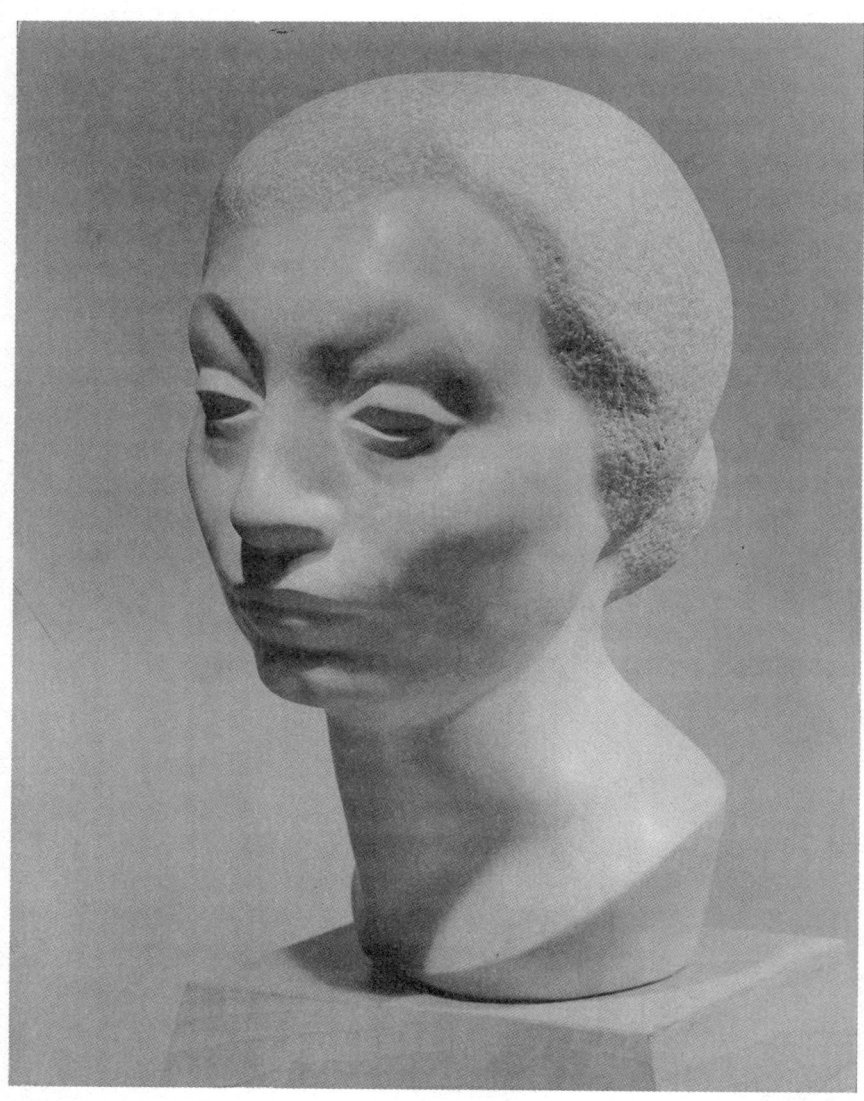

Aline and her husband were associated with a who's-who of early to mid-century artists, including the renowned Japanese sculptor Isamu Noguchi. In need of money during 1937, Noguchi offered to make this bust of Aline in exchange for a $500 loan. *Isamu Noguchi, Aline MacMahon, 1937. 14 3/8 x 10 5/8 in. (36.5 x 21 x 27 cm), Botticino marble. Billy Rose Theatre Collection, The New York Public Library at Lincoln Center. The Noguchi Museum Archives, 01527. Photo: F.S. Lincoln.* ©INFGM / ARS.

will and deference the studio had allotted her previously was now shelved and made no secret. "It is perfectly patent that Warner Brothers are not going to do properties I care for," she recognized. "I must adjust myself to this firm fact and find some peace in myself regardless. I have so many, many blessings—it is shameful to be so complaining."[28] Aline MacMahon would appear in just five more pictures for Warners; all five were slight domestic comedies, and in each her costar was Guy Kibbee.

There was without question chemistry between those two brilliant troupers. Both had extensive stage experience, and each had arrived in Hollywood within months of each other. Kibbee, with his portly frame and bald pate, was often typecast in comedies as a buffoonish lout or ineffectual husband, but could also be sly or calculating, as in Lewis Milestone's *Rain* or Capra's *Lady for a Day*. At Warner Brothers he was among the best loved of their character players, men and women who were so talented and appeared so regularly on America's theater screens that they carved out a loyal audience that sometimes rivaled those of the industry's biggest stars.

Aline's general lack of enthusiasm in teaming with Kibbee was not a reflection on her costar, but rather the weak stories and scripts in which Warner Brothers presented them. In the 1960s Aline thought back on the eleven pictures the pair appeared in together. "Guy was a darling to work with," she said. "All those pictures were great fun, but the parts were repetitive and it was just too dull to keep doing them."[29] For his part, Kibbee likewise held Aline in very high esteem. "I don't know how much I help Aline MacMahon," he was quoted saying in 1934, "but her comedy sense is so perfect that it's a privilege to work with her. In all the years I have known and worked with Aline, I have never seen her play herself in a single scene."[30]

The Merry Frinks, based on a story by Gene Markey, was the first of these frothy team-ups to be extruded from the Warner Brothers assembly line. The story is simple. Hattie (Aline) is the put-upon and unappreciated matriarch of the Frink family, riding herd over a sordid collection of semicomic ne'er-do-wells, cranks, crackpots, boobs, and reprobates. Her husband Joe (Hugh Herbert) is an alcoholic slacker. Her elder son Emmett (Allan Jenkins) is a rabid Communist, while the other is a budding criminal who also wants to be a prizefighter. Meanwhile, her daughter is dangerously infatuated with a sleazy hood (Harold Huber), and even her elderly mother is a mewling, complaining old crone. Compounding this bedlam is the arrival of her long-lost Uncle Newt (Kibbee), an eccentric blowhard who has just arrived, he claims, from Bali. Kibbee is in the film only long enough to provide a few laughs, then conveniently die, leaving Hattie his fortune of nearly a half a million dollars. (Maybe he wasn't such a blowhard, after all.) But Newt—having been horrified by Hattie's treatment at the hands of this sideshow of selfish louts—stipulated that the inheritance will only transfer if she leaves the house and disowns her family. To which Hattie instantaneously and unreservedly agrees.

If this all sounds like a coarsely chopped version of *You Can't Take It With You*, therein lies interesting ground for supposition. Before Frank Capra's film version, *You Can't Take It With You* debuted on Broadway in December of 1936. The play was written by Aline's close friend Moss Hart with George Kaufman, who Aline knew well from the original production of *Once in a Lifetime*. As we know, Kaufman and Hart were in Hollywood at exactly the time that Aline was making *The Merry Frinks*, and may have visited the set with its star. This is not to imply that one of the most successful writing teams in Broadway history plagiarized *The Merry Frinks*—the idea of the eccentric family was not exactly new, even in 1934—but it does make one wonder if it couldn't have been a subconscious springboard for the writers when they were contemplating the project that became *You Can't Take It With You* just two years later.

The last act of *The Merry Frinks*, where Aline abandons her family for wealth, then discovers that the high life is no life for her, is again typical of the theme of class schism at Warner Brothers. When Hattie is momentarily taken in by a dapper confidence man, it is left to the simple, honest family folks to ride to the rescue before she is fleeced of her inheritance. Thus, order is restored; Hattie returns home, and the corrupting power of money is subdued by familial love. We can only assume that the inheritance—which Emmett (now a *disavowed* Communist) has managed to allow Hattie to keep—will be squandered by the family forthwith.

The Merry Frinks reminds us that the Golden Age of Hollywood was often more gilded than gold. With a weak script and flat direction, the film was destined to evaporate from memory shortly after its theatrical cycle had passed. "They don't come any worse than this one," an Indiana theater owner wrote. "If they do, I have not seen it. It is poor from start to finish. Reaching for laughs and not getting them. Should have been sealed in a can and left there."[31] Aline recorded her own divided thoughts, lamenting the defects and appreciating the compensations of the production. "The rushes drive me into deep caverns of depression," she said. "But much that happens on the set amuses and interests me. Hugh Herbert—a very adroit low comedian is a positive challenge to another actor. Quite aside from his skill at snatching comedy parts in a scene, his method is so naturalistic, so delightful, that he illuminated a great deal for me and has given me a new zest for playing the part—tripe though it is," she concluded.[32]

After three years in Hollywood, Aline's attitude concerning her job—outrage and conciliation—had ossified into something like dogma. "I am appalled at the immediate prospect in my career," she wrote during the filming of *The Merry Frinks*. "I am being starred in the most inferior material imaginable, with a campaign in which nothing new or noteworthy will be stressed, and by a company which has caused me real personal anguish and has spent a minimum of money on my exploitation and my vehicles." When Aline met the prolific old-time character actor J.M. Kerrigan during the filming of *The Merry Frinks*, she complained so bitterly about Warner Brothers that Kerrigan was forced to put her predicament into brusque perspective. "To hear actors complain about pictures," he told her, "you'd think that in the theatre they went from one distinguished success to another. I found damn few decent plays to do in the theatre, I remember."[33]

There is no doubt that Aline wished for the kinds of complex roles being provided for Bette Davis or Katharine Hepburn, and was irked that her talent was being squandered on the cheap vehicles assigned her at Warner Brothers. Or perhaps deep down it was the realization of her own ambition that actually hurt the most. "If I catch myself retrogressing in my work I will quit and to the Devil with the whole lot of them," she insisted. "But I suppose I'll go on taking the money, just the same."[34]

Back in New York during her spring hiatus, she peppered studio executives with messages begging to be given better scripts upon her return in June. Then in May, without any personal communication from the studio, Aline spied a blurb in the trade press reporting that her next picture would be yet another class-conscious domestic comedy costarring Guy Kibbee, *Big Hearted Herbert*. The moment she heard the news, Aline shot off an angry telegram to Jack Warner: "Newspapers announce me for 'Big Hearted Herbert.' This is exactly the sort of material which I objected to in my telegrams of April 11 and 18. Is it true that I am cast for it?"[35] There is no doubt that Aline was justified in her pique at the situation. Her role in *Herbert* was another matronly, put-upon wife with little nuance except what she could inject into it. When she returned to Los Angeles and the assignment was confirmed, Aline was so upset that she resolved to end her association with Warner Brothers. But she would find that the severance of her contract would not be so easy to accomplish.

ALINE MACMAHON

The summer of 1934 was an awkward time for Aline to attempt a parting with Warner Brothers. From her very earliest days in Hollywood she had been a darling of the critics, and was now, as the *Chicago Tribune* put it, "at the peak of her career."[36] In December 1933 *New Movie Magazine* had announced her as one of the ten best new stars of the year ("Ahh, what an actress," they said) alongside Katherine Hepburn, Paul Muni, and Dick Powell, and other fan magazines readily agreed. "Aline MacMahon is one actress who has no competition in her own line of parts. Too versatile to be typed, she has a method so distinctive that her brand of comedy has become identified as her own."[37] In June 1934 the *Los Angeles Times* called her one of the three best actresses in the country,[38] and in July she received very special honors from fans in Great Britain: "Aline MacMahon has won a poll conducted by a leading London newspaper, which names her as 'the most versatile character actress on the screen.' In view of the special renown which British character acting has always enjoyed, the result was a notable tribute to the American actress." *Variety* called her out in an article about the industry's trend away from helpless females of the silent era. "That's what people like now—women who are down to earth—an Aline MacMahon, who knows what it's about. She doesn't have to be a beauty. Let her be regular, be natural, and she'd better not be a crybaby. Be herself."[39] Even her nemesis Rufus LeMaire could not fail to place Aline on *his* list of "the ten smartest actresses in Hollywood." "She knows what she wants," he said, "knows how to get what she wants, and knows what to do with what she wanted when she gets it." At the same time, she was receiving prestigious offers from every quarter. MGM wanted her for a two-film-a-year contract. Phil Moeller, who had fired Aline from *Mourning Becomes Electra* at the Theatre Guild, asked when she would be available to return to the stage for him. Paramount wanted her for a loan-out. Charles Hopkins was interested in getting her for a play in the fall of 1934. G.W. Pabst, the superb German director of *Pandora's Box* and *Kameradshaft*, hoped to entice her to Europe as he had to great success with Louise Brooks. And Rufus LeMaire himself—now a fledgling producer—showed interest in two scripts that Aline had commissioned at her own expense, biopics of sharp-shooter Annie Oakley and Puritan-era religious reformer Anne Hutchinson, and also put out feelers for her to travel to London for other projects.[40] But regardless of what Aline thought, Warner Brothers was not stupid—they knew exactly what other studios, producers, film critics, and the public knew—that they had a highly talented and sought after player on their payroll. They had no intention of releasing her—and with Aline's contract renewal at the studio's option, she was stuck—if they paid, she must play.

However, Aline MacMahon was nothing if not persistent. "I put up a good fight to get out of my contract this A.M.," she recorded just days after returning to LA in June. "But I didn't pull it off. I can only hope that they will let me out in October." Just a month later Aline, still angry and growing ever more desperate, made a direct call to studio production manager William Koenig, with a new tactic. Now, she offered to buy out the balance of her contract unless the studio intended to give her better parts. Irked by Aline's perceived ingratitude, Koenig told her that the proposal was "absolutely impossible" and alerted Hal Wallis to the situation. After reading Koenig's memo, Wallis removed his kid gloves and banged out a reply to Koenig. "We will certainly NOT consider releasing Miss MacMahon from her contract," he wrote angrily. "There is no reason for it and there is no reason for her requesting it and, just as soon as we get her next story ready, we will notify her to come to work."[41] When the studio did exactly that, Aline again weighed money versus pique. "I've been on the edge of throwing the whole thing over and letting them sue me," she said. "On the other hand I didn't do it. Why? Because it is too fantastic to get in a fever about an innocuous movie, so negative it can't possibly be *importantly* bad—and they will pay me $13,750 for fifteen days work." Just where Frank Orsatti was during all this is a mystery, but in spite of her long experience, Aline was no match for the weight of the Warner Brothers organization. She would have to shoot *Big Hearted Herbert* and take the money that was both a comfort and a thorn in her side.

Just as Aline began work on *Herbert*, something was taking place that would mark the summer of 1934 as a major turning point in the history of Hollywood's studio system. For months the Catholic Legion of Decency had been agitating against what it considered deep immorality in motion pictures. Films like Aline's own *Heat Lightning*, with its allusions to rape, infidelity, loose sex, and unpunished murder, had pushed the organization to threaten a boycott of the studios if they didn't rein in such excesses. Although a published, semibinding morality code had been in existence for many years, it was often toothless or timid in its censorship. *Heat Lightning* itself had run afoul of the old system, enduring pages of suggested cuts that were largely ignored by the studio.[42] In June, Aline recorded the mood of the industry as the League's threat of a boycott grew in strength. "I was at a dinner party last night, and all the talk there was of religious force in censoring films and a Catholic blacklist. It appears that the studio heads are very concerned about this problem. I think we may be in for a nasty period of censorship and religious intolerance—but of course the pictures brought it on themselves."[43]

Aline's Victorian propriety may have given her some sympathy for the cause of good taste—this was, after all, the woman who felt uncomfortable doing a scene in her combination—but she was much more aware of the necessity of art to have its voice unfettered. "The movie industry is pulling itself to pieces over the censorship situation," she reported. "They took out the 'damn's' from our script [*Herbert*], and we can't say 'Good Lord'—no more 'Lord's'! There's a whole list of contemplated pictures shelved for the time being. Of course it will pass, but there appears to be some fundamental earthquake in the public consciousness that has all the industry well shaken up. At heart they fear a pogrom—being 100% Jewish and being clearly to blame for the sins against morality and taste. I love to see them run, personally, but I fear the power of ignorance as much in a prohibitive aspect as in an active."[44]

Aline was wrong in her assessment that the censorship movement would soon pass. The new film morality—and its power to punish—that was instituted during the summer of 1934 would last more than thirty years, and constitute a drag on development in the American arts for decades. The one saving grace of the new paradigm is that it instantly carved out a unique, vibrant age for film historians to study. Hollywood had just simultaneously abandoned—and created—the pre-Code era.

Big Hearted Herbert—the story of a brash, opinionated, "self-made" husband (Kibbee) and his long-suffering family—came and went without fanfare in Aline's career. Its primary charm is a sequence worthy of the classic domestic comic strips of the era, such as *Blondie* or *Polly and Her Pals*. (Aline, in fact, would have made a superb Maggie from George McManus's marvelous *Bringing Up Father*.) When Herbert meets the ivy-league parents of his daughter's Harvard-educated fiancée for the first time, his inferiority complex is so acute that he insults the young man's family and nearly scuttles the romance. In payback, his wife, Liz (Aline), engineers a turnabout. With Herbert bringing home an important client from his manufacturing business, she and the children turn the house—and themselves—into a tawdry parody of the lower-class life Herbert fears to project. Here, Aline is at her comic best, transitioning from sweet suburban wife to uncouth scrubwoman. With delicious crudeness she teaches her husband a lesson in manners (after slyly alerting her guests to the plan) and asserts her power within the marriage—ultimately somehow, lovingly. At sixty-six minutes *Herbert* is not much more than a long sketch, but it is an amusing one. "This is good natured, if not exactly devastating farce," the *Daily Eagle* said, "and it is fortunate in having the services of two such expert actors as Mr. Kibbee and Miss MacMahon."[45]

When shooting was done Guy Kibbee made certain to corral Aline and let her know how much he appreciated her work in the film. It was the exact kind of old-world courtesy that was certain to make Aline emotional, especially coming from someone she liked as much as Kibbee.

After a series of gains following the relative success of the bank holiday and the launch of Roosevelt's New Deal, the American economy had slipped once again in late 1933 and moved sluggishly during 1934. The rules and regulations of the National Recovery Act often put labor and business at odds in many areas, inciting violent disputes with textile workers that saw the National Guard called out in seven states.[46] A growing perception that the new administration was propping up capitalism instead of the working man made Aline—and other Communist thinkers—wonder if their New Deal honeymoon was over. Soon after reading the report of a swanky, black-tie meeting of the Los Angeles Chamber of Commerce chaired by former Assistant Treasury Secretary Frank Vanderlip, Aline was convinced. "Vanderlip assured them Roosevelt is out to protect Capital," she told Clarence. "I think Roosevelt will go down in history as the greatest enemy to progress America has had. Just when it might all have gone to pieces, along he comes with his fancy phrases and—snap!—the little fellows are caught so tight in the trap that they will never get free.[47] I will start working on my Russian—and we will emigrate there one of these days."[48] Aline's idea that Russia would be a model of fairness and comradeship was as ill formed as her idea that other studios—or even a return to the stage—would be better than her treatment at Warner Brothers. Her idealized vision of art *and* politics seems painfully naive in retrospect, but the distance of history reveals infinite examples of people, movements and entire societies caught up in the seductive power of the big picture without regard to its real-world application.

All through early summer, Aline MacMahon (Labor) was thinking of ways to gain leverage over Warner Brothers (Capital). After finishing *Big Hearted Herbert*, she now offered the studio an increased cash buyout payment of $6,000 to be released from her contract. The studio again ignored her overture, this time with a measure of imperious disdain. In July she asked Clarence about her options. "Shall I refuse to play the next picture if they don't let me out? If it is with Kibbee I am convinced they can destroy my career in pictures by co-featuring me as middle aged mothers with Guy Kibbee." She also went as far as to seek counsel from Kibbee himself on the subject. "I asked Guy if he thought I could be disagreeable enough to persuade W.B. to let me out of my contract," she recorded. "He said that Cagney and Allen Jenkins have achieved new records in being disagreeable, with no effect whatsoever!"[49] When nothing else worked, she returned to the ploy that had procured a release from her Shubert theatrical contract a decade earlier: "I told them I cannot sleep at night and I am close to a nervous collapse." This time Warner Brothers didn't even bother to blink. As good of an actress as Aline was, they knew immediately what she had already confided to Clarence: "It's all a fib, of course," she admitted.[50]

As feared, Aline's next assignment was to *again* play the middle-aged wife of Guy Kibbee. According to the *Los Angeles Times*, "Aline MacMahon and Guy Kibbee, experimentally united for 'Big Hearted Herbert,' have impressed the higher-ups. Not only are they to be seen in 'Babbitt,' but yesterday a third joint vehicle was put on the schedule for them."[51] In spite of Warner Brothers' apparent lack of vision concerning Aline's career, the studio might have made something special of *Babbitt*. Sinclair Lewis's immensely successful 1922 novel was already enshrined as one of the finest books of the postwar era, and in 1930 it had helped make Lewis the first American author to win the Nobel Prize in Literature. In the right hands, this story of an ignorant, social-climbing, small town conformist innocently drawn into financial and social disrepute would have been perfectly served with Kibbee as George Babbitt and Aline as his wife, Myra. Unfortunately, Warner Brothers decided that *Babbitt* would likely alienate those small town audiences and reconfigured Lewis's darkly cautionary tale of social pressure and conformist zeal as nothing more than another domestic comedy to be sold to the yokels of the heartland—the exact demographic Lewis was satirizing. After reading the novel and then being shown the screenplay, Aline's disappointment was profound. "I read 'Babbitt,'" she wrote, "and it is a splendid thing—very moving and tragic. Then [producer] Sam Bischoff showed me the script and I had a fit. It is a brutal mischance that has led Warner's to discard the book and keep only the title for this trite semi-farce. It is another Hollywood mistake, but this time a big one."[52]

If Warners had resolved to follow the novel more closely and place a quality director on the project, Aline might have accepted again appearing as Guy Kibbee's matronly spouse. But with all literary nuance removed from the script and her character confined to the beginning and end of the film, she felt it impossible to continue. On August 15, she marched to William Koenig's office and tossed the script for *Babbitt* on his desk, telling the studio manager that she would not play the part. By now Koenig and Hal Wallis were exhausted by Aline's continuing efforts to obtain a release and in no mood to placate her. Wallis immediately dispatched a letter enumerating the kaleidoscopic whirl of legal dangers in store for such insubordination ("we shall hold you responsible for all damages which may accrue to us as a result of your refusal") and urging her to report for work on the August 20.[53] Here again, Aline's resolve was not the equal of her outrage, and she grudgingly capitulated. As in her past opportunities to make a stand, she would only take the ball so far before giving up the game.

The film version of *Babbitt* is a prime example of the downside of the studio system. Well cast and easily adapted to the screen, this wonderful novel was instead bastardized by business pressures. *Babbitt* needed a sensitive hand in both writing and direction, something Warners did not truly have during the early 1930s. At that moment the studio was largely devoted to the kind of muscular, blue-collar storytelling that had garnered them box-office success with gangster films, frothy musicals, cutting social commentary, and tales of modern urban life. As good as their directing stable was, William Wellman, Michael Curtiz, Mervyn LeRoy, and Al Green were generally more suited to sensationalism than subtlety. *Babbitt* was assigned to William Keighley, a man who genuinely admired Lewis's book and desperately wanted to do it well, but who was limited in his abilities and could not slow the headlong rush of the Warners assembly line. "Keighley was heartbroken with the script, and so was I," Aline said. "It was a terrible perversion of the book."[54] With a feckless script and uninspired direction, the film failed to capture Lewis's devastating satire, or its deeply buried sympathy for the invisible cage constructed out of George Babbitt's own ignorance. Aline understood the troubles with the film only too well. "I re-read Babbitt, trying to find some way of bending the character into a semblance of the original Myra Babbitt, but there's no hope or possibility. I feel as if I am cheating Mr. Lewis," she said, optimistically adding, "but he probably has a generous loathing of the movies and never will see the picture anyway."[55] Looking back years later, her disappointment was undimmed. "It was a sad chapter. That was a really sad one."[56]

During the shooting of *Babbitt*, Aline was visited by Warner Brothers casting director Max Arno. He was there to sound out Aline about a new film that would impact her upcoming hiatus period. Her record of the events surrounding their meeting not only spotlights Aline's strained relationship with the studio, but illuminates some of the little-known process of casting during the studio era.

Mr. Arno came over to the Vitagraph studios this morning to persuade me to stay another month and play what he described as an excellent role in a picture Barbara Stanwyck is to star in. I said that I didn't care to play the part—a thwarted nurse, strangely in love with a helpless cripple whose wife (Stanwyck) is having an affair with his brother. I said, "No—you've lost your chance to talk excellent parts to me—as far as I'm concerned there is nothing but the definite time I have off, the moderate money, and the fact that I can get out in a year." Then [Hal] Wallis sent for me—very much hurt—and gave all the easy arguments: he can't help what the New York office does—they can't help what the exhibitors do, etc. So I made it a little stronger for him. "Next year is one long dose of bitter medicine as far as I'm concerned," said I. Now we will see. I may have influenced them not to pick up the option. Poor me—I still hope.[57]

In spite of her fragmented appearance in *Babbitt*, critics again appreciated Aline's contribution to the film. "In less able hands, this wifely role might have easily been caricatured and patronized," *Variety* said on release. "It rings true in every detail." Various other critics described Aline's performance as "gratifying," "keenly accurate," "supremely competent," "fine and finished," and "played with intelligence and discretion." As to the rest of the film, reviews were mixed, at best. "I don't feel this is final or fatal," Aline wrote of *Babbitt*, "but it is such a waste of high hopes and sincere endeavors."

11

ONE WAY PASSAGE

In September 1934 Aline returned to New York for her quarterly hiatus just as two of her *Once in a Lifetime* compatriots—tour company director Robert Sinclair and producer Max Gordon—were riding high on the success of their Broadway stage version of another masterful novel by Sinclair Lewis, *Dodsworth*. The play was anchored by Walter Huston as Samuel Dodsworth and featured a small but pivotal part for Richard Boleslavsky's friend and Method teaching partner, Madame Maria Ouspenskaya. Just a year after the demise of the American Laboratory Theatre in 1930, Ouspenskaya had opened her own acting school in Manhattan and the same financial troubles that Boleslavsky had endured also drove her to take stage work in order to subsidize it.[1] By 1934 she had taught perhaps hundreds of students her version of Stanislavski's system, and it was at last making some modest inroads on the American stage. The most significant development of the era was the establishment of the Group Theatre and teaching school by two of Boleslavsky's students at the Lab, Lee Strasberg and Harold Clurman, and a casting director at New York's prestigious Theatre Guild, Cheryl Crawford. The Group, wanting to distinguish themselves from the Lab, adroitly rebranded Stanislavski's system as "the Method" and mounted their first production, *The House of Connelly*, in September 1931. In the cast was perhaps the next earliest well-known product of the Method after Aline MacMahon, Franchot Tone, and one of its greatest teachers, Stella Adler. Seventy years later, author Mel Gordon wrote that the formation of the Group "influenced and continues to influence the teaching of acting in the international marketplace of the performing arts. It has spawned an army of the innovators."[2] Of course, the Group itself was a conglomeration of innovators spawned largely by what Boleslavsky began in Pleasantville during the spring of 1923. By the time the Group was gaining notice, Aline MacMahon had long since conquered the Broadway stage and made a critical and popular name in motion pictures. America's other Method adherents were only now starting to catch up.

While Aline was in New York, a letter arrived at the Steins' home from Warner Brothers. In tersely worded legalese the correspondence announced the studio would renew Aline's contract option for another year.³ It was a grave disappointment. "Playing sympathetic characters will henceforward probably be Aline MacMahon's sovereign duty," the *Los Angeles Times* reported. "Warner Brothers have taken up the option on her contract, and she is expected back soon from New York, the production in sight being 'While the Patient Slept,' to co-star Guy Kibbee."⁴ ("I see more of you than your husband does," Kibbee told her when she arrived on the set.)⁵ An increased salary of $3,000 a week may have contributed to Aline's strangely calm acceptance of this distressing news—at least until November, when she returned west and stepped through the gates of Warner Brothers' satanic mill once again. "I set off for the studio so gaily today," she began, "and—ugh!—a great blanket of dismal fog envelops me when I get there. My eyes smart, my cheek muscles congeal—I don't like those people. I come away feeling debased, nauseated. I cordially detest them. I will do my job, and adapt Daddy's slogan," she said, paraphrasing his recurring lament: "*Nothing* makes me sick."

Two items buoyed Aline's dour mood as her autumn schedule began. One was Metro-Goldwyn-Mayer's interest in having her test for the plum role of O-Lan in their proposed film of Pearl S. Buck's Pulitzer Prize–winning 1931 novel of Chinese peasants, *The Good Earth*. Aline, an ardent Asiaphile and an admirer of Buck's writing, was thrilled at the idea, but discovered that Warners had already refused MGM the use of Paul Muni to play the lead (which they eventually allowed), and expected that if requested, her loan-out would also be blocked.⁶ Even so, she tasked Frank Orsatti—whom she now referred to as her "so-called agent"—with working out the details of a screen test. Orsatti obliged, and in November, MGM chief Irving Thalberg personally asked Warner Brothers permission to test Aline for the role. Then came the waiting.

Meanwhile, production on *While the Patient Slept* was momentarily stalled, and Aline was delighted to have idle time to receive an important guest in California, her friend Aline Bernstein. Since their early days together at the Neighborhood Playhouse, the pair maintained a close relationship. "Aline [B.] looks lovelier, clearer eyed and fresher spirited than she has looked in five years," she wrote when Bernstein arrived in November. "I am fascinated by her 'problem,'—no wonder everybody wants to be a psychiatrist—no novel can compare with it." The "problem" Aline spoke of was the tempestuous, often hurtful ardor still simmering between Bernstein and author Thomas Wolfe following their breakup in 1930. Between the dissolution of their affair and Wolfe's early death in 1938, Bernstein endured years of abuse, heartache, and anxiety. She was prone to deep mood swings, and her visit to Hollywood was no exception. Aline did her best to keep Bernstein's spirits up—including arranging a reunion of twelve Neighborhood Playhouse alumni then living in and around Los Angeles. However, after just a few days Aline saw through Bernstein's thin veneer of mental health. "She is in the grips of something very big—very terrible, and her sick eyes make you want to cry. I will make it possible for her to have a lovely visit, but watching and listening have convinced me I can do no more."[7]

Now, snapping nastily at the heels of Bernstein's fragile mental health came another tragedy. Bernstein's daughter Edla suddenly lost her young husband in an accident, leaving her with no insurance and no means of support. Bernstein immediately devolved into a deep depression, and Aline feared that it would trigger dire consequences. Simultaneously, Aline also fretted over "little Edla," for whom she felt something like a surrogate mother, although there was only a six-year gap between them. Fearful that Edla would be forced to return to the family home—an often-toxic environment for her—Aline wrote to Clarence with a proposition designed to keep Edla independent. "Please give a little consideration to this idea," she asked. "I would like to set aside $2,500 for Edla—and give her $50 a week for a year out of it. You know I love them [the Bernsteins] more than anyone I know who is not kin. [The opportunity to help Edla] is what having money means to me."[8]

During this period Aline is so concerned about the Bernsteins and their troubles that her psyche appears to have little energy to complain about Warner Brothers. Under other circumstances, her ire at being assigned to again costar with Guy Kibbee would be overflowing, but during the filming of *While the Patient Slept*, she developed a sense of proportion about what we would now call "First World problems." "The work goes well enough," she noted. "Stupid stuff, nice director [Ray Enright], easy picture—the old Warner Brothers set up. But this tragedy makes these little worries very tiny indeed."[9] When Edla soon arrived in Hollywood to reunite with her mother and leave the painful memories of New York behind, Warners executives saw to it that Aline had the day free to greet her guests at the train. "Wasn't that good of them?" she asked, warmly.

The production of *While the Patient Slept* was soon trudging along in assembly-line fashion, and Aline found it tolerable as a distraction. A mere program trifle, *Patient* was meant to be the first in a series of B pictures featuring Aline as nurse Sarah Keate, the amateur sleuth created by mystery author Mignon Eberhart. In 1934 all of Hollywood was trying to duplicate the recent box-office success of MGM's breezy comedy / detective vehicle, *The Thin Man*. On *Patient*, this meant injecting a large dose of humor into the screenplay, and once again repeating the undeniable comic chemistry between Aline and Guy Kibbee. Here, nurse Keate is attending a dying millionaire whose rapacious offspring are gathering like piranha around a bloody carcass. As one might expect from such a hackneyed premise, the rest of the story is as generic and forgettable as a book of railroad timetables. During the bedside vigil, a murder brings Detective Lance O'Leary (Kibbee) to the house. Keate and O'Leary are well acquainted, with the nurse having previously helped the detective solve other cases. During these collaborations the pair have built a not-quite-love / slightly-less-than-hate relationship, which gives them the impetus to playfully spar like a cut-rate Nick and Nora Charles. (When one of the heirs asks the detective, "Are you insane, O'Leary?" Keate looks at him, waiting for a response. "Don't let the question embarrass you," she urges.) It was simple work, and Aline found it great fun on the set with Kibbee, but by now she had given in to a strange apathy. "I have a great resignation at the lousy Warner Brothers stuff I am doing—and another feeling—that I will not fight for anything out here. Later, when I am free will be the time for fighting." A chance meeting at a dinner party late one night in December challenged Aline's apathy, and made her seriously consider a return to the stage. There, Aline had a wide-ranging and very satisfying conversation about the American stage with the great character actor Sir Cedric Hardwick. Riding the euphoria of high-minded theatrical talk, Aline's sense of humor—yes, she had one—made an appearance, and old-world it was, too: "I believe I may want to go back to the stage after all. 'After all what?' After all the terrible pictures I've done," she said.

By now Warner Brothers was displaying a shocking and inexplicable indifference to Aline MacMahon's career. Perhaps it was spite over her recent set-to with management, or just the simple expedience of a factory schedule, but Warners appear to have given up trying to position her as anything other than a middleweight comedienne. Everyone knew that Aline was a special talent, but after just a handful of minor failures they appeared to have lost their taste for the treasure hunt. "Latest rumor is that I start another picture in January called 'Mary Jane's Pa'—and *Guy Kibbee* plays the part," she announced. "In other words, what I desired not to happen is happening! All my pictures this year will be with Guy, and when I go back to the theatre I will be established as a middle-aged actress of homely characters. I suppose there are worse fates," she allowed, "I am very fond of Guy, but the theatre I was aiming for is so far away now. It's as though a golden whip had a thousand unexpected scourges and each new cut reminds me that I will pay and pay and pay for the $75,000 I'll get this year. However," she added, downcast, "I am determined to stick it out."[10]

For Aline, the shooting of *Mary Jane's Pa* was strangely fraught with Freudian incident. The film, a domestic drama with Aline as the abandoned wife of a wandering Guy Kibbee, gave her a strong character to play, but not much more. Once more unchallenged by the simplicity of the work, Aline found herself time and again forgetting lines and unable to recover them. A dedicated self-therapist, Aline attributed it to internal sources. "It's the only way my poor, tortured, unwilling subconscious has to express itself," she posited. "I was delighted to find I still have one court of appeal."[11] She also again succumbed to the deeply ingrained neuroses that appeared to have diminished in recent months. "Today was a day when I thought—what I am doing is all I can do. I have no beauty, no glamour. To be honest and wholesome in a bucolic study of middle class America is my only sphere. There isn't any bubble in me these days—not that kind of frothy bounce—whether it's maturity or ennui, I can't say. I should thank God for being rewarded at $3000 a week for my supreme mediocrity."[12] Today, we would recognize Aline's feelings as a minor case of depression, likely a result of her continuing remove from Clarence, and a feeling of dissatisfaction in her professional life. "I have lost my way," she wrote. "My really sad moments come when I think I don't care. I am shockingly full of self-pity, too . . ." She would, as usual, rebound—but never quite be free of sadness and doubt.

During February 1935 Aline MacMahon could often be seen scouring the second-hand shops of Los Angeles's Chinatown, searching for period-appropriate clothing to wear in front of MGM's cameras for her test as the peasant wife O'Lan in *The Good Earth*. Three months had now passed since Metro's initial interest, and they were at last ready to proceed. "Thursday [February 7] I made the test for 'The Good Earth,'" Aline recorded. "It was a great pleasure—they had *every* facility there. The best cameraman in Hollywood, a Chinese man, Jim [James Wong] Howe, made the test, and I worked with a Chinese actor and child."[13] The day after the test was shot Metro executives called her back for a peek at the footage, which was more than Aline had even hoped for:

> I saw the test and I think it is excellent. I look extraordinarily Chinese, and a peasant—simple, elemental Chinese in the bargain. O'Lan must have been just like that! Everything about it pleased me—mood, voice, diction—the quality of it seemed just right, and above all I am glad to know that in spite of all the dreary tripe I am doing, there *is* an actress there—and some of the things I intended to be and do with myself, I *can be* and *do*! Now, whether they like it—whether it will ever happen, who can say? I made O'Lan as primitive as possible—there is no beauty in it, except the beauty that all natural, true art has. They may be revolted by that plain, broad face—the droopy mouth—the wooden body—but I think it is just right, and I am very glad I took the test, even if nothing comes of it.[14]

Two days later—the day before Aline was scheduled to trek east for three months in New York with Clarence—Irving Thalberg personally called to relay his thoughts about the test. "Thalberg says the test was interesting. He thinks he could do something with me in the role, but he is not entirely convinced and wants me to make another test with different dialogue."[15] Again presented with the choice of career imposing on marriage, Aline quickly graphed her position on a chart relative to the intersection of art and love. She was in no mood for Hollywood's charms. "I'm perfectly willing to make any number of tests," she said, "but I don't intend to stay here to do it." And off she went.

While Aline MacMahon nestled once again into domesticity on Central Park West, her Hollywood career was poised like a weathervane in anticipation of a prevailing wind. All during the spring she dreamed that her highly paid indentured servitude with Warner Brothers was at an end, but each time she awakened to find that the studio was still, for the moment, her master. MGM had maintained an interest in giving her another test for *The Good Earth*, but promised nothing more. Ken MacGowan tentatively offered her the part of the Queen Mother in a film version of *Hamlet*, a pipe dream never to be made at his home studio, RKO.[16] Fox producer Patterson McNutt discussed a filming of *Miss Lulu Bett*, the novel by Zona Gale, which failed to even make preproduction, and read—but did not buy—a screenplay that Aline had commissioned from Agnes Morgan, set during the American Revolution. More interesting still was the idea from a New York broadcaster for Aline to star in a weekly radio program to be produced in Manhattan, an opportunity that would be hard to resist, if only Warners would cancel her contract.[17]

With the release of *Mary Jane's Pa* in April, Warner Brothers found that after some initial success, the teaming of Aline with Guy Kibbee had grown stale with audiences. "Not the best or the worst from this team," one theater owner noted, "but they have ceased to be box office for us. The picture did not pull, nor did it please generally. Aline MacMahon deserves better roles than this," he concluded. Just months earlier *While the Patient Slept* had elicited this: "It will please the less discriminating mystery lovers in cheaper class neighborhood houses. It will prove a minus quantity in better class districts. Isn't the public becoming a wee bit soured on seeing these same players in every other Warner's film?" Exhibitor's comments on *Babbitt*, in theaters at the same time as *Pa*, also confirmed the waning interest of the public. "Nothing to rave about. No business for us. Nobody had much to say. Just a night's entertainment if there isn't anything else doing."[18]

More than all of Aline's complaints, it was these kinds of comments that gave Warner Brothers reason to reconsider their position on her contract. After she turned down the Warner Brother's offer of a six-month hiatus for her to explore freelance work with other studios rather than outright release, the studio at last granted Aline's wish, releasing her into the uncertain wilds of Hollywood. Her contract, which should have expired in November, was retroactively terminated with the end of shooting on *Mary Jane's Pa*. "Aline MacMahon has decided that 'the far field looks greener,' and to that end she has decided to freelance. Miss MacMahon feels that she may secure more diversified opportunities by general activities in the studios,"[19] the press reported. The severance appears to have been a mutually respectful one, with both Roy Obringer and Jack Warner himself sending regards to Aline after all was done. "It has been extremely pleasant to have had your acquaintance during your association with us," Obringer wrote. "And I sincerely wish you happiness and success in the continuation of your professional career."[20] In response, the freshly released star replied, "Dear Mr. Obringer—thank you for your nice note, and thanks for more than I can express, for your courtesies and understanding of my darker moods this past year."[21] Before she parted, Aline made certain to plant a seed she hoped would bear fruit, politely suggesting that she be considered for a part in Warners' upcoming film of the runaway bestseller of the season, *Anthony Adverse*. In her thank you note to Jack Warner, she cheekily asked, "Won't you please instruct your publicity department to send out the following announcement: 'Warner Brothers pictures and Aline MacMahon have mutually agreed to a cancellation of contract. Miss MacMahon wants the freedom and wider choice of material which comes by freelancing. The separation is a friendly one and there is an excellent chance that Miss MacMahon will play 'Faith' in WB's production of 'Anthony Adverse' next season."[22] Jack Warner not only ignored this request, but when time came for casting, Max Arno instantaneously forgot that Aline had ever even worked at Warner Brothers. He instead hired newcomer Gale Sondergaard for the role, and in her film debut Sondergaard won the inaugural Academy Award for Best Supporting Actress, beating out Madame Maria Ouspenskaya in *Dodsworth*. When she heard the news, Aline was conciliatory. "She's a good choice for it. But it hurts to miss out on a role I want to play."[23]

Although Aline's decision to leave Warner Brothers would not exactly pan out as she hoped, it was only but for the studio to produce a press release confirming that it was a sound choice. Just weeks after Aline's severance, Warner Brothers announced that they would now pair Guy Kibbee with Zasu Pitts in another low-budget, class-conscious domestic comedy, *Going Highbrow*. It is almost certain that Aline's next assignment would have been (and quite possibly *was*, before she broke her contract) to *Highbrow*, and it proved that the studio's producers were now only comfortable casting her as a low-brow comedienne. For Aline, this was a final confirmation of the righteousness of her decision to leave the studio.

Happy to be away from the repetitive farces of which she had tired, Aline told a reporter, "I want to play worthwhile properties. I want to do the sorts of things as a woman that George Arliss has done as a man. For instance, Florence Nightingale, or Candida, or a story of a woman political leader—parts that are distinctive and definite and clear-cut."[24] Of the man who had become her dominant romantic partner on screen—a man with whom she never shared a kiss, or a true moment of passion—Aline had only this to say about Guy Kibbee: "I'm sorry our pictures together weren't better."

In the end, the failure of Warner Brothers to find worthwhile properties for Aline MacMahon was perhaps more a lack of imagination than a lack of will. With the possible exception of Bette Davis, nearly everyone in their stable endured the indiscriminate cudgel of typecasting. With each Cagney gangster film, Flynn adventure story, or Guy Kibbee hayseed, the Warner brothers again reminded us that they ran a factory. When a successful product was synthesized, it would be marketed again and again until the public stopped purchasing it. Once used up, it would generally be discarded. To be fair, even from the distance of history it is not entirely obvious what Warner Brothers could have done with Aline. Audiences appeared to have wanted her most as the salty comedienne in high-quality productions such as *Once in a Lifetime* or *Gold Diggers of 1933*. But those vehicles are like uranium ore—exceedingly difficult to locate and time consuming to refine. If Aline MacMahon had only wanted to be a comedienne, she could have had the career of Marie Dressler, Zasu Pitts, and Faye Bainter rolled into one. But instead she wanted to be Arliss, and her perceived lack of sex appeal kept the studio from using her in the kinds of drama in which Davis, Joan Crawford, or Norma Shearer had so often succeeded. Aline's commitment to "important" drama would vex her employers and keep her in a state of perpetual disappointment for years to come.

In May 1935 Aline returned to Los Angeles with many possibilities, but no concrete projects on the horizon. Fortunately, she found the dubious unknown far more invigorating than familiar security; despite her recent frustrations, she was still deadly focused on claiming the opportunities that she felt were denied her at Warner Brothers. "I am so happy to be arriving to a future of 'I know not what' instead of a future of 'I don't know what!!'" she said.[25] "My Dream Department was practically gutted in the Warner experience, but those old dreams are re-commencing.[26] I am reading, thinking, dreaming, growing brown, sleeping well, gathering up my forces. I have about 60 minutes of despair each day—but hope to cut that to 30 soon..."[27]

By early June Aline's despair had actually grown rather than ebbed. The ink wasn't even dry on her severance check from Warner Brothers when the *Los Angeles Times* included her on their list of "fading stars," along with Leslie Howard, Dolores Del Rio, and Ruth Chatterton. The same month a different *Times* columnist said that the fate of her career was "trembling on the brink,"[28] and perhaps it was. Weeks earlier Aline had refused a part opposite Joan Crawford in W.S. Van Dyke's *I Live My Life*, and no other offers had yet appeared to fill the vacuum. Her reasons for rejecting *I Live My Life* were uncontestable; the script, written by the usually reliable Joseph Mankiewicz (*All About Eve*), was absurd nonsense about an insipid socialite (Crawford) falling in love with uber-dull archaeologist Brian Aherne. Aline had no regrets about passing on the role ("it is pretty silly stuff," was her polite read), but when MGM called to say they had fired her replacement and proceeded to raise Aline's salary offer to $5,000 a week, she accepted. "It seems most prodigal to defy one's luck to such an absurd point. You get a terribly sinking feeling when day after day no offers come through."[29]

At MGM Aline quickly discovered that all Hollywood studios were not created equal. From the start of the production, she spent days and days idle while collecting her largest salary yet for a part so meaningless that it could be neatly excised from the story and not even leave a shadow behind.[30] Then, the day before she was to shoot her first scene, a large box of white flowers was unexpectedly delivered to her dressing room. "They were from Joan Crawford," Aline wrote, "with a very gracious note of admiration and pleasure that she is to play with me. I called on her to thank her, and she said that they are going to take all her scenes over again (after she's already shot for two weeks) because she didn't like the cameraman we had." Born and bred at a studio that recycled bent nails from deconstructed sets, Aline was astonished by MGM's willingness to bend to the will of the artist: "This never happened at Warners!" she exclaimed.[31]

But Crawford's retakes did not help. *I Live My Life* is like a high school production of *The Man Who Came to Dinner:* ill advised, painful to watch, and highly embarrassing in retrospect. As Betty Collins, Aline does, however, contribute the only scene to arouse any pleasure. Sick with the flu, and forced for no apparent reason to travel to a mansion in the country, Betty teeters dangerously with illness ("I'd like to be left alone with a hot water bottle for about three weeks," she says), then passes out on a divan in the sitting room. What Aline does while Betty is asleep is—sincerely—more interesting than the performance of every other actor in the film.

Just as *I Live My Life* was preparing to wrap, Aline received the devastating news from New York that Aline Bernstein had attempted suicide by taking an overdose of sleeping pills. Although Bernstein's turbulent romantic liaison with Thomas Wolfe had largely expired, the two were still engaged in a charged and dangerous coda to their relationship. The incident followed by less than two weeks an aborted suicide attempt on July 12 at the office of Scribner's & Sons publishing house. This second and far more serious occasion remained largely unknown in the microscopically examined history of the couple until 1998, when details were uncovered through examination of Clarence's correspondence for a book on his career. "Aline [B] has done it at last," he wrote. "She took an overdose of her sleeping medicine and there seemed very little hope for her, but she has come out of her coma."[32] Both Aline and Clarence were profoundly disturbed by the event, being particularly worried about Bernstein's daughter, Edla, enduring another trauma so soon after having lost her husband. Immediately Aline circled the wagons to protect Bernstein's privacy and reputation. Just days after the attempt, Lee Simonson, a theatrical production designer within close orbit of the Stein / Bernstein NYC circle, coincidentally arrived in Hollywood looking for work.

"I have told Lee that she [Aline B.] has pneumonia," Aline counseled Clarence. "I have told others the same thing. We should all be extra careful to say pneumonia. We must think about Aline's recovery and how she will feel about what she has done. It seems to me it should be a secret between the family and us—and nobody else. Don't you agree?" He did, and the Steins took Bernstein's secret into their graves.

In August 1935 Aline returned to New York. At that time, the strain of Clarence's work and his periodic separations from Aline were particularly wearing on him, and he was beset by increasingly frequent bouts of manic depression. Throughout his life Clarence had regularly exhibited signs of nervous tension and anxiety. In 1900, just before entering college, he had endured a mental collapse serious enough for him to take months recuperating at a friend's farm in Florida. Now, his fragile mental and physical health was taxed in commuting between Washington, DC as a member of a national planning commission, and Wichita, Kansas, where he was developing their new Art Institute. Simultaneously, he was also planning and overseeing construction of the Hillside Homes apartment complex in Queens, NY.[33] By September, Clarence was in a manic phase ("I don't know when I have been so full of energy all through the day. It's grand!"), but as these projects drew to a conclusion, he soon endured the loss of five separate commissions, including designs for the new Pasadena Art Museum, despite the considerable energies Aline had expended lobbying board members on his behalf. And although Aline continued to express her sincere love and admiration in every letter that passed between them ("I am on the porch, looking out over the emerald valley and wishing—wishing—you were here. How can I be happy with you so far away? I love you and you love me—ergo, I am happy"), it was scarcely enough to assuage his ongoing battle with loneliness. A dangerous darkness was soon approaching.

Throughout their lives, the Steins carried on an ardent love affair with New York City. Manhattan held everything that made living meaningful to them: museums, theater, architecture, concerts, restaurants—everything except, perhaps, the genuine untamed vastness of nature. To fill this final need, that July the Steins purchased a small, run-down summerhouse on thirty-one acres in Yorktown, Westchester County, thirty-five miles north of Manhattan. It would be their retreat from the world of subways and traffic for decades to come. Just weeks after closing the deal, Aline cheekily sent Clarence her hand-drawn blueprints for design, renovation, and expansion of the tiny, four-room cabin, momentarily forgetting that she was married to one of the nation's most prominent architects. The house and its forest environs would soon become known as *A Thousand Years*, an allusion to the book Aline was then reading, Murasaki Shikibu's millennium-old Japanese novel, *Tales of the Genji*. It was also an ongoing reminder of the phrase the Steins invoked to put their perceived travails in proper perspective: "We must look upon our troubles in the light of a thousand years," they would remind each other. *A Thousand Years* soon became an oasis for the Steins—it was a retreat, a creative haven, and a gathering place for artists, thinkers, and family alike, and would stay in their hands for more than three decades.

At this time Aline was still gravely disappointed with film work recently offered, and in her failure to interest producers in scripts that she had personally commissioned. Among these unfulfilled projects were *Revolution 1776*, passed on by Daryl Zanuck; *Nurses on Horseback*, refused by Paramount; *Spinster of This Parish*, uninteresting to producer Patterson McNutt; and—for the moment—*Kind Lady*, to which her friend Kenneth MacGowan said "no." Meantime, Moss Hart was thinking of casting Aline as the Queen in his upcoming musical hit *Jubilee*, but the part was instead given to Mary Boland. And after speaking to director John Stahl, Aline opted out of the role of Nancy Ashford in his 1935 version of *Magnificent Obsession*, even though Universal was willing to match her exorbitant MGM salary. "The picture is emotional bilge," she said. "All about a blind woman and a rich wastrel—oh my God, what stuff!" Last, she craved a part in Sean O'Casey's *The Plough and the Stars*, to be directed by John Ford at RKO. Luckily, Aline was passed over for the part—if she couldn't take the brusque direction of Mike Curtiz or Archie Mayo, it is certain that she would have *hated* Ford, who drank heavily during the production and treated *Plough's* star Barbara Stanwyck as if she were a mule. The battle of wills would almost certainly have been far more exciting that the finished film.

Little by little, these disappointments were continuing to erode Aline's mercurial confidence. During her rise on the New York stage and her early years in Hollywood, the mounting acclaim and opportunity to prove herself as an artist intoxicated her. But as the work provided fell well below the threshold needed to challenge her, despair again set in and took up residence. "Once I had such resources," she lamented. "Such a rich promise of virtuosity—but it is gone—buried under an avalanche of sincerity. The doom of simplicity is on me. I am earth bound. I tell myself that it is because of the past year of fatally dismal roles. I hope it will be born again—the imaginative creation—but from the very core of me I have nothing to say in my work or to people. Something got broken this last year. I am dead."³⁴ Here, one might think back to Aline's contentious relationship with her aunt Sophie, who reveled in conquering a nearly unreachable ideal, and often alienated her niece by insisting that she do the same. Through her gray haze of disappointment, Aline could just *barely* see that throughout her career she had done exactly the same as Sophie, and it was this striving which kept her creative spirit alive. "If I had a tangible goal," she concluded with a glimmer of recognition, "I might survive to reach it, but I have got off the track where I was going—of what I was meant to be—and I'm terrified I can't get back on the main line."

Fortunately, while working on *I Live My Life*, MGM had offered Aline the role of Aunt Lily in their production of Eugene O'Neill's story of turn-of-the-century America, *Ah, Wilderness!* The opportunity for a good part in a quality project—as well as her affection for both Mr. O'Neill and his writing—helped reinvigorate the spirit that she had found waning in recent months. "It is the best chance I've had in over a year," she said, at last enthusiastic for something. In September she left New York for the West Coast, reporting to MGM just as rumors boiled as to the identity of the actress who would play O-Lan in *The Good Earth*. Although Aline was not yet out of the running, Irving Thalberg was testing everyone in sight, and smart money was now riding on Francine Larrimore, who had originated the role of Roxie Hart in the Broadway production of *Chicago*. Even long-odds bettors were not staking money on Luise Rainer, unhappily toiling on *The Great Zeigfeld* just a few sound stages away.

The production of *Ah, Wilderness!* proceeded with the kind of genteel charm that the story itself possesses, wherein simple family problems result in complex lessons learned. It was Aline's first time in front of director Clarence Brown's camera, and she was enthusiastic. "The first day of so-called work. All pleasant—Mr. Brown is very nice, so quiet and sure. It's nice material, and I'm delighted."³⁵ Likewise, being outfitted in period costume appeared to please whatever remnant of a little girl was still residing within her—if indeed there had ever really been one. "Wait till you see me in my 1906 motoring costume!" she told Clarence. "I look like I belong at the Vanderbilt Cup Races!"³⁶ She was tickled when the MGM crew regularly praised her work ("Mm! I love it! It's a great satisfaction"), and found nourishing warmth in her costars. "Did I write you how sweet Lionel Barrymore is? He is terribly crippled—arthritis, I think—but he is so gentle and thoughtful, and nothing star-ry about him. He's *very* good as the father, too." Of another she said: "Spring Byington is also *very* good in the picture. I'm glad for her—she's one of the nicest people I've met here." There *was* one cast member, however, on whom she was divided. "Wallace Beery is *not* so unselfish," she recorded. "He's very much the star—very adroit in getting the best camera spot. And his idea of fun is to set off firecrackers under people who are asleep. He's a very resourceful actor, however, and I enjoy watching him take the stage—and *preventing* him!"[37]

Ah, Wilderness! was a success for MGM, buoyed by its cast, and the understanding direction of Clarence Brown. But the focus shined most on Beery's brash performance as Aline's drunken beau, Nat. Aline's scenes with Beery are nice, but Aunt Lily was so nearly a caricature of the thwarted lovers she had played before that critics scarcely mentioned her. Upon release Aline found the film a charming one, but watching Aunt Lily stirred up an emotional hornet's nest. Even though the MGM family praised her, she could not truly accept anything less than internal approbation. "I'm profoundly discouraged," she complained. "There's nothing about me that is alive or attractive. How I dislike myself in it. It may have something to do with the character I played—again the wistful, the thwarted, the pathetic creature. Perhaps I am unwilling to face the actress I am. I think I've made a mistake working for truth all these years. I may not be enough of a virtuoso at the core to be truthful. Before movies actresses had troubles, but not the struggle of acquiescing to one's proven limitations. When will I be mature enough to accept myself?"[38] "Never," perhaps, was the answer with which Aline wished to punish herself.

After these two films, the powers at MGM decided they liked Aline, and those feelings were warmly returned. "They are dears," she found. "Quite the nicest people I've worked for."[39] Only days into shooting Ah, Wilderness!, producer Lucien Hubbard called her to his office to discuss another project with the studio. He wanted Aline for the lead in Kind Lady, a suspense story by Hugh Walpole about a wealthy spinster who is held hostage in her home by a group of con artists. Although Aline had attempted to interest others in the property (there is some question as to whether she owned the rights herself), when time came to commit to the project, she was suddenly lukewarm. "If it weren't for the big salary, I wouldn't even consider 'Kind Lady,'" she admitted. "But it is for Lucien Hubbard, and he's an exceptionally nice fellow. I went in to see him—to let him convince me—and the first thing I knew I had said 'I will do my best.' 'That's plenty enough for me,' said he."[40] And it was done. Unfortunately, Kind Lady would be her last project with MGM for some time.

Of Aline's other opportunities gestating out in the wailing limbo of development hell, *Anthony Adverse* was still uncast, and Francine Larrimore had

After leaving Warner Brothers, MGM starred Aline in *Kind Lady* (1935), as a trusting middle-aged spinster taken advantage of by Basil Rathbone and a group of loathsome criminals. Studio publicity material.

signed a contract to star in *The Good Earth*, which would eventually amount to nothing more than lucrative step-aside money for her. Meanwhile, after RKO's refusal to proceed, Aline's friend Ken MacGowan had been peddling his production of *Hamlet*—for which he wanted Aline to play Gertrude—all around Hollywood. In October Mr. MacGowan was forced to report to her that it was not to be. "I can't get 20th Century Fox to do 'Hamlet,'" he told her. "Zanuck said 'Hamlet' on a billboard is like an advertisement for smallpox." And so it went.

Now in the third year of Franklin Roosevelt's presidency, the country was sitting on an economic plateau somewhere above fear, but well below recovery. As a result of the great dust storms of 1933, '34, and '35, migrants were on the move west to California, and the hunger of millions of Americans was still an overriding concern of liberals and Communists—and the Steins. Upton Sinclair, the Socialist writer of *The Jungle*, had made an unsuccessful run for California Governor as a Democrat the previous year, and was agitating for equality through his End Poverty in California movement. The Hollywood studios considered Sinclair a dangerous liberal and had pressured their employees to vote for his opponent, Frank Merriam. They then set out to sabotage Sinclair's campaign further by creating propaganda films of grubby-looking migrants arriving on the California border. Roosevelt himself had been losing ground in Communist circles for some time, and only Stalin's entreaty for his followers to align with liberal democratic governments as a bulwark against the rise of fascism in Germany and Italy kept the far left in orbit around him.

In October, Sinclair Lewis's antifascist novel about a totalitarian takeover of the United States, *It Can't Happen Here*, was released. A fan of his other novels, including *Babbitt* (which Warner Brothers had so denatured), Aline immediately devoured it, and perhaps did not see the perfectly similar totalitarian danger in Communism as she did in fascism. Prior to its release MGM had secured the film rights and Aline quickly lobbied for the role of Lorinda Pike, the activist firebrand who loves the book's "hero" Doremus Jessup. It worked. "Lucien Hubbard asked me if I'd like to play in 'It Can't Happen Here'—Sidney Howard is doing the adaptation, which might make it a splendid scenario." Sadly, having been warned about potential financial losses from backlash in the German and Italian markets, Louis B. Mayer scuttled the production, ruining Aline's opportunity, and proving that fascists already held some level of economic control over corporate America's decisions.

This was the political landscape that Aline's social conscience was cautiously navigating during the autumn of 1935. When her friend Marian Thompson arrived from New York, Aline was confronted with a deep sense of urgency about her worldview, and how to resolve it. "Marian is so full of Communist fervor," she wrote. "A light has dawned, and she wishes to work actively for the Party. When she talks I have a feeling of bewilderment. First— it seems incredible that anyone does NOT believe in the necessity of a government for the benefit of all—and then, the question: do I care enough to see it happen to *suffer* for it? It is so logical—quite inevitable—that the future will have to be a Soviet in some form and the time between now and the Golden Day will cost the active revolutionists perhaps even their lives. 'Tis puzzling," she concluded. Here again, Aline demonstrates that she can neither fully commit to a cause, nor remain neutral and accept the brand of cowardice—or worse still, indifference. Aline was so conflicted on this issue that when she was again confronted with a choice, she allowed herself the rare luxury of consulting a higher power. "[Screenwriter] Marian Spitzer called today. She is getting a small group of people to meet once a week and discuss social revolution. Do I care to join them? Well, Clarence—do I?" she asked.[41] Her husband's response was as uncertain as the question. "You ask, do you want to meet with a group of serious pinks? Why not? I have always thought I was going to be a Red, if ever I had time to decide what shade really matched my own point of view. But first I had to find out just what that point of view was. It keeps moving, except during long periods of active work when it goes to sleep. And yet I am always sure that tomorrow or the day after I will join a revolution. So, perhaps you better go and find out if I am going to be making a mistake or whether you are coming along."[42]

Throughout mid-October Aline was annotating her script for *Kind Lady* with notes and observations based on the Method technique she had learned in Pleasantville during 1923. In the film Aline is Mary Herries, a wealthy socialite who lost her lover in the First World War and has largely retreated to a solitary life in her London brownstone. When she encounters a poor war veteran (Basil Rathbone), she perhaps sees something of her old flame and invites him in as a charity case. Mary is momentarily beguiled by his keen observations about her art collection, but too late she realizes that he is merely a confidence man planning to take her paintings, and perhaps her life. Soon, she is held prisoner by Rathbone and a group of reprobates so loathsome that they appear to have been liberated from a local asylum. Although Mary is portrayed and outfitted here as a middle-aged spinster, MGM's costuming and make-up departments have treated Aline with great care. In the early scenes especially, we can see her genuine beauty, and it again reminds us that there was a potential middle ground between sex symbol and matron if someone had cared to exploit it.

Kind Lady began shooting on October 29, under George B. Seitz's direction. With nearly eighty films already under his belt in a twenty-year career, Seitz had still never quite developed beyond a journeyman, and Aline saw it

Aline and Basil Rathbone (seated, left) filming a scene in *Kind Lady*, made following her departure from Warner Brothers. Studio publicity material.

her first day on the set. "The picture will be mediocre regardless of cast," she said. "The director is nice, but he doesn't know anything." Immediately after watching the early rushes, she felt well justified in her opinion. "The picture *can't* be any good. So nice to work for Mr. Hubbard, but Seitz hasn't got it. I see so much in the direction that seems to me mediocre. I must work with better people. I *must*."[43] At this stage of her career, Aline might have tried to leverage her name and experience to perhaps change the course the picture was taking. She did not wield Joan Crawford's power to insist on retakes after two weeks of shooting, but Lucien Hubbard was an undisguised fan, and it appeared that MGM might be grooming her as a new star in their stable. Yet Aline could never break the bounds of propriety, especially among a company that she found especially charming. "My problem is that I cannot push my advantage," she admitted to Clarence. "I could impose some of my convictions on this particular piece, but the very fact of my being able to puts me in the position of being ungenerous if I do. It sounds complicated, but it's all the difference between acting like a star and letting the director do the directing."[44]

Typically for Aline, she underestimated, perhaps not the director, but the MGM production crew as a whole. While *Kind Lady* does betray elements of Seitz' silent-era work—the passive damsel in distress, mounting tension, and a last-minute salvation—it also delivers creeping suspense, odd grotesquerie, and a satisfying climax. (One reviewer reported that her audience broke into "spontaneous and relieved applause" when Aline was rescued at the end of the film.) Unfortunately, Seitz and screenwriter Edward Chodorov (*The World Changes*) missed an opportunity for the ordeal to revive Mary—to return her to the wider world from which she had been divorced for so long. And Mary never quite takes a firm hand in her own salvation, instead playing the typically helpless female character. Chodorov should have known better; even in 1935, women were far removed from Hugh Walpole's Edwardian-era sensibilities. When it was all over, Aline again demonstrated her continuing pattern of despair and conciliation. "Finished the picture today. Some of it is first rate, and I am pleased with myself. I'd like to have a second chance at several scenes. There are a few where I lost the person I was playing and became myself. For such errors it is good to have the theatre—the movies are as final as architecture!"[45]

During the making of *Kind Lady*, letters were flying like buckshot between Los Angeles and New York about a grand adventure that the Steins had been considering for a long time—a trip around the world. Even before Aline and Clarence first met, both considered travel an essential feature of a fulfilled life. But once Hollywood had beguiled Aline, opportunities to visit and experience novel cultures had been sidelined by the couple's respective professional responsibilities. Moreover, 1935 was still the era of the steamship, meaning long ocean voyages that begged travelers of means to stay as long and see as much as possible once their far-flung destination was reached. It would be foolish indeed to take an extended ocean voyage and spend less time on land than on the sea. But now, with Aline fully convinced that *The Good Earth*'s O'Lan was the uncontested property of Francine Larrimore and little new work on the horizon at Clarence's architectural firm, that time at last appeared to be available.

Aline advocated diligently for extended time spent in Japan and China, but in their blizzard of letters, Europe, Mexico, South America, the East Indies, Java and Bali were each discussed, contemplated, and planned. After research that included Chinese and Japanese travel bureaus, discussions with expats, and detailed information from MGM's cameraman George Folsey (who had spent months in China filming second unit material for *The Good*

Earth), the Steins settled on a comprehensive four-month sojourn that circumnavigated the globe. In early December they sailed from New York to England, then on to the Continent, visiting Clarence's colleagues and friends in Europe. From Amsterdam they went by rail to Genoa, where they boarded a Dutch ocean liner to Egypt, passing through the Suez Canal en route to stays in Bali, Java, and Siam (Thailand). The final leg of their trip had them reach China in March for a month-long stay in Peking (Beijing) before returning to America at San Francisco in April.[46] This amazing adventure became an indelible landmark in Aline MacMahon's life, a fulfillment of the wanderlust that was instilled by the simple glass slides that she so admired at Brooklyn's PS 103, two decades earlier. In the timeline of the Steins' life, however, the voyage appears like a discolored stratum scratched across a mountainside, denoting a seismic upheaval of the epoch. Dark forces were marshaling to conspire against them, and changes will soon impact health and career, each never to be quite the same again.

12

THE WORLD CHANGES

In later years, the Steins insisted that the origin of their trip around the world was nothing more than simple pique. "I was all set to play O'Lan in 'The Good Earth,'" Aline told a reporter in 1977. "And then they found Luise Rainer, who they thought was better than I for the part. They took it away from me, gave it to her and my heart was broken. So Clarence said, 'We'll get even with them. We'll *go* to China!'"[1]

Now, although this story was good dinner party conversation, Luise Rainer was—literally—not in the picture when Aline and Clarence booked their tickets and headed east. That autumn, *The Good Earth* was still the supposed property of Francine Larrimore, and Aline herself already knew that MGM's production head Irving Thalberg had reservations about her in the part. Neither Clarence nor Aline had then mentioned the idea of travel based on spite. But, like many recollections, in the years of telling and retelling it eventually became a kind of truth. "The wonder of the trip is beginning to grow," Aline remarked just weeks after returning home. "It will be a legend soon."[2]

Throughout her life travel invigorated Aline MacMahon, but China *entranced* her. This was an era before the country had truly modernized, and when the Steins arrived in Shanghai it was still a buzzing warren of *hutongs*, narrow streets fronting centuries-old courtyard buildings that would soon be largely demolished and lost to history. The couple took such a house at 10 Kon Tai Hutong, and settled in to live among the population rather than remove to hotel life. The culture and its people had a profound effect on Aline, which she poetically expressed in a letter to Jennie Mac, written in the late winter of 1936.

Dearest mother—
We have met China and we are hers. Yesterday was the China of our dreams. We went to Ka-ding, a little town about thirty miles

Aline outside "the little house at the end of a lane" that she and Clarence rented in Shanghai during the spring of 1937. Donated to Cornell University by Aline MacMahon without copyright.

from here and walked from the south gate to the north gate through winding cobbled streets only wide enough for a rickshaw, with the balconies of the tiny houses meeting overhead, and the curling roofs and the window panes of seashell, and the temples and the stone bridges. My God, it was the China of storybooks and our fondest imaginings! At dinner, from the casement windows of our restaurant there was a medieval scene comparable only to Elizabethan England—the mail boat went past on the narrow canal as a conch shell marked its approach, and across the street we could look into the chambers of the opium smokers. Later we saw the keeper of the Temple of Confucius, who is eight feet tall and must be a eunuch, and all around us was the cold spring rain and the willow trees were vaguely yellow, and the bamboo glades just turning the first green, and there were men in straw capes and cartwheel hats sitting motionless on gondolas, while the cormorants watched the water for their prey.[3]

Ever the artist, Aline drank in all the details of Chinese life, watching her neighbors and other locals with the mindful eyes of a student of Stanislavski. At Suzhou she again mused poetically about the sights and sounds of the country. "What a superb day—the dreamy beauty of the old stone gardens and the baby leopard and the fur robes on the line and the little boy with his white bearded teacher at work in the pergola above the lake."[4] In Shanghai, the Steins were lucky to have the hospitality of a group of American expatriates who Aline knew through the film industry and her Neighborhood Playhouse days. The connections resulted in close contact with Chinese life, and at least one other very memorable encounter: "The days here are interesting and social. We met Mei Lanfang [legendary Chinese opera star]—and Charlie Chaplin!! And Paulette Goddard!—on their way to Bali—and at the same tea party we lunched with Lin Yutang, who wrote 'My Country and My People'. All this happened through Mrs. Fritz, who I met years ago at the Lewisohn's."[5]

After a tour of the countryside that ended with a long stay in Peking (Beijing), the Steins finally left China. But in truth, China never left them. "I found the Chinese people to be just folks," Aline said. "Most of the Chinese ladies I met are, in their ideas, what one might call late-Victorian, but even so there is some conflict between oldtime conservative women and progressive ones."[6] It is easy to see why Aline loved China so—they were indeed folks just like her.

The Steins 1937 trip through China was a touchstone of their married life. Aline was entranced by the country, calling it "the China of storybooks—the China of my wildest imaginings." Next to Aline is Lin Yutang, the influential Chinese novelist and philosopher. Donated to Cornell University by Aline MacMahon without copyright.

Aline enjoys a rickshaw ride while living in China. She and Clarence met Charlie Chaplin and Paulette Goddard in Peking, while the world press was scouring the Far East to find them and determine if they had married. (They hadn't.) Donated to Cornell University by Aline MacMahon without copyright.

The World Changes

Disembarking at San Francisco in April 1936, the Steins vowed to return east as soon as possible. ("We must get back to Peking [by 1938]—and, oh! dream of a life—a trip with the Liang's into the interior!") But just two years later China was at war with Japan, and a world war soon followed. After the end of hostilities, the Communists closed China to the West, and the Steins found that, sadly, they could never return. "It was the most beautiful, extraordinary life in China," Aline said in 1977, wistful at the memory. "It has the bluest sky I've ever seen."[7]

By the time the Steins reached San Francisco, the hunt for O'Lan was finally over. Luise Rainer would soon receive an Oscar for her portrayal of the Chinese peasant, the second of two consecutive Best Actress awards she received. But Aline's opportunity to know the land and people of China firsthand was more significant still, and changed her life in ways she appreciated more and more over the years ahead. "That winter in Peking with Clarence became the source of our life, so to speak. We had that for reference," she insisted. "That was bigger than any acting experience or any literary experience or book. Until then, truly, I would rather have played 'The Good Earth' than gone to Peking. But I learned in 1936 that it was better to go to Peking. That was my big discovery—that I truly and truly would rather go to Peking with my husband than play O' Lan in 'The Good Earth'. At the time I didn't know it."[8]

Now back in the States and with no film work lined up, Aline encamped on Central Park West for the summer. When she at last returned to Hollywood in September, Aline had been absent for ten months, a dangerous eternity in the studio era. Movie audiences saw new faces filling the void where she had once been so familiar, and the Orsatti Brothers had nearly forgotten that they ever represented her. While passing through Illinois en route to Los Angeles, Aline observed a landscape still struggling with the effects of the Dust Bowl, and recorded an unintentional metaphor of her own withering career. "This parched land is getting its first rain in weeks—but it is too late for the crops—you never saw such desolate fields. It scares you to see what nature can do to man when the Gods are harsh."[9]

Columbia Pictures had called Aline west for a featured role in *When You're in Love*, starring Cary Grant and a leading American opera star of the moment, Grace Moore. Written and directed by frequent Frank Capra collaborator Robert Riskin, the film is a rather tepid comedy spiced only by a lively cast (also including Thomas Mitchell and Lewis Stone) and islands of sparkling dialogue from Riskin's pen. The scenario is a mélange of only-in-the-land-of-romantic-comedy nonsense about an Australian opera star (Moore).

who has been deported from the United States to Mexico and can only return for a big concert if she marries a US citizen. Aline is the fixer charged with finding an ersatz husband (Grant), who in short order falls in love with Miss Moore, and vice versa—after they first hate each other, of course. *When You're in Love* is built around the now nearly forgotten Moore, a charming but rudimentary performer, except, of course, for her voice.

As a popular diva, Miss Moore felt obliged to act in Hollywood as a diva should, and quickly exercised her star power at the studio. She was boisterously outraged upon discovering that the main hairdresser on the picture was also working with Aline, and not *her* exclusive property. "Cruelty makes me feel sick, so I retreated to my dressing room," Aline calmly reported after the incident. "They can call me there just as well as from the stage."[10] Again, when Miss Moore also halted production to berate Riskin and others over a minor mishap, Aline did not condemn her too harshly—she had seen that kind of behavior often enough during her career. "Our *star* showed her claws this morning," Aline wrote. "Everyone on the set felt so uncomfortable—but the tradition is hallowed by generations of ill-tempered temperamentals. Miss Moore is a *star* of the old school—Victorian legend, *Opera Comique*, Paris and Monte Carlo," she explained. "She is blonde and curving and elaborate and fussy and fearful—all the Geraldine Farrar stuff which seems quaint in 1936. I could be pretty sore if I really set my mind to it, but she puts it over."[11]

In spite of her uneven temperament, Aline found that Moore could also be a gracious coworker. "I am going to [*When You're in Love* co-director] Harry Lachman's house tonight for a party in honor of Grace Moore and her husband. He and Miss Moore came to me together—each was too shy to ask me—and they thought that between them they'd have enough courage! I must have a terrifying shell. Anyway—they were so sweet in their invitation, I couldn't refuse."[12] The next afternoon Aline reported to Clarence on the night's festivities. "I went to the Lachman's—it was a dinner party for *fifty*— Myrna Loy, Gloria Swanson, Mary Pickford, Loretta Young, and Harry Cohn, head of Columbia—and Adolph Zukor, head of Paramount, and others! Loretta asked for you especially—remembers you so well and thinks you are charming." Even at a party overflowing with unique guests, Aline found it particularly hard to engage on a meaningful basis. "I stayed until 12:30 when I suddenly found I had nothing to say to anyone, so I got my coat and went home. I couldn't quite make the effort to be conversational with so many and so famous people whom I had never met. It was kind of them to ask me, but

I really didn't enjoy it. Good food and champagne to drink, but I am too old for the thrill of famous faces, and not ambitious enough to be nice to people for professional purposes. I'm sure I'd have enjoyed any or all of them singly—or in a party of five or six—but fifty!! Whew!"[13]

The very next evening Aline was nestled among a crowd of 7,000 people at one of the earliest large-scale gatherings to denounce the rising influence of Nazism in America. As a liberal, Communist-curious citizen, Aline was there to hear speeches by prominent religious and political figures of the day. "The best thing," she reported, "was the subtle connection made between religious intolerance and the intolerance of the majority for the opinion of the minority. [The chairman of the committee] kept reminding the audience of the freedom of the minority. That's the best liberal education I know. It was a relief to have the matter discussed openly and to feel there is some weight of numbers behind a protest."[14] And although Aline backed Franklin Roosevelt in the November election (while Clarence professed a liking for the Socialist candidate, Norman Thomas), the gravity of Aline's liberal conscience is gradually changing her orbit as the war approaches.

When You're in Love did a grand total of zero for Aline's diminishing career, and Robert Riskin's inability to hold a proper schedule (filming dragged on through December) summarily snuffed out his efforts to become a director. The film did remind a few critics of the work Aline had done before Warners made her Guy Kibbee's long-suffering wife. "I want to give credit to a splendid character actress, Aline MacMahon," one theater exhibitor wrote. "Miss MacMahon was starred in one picture by Vitagraph [actually six] and, without detracting from her ability, she was not successful at the box office. But in every picture in which she has had a supporting role—as in this one— she reaches greatness as a comedienne in her subtle manner of putting over her characters."[15] Beyond that there was silence.

During *When You're in Love*, Aline was looking for another film to fill out her schedule for January. At the same time she was growing worried about Clarence's increasing manic depression, which was reflected in his nearly daily letters. Beginning the summer the Steins returned from China, things had taken a downturn for him. In June 1936 his close friend and creative partner Henry Wright died suddenly at the age of fifty-eight. His commission for Topeka's art museum was scaled down due to money troubles, and no new projects were on the horizon. During the fall Clarence's only work was the design of a house for his sister Gertrude, and a commission for a new movie theater from his brother-in-law, a New York film exhibitor. Simultaneously, he

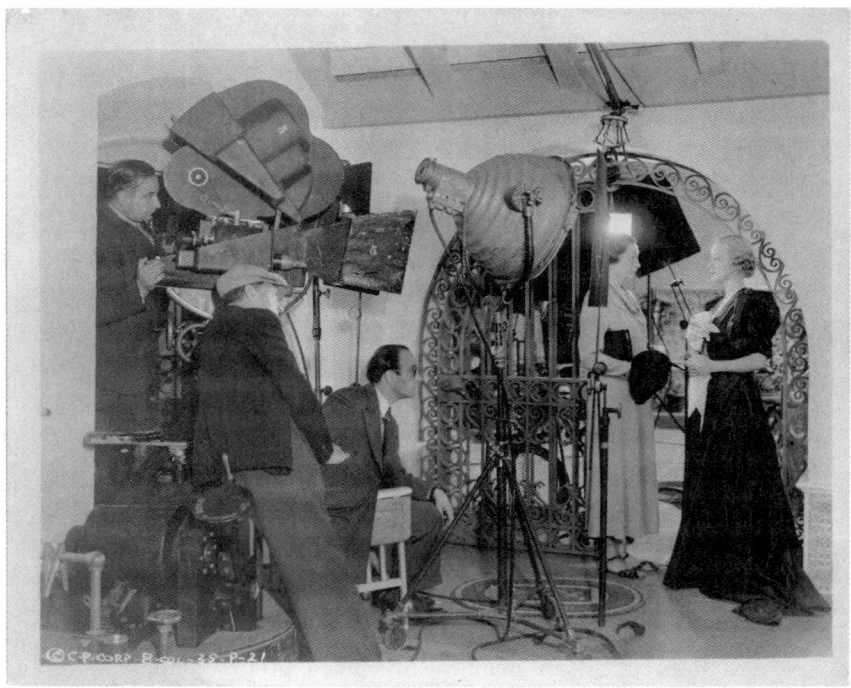

Aline with Grace Moore on the set of *When You're in Love* (1937). Note Aline's flat shoes; at 5'9" she often towered over her female costars. Seated is director Robert Riskin. Studio publicity material.

was attempting to write a book on city planning, which became almost emasculating in its refusal to cooperate. "I have been way, *way* down," Clarence wrote. "This damned book! Why must I inflict it on myself and the world? I am sure I will never be able to write anything that makes sense. There is that, and no jobs, and general blues. Today has been an all alone day, home in my pajamas. If only I had a job."[16]

Aline was entirely sympathetic to Clarence's troubles, even secretly speaking to his friend Benton MacKaye about her fears. When Clarence visited Los Angeles in November, Aline could see a different kind of darkness circling her husband. "You seem so sad," she wrote when he returned east. "And I am too. I weep for you my dearest—it is a horrible mood. I know it all too well. But you will pull yourself out of it. Don't think I take this lightly—I mean weep literally, my poor dearest. The windmills will blow away—they must!"

The World Changes

On New Year's Eve, 1936—exactly six years after she first set out for Hollywood—Aline was taking fittings at Paramount for her next film, *The Years Are So Long*. Simultaneously in New York Clarence was scribbling a letter in strangely unruly handwriting about the possibility of a commission to design the world's first costume museum, being spearheaded by Aline Bernstein and Irene Lewisohn.[17] A few days later, on January 4, Clarence Stein's depression and anxiety finally overcame him. Unable to write, work, or even rouse himself from bed, he turned away from sanity and retreated into the dark place that became known as his "time of troubles."

Clarence Stein was the love of Aline MacMahon's life. Perhaps her only love. In her writings, and in her actions before and after his death in 1975, it is clear that she was utterly devoted to the man that embodied so many of the positive attributes she admired. When she received word from New York that her husband had suffered a complete mental collapse she was frantic. Although there were many people in New York to look after him until she arrived, Aline immediately booked a cross-country flight rather than take the *Chief* home. She called Paramount to inform them that she would be unable to honor her contract, then endured a sleepless, twenty-hour ordeal of droning flight, fear, and deadly imagination.

By the time Aline arrived home, Clarence had been admitted to the Neurological Institute of New York. His mental state was so tenuous that he was obliged to remain almost three months under the daily care of both a neurologist and a psychiatrist. During this time he was subjected to a battery of electroshock/electroconvulsive treatments (EST) that were among the earliest of the technique ever used in the United States. Between the EST—which appears to have been helpful in this case—and his sessions with Dr. Edwin Zabriskie, he eventually recovered well enough to be moved to the Silver Hill Sanitarium in Connecticut for further observation and treatment. During the first month of his stay there, Aline took rooms nearby and looked after her husband's need for continuity and togetherness. There is no doubt that the years of long separation from Aline seriously contributed to the collapse of Clarence's mental health in a way that neither truly anticipated. Clarence's devotion—dating back to the first months they met—was a powerful force in his life. Over the years the gloom of removal from his lover built up in his system like granules of arsenic alongside other stresses and anxieties. Aline's regular visits home offset the poison for a time, and would now also eventually help him heal. "Aline has been here," he wrote to Benton MacKaye, "and we have had a grand time just being together. I have been gradually getting back to things recently." However, when Aline momentarily returned to New York in April, Clarence was nearly inconsolable. That afternoon he scrawled a letter to Aline; instead of recording the date at the top of the page, Clarence scratched the heartbreaking notation "There are no dates here." The letter began, "You are only gone a half hour and I am so homesick for you."[18]

It was now dawning on Aline that in some ways she must handle her husband as if he were a sick young child who desperately needed his mother's reassurance. It was late May before doctors allowed him to be released to her care and resume a light work schedule, but it would be much longer before Aline would feel confident enough to leave him for any significant distance or time. From 1937 to 1940 she would appear in just one film, the dismal B-picture *Back Door to Heaven* (1939), made at nearby Kaufman Studios in Astoria, Queens. Of it, one theater owner said, "It is an exhibitor's taste of what it must be like in Dante's Inferno. In fact, I think that would be more pleasant than having to meet your customers on their exit."[19]

As a result of her sudden remove from Hollywood, Aline had lost a key role in one of the finest films of the 1930s.[20] Faye Bainter was hurriedly called on to replace her in *The Years Are So Long*, which was soon retitled and released to theaters as *Make Way for Tomorrow*, Leo McCarey's sorrowful chamber piece on aging and familial relationships. The gap also marked the end of her fleeting opportunity to be a star, or even an important character actress. "I left the day before I was to start [*Make Way for Tomorrow*]," she remembered, "and it took Clarence nearly a year to get back on his feet. By that time I had a long break in my career, and when I went back I did not come in on the starring level, and I never did again."[21] Although she eventually tried to secure another "home and away" studio contract, the caste of Hollywood had changed dramatically since she left for China. By 1939 the handwriting was on the wall in tall letters. "Orsatti thinks I can get work, but no chance for a contract on my terms. He says the whole game has changed. 'If they can't get the one they want for a part they simply take the next nearest actress to fill the role.' Apparently all the palmy days are passed," she reported.[22] "No one will contract to keep me working if they are restricted in time and between certain dates."[23]

Those four lost years were not entirely unproductive for Aline. Largely tethered to New York for the sake of her husband's health, she now took advantage of the opportunities that broadcasting and the stage still offered her. Between 1937 and 1939 regional theater audiences could see her in, among others, *Away From it All* in Carmel, NY, *Liliom* in Ann Arbor, MI, *The*

The World Changes

Beaux Stratagem in Charleston, SC, and *Candida* at the Berkshire Playhouse, where she had last appeared in 1930. On radio she was heard on Colgate's *House Party* and the *Sealtest Ice Cream Radio Hour*, both produced in Manhattan. Her most obscure and ultimately disappointing project during this lost period is an almost entirely unknown opportunity to work with one of the great figures in interwar American arts, the boy genius Orson Welles.

Aline had first taken notice of Welles in Katherine Cornell's 1934 national tour of *Candida*, and followed his subsequent rise as a director, writer, and actor on the New York stage with great interest. During the summer of 1937 Aline met the young man whose acting she had so admired in California, and found that he admired her in return.

In Aline, Welles immediately saw a great opportunity. Among his favorite plays was the dark, Jacobean revenge tragedy *The Duchess of Malfi*. Described by Welles himself as "one of the great horror plays of all time," *Malfi* features no fewer than seven murders, and contains a difficult lead part for any actress who is not a thorough, classically trained professional. Struck by the idea of staging *Malfi* with Aline as the Duchess, Welles proffered an invitation for her to join his newly formed Mercury Theatre Company. Unfortunately for Aline, *Malfi* was then just an indistinct blur on the horizon of the Mercury schedule, to come after the closing of the company's maiden hit, *The Tragedy of Julius Caesar*, and a proposed production of *Five Kings*, Welles's massive pastiche of all Shakespeare had written of his immortal creation, Falstaff. In September 1937—six months before they could even go into rehearsal—Aline was publicly announced as the lead in *Malfi*, and in the Mercury's following production, *Heartbreak House*.[24] Fortunately, Welles's production of *Caesar* was so successful it ran through May 1938, and the delay convinced Orson to table his production of *Five Kings* in order to mount *The Duchess of Malfi* with Aline MacMahon.

In early March 1938 Aline was researching *Malfi* at the Carpenter Library on the Barnard/Columbia campus when she was corralled by a curious reporter from the university newspaper. "I am very absorbed in working under Orson Welles, who is perhaps the most exciting talent in America at the present time," Aline said. "I'm a little reticent to talk about 'The Duchess of Malfi,' because it isn't yet certain that it will be produced," she continued. "It will have to wait at least for the recordings of 'Julius Caesar' to be made."[25] It was not until mid-March 1938 that Aline was called in for rehearsal and casting. Norman Lloyd, then a Mercury company member, remembered the first run through. "Orson called the rehearsal for midnight; I found myself sitting with eighty or ninety actors, looking at each other and wondering what was going on. There were only eight parts in the show. Orson came on stage from a late dinner and said, 'This is only going to please a few friends and myself,' and called eight of us on the stage to read the play, leaving everyone else who had been told they might be in the 'Duchess of Malfi' sitting in the audience. We read the play, but it didn't go too well; there were five other actors sitting ready to play each part should Orson want to make changes."[26] Among those present and ready to pounce at the opportunity were a young Vincent Price and his wife Edith Barrett. Decades later Price was still stung by what happened at the second rehearsal, scheduled for the following night. "Orson didn't show up!" he said, irritated at the memory. "*He didn't show up.*" Without telling anyone in the company, Welles had simply abandoned his plans for a production of *The Duchess of Malfi* following the first rehearsal. "He just decided that he didn't want to do it, but he didn't tell the actors. He was completely undisciplined."[27]

Orson's impulsiveness left the ad hoc cast of *The Duchess of Malfi* suddenly without work that they had expected. A few, including Price, Lloyd, and George Couloris, were angry and vocal enough that word got around to Welles, who, with imperious pique, explained what they—and by extension, Aline—could expect from him. "Some of you may have thought that as a part of the Mercury theatre, it owes you some obligation," he began. "I want to state, here and now, that I AM the Mercury theatre."[28] *Malfi's* unceremonious cancelation stoked the never-ending questions about both Welles's unpredictability *and* his completion anxiety. Later, hoping to reframe his image as an unreliable collaborator, Welles addressed his abrupt cancelation of *Malfi*. "We didn't have a strong enough company," he insisted. "No matter what people say, that's why we didn't do *Malfi*. I saw they weren't up to it, and I didn't have people for three of the leading parts. They just weren't disciplined, classic actors."[29]

It is safe to assume that Aline was the single solid link among the four leads, since she had strong training and plenty of time to do extensive preparation. And, when time came to begin the Mercury's next production, Bernard Shaw's *Heartbreak House*, Welles reiterated his offer for her to take the female lead as Hesione Hushabye. Unfortunately, irked by what she considered Orson's casual disregard for basic professionalism, and acutely aware of her need to protect Clarence from undue anxiety and stress, Aline turned down *Heartbreak House* and an ongoing relationship with the Mercury Theatre.[30] It is a tragic lost opportunity that Aline did not remain in the Mercury company. As a creative force, the Mercury would have been a perfect fit for Aline, but Welles's volatile nature also assured that her service would not have lasted too long. A month before the scuttling of *The Duchess of Malfi*

Aline had already recorded her feelings about working with such a mercurial collaborator. While in Los Angeles looking for freelance motion picture work and finding only the flimsiest of roles available, she complained: "Far better to let the Mercury trample my feelings in the dust and be where there is some creative life and hope."[31] Aline did, at last, get a chance to work with Welles in 1939, when she appeared in the Mercury Theatre of the Air / Campbell Playhouse radio drama *Counselor at Law*, starring and directed by Orson.[32] She played the lawyer's wise secretary, an unrewarding throwback to the era of *The Mouthpiece* and *Five Star Final*. It seems that Welles and the Mercury offered only the *promise* of creative life and hope.

It was the morning of September 1, 1939, when Aline MacMahon arrived at 20th Century Fox Studios to test for an important role in what would be one of the most honored films of the coming decade. At that exact moment in Europe, however, the dangerous chess pieces that had been marshaling in Germany since the Steins' visit in 1931 were now moving in their first deadly gambit. As she reached the soundstage, Aline heard technicians chattering above an international radio broadcast reporting that Luftwaffe and Panzer divisions of the Third Reich had opened a Blitzkrieg attack across the Polish border. Although it would be more than two years before the first imprint of American boots marked the Continent, World War II was suddenly underway.

The war would consume the world's attention and awaken Aline's social conscience more than ever before, but on this, the first day of a carnage that would last six long years, Aline was also concerned with the work for which she had prepared so diligently.

> Amid Europe's bombs bursting, I took the test for Ma Joad in "The Grapes of Wrath." When I got to the sound stage it seemed impossible that there would *be* a test—everyone was so intent on the radio, and so entirely uninterested in anything else. The cameraman had never read the book—Pa Joad was at least half a foot too short for me, and there was no "Al." I thought—"shall I take off the costume and quietly steal away?" but decided to stand by, and was rewarded. The director turned out to be a youngster I had known and liked from Warners—and as soon as I started to rehearse you never saw such a rapt audience as the camera men and all the crew. We worked all morning and everyone on that set managed to tell me that if I didn't get the part they will never have faith in tests again. The cameraman said "God damn it! That's what I call acting!" Well, we

will see. I met [GOW screenwriter] Nunnally Johnson after lunch—he said it is between Beulah Bondi and me and he is impartial, but is delighted to have two such wonderful possibilities. I'm glad I came to make the test—it was right even if I don't get it.[33]

Although it wasn't long before the Hollywood grapevine revealed that Fox production head (and long-standing MacMahon fan) Darryl Zanuck liked Aline's test "very much," she still heeded the negative voice that regularly colored her enthusiasm during eight years in Hollywood. After hearing that Beulah Bondi was also being considered for the role, but would not be required to make a test, she turned defeatist. "I read in that my doom," she said. "It means that my test has to be a bull's eye, and there is so little chance of a test ever being so."[34] In the months that followed, Aline fretted over the decision, waiting for some word from director John Ford and the studio, but it was not to be. In the end it wasn't Bondi that scuttled Aline's chances, but instead Jane Darwell who received the role, and a well-deserved Oscar for her performance as Ma Joad.

By the time Frank Orsatti relayed the bad news about *The Grapes of Wrath*, Aline was already talking to designer/director Robert Edmond Jones about a return to Broadway after eight years off the boards. The two were acquainted from their work on the 1931 production of *Mourning Becomes Electra*, where director Phil Moeller had released her in rehearsals. Jones was then readying the Broadway debut of Vincent Carroll's *Kindred* and wanted Aline for the female lead opposite Barry Fitzgerald. Set across two generations, *Kindred* follows Mary Griffin (Aline), a young woman whose fiancée suddenly leaves her for another woman and subsequently commits suicide. Years later, Mary encounters her ex-fiancée's son, forcing her to grapple with unwelcome thoughts about what her life might have been. Aline's return to Broadway was reported with great affection in the New York press, but a warm feeling alone is not enough to nourish Broadway audiences. *Kindred* closed after a mere sixteen performances.

Throughout the 1930s, meanwhile, the Group Theatre had continued, with varying degrees of success, to bring the Stanislavski Method to American stages. Richard Boleslavsky, the instigator of everything the Group became, died suddenly in January 1939, at the age of 47. Meanwhile, a handful of its graduates, including Franchot Tone and Lee J. Cobb, followed Aline's lead to modest success in Hollywood, but by 1940 the Group had endured a series of costly failures and internal disputes that would soon destroy the company and scatter its members to the winds. When Stella Adler moved west in 1937, Aline was already fearful of the stability of the Group. "Stella has come today to break into the movies," she lamented. "Oh, Clarence—is that the end of the Group Theatre? Franchot Tone and J. Edward Bromberg, and now Stella?"[35] Aline needn't have worried—Hollywood's indifference to Stella Adler was comprehensive. Over a twelve-year period the great teacher of the Stanislavski Method managed only four minor film credits and soon hied back to New York for good.[36] Only a year later however, one special talent *did* emerge from the Group to electrify the silver screen and bring the Method to national consciousness more than any other; he was a brash, working-class kid from New York named Julius Garfinkle. In 1938 Warner Brothers plucked Julie from the Group, signed him to a seven-year contract, and changed his name to John Garfield, whereupon he quickly became one of the studio's top assets.

Aline MacMahon and John Garfield shared a number of similarities in both career and social conscience. Each had come from great success on the Manhattan stage to sign contracts with Warner Brothers. Both used personal leverage to pry special concessions from the studio (Garfield insisted on time off to return to the stage), and each held similar interests in America's liberal socialism, leading both to endure serious professional consequences when postwar Communist hysteria was at its height. In 1940 Garfield exercised his contract clause to appear on Broadway in the light fantasy *Heavenly Express*, and Aline was cast beside him. In the play, Garfield is the ghost of a beloved hobo who is now the conductor of an invisible passenger train that transports those who have died riding the rails to the pristine afterlife of the Land of Constant Comfort. When he finds that the kindly proprietor and cook at a roadhouse frequented by wandering bindlestiffs (Aline) is soon to die, Garfield resolves to collect her too. As the company toured the play through eastern locales in the spring of 1940, they found that no matter how warm and magical the concept, fantasy is a difficult thing to put across on stage. "I judge our chances of success very slim," Aline declared as they momentarily lit in Columbus, Ohio. "Everything we thought of the play when we read it first is still true. It is very entertaining and unusual, but it isn't an expert job and the wise boys will fall upon it. Actually, it *just isn't* good enough."[37] Her usual defeatist attitude aside, Aline was hoping to find a long-term home on Broadway after her years toiling in Gomorrah. "I'm so glad I've done it. So much fun and such a *great* gang to be with." Even as the only woman among a cast of seventeen men, Aline found the situation not the least bit disconcerting, in spite of the usual male tomfoolery. "I wouldn't trade one day of rehearsal of 'Heavenly Express' for four weeks of picture money," she said.

A fringe benefit of the *Heavenly Express* tour was Aline's opportunity to return to her birthplace for the first time in decades. When the company stopped in Pittsburgh, Aline visited McKeesport, and returned to the family home, still occupied by her Uncle Abe. "The city smells like the Pittsburgh of my childhood, but I really remembered nothing of my birthplace—just the house itself and the back yard and porch—otherwise it is just the usual ugly small American town."[38] Seeing her uncles Abe and Isadore was a genuine treat for Aline, and they passed the day with tales of old McKeesport, her father and grandfather, and of course, the precociousness of young Aline herself.

When *Express* at last reached New York, there was an enormous amount of positive publicity surrounding John Garfield's reemergence on Broadway. For both he and Aline it was seen as a return home, away from the fatuous world of Hollywood. But more importantly, the press barrage signaled a passing of the invisible Method baton from Aline into the hands of John Garfield. When Aline brought the Method to the stage in 1923 and the screen in 1931, there was no cachet—not even a true understanding of what Stanislavski's system meant to the art of film acting. For a decade after her first use of the technique at the Neighborhood Playhouse, Aline was nearly the sole popular proponent of what was then only an esoteric discipline, the pioneer of a new trail that few knew was even being blazed. By the late 1930s, however, John Garfield was the media darling of a well-publicized, ongoing teaching and performing troupe who had also popularized a permanent, new name for Stanislavski's system: the Method. For the moment *he* was now the dominant face of the ongoing revolution in acting.

Even with the spate of positive publicity, the outlook for *Heavenly Express* still appeared grim. Writer Albert Bein could never quite crack the prologue and intro of the play, and the fantasy elements—while entertaining—never resolved into anything more than a series of vignettes. "'Heavenly Express' is no more than the five best plays of what has been a tired season," the *Evening Star* said. "But chances are it is no great shakes as a work of literary art."[39] It is divided into acts exactly like a play, but it is not a play. There is nothing wrong with it except that it is unfathomable, and dares you to fathom it." However, when John Garfield's old friend playwright Clifford Odets attended an early performance he saw something altogether different and inspiring. "As usual the critics are profoundly at fault," he wrote to a friend. "As profoundly as our civilization cripples all mankind. The production is creative in all of its parts, and its impending failure has so depressed and saddened me that I was almost speechless when I went backstage. The cast was having a meeting—the usual sort you have after opening a play with creative merit [but not financial success]. You call a meeting and tell the actors that you can only continue running if everyone will take a pay cut."[40] This is exactly what the producers asked, and what the cast did. *Heavenly Express* still closed after only twenty performances.

Aline's short-lived experience with *Heavenly Express* did result in a pair of modest compensations; one was her friendship with John Garfield, who gave her an entrée to return to Warner Brothers when they both appeared in the proto-noir *Out of the Fog* the following year. The other was an opportunity to participate in something she had been contemplating for a long time—a low-cost, national theatrical co-op to be based in New York.

At the end of *Heavenly Express*, Aline and director Robert Lewis corralled a group of actors to found "a new acting group, starting in the barn theatres this summer."[41] Since her youth, Aline had wanted to replicate the creative and socially aware atmosphere of the Neighborhood Playhouse, with high-quality productions at a modest cost that would encourage a culturally and economically diverse audience. Just a year earlier Congress had defunded the Roosevelt administration's Federal Theatre Project (FTP), claiming it was using citizen's tax dollars to perpetuate supposed radical and Communist ideas such as racial equality. As a result of the abrupt cancelation of federal support, 8,000 actors, writers, designers, and craftsmen were instantly thrown out of work, including Robert Breen, the head of Chicago's chapter of the FTP. Unemployed and wanting to recreate the spirit of what he had done in Chicago, Breen soon traveled to New York to join forces with Aline and Robert Lewis. By August the framework was in place for a nonprofit, all-Equity company charging as little as 50 cents to see productions with performers such as Aline, Jacob Ben-Ami, Flora Robson, and Aline's friend and soon-to-be blacklist mate, Sam Jaffe. With the Old Irving Place Theatre engaged, and a lengthy schedule of plays announced, it seemed as though Aline's dream would be realized.[42] However, even after Actor's Equity agreed to allow their members to work in a co-op capacity, it was profoundly difficult to convince other unions to follow suit. When the stagehands Local 1 remained "unalterably opposed" to the arrangement, the writing had appeared on the proverbial wall, and Aline's idealism took another disheartening reality check.

By early 1941 the war in Europe had been raging for eighteen months, during which Germany ran riot across the continent, capturing Poland, Norway, and France. Although still carefully "neutral," elements of American government were openly preparing a war footing in anticipation of being drawn into the hostilities. As an expert in architectural planning and logistics—and in spite of his reasonably clear Socialist tendencies—the federal government enlisted Clarence as a consultant to the Housing Defense Committee in Washington, DC, a position he enjoyed throughout the war. Meanwhile, in Hollywood Aline was awaiting word of her return to a major studio, big screen part. During Clarence's illness, her only film appearance was in the threadbare *Back Door to Heaven*, shot in New York. With his work and health largely returned to stability, Aline encamped in Hollywood, and in February Warner Brothers called her to test for *Out of the Fog*, to star her *Heavenly Express* costar John Garfield. "There's a good job at the studio for me," Aline told Clarence. "But it's at Warner Brothers, and I raise an eyebrow."[43] Unfortunately, Aline now discovered just how radically things had changed during her absence. Once, she was the studio's go-to choice for high-quality character parts, but now she was forced to wait while Warners also tested Beulah Bondi, Faye Bainter, Margaret Wycherly, and numerous others for the part. After four years away from Hollywood, Aline was desperate to return to the intoxicating validation of appearing in front of the camera, and the absence of Warners' confidence whittled her often-fragile ego even further. Just *how* deeply it was compromised is found in a letter written following Aline's chance encounter with one of the great performers of the twentieth century. "I was invited to dinner last night and Vladimir Horowitz was there. He's the genius of the moment—the pianist who is Toscanini's son-in-law. It touched me to see a man in his full powers as an artist, at the top of the ladder, simple and gorgeous. To be the best among the best—that's what saddens me about my work. It's not only pride—not only Princess Aline—it's being out of the Big Race. Well, it's an old wound, my lacerated soul, but it's nearly healed. I had meant to be so good—how did I lose my way?"[44] In just a few short years Aline's certain—if guarded—belief in her powers as an artist has collapsed into resigned self-pity.

During the studio's indecision about her test on *Out of the Fog*, Aline had taken advantage of the idle time to visit Mexico, where she vacationed and helped scout locations for an ethnographic documentary to be made by her friend Herb Kline. Aline's friendship with Kline is instructive of the political circles in which she was involved just before America's entry into World War II. His film, *The Forgotten Village* (1941), counted a who's-who of leftist political thinkers in its cast and crew. Kline himself, already a well-known liberal documentarian for his films on the Spanish Civil War and the rise of

The World Changes

Nazism, eventually came under the scrutiny of the House Committee on Un-American Activities and was blacklisted during the 1950s, not to return to filmmaking until 1970. John Steinbeck, famous for his support of unions and other liberal causes, wrote the screenplay, while Burgess Meredith—also blacklisted during the HUAC hysteria—narrated. Even the film's composer, Hanns Eisler, was later caught in the HUAC net and forced to leave the United States. Aline's acquaintances with these artists—and her long-lasting devotion to liberal ideals—will lead to the same consequences for her following the war.

Aline's time submerged in a foreign culture was again transformative. The food, the exotic locales, the pace of life, and people of Mexico were of such interest that she again returned to the idea of becoming a film producer. "I've just sent off the scenario I've been cooking up about a series of travel shorts on Mexico, Guatemala, etc." she reported, asking Clarence to forward the scripts to his brother Arthur, a very successful film exhibitor in New York, for comment.[45] "If Arthur thinks it impossible as an idea, I hope he'll not pull his punches," she counseled. Arthur Stein did not pull his punches. "You know without my telling you," her brother-in-law said, "that there is no money to be made in shorts. Not even Disney's, much less travelogues. Pictures of this sort should be financed by the organization for cultural relations with South America. One thing is certain: if you are to do it, you MUST obtain a national distributor *prior* to production. You will not persuade a film studio to distribute it when they have more shorts of their own than they know what to do with."[46] Arthur's punches had the effect of a sparring partner knocking out the champion in preparation for a big fight. The production was summarily canceled.

After weeks of dithering, Warners producer Henry Blanke at last tired of testing actresses for *Out of the Fog*. He declared Aline to be "the absolute best for the part," and proffered a contract.[47] Even though Clarence was now long removed from his breakdown, he was still expressing loneliness and frustration at separation from his wife. At this, Aline rather forcefully explained her own frustrations and desires. "Yes, dear, it is silly for us to be at two ends of the country, but I *need* to work. I'm sorry you are lonely, but dearest, *when I get work, I am going to do it*, so you might as well get used to the idea. Let's just ride with the waves a little—I gave up work easily enough once before—only I've been so idle—and very blue. My stock is *way* down. I don't know if I can get [a significant amount] of work, but if there *is* work here I just *have* to do it."[48]

Aline's role in *Out of the Fog* was minimal, featuring only a handful of scenes as the wife of Thomas Mitchell, a good-hearted man who is forced by circumstances to murder shake-down artist John Garfield. But *Film Daily* had not forgotten her, and was not fooled by the brevity of the part. "Aline MacMahon makes the brief role of the tailor's nagging wife outstanding," they said.[49]

Although there was some talk about other work with Warners during the shooting of *Fog*, nothing materialized. Orsatti made efforts at other studios where Aline mercifully dodged proposed assignments to such crackerjack productions as *The Smiling Ghost*, *Ladies in Retirement*, and *Remember the Day*, before failing to avoid *The Lady is Willing* at Columbia. The film, a tepid farce about Marlene Dietrich engineering a marriage of convenience to Fred MacMurray in order to adopt a baby, was only good for Aline as far as her finances. She played the sassy aide-de-camp to Dietrich, and audiences likely forgot Aline was even in it by the time they passed the concession counter on the way out of the theatre. For someone who was once the darling of critics and audiences, her roles have now returned nearly to those of a novice breaking into the industry, and at a lower rung than she was on in 1931. "When you start again from the bottom, you start from aways down," she said.[50]

Meanwhile, as Aline was making *Out of the Fog* and trolling work at the studios, a group of investors were finalizing plans to create a Garden City–style complex in Los Angeles. Enamored of the emerging Green Belt movement, the group had hired America's premier progressive architect for the project, Clarence Stein. In an incredible stroke of serendipity, the site of this new development—Baldwin Hills—lay less than ten miles from both Aline's home in Brentwood Heights and the house that Jenny Mac was living in just off the Sunset Strip. During summer and fall of 1941 Clarence was able to have extended time with Aline on his visits to inspect the project, and by early December construction was finished. Although history has since narrowed its focus of the day to but one event, on December 7, 1941, other things were happening in America while Japanese aircraft loosed bombs on the US naval base at Pearl Harbor, Hawaii. That day, Baldwin Hills' first residents arrived at their new homes to the drum call of a nation headed to war.

By the time Pearl Harbor thrust America into the Second World War, the Steins had been creeping around the edges of a phantom mobilization effort for many months. In addition to his work in Los Angeles, Clarence was also regularly commuting to both Pittsburgh and Washington, DC for work with the government Housing Commission, while Aline was engaged across a spectrum of causes. In the summer she had worked with the local Red Cross, and was simultaneously supporting British War Relief. That season she also

The World Changes

exhorted Clarence to sponsor at least a pair of refugees from Europe—a long and complicated process that involved financial responsibility for the incoming applicant. "I think we can do it," she wrote, "in fact, we could take a couple. I want to climb down from my ivory tower."[51] The Steins did not bring refugees from Europe, and although Aline probably thought of it as another failure of her will, the entire idea was likely just wishful thinking on her part.[52] "I'm a notorious non-stick-to-it-er," she admitted.[53]

Throughout 1941 Clarence Stein had been extending himself far further than his doctors had advised. His numerous architectural commissions and ongoing work for the government were onerous ("I can't be away now. Ten men working on the job and I have to keep pouring out ideas and decisions to keep them going.")[54] and required a transcontinental travel schedule that taxed his mental and physical health to their limits. In January 1942, Clarence crashed into another deep depression, and Aline immediately flew east, where she remained for three months to oversee his care, again stalling a possible comeback run in Hollywood. This downturn was not as severe as his previous manic episode, and within a few months he was able to return to work. This episode resulted in Clarence being diagnosed with neurasthenia, a nervous condition sometimes known by the revealing moniker "Americanitis" for the modern-era high-pressure stress of urbanization and business competition that are at its roots. The clinical description of the typical neurasthenia sufferer is "an upper-class professional with a sedentary occupation," which could not have been closer to the silhouette of Clarence Stein. And no less an authority than Sigmund Freud also seemed to describe Clarence when he concluded that in neurasthenia "an infrequency of emissions"—a quaint euphemism for a lack of sexual release—contributes to the tension that leads to nervous collapse. With Clarence regularly separated from Aline for as much as six months at a stretch, we must reluctantly conclude that in spite of the good doctor's obsession with sex, Freud may have been onto something in this case.

On returning to California in April 1942 Aline found Hollywood's war effort already proceeding as fast as the German Blitzkrieg and she was itching to be part of it. "All about us people are going off to the War, and training to be welders, air-raid wardens, and plane spotters. I am inquiring about stenography and book keeping tonight," she said. "Here we are in the world's battle, and I need to have a place to make a contribution. It occurs to me I might be more useful as a film cutter, and I'll look into that, too. There is likely to be a shortage if all the young men go off to war." Quickly thinking better of preparing herself for factory work, Aline was soon concentrating on establishing entertainment options for local troops through the American Theatre Wing, an organization that had spearheaded similar efforts during the Great War.[55] "I am harassing the Theatre Wing Committee," she reported in April. "I sent off letters to Mark McClosky and Moss Hart telling them I can raise the first $1000 to start a new project—I care very much about getting theatre into the war communities. Still, I feel it's not enough to do. We are a war machine first, and then a machine to make the war machine—and then there's the problem of how to live and serve the machine that makes the machine."[56]

Ruminating about the ultimate future of fealty to the machine, Aline seemed strangely—naively—hopeful that the outcome of the war could be the institutionalization of her ill-considered idea of American Socialism. "The future will have to be a Soviet in some form. [There will certainly be a government takeover of the banks and real estate] and the first thing you know we will be socialized and the war won—and then we will have a set up to build the cities of the future. Pre-suppose the socialized state and act now!" she advised her husband.[57]

While Aline contemplated the metamorphosis of democracy in America, she hadn't yet given up on the blue-chip capitalism of the beast known as Hollywood. The spring of 1942 found her on a set at Metro filming *Tish*, the first of a proposed series of films featuring characters from the pen of Mary Roberts Rinehart. The director was Sylvan Simon, a rudimentary studio drudge who also happened to be Aline's cousin, made good (well, adequate) in Hollywood. Of the film, the less said the better, as Rinehart's charming, turn-of-the-century stories of small-town eccentric Tish Carberry are chopped into a hash of cheap sitcom situations and mechanical, emotionless melodrama. Aline had long avoided appearing in front of Simon's cameras, having seen her cousin's professional limitations before. "Sylvan showed me his latest picture," she reported to Clarence after seeing 1940's *Keeping Company*. "And it is a STINKAROO! The banality and extreme lack of taste is a little overpowering." Still, there were numerous elements in *Tish* that Aline found too delicious to pass up. The film reunited her with Guy Kibbee, her beloved trouper from the Warners days, and Zasu Pitts, who Aline so respected even before their time together on *Once in a Lifetime*. There was also the opportunity to work with another old-time stalwart, Marjorie Main. ("Such a fun day," she reported. "Marjorie cannot remember all she has to do and say in a scene—and we get so silly and hysterical. She is the worst I've ever worked with, but such a nice scattered soul!")[58] Most of all, it was Aline's

The World Changes

one and only chance to appear on screen with Jenny Mac—hired for a bit part by her nephew—that convinced her to take the plunge. Unfortunately, even the inspired teaming of Aline with Marjorie Main (Tish) and Zasu Pitts was not enough to counterbalance the dismal script and Simon's woeful direction. After seeing the rushes Aline commented, "It's moderately funny in what is called 'zany' style—it may be successful, but it has little taste or subtlety." The only noteworthy incident in the shooting of Tish was a heated argument with the studio about Aline's place in the film's credits. At this, she was mortified. "Corregidor has fallen and I'm still worrying about billing on a picture called *Tish*."[59]

In the summer of 1942, Aline's life was—at least on a personal level—divided against itself. One constant—unhappiness with the quality of her jobs—was at a high water mark, and caused her to consider retirement from films, or at least the release of the Orsatti Brothers from their duties. But Aline also grudgingly knew that her inability to get good parts was mostly of her own making. "You know," Orsatti told her, "the problem is that you go East each time after a picture and when they want to talk to you I have to say that you are in New York." And while she still wanted—and needed—to be with her husband ("I just wish I could be with you and put my arms around you. You are a darling of darlings, and I love you"), Aline MacMahon had also become nearly as much a creature of California as she was a New Yorker. The perfect, if unspoken, solution would have been for Clarence to relocate his architectural firm to Los Angeles, but Aline knew that this was not to be. "I would never want you to live anywhere other than NYC," she told him. "It is your town."[60] Clarence's ability even to visit Aline was limited during the war years, much to their mutual dismay. On Aline's birthday in 1942, she fantasized about the one present she could not have. "I thought you might surprise me for my birthday with a visit," she chided after he failed to appear. "I put two small bottles of Champagne on ice. Perhaps I'll open one little bottle for dinner and drink to you only with a good glass of wine."

Tish was Aline's last serious film work for more than two years. With the war now consuming every waking thought of most Americans, Aline had difficulty justifying what she considered the trivial nature of simply making money in Hollywood. "I want to do something to help the way of events, however modest my contribution is," she said. Fortunately, the seeds she had recently planted were beginning to peek through the soil. Moss Hart was now working in Washington, and had taken up Aline's detailed idea for the American Theatre Wing to put on quick stage shows to be performed at plants and factories doing war production work. With Aline's $1,000 in seed money, a test show was scheduled for June 8 at the Wheeler Brother Shipyards. Hart named it *The Lunch Hour Follies* and wanted Aline to return to New York for its debut. "Is there a chance of you being back in time?" he asked. "I'm not sure, but we'll all report fully because this is your baby." Aline desperately wanted to be there to see the fruits of her handiwork, but at that moment she was cooling her heels at MGM, waiting to start shooting on Herb Kline's feature film debut, *Journey for Margaret*. But once again her inscrutable luck had other plans.

Just as the first try-out of the *Follies* was about to be presented, Clarence Stein again succumbed to the weight and stress of his workload, and this breakdown proved much worse that it had been in January. For all of Aline's regular and loving warnings about his health, her husband had overtaxed himself. "I took on too much of a job and went at it too vigorously," Clarence admitted, "and it got ahold of me psychologically." He soon returned to the Silver Hill sanitarium and at the urging of his doctors later removed to a hospital retreat in Arizona.[61] And although he occasionally returned for short visits to *A Thousand Years* or on Central Park West, it would require almost a year for his full recovery.

When Clarence relapsed in June 1942, Aline abandoned her opportunity on *Journey for Margaret* to return to New York. As when she missed out on the Broadway debut of *Once in a Lifetime*, this sad circumstance inadvertently provided rewarding opportunities in compensation. Being largely moored to New York meant that she could now work full time finalizing and overseeing her long-lasting contribution to the war effort, *The Lunch Hour Follies*. While Clarence rested in the hospital, Moss Hart took Aline to visit the Labor Department of the War Production Board in Washington, where she discovered some of the problems of the factory executives and workers. She and Hart were able to convince the Labor Department to provide $10,000 in funding, and Aline was installed as chairman of the Planning Committee. The pair immediately began pulling strings connected to well-known people, and soon George Kaufman, Kurt Weill, Maxwell Anderson, Robert Rossen, and many others were working pro bono on comedy sketches, blackouts, and music for the shows. "'The Follies' is more than just entertainment. We developed a rounded program," Aline explained to the press. "We aren't just sending out vaudeville units. We get over a message to the men. We produce sketches that have meaning and value in speeding production and boosting morale. The plant executives discuss whatever it is that might be a problem and we build a sketch around it. It goes over a good deal more than any amount of lectures!"[62] *The Follies* were soon performing up and down the East Coast, from Massachusetts and New York to Baltimore and Norfolk, and Aline was at last in the heart of America's home front war effort.

As the *Follies* were gaining momentum in the autumn of 1942, Aline was rehearsing for another return to Broadway, an opportunity that would have been unavailable if she had stayed in Hollywood. *The Eve of St. Mark* would be—for a time—Aline's longest running stage success, and temporarily renew her faith in art, culture, and career.

The Eve of St. Mark takes place on the embattled Philippine island of Bataan, which had fallen to Japanese forces in April, just six months before Maxwell Anderson's drama opened at the Cort Theatre. On the island, young Quizz West is manning a coastal artillery battery while the enemy bombards their positions as a prelude to invasion. In his nightly dreams, Quizz visits his small-town family and sweetheart, desperate for an answer to his quandary: Should I stay on the island to fight—and likely die—or retreat? "The play is about our soldiers on Bataan," Aline explained, "with the story moving back and forth between the Mid-West and the Philippines. My part? I play the boy's mother, Nell. It's not a long one, but it's the kind of part I've always wanted, and I think it is beautiful.[63] Mister Anderson's lines are something I believe in, and that is more than any actress has a right to expect."[64] The New York critics agreed. "Mr. Anderson has done more than any other dramatist to bring poetry back to the modern theatre," one said. "True, it is not a play in verse, but certain scenes between the soldier hero and his mother (Aline) attain the simplicity of dramatic poetry."[65] *Eve* was the first major play to feature a story of Americans in the war, and it attracted an audience thirsty for tales of their boys overseas. But rather than John Wayne–style heroics, it instead delivered a complex story of patriotic sacrifice. In the third act, after Quizz has been declared missing in action, his two younger brothers implore Nell to allow them to join up and continue Quizz's work. "It's wrong when there is only one important thing to do in the world," one says, "to look the other way and let someone else do it. I want to pay my ticket."[66]

As she often was, Aline turned out to be wrong in her assessment of the show's potential. "I didn't have 'The Eve of St. Mark' figured for success," she admitted. "I thought it was important and I wanted to do it, but I thought it was too sad a play to go over big. I still think it might have been but for the fighting message that we accented with the writer and director in rehearsal."[67] Understandably, the gentle propaganda of *The Eve of St. Mark* was exactly

In *The Eve of St. Mark* Aline played the mother of a soldier in the Philippines waiting for the coming Japanese invasion. Opening on Broadway less than a year into WWII, Aline was devastated as, one by one, her young male costars were drafted and sent to the war, some never to return. *Wisconsin Historical Society, Vandamm Studio, ID #149061.*

what American audiences needed during the first year of a war that had already seen a long series of failures and defeats. It connected them to their boys in the Pacific the way that newsreels couldn't and with honesty and language that Hollywood movies wouldn't. Burns Mantle spoke for most critics when he wrote, "The best play of the season so far is 'The Eve of St. Mark.' It is a simple, human, warm and moving drama."[68] Aline echoed Mantle's sentiment, and revealed the true loyalty of her heart. "It's pretty important at a time like this, to have the kind of part you've always wanted and a play that says something," Aline said. "Doing this gives me the feeling that I am doing something exactly right for wartime."[69] New York City opened their hearts to *Eve*, and for the next eight months, Aline daily walked the twenty blocks from 1 West 64th Street to the Cort Theatre, basking in the warm glow of one of the seasons' biggest hits. But the military's need for young men was voracious, and every few months there was a sudden, sullen void in the cast. "Last night we rehearsed a new 'Neil,'" Aline reported, after another actor resigned in order to join the fight. "Our boys just keep going off to war."[70]

Those months with *The Eve of St. Mark* were among the busiest of Aline MacMahon's life. There was, of course, the daily grind of 307 performances of a hit play, and the ongoing, exhausting work of scheduling and overseeing *The Lunch Hour Follies*. But Aline was also embroiled in another attempt to create a national theater system, embryonically known as the Cort Experimental Theatre Group. "It's just the company here so far," she said from backstage at *Eve*, "trying to do what we can about bringing new talent into the theatre." The idea was to find new plays and bring them to New York audiences, then export them to other parts of the country—something Maxwell Anderson was already allowing with *The Eve of St. Mark*.[71] "We're all reading plays whenever we get the chance," Aline explained. "If we can find a script we'll try it out for several performances and let the managers come and look."[72] Meanwhile, lurking behind all this activity was also the ongoing anxiety and trauma of her husband's uncertain recovery taxing her emotional resources. Or perhaps the activity was helping banish it. It wasn't until April 1943 that Clarence finally returned to New York, and some sense of normalcy at last returned to the Stein household.

13

WE FIGHT IT ROUND BY ROUND

On July 1, 1950, a man named Louis Budenz sat in an obscure government office with an agent of the Federal Bureau of Investigation. Balding and putty-faced, Budenz was a longtime labor leader and Communist Party member who in 1945 had renounced the party and was now a paid informant for America's national law enforcement agency. With a stenographer at his side, Special Agent William McCarthy plumbed Budenz's insider knowledge for information about Aline MacMahon's connection to the Communist Party. Budenz's testimony that afternoon prompted the FBI to begin long-term covert surveillance of Aline MacMahon and Clarence Stein—investigations that would continue sporadically for almost fifteen years:

> Miss MacMahon was represented to me in the late 1930's as working closely with the Communist Party, this representation being made by Robert Reed, an actor who was then in charge of [Communist] infiltration of Actor's Equity.[1] Although I had heard of her in a favorable light [as Communist friendly] from that time forward, I was not definitely advised that she was under Communist discipline, until about 1943 when Reed advised me so. Later on I was officially advised that Miss MacMahon was an adherent of the Communist Party. These advices continued until I left the Party in 1945. She has been quite active in a number of Communist fronts.[2]

There is no doubt that Aline MacMahon had long held a great hope for Communism, and a belief in the Soviet government that was greater still in its naivete. But it was a lie that she had ever been a member, or was under the direct influence of the Communist Party. At most, she was seduced by Russian interwar propaganda that touted the Soviet state's supposed racial and gender equality, peace, and stability. Aline's liberal influences and innate compassion made her an easy convert to the belief that their system would lead to what she called "a more equal world." During the war years, with the USSR an ally in our war against fascism in Europe, it became de rigueur among liberals to openly support the Soviets, and Aline was no exception. Far from the woman who once timidly asked her husband if she should attend a discussion of Communism among friends, during the late 1930s and throughout the war Aline became more publicly outspoken in her leftist activism, while privately saying, "I would feel at home in Russia. I hope we get to go there."[3] Unfortunately there were forces within the US government secretly watching the American Socialist movement, and taking detailed notes on their activities.

As early as 1938 the House Committee on Un-American Activities (then also known as the Dies Committee) was in possession of information about Aline MacMahon's affiliations with "Communist fronts" that cast her as a Red Sympathizer. According to declassified records, among the supposed (and actual) Red fronts with which Aline worked was the League of Women Shoppers, a pro-labor consumer's rights organization that the Dies Committee claimed was sponsored by the USSR and cofounded by Aline MacMahon in 1935.[4] Also in the Dies files were details of a 1938 antifascist letter called the "Declaration of Democratic Independence," created to convince Congress and the president to sever all economic ties to Germany and Italy, signed by Aline and nearly sixty other movie industry professionals.[5] After the war, America's anti-Communist crusaders would cynically reinterpret this antifascist stance as prima facie evidence of Aline MacMahon's *pro*-Communist sympathies.

Also cited in Aline's FBI file was her signature to an open letter that appeared in the Soviet newspaper *Daily Worker* in August 1939 calling for greater unity and closer cooperation with the USSR. The letter, titled "To All Active Supporters of Democracy and Peace," read, in part: "[Anti-Communists] have encouraged the fantastic falsehood that that the USSR and the totalitarian states are basically alike. Some sincere American liberals have fallen into this trap and assert that the fascist states and Soviet Russia equally menace American Institutions and the democratic way of life. The Soviet Union considers political dictatorship a transitional form, and has shown a steadily expanding democracy in every sphere. Soviet aims and achievements make it clear that there exists a sound and permanent basis in mutual ideas for cooperation between our nations on behalf of world peace and the security and freedom of all nations."[6] Aline's signature on this document is, at least, naive—even by the standards of the day. The Soviet state had no such ambitions toward democracy, nor an interest in peace that would be anything other than a subjugation of the nations within their sphere. As with the "Democratic Independence" letter, Aline and the 400 notables of science, religion, education, politics, and the arts who also signed it soon found it forged into a cudgel in the hands of anti-Communist politicians.[7]

While Aline publicly flexed her liberal muscles throughout the war years, the government's sub rosa information-gathering efforts quietly continued. Chronicled in Aline's file is her work with a long list of Communist or Communist-influenced artists who were later blacklisted or testified before the House Un-American Activities Committee.[8] She appeared with the controversial African American actor and activist Paul Robeson on a CBS radio broadcast outlining the forces of systemic racism that led to the Detroit riots of 1943. During the 1940s she worked with two of the so-called Hollywood Ten accused of Communist influence in the film industry. With writer Albert Maltz, Aline helped add new scenes and dialogue to an import of director Sergei Eisenstein's silent Russian classic *Battleship Potemkin*. And as a teacher in the Actors' Laboratory Theatre in Los Angeles she worked alongside John Howard Lawson and others who would be blacklisted or testify before HUAC following the war, including Lee J. Cobb, Lloyd Bridges, Jeff Corey, Howard Da Silva, and Marc Lawrence. In all, Aline was connected to at least a dozen so-called fronts, including The Council for Pan-American Democracy, The Artist's Front to Win the War, The Allied Voters Against Coudert, The Progressive Citizens of America, The Joint Anti-Fascist Refugee Committee, The Russian American Club, The Los Angeles Committee for a Democratic Far East Policy, and others with similarly unwieldy titles. The FBI even managed to cite *The Lunchtime Follies* as a Red-influenced group, presumably because it was organized by Aline and aided the war effort to defeat the Nazis.

By the end of WWII the information in Aline's supposedly confidential file was scarcely more secret than the Manhattan phone book. Agents of the FBI had begun leaking details of her Communist affiliations to newspapers and nongovernmental organizations, and in 1945 the *Chicago Tribune* publicly denounced Aline as a Communist influence within the Actor's Equity union. "Leading the fight to drive Actor's Equity into the ranks of Communist labor unions are at least four 'whips' in the executive council. Aline MacMahon, along with Sam Jaffee, Philip Loeb, and Paul Robeson have well documented pro-Communist records in the reports of the Dies Committee."[9] The fight between liberal and conservative factions in Equity would continue for years.

Ultimately, this microcosm of political backbiting would fill many newspaper column inches with tales of secret plots to overthrow democracy through the venerable profession of making faces on the stage.

After *The Eve of St. Mark* finally closed in the summer of 1943, Aline did not return to Broadway for more than a decade. Following some radio and film appearances connected to the war effort, she was called back to Hollywood for what would be the double-edged highlight of her war-era career. Aline's work in MGM's adaptation of Pearl Buck's novel *Dragon Seed* garnered the only industry-sanctioned recognition of her years on screen—an Oscar nomination for Best Supporting Actress—but also the dishonor of appearing in one of the most racially inappropriate and embarrassing films in Hollywood history. It should come as no surprise that MGM elected to populate Buck's story of Chinese peasants fighting the Japanese invasion of 1937 with white actors. "Whitewashing" was a common practice during the era, composed of various ratios of market forces (i.e., "greed"), mute insensitivity, and sheer racism. Also, the studio had achieved enormous success a few years earlier with primarily white actors carrying Buck's *The Good Earth* (the lead role of which Aline had lost to Louise Rainer), after a halfhearted attempt to hire an all-Chinese cast. (After failing to find enough Chinese actors for *The Good Earth*, producer Irving Thalberg defended his choice to use mainly Westerners. "I'm in the business of creating illusions," he said.) In addition to the obvious racism, *Dragon Seed* also stands out simply as a truly bizarre example of the casting director's art. Besides Irish/Jewish Aline MacMahon, the film's leading roles are filled by a baffling assortment of ethnicities. Among the actors playing Chinese characters are Katharine Hepburn (New England American), Walter Huston (Irish/Scottish), Akim Tamiroff (Russian), Henry Travers (British), Turhan Bey (Turkish and Czech), Anna Demetrio (Italian), J. Carrol Naish (Irish), Robert Lewis (Jewish), and Agnes Moorehead (Irish American). The disparate welter of dialects and accents among the "peasants" of *Dragon Seed* conjures not rural China, but instead the heterogeneous chatter of turn-of-the-century Ellis Island—barring, of course, that any actual Chinese immigrants had arrived that day.

For all her liberal ideology and love of Asian culture, Aline appears to have had no misgivings about playing Asian characters in either film. This apparent obliviousness of a supposedly enlightened person is another reminder of just how deeply ingrained racism was in the culture and economics of studio-era Hollywood. If anything, Aline seemed to think that her travels in China gave her—at least on a surface level—an insight into a more honest portrayal of Lin

Tang's wife in *Dragon Seed*. "A visit to China is what helped as much as anything to imbue me with the feeling for my interpretation in 'Dragon Seed,'" she claimed.[10] Unfortunately, Aline found her first serious work in front of a camera for two years a tiresome slog ("The picture lumbers on—not very satisfying, this one—but I'm doing my best"),[11] and it took weeks for her to decipher the cause. When the director George Conway was laid up with the flu, she suddenly understood. "The morale on the picture is greatly improved by Conway's absence," she said. "Oh, what a boon it has been to us—his understudy is a gentle, sensitive fellow named Harry Becquet, and really, the difference in the mood of the set is striking. I hadn't realized how much he [Conway] is to blame for the air of worry hereabouts. Everyone is light-hearted suddenly!"[12] Typically, once Conway returned and Aline saw the picture partially assembled, she was disappointed in her work. "I tried hard, but I didn't get much help from 'them,'" she said. "I may get by, but the fact is it is the work of a talented amateur. I feel disappointed, but not crushed."[13]

It is not much to say that Aline stands out among the cast of *Dragon Seed*. For all their sparkling talent even Katharine Hepburn and Walter Huston are well-nigh preposterous, and Aline perhaps only looks more sensitive and less vulgar in contrast. On the film's release, the era's monolithic block of white Academy voters seemed to agree, and honored Aline with the only Oscar nomination of her career. The critics were also kind to Aline, but not to *Dragon Seed*. Even as they noticed the strange jigsaw puzzle of actors and accents, however, they failed to mention—or likely even understand—the racism on display. After decades of watching Asian characters portrayed by Myrna Loy, Lon Chaney, Boris Karloff, Edward G. Robinson, Paul Muni, and Warner Oland, they were likewise guilty of the unconscious inertia of racism in Hollywood.

Although Aline eventually lost her Oscar bid to Ethyl Barrymore in *None but the Lonely Heart*, it was another, private review that most buoyed her spirits. It came from two people who would be expected to know best, and also to know better. Just after *Seed* was released, Aline was trying to secure the performance rights to an Asian-themed memoir then being serialized in *Asia* magazine. "The author's representative is Richard Walsh," she wrote. "He is Pearl Buck's husband. He wrote me that they think I'm *superb* in 'Dragon Seed,' no less!"[14] Even Buck, who understood and admired China's culture and people as well as anyone in the West, and had implored MGM to use only Chinese actors in *The Good Earth*, appeared to accept the reality that *Dragon Seed* could only be transferred to the screen if it obliterated any true connection to the people it portrayed.

Aline finished her war-era work with the troubled production of *Guest in the House*, an absurd melodrama about a dangerous sociopath (Anne Baxter, in the role that likely contributed to her casting in *All About Eve*) who manipulates and nearly destroys everything she touches. In spite of Aline's generic role as the spinster aunt who is the first to understand Baxter's potentially deadly machinations, her mood was high. "The first day of 'Guest in the House' was a delight," Aline reported. "Such nice people! Mr. Stromberg, the producer, sent me two dozen roses! And the director, Lewis Milestone is very nice—very gentlemanly and contained. There is an air of ease and relaxation—all very nice."[15] Within a few weeks, however, Milestone was already well behind schedule and tensions were mounting on the set. "The picture moves along slowly," Aline said. "[The producers] are getting somewhat harassed and jumpy. When things begin to seethe, I settle down with a good book, or I mend stockings in my dressing room and let them reach a boiling point by themselves."[16] To make matters worse, two months into filming, Milestone suddenly collapsed on the set and found himself remanded to the hospital with acute appendicitis. "We don't know what this will do to the picture," Aline mused. The appearance of replacement John Brahm did not end the difficulties. "I wish you could see the chagrined actors," she continued. "Especially those pets of poor sick Mr. Milestone. He let some of the mediocre talents impose on him—they were writing their own lines—and now all that is over and boy are they *sore!*"[17]

As filming continued past the June invasion of Hitler's Europe by Allied forces, Lewis Milestone returned to find *Guest* in a similar state of desperate upheaval. "Milestone is about to re-write and re-direct a good deal of the picture," Aline recorded. "Now he blames the pinch hitter—John Brahm—for throwing the game! As if three weeks work could ruin twelve weeks that went before. What an alibi business!" In all, *Guest* endured the hands of four directors ("The new director, Andre De Toth is very authoritative, but he likes it *juicy*"), and by release it barely resembled the film that Aline had signed on for. "Who would have thought they would rewrite the *entire* script and finally not even do the scenes for which I was engaged to play the part? And at such prices!"[18] Aline's paucity of screen time was, perhaps, fortuitous. As Bosley Crowther noted, "Aline MacMahon remains in the background, which is a happy place for one in this film."

Following *Guest in the House*, it would be two long years before Aline MacMahon appeared in front of film audiences. The reason for this professional void is yet another heartbreaking trauma in the life of the Steins. Buried deep in Aline's personal archives is a terse note written in her hand that tells the tale. It says only: "Unhappy years. C.S.S. unwell. Rocky recuperation."

After spending January vacationing in Florida, the Steins had returned to New York City early in 1945. The end of the war was now in sight, as the Allies repulsed a final large-scale German offensive in the Ardennes Forest. By April Berlin had fallen, and shortly after the German Army at last surrendered. As May limped on past VE Day, there were still men fighting and dying in the Pacific theater. And on 1 West 64th street, Clarence Stein endured another unstoppable mental collapse.

As severe as the previous episodes had been, the 1945 incident was longer lasting and more deeply disturbing, requiring Clarence to endure nearly two months in New York Neurological Hospital. During those long weeks, Clarence Stein could be found, on a semidaily basis, strapped to a gurney in an exam room with electrodes positioned at his temples. Then, for as long as sixty seconds, a stiff electric current would be passed through his brain. In the early days of electroconvulsive therapy, the current applied was high, and information on just what was happening inside the brain was nearly nonexistent. The treatments momentarily destroyed Clarence's short-term memory, and for almost a month after his transfer from NYNH he lived in a long, dark tunnel with only a pinpoint of light at its end. "It probably will be a long time before I know just where I have been," he told Aline. "It is still very mysterious."[19]

With nothing to do while Clarence was still receiving treatment in the hospital, Aline returned to Hollywood, looking for work. Since 1937 the costs of his periodic hospitalizations and psychiatric treatment had mounted heavily, and even the savings of two well-paid professionals were being depleted. Things were bad enough for the Steins to consider giving up the lease on 1 W. 64th Street in favor of more modest lodgings, and Aline felt pressure to offset their recent outlays by returning to profitable employment. But the time off had changed her professional outlook yet again. "My career seems to be dormant," she said. "No jobs on the horizon here. I am cross to think that just now, when a little income would come in handy no one wants to give me any. I am confident we can have contented and useful living even on a restricted budget. In many ways we will thrive on the simplicity—it may even be better."[20]

In July Clarence was transferred from the Neurological Hospital to Silver Hill Sanitarium. While he was there, the atomic bomb laid two Japanese cities to waste and World War II came to an end. The final victory over Japan was both a relief and a terror to Aline. "What do you think of the 'atomic bomb?'"

she asked Clarence. "Does it horrify you as it does me? Do you think it makes America the menace of the world? Or ought we be realistic enough to say, 'if there is war, let us be the most warlike.' In that way we safely win. But can you imagine what we would be saying of the Germans if the atomic bomb were *theirs*?"[21]

In some ways World War II claimed Clarence as another casualty, his war-related government duties having contributed mightily to his stress load and overwork. By extension the war also injured Aline, whose career was severely compromised by the toll it took on her beloved husband. But there was never a moment of recrimination or self-pity in either of them. "I am not done, that is sure," Clarence insisted. "I have important things ahead of me. I can't see life otherwise. The fog is rising." In response to this dogged determination, Aline again revealed her admiration and love:

> Your letter means a great deal to me. You are good—so fine—and to write a letter of spirit and to even make me laugh in the midst of this ill-ness. Like Ling Lao in "Dragon Seed" I say, "Now where is there another like him?"[22] Remember—it will come right. We are still way ahead in life. *Way* ahead. A little healthy dimming of the luck is in order.

In all, this dimming of the Steins' luck would last more than two years.

During 1945 and nearly all of 1946 Aline traveled back and forth between Manhattan and Los Angeles with nothing to show for it but a pile of ticket stubs for the *Super Chief*. Although she made a sincere effort to produce a stage version of the memoir *With My Daughter's Indian Family*—even enlisting help from Moss Hart, Maxwell Anderson, and Pearl Buck herself—it got no further than a tryout at Stanford University under the direction of her friend Cowles Strickland.[23] Meanwhile, greater dangers were gradually marshaling their forces toward a political conflict that in its social impact was nearly as frightening as the war just ended.

When the *Chicago Tribune* called out Aline MacMahon and other executives in Actor's Equity as Communists in October 1945, it was among the opening salvos of a civil cold war in America that would last nearly two decades. The impetus for the Equity dispute was the accusations of council member Frank Fay, who called for an investigation of five other AE members over what he considered "anti-Catholic" activities. Fay clearly had other axes to grind, and after being threatened with censure by Equity, he revealed his true target, calling the union's actions a "Communist smear," something that the *Tribune* and other papers reported as if a holy truth. Aline was not available to be in New York when the matter came to a vote in December, but made her feelings known, nonetheless:

> I deeply regret that I am in Los Angeles today. I would like to be present and say to all our members that it is my deep conviction that Frank Fay is acting in bad faith in this matter. All this talk about religion is only a cover up. I believe he is conducting a smear campaign against all of us who have a liberal point of view. Frank Fay has proved by his mis-statements and frequent newspaper interviews that he is irresponsible, and I submit that he should be requested to resign from Equity Council.[24]

Fay was eventually censured, but his aim was achieved—the five Equity members he singled out were scrutinized by the House Committee on Un-American Activities, and at least one, Margo, was later blacklisted.[25] Additionally, Aline and the other three Equity members publicly named as Communists were put under the FBI's most powerful microscope.

It wasn't until the autumn of 1946 before a Hollywood studio remembered that Aline MacMahon was still alive. The film was *The Mighty McGurk*, which was as close to a "B" picture as Metro-Goldwyn-Mayer ever turned out. This threadbare story of a blowhard ex-Heavyweight Champion turning over a new leaf feels as if it was pasted together out of other screenplays over a lazy weekend, and the casting of Wallace Beery in the title role only amplified the film's clichés. Even twelve years after their first teaming in *Ah, Wilderness!* there was still an entertaining chemistry between Beery and Aline, but it is all in service of mediocre nonsense wherein the rough-hewn Beery helps unite a pair of crazy, star-crossed kids, adopts a precocious preteen wastrel, marries his long-suffering, tough-as-nails belle (Aline), and joins a local chapter of the Salvation Army. If your tolerance for hokum is up to it, *The Might McGurk* entertains, but do not expect to be edified.

During the largely idle years of 1945 and 1946, Aline MacMahon sought opportunities to fill her time where she could manufacture them. Now living in a cottage alongside Jennie Mac's small house in Los Angeles, mother and daughter bickered and reconciled, argued and appreciated each other. There were social engagements, concerts, cultural events, and political activities, including Aline's speech at a major rally on behalf of former vice president

Henry Wallace's 1948 Progressive Party presidential bid that received angry scrutiny from the political Right and amplified her Communist profile ever more. Expecting Clarence to come west after his release from Silver Hill, she turned down a series of plays in New York, including the lead in *On Whitman Avenue*, about an African American family renting a flat in a home in an all-white neighborhood.[26] Still itching to work, but with nothing suitable offered, Aline gradually became more deeply involved with the Actor's Laboratory Theatre, the West Coast Method-teaching offshoot of New York's Lab, opened in 1941. There, she was performing, directing, and teaching alongside a who's-who of future HUAC blacklistees, including Lloyd Bridges, Jeff Corey, and Howard Da Silva. "I have been occupying my time with visits to the Actor's Lab. I'm counting on it to keep me diverted," she said. "I am very much impressed with the school—I only hope I am up to the job. I like them all so much."[27] There was, of course, much talk among staff and students about liberal causes and ideals—but it is unlikely that Aline engaged in any serious party-level discussions. She was content simply to see the young actors beginning careers and paying attention to the world around them. "L.A. is the home of the 'America First's' and the Gerald K. Smiths," she noted,[28] "and it is good to know that some young people are awake to the menace and just as lively agin' it as the other side are 'for.' Capitalism is cornered, Labor is awake and the stock market fall simply proves that the halcyon days are over."

The migration of elements of the Lab to Los Angeles again widened the profile of the Method in America. For the moment, John Garfield was still the face of the new style in film and stage acting, and enjoying a run of popular postwar films, including *The Postman Always Rings Twice*, *Body and Soul*, and *Gentleman's Agreement*. But by the late 1940s other Method players were also finding success on the screen. These included Montgomery Clift, an alumnus of the Actor's Studio who would momentarily wrest the Method baton from Garfield before it was, in turn, seized from him.

Heading to Hollywood following a successful career on Broadway, Clift's first film was Howard Hawks' *Red River*, playing against John Wayne. Long considered one of the classic studio-era westerns, *Red River* displayed the tension produced by Clift's intense Method style sparking against the flinty charisma of Wayne's casual roughness. When it was released in 1948, *Red River* made Monty Clift a major star. But before *Red River* could make it to theater screens, Clift completed another picture that placed him in front of movie audiences first, *The Search*, shot on location in Europe among the ruins of the destroyed German Reich. When a telegram arrived at 1229 Ozeta Terrace in

May 1947 with an offer to join the cast of *The Search*, it meant that Aline MacMahon would again costar with one of the new icons in the long march of the Method: "There's been an inquiry from Switzerland—the man who made 'The Last Chance' [1947], Richard Schweizer, will produce a picture about displaced persons.[29] Fred Zinneman—an excellent Metro director, now in Switzerland, will direct. They asked if I'd be available June to September. Of course I said I am definitely interested."[30]

In spite of a modest salary ($1,500 a week on a four-week guarantee), Aline was beguiled by the compensation of traveling Europe in first-class accommodations on Metro-Goldwyn-Mayer's dime.[31] And there was also the opportunity for Aline to be involved in something she considered important: *The Search* was an effort to articulate the plight of Europe's displaced children through the story of a single boy (Ivan Jendl) separated from his mother (Jarmila Novotna). "I was the American field worker in Germany, in charge of repatriation," she said. "It was not a great acting part,[32] but I decided to accept the offer because I had admired the producer's last picture [*The Last Chance*] so much."[33]

By July 5 a contract was in place and Aline was heading to Stockholm in a first-class cabin on the luxury liner *M.S. Gripsholm*. With Clarence back at home but unable to be away from work, Jennie Mac came along for the ride, and the pair roomed shipboard with Sally Kirkland, the fashion editor of *Life* magazine. During the first night at sea Ms. Kirkland—until then a complete stranger—blurted out an astonishing piece of gossip to Aline—the kind of gossip that almost certainly should have been relayed to the CIA, the Department of Defense, and the Secret Service. "Our cabin gal is very lively," Aline said of Ms. Kirkland. "And she talks in her sleep. Waking up suddenly, she told me that the Russians will announce their atomic bomb in two months." Then, with tongue apparently in cheek, Aline told Clarence, "If I hear anything important, I'll wire you."[34] Kirkland was somewhat off in her prediction—the Soviets did not detonate their first device for almost two years—but one wonders what the US intelligence apparatus would have made of a New York fashion editor claiming to have inside information about the Soviet bomb program at the same time that Julius and Ethel Rosenberg were feeding top-secret information to Russian operatives in Manhattan.

Arriving in Stockholm on July 18, Aline found that the making of *The Search* and her appearance in it was major news across Scandinavia, and the local MGM representatives treated her and Jennie Mac as if they were visiting royalty. With a week before shooting began, mother and daughter went

We Fight It Round by Round

from city to city, sightseeing en route to the film's first location in Zurich. In Sweden they were squired in limousines, feted with parties, and put up in hotel suites "the size of Grand Central Station." But after making their way to Copenhagen, near the German border, Aline was reminded that postwar Europe was actually a cruel and forbidding place, where the true horrors of war—the up-close, inescapable sights and smells of demolished cities and human wreckage—were omnipresent. Even her work with returning soldiers after WWI did not prepare Aline for the sober reality of the carnage of black and white newsreels brought heartbreakingly to color and life.

Aline and the tiny company of *The Search* were among the first civilians allowed to shoot in postwar Germany, and for her the making of the film was also the revelation of the unmaking of a continent. "I have seen the infernal and the blessed lands," she recorded for Clarence. "Sweden and Switzerland—and south Germany. In Switzerland everyone is well fed—some superbly so. In Germany, just 40 minutes away, even the Bosses are in torment. I'll have to wait to see you to do justice to the rotting carcass of Frankfort, and the kind but sad sacks who sit about in the Press Club there, and the disillusioned, hopeless air of the Military-who-Occupy, and the emotional wallop to your hope for the human race which this moment in history at Frankfort gives you. Even at Malmo [Sweden] we felt the lingering fear of the Nazis. The waiters bowed too low—the porter was too efficient—and all the boys in bellhop caps had to run too fast. And here in Copenhagen where they lost and were conquered and have too little of everything," she wrote, "the Nazi smell still pervades."[35]

By the time she alit in Zurich for her first shots on *The Search*, Aline was herself becoming disillusioned. "Many things have occurred that give us pause. Our extras are *real* displaced children and we ask them to re-live the horror of their own experiences. How we will manage on location in Germany I can't imagine. 40 children as extras, 24 staff and crew—and there's no food, no soap, no running water where we'll be. We'll have no telephones or even postal service for weeks. But we will struggle on."[36] On leaving Zurich and driving through Bavaria to Munich, the things that gave Aline pause turned darker still. "It was a church holiday," she began. "Everyone was in his best clothes, and lovers and lasses walked arm in arm in the dusk—a long twilight with an orange sun—and it is hard to believe that Dachau is only 15 Kilometers from us—and that the gay peasant in his so-quaint costume never lost one minute sleep over the torture and destruction of how many thousands of the human race." In Munich she observed the bitter fruit that

Nazi aggression had visited on the populace. "You cannot begin to imagine the desolation," she told Clarence, "the blocks of desiccated buildings, sometimes with one light in one room where four walls still stand though all the others are in rubble for *miles*. Absolutely razed to the ground."[37]

Another incident brought home the unseen circumstances of the people who—unlike Aline—were not being fed and housed by Metro-Goldwyn-Mayer and helped by the United Nations. Aline was returning to Munich late at night following a research visit to a UN Refugee Camp. "I had spent three days there with the head of the center, Rachel Greene. My driver, a wild renegade Ukrainian named Mike was at the wheel," she recalled. "Around 11:00pm he suddenly drove off the road into the pitch black woods! He was trying to run down a fawn at the edge of the Reichsautobahn. I begged him to stop. Mike looked at me and said, disappointed, 'But it's so good meat.'"[38]

During the making of *The Search* Aline's letters home are fewer in number, but dense with the difficulties and intrigue of filmmaking on a shoestring in locations that would vex the best-equipped studio productions. The entire production staff numbered only twenty-four hands, including technicians, cast, and crew. When the company attempted a scene requiring 600 extras, ten trucks, and two ambulances, there was no assistant director to organize the sequence. "In Hollywood we would have had four, at least," Aline noted. "The disorganization of this project is really formidable. They are a little film company and simply aren't up to the undertaking." On another occasion seventy-five children arrived for a night shoot only to discover that the film's independent producer, Lazar Wechsler, had neglected to provide food or beds for them. Additionally, no one had checked to see if the local electrical power would carry the lights. At 1:00 A.M., with the children asleep in trucks or on the ground, the answer came. "It can't," Aline reported. "And we've lost two more days."[39]

Lazar Wechsler was a roguish character of the first order, part scoundrel and part noble fool. "He's a darling—very difficult—and I hope he is honest. It will be quite a blow if he isn't, as I like he and his wife very much."[40] Aline soon discovered that Wechsler was positively *not* entirely honest. In the cast of *The Search* was a first-time actor, the well-known Czech opera singer Jarmila Novotna. ("A remarkable woman" Aline said.) During the process of signing her first ever film contract, Novotna insisted that a certain important clause be inserted, which the producer duly included and had her initial. Then, while Novotna was distracted, Wechsler crossed out her clause and wrote an entirely new one just underneath, giving the appearance that she had approved it. When Novotna discovered the deception and confronted him there was no shame or contrition; Wechsler simply advised her to sue him. Later, as shooting continued week upon week, Wechsler fell so far behind in salary payments that the principals were forced to momentarily go on strike. "Fred Zinneman, Jamila Novotna, Monty Clift, and I paid our fascinating Mr. Wechsler a visit at his hotel today, and we gave him a sad half-hour. He is very attractive, brilliant, creative and has a strong sense of social justice. But as we pointed out to him—social justice begins at home. The fact that we confronted him—unprepared—together—floored, humbled and depressed him. For the morning, at least. We were right, but I didn't enjoy the victory. It is not nice to see anyone crawl—I wouldn't like to have to do it again."[41] Payments were eventually made—as was the film—but not before the ongoing delays nearly scuttled Aline's ability to appear stateside as the nurse in 1947's legendary production of *Medea* with Judith Anderson in the title role.

Before Aline had even left the States, producer Robert Whitehead contacted her about appearing in his revival of *Medea*, the classic Greek tragedy by Euripides. With *The Search* scheduled to shoot in July and August and *Medea* not slated to open until late October, Aline eagerly accepted what she considered a great opportunity. But when *The Search* was still shooting into September with no end in sight, Aline was reluctantly forced to bow out of *Medea*. "Production confusion forces I protect you by release our contract," she wired Robert Whitehead. "No confidence local promises. Heartbroken."[42] Still, no matter how hard she tried, Aline could not bring herself to dislike Lazar Wechsler. Even if just through incompetence, the lovable rogue had relieved Aline from a burden she didn't quite understand until it happened: she did not want to rush back to New York and take on *Medea*. "I think I'm tired," she admitted. "Not physically, but tired of the effort it takes to keep on winning. I will be glad to relax and be there on opening night and very happy at [my replacement's] success." Amazingly, Wechsler *was* able to finish *The Search* in time for Aline to return to the states for *Medea*'s preview engagement in Philadelphia. Unfortunately, Aline simply discovered that she was too tired to continue through the Broadway run that eventually lasted over two hundred performances.[43] Now nearing fifty, Aline was no longer the creative dynamo who signed on to *Once in a Lifetime* just days after returning from India, or the woman who left New York for Hollywood on New Year's Day with just a few hours' notice. She asked to be released. "I have been feeling a little older lately," she advised Clarence, "awfully 'settled' and not regretful that I am."[44] More and more, Aline MacMahon now wished to slow down and live at her own whims.

Sadly, Aline's thoughts on her costar and fellow Method devotee Montgomery Clift are sparse, even among her private letters. It is not unusual that her contact with him appears slim. Clift became well known for sometimes shying away from other cast members while working privately with his longtime acting coach, Mira Rostova. But after reading Robert LaGuardia's 1977 biography of Clift, Aline was confused by claims that Rostova had been highly influential on location during the making of *The Search*. "I am amazed, because I was with Monty while we made the movie, and I truly was not aware of anything going on. [The book] describes Rostova as being there all the time, but she'd never met the company and she always stayed in the hotel room. Well, I can swear to the fact that I never knew she was there and we made that movie for weeks and weeks in Germany. I think it's very possible that she was there while we were in Zurich, but I do not see how it was possible to have her in Munich. The city was a shambles. They did find a place for us at the Munich Press Club and Monty was there. But there was no place for Rostova. I don't see how she could have been there at the time. Impossible. And in Ingolstadt, that's a little ancient German village with just one hotel. I don't understand that at all."[45]

At the time of its release, *The Search* was highly lauded for the honesty and naturalism with which it treated its subject matter. *Newsweek* named it "one of the finest films in years," Louella Parsons called it "a wonderful motion picture," Walter Winchell said it was "memorable," and Norbert Lusk suggested "everybody the world over must see this picture." Now, there is no doubt that *The Search* is a sensitive and absorbing film. But at the risk of seeming cynical, it is perhaps overpraised. It is of course impossible to untie contemporaneous praise for *The Search* from the era in which it was made. Like most films that observe a recent tragedy, it is hard for critics to dissect something so concerned with the fresh, raw pain of the survivors of that tragedy. The truth is that *The Search* suffers at times from an odd remove, relating the backstories of lost children with droning declaration, and with a cloying music score that fails to elicit a proper emotional response. Especially curious is the finale in which our young boy (Ivan Jendl) is at last reunited with his mother (Novotna) after the horrors of wandering alone in postwar Germany. The entire scene—from mother's recognition to final fade out—lasts perhaps ten seconds, and plays without a close-up or a serious emotional reaction from Novotna. It is entirely possible that Fred Zinneman was attempting to portray the deadened emotions precipitated by war, but more likely it is simply that as a first-time actor, Novotna was not up to the task. Fortunately, *The*

Search does provide some moments of genuine warmth and honesty; as the GI who befriends little Ivan Jendl, Clift brings real energy to their relationship, something sorely lacking elsewhere. And when Novotna is mistakenly told that her boy has drowned, Aline's earnest, tender consolation provides the only genuine up-front emotion in the film. Unfortunately, Zinneman brushes past this moment with the directorial equivalent of a sidelong glance. Ultimately, *The Search* feels like a potentially great film that never realized its emotional or political possibilities.

Leading up to the new decade of the 1950s, Aline meandered quietly. In Hollywood, demand for her services was light ("I do admit I think my halcyon days of big salary are on the wane," she said), and in the summer of 1948 she returned to Stanford University as an artist-in-residence, something she would do periodically over the next few years.[46] In late 1948 Samuel Goldwyn hired her as the matriarch of the McCoy family in *Roseanna McCoy*, a sort of *Romeo and Juliet* of Appalachia set amid the famous Hatfield/McCoy feud. The production was terribly troubled, with multiple directors and screenwriters—as well as another leading lady in her first film, this one just a wisp of a girl, Joan Evans.[47] "Our leading lady is a child of fourteen," Aline wrote. "And the script is written with scenes of a great deal of feeling and intensity. Being only fourteen the girl is—in life—a very nice, restrained, intelligent young lady—but neither spontaneous like a child, nor impassioned like a woman. At this point we all wonder if she can do it. And if she can't, what will we do about it?"[48] The result of this miscasting was, in the words of Evans's adult costar Farley Grainger, "a complete lack of sexual tension between our Romeo and Juliet."[49] Sadly, *Roseanna McCoy* is a dreary, leaden bore, and one of the weakest pictures in Sam Goldwyn's long and storied career.

As the 1940s staggered to a close, a magical opportunity in the career of Aline MacMahon presented itself. That year she was hired by Nat Karson to play Queen Gertrude in a stage production of *Hamlet*, her first opportunity since Richard Boleslavsky's 1930 one-off production of *A Midsummer Night's Dream* to play Shakespeare as a professional. While the production toured the Atlantic coast, intrigue was simultaneously afoot in Hamlet's home of Helsingor, Denmark. Helsingor, immortalized in Shakespeare's play as "Elsinor," has hosted a world-renowned Shakespeare festival at Kronborg Castle—the real-world setting of the play—annually since 1816. In preparing the festival for 1949, the Danish government made it known to the US State Department that they wanted an American theater company to be engaged for the first time. By coincidence this information passed across the desk of an officer from the

State Department's Cultural Affairs Bureau who happened to be a friend of director Robert Breen, head of the American National Theater and Association (ANTA). She quietly passed this confidential information to Breen, who was then performing his own version of *Hamlet* with ANTA at the Barter Theatre in Virginia. Breen immediately marshaled his political connections to see that his company would be selected to bring *Hamlet* into the very home of the most famous character in Western theater. And he wanted his friend Aline MacMahon, fresh off her performance as Gertrude, to accompany him.

Only a year after Aline's work in *The Search*, travel in postwar Europe was still a limited and difficult endeavor. But, with the engagement cosponsored by the State Department, the US Air Force, and the government of Denmark, Aline had soon returned to Copenhagen, en route to Helsignor. "It was an extraordinary experience," Aline said of playing *Hamlet* outdoors in the courtyard of Kronborg. "It was a big order, to play Shakespeare for the first time—but oh!—it made such a difference to play it at the castle.[50] I felt very romantic about all that—extremely. Oh, it was wonderful!" After two weeks in front of festival audiences in Helsignor, the US Air Force next took the company on a splendid tour through Germany where Aline played for US troops stationed in the American zones.[51] Transported and provided security by the Air Force, the movements of the *Hamlet* company were far more restricted than the crew of *The Search* had been. But even with strict rules governing fraternizing, travel, food, money, and mail, Aline was thrilled. "We toured the camps, and we were honored guests of the Air Force and we were treated to champagne and vintage wines everywhere." This engagement may have been the apotheosis of everything Aline wanted out of the profession of acting: a significant part in a quality production of an important play, performed to appreciative audiences at an exotic location that was deeply connected to the source material. Even the American soldiers, who were expected to be more interested in Bob Hope than Will Shakespeare, proved wildly enthusiastic. "At the end of each show everyone stayed on to demand curtain calls of the cast, giving a rousing ovation."[52] Aline's final thought on the engagement was simple but exultant: "It was *extraordinary*," she said."[53]

But even here, among representatives of cultural exchange for their own government, the specter of the gradually looming anti-Communist movement was at play. Upon return to the United States Clarence Derwent, the president of Actor's Equity and the production's Polonius, was detained by authorities and subjected to a six-hour interrogation concerning his alleged

We Fight It Round by Round

In 1949 Aline traveled to postwar Europe to perform *Hamlet* at Kronborg Castle, the real-life inspiration for Elsinor Castle. Aline is on the bottom step and, at the top, fifth from the left, is fellow cast member Ernest Borgnine. *New York Public Library, MacMahon / Abel photo file*. Donated to NYPL by Aline MacMahon without copyright transfer.

Communist affiliations. Aline, who knew Derwent well, having served with him on the Equity Board, refused to leave, and with the entire company behind her, remained, waiting nervously for Derwent to be released. When he was at last sent out Aline was chilled. She quickly understood that the government's microscope was poised everywhere.

Late in 1949 Aline returned to Warner Brothers for a tiny role in the Burt Lancaster swashbuckler *The Flame and the Arrow*. There, as she had been before, Aline found her passion aroused by a man with the type of masculine charisma that was in no way part of her married life. "Burt Lancaster is a darling—attractive, talented, wonderful looking—and intelligent, too," she said, unreservedly. "He really is unreal. He has a clever mind and an exceptional ability to make his own deductions. He is an acrobat, you know—of *extraordinary* beauty, and very expressive and high tensioned." Then, without guile or equivocation, Aline wrote to her reserved, intellectual husband four words that revealed the unfulfilled ardor percolating beneath her prim exterior. "Well, I am *his*," she said. "It is a *very* exciting project."

The only diminution to the high esteem that Aline felt for Lancaster was her disappointment at his lack of resolve in the perfectionism of picture making. She knew that he worked exceptionally hard at his craft, but when Lancaster flatly admitted that he treated *The Flame and the Arrow* as little more than Saturday afternoon adventure picture—Aline reacted like a wife who discovered her beloved husband in bed with a prostitute. In Lancaster Aline saw the ideal man—intellectual, talented, handsome, and energetic, and was disappointed that he presented himself as a mere pieceworker instead of an artist. "He doesn't know that Cimabue should have been disinterred to compose the scenes," she said, "and Dante to write the dialogue—and he must constantly compromise his own standards because 'it's too expensive' to rehearse or to explain the period attitudes to the extras."[54] Whatever Aline hoped for *The Flame and the Arrow* and its star, the film *is* little more than a low-budget reworking of *The Adventures of Robin Hood*, with Lancaster as Robin and Virginia Mayo as Marian—highly entertaining, yes, but hardly a potential masterpiece. It is interesting to consider that the limitations of time and resources on *Flame* may have influenced Lancaster as he soon developed into an expert producer and star of many high-quality films. Aline, meanwhile, thoroughly enjoyed herself. "I am crazy about the whole group. My part is small and I'm not especially noteworthy in it, but the whole project delights me."[55]

Late in 1949 the final direct teaching connection to Konstantyn Stanislavski's system passed. Madame Maria Ouspenskaya died after receiving severe burns and suffering a stroke in a house fire that started when she fell asleep while smoking. By now the Group and a few other New York schools were the primary domain of the Method, all run by Americans who had learned at the feet of Boleslavsky and Ouspenskaya. Even then the Method teachers were splintering into factions, each adding their own ideas to the technique, exactly as Boleslavsky had predicted they must in order to survive.

The following year Aline made her first appearance on the emerging medium of television in an episode of *The Philco Playhouse*. With television quickly infiltrating into millions of homes, there was a palpable fear of impending irrelevance brewing in the studios, but Aline was unconcerned. "The talk is that television is going to finish off Hollywood," Aline said. "I don't see why. All the smart ones are there—I think they'll just take television over."[56] Aline was prescient in her calm assessment of the future of the

We Fight It Round by Round

On the set of *The Flame and The Arrow* (1950). Aline was smitten with the electric masculinity of the film's star, Burt Lancaster. "I am *his*," she said. Unknown photographer, candid, unpublished.

industry; with the studios' new television production divisions and sales of broadcast rights to their film catalogs, they eventually did just that.

Meanwhile, a far more insidious enemy was then stalking Hollywood. The anti-Communist information gathered by the US government since the end of the war on the entertainment industry was now being accessed, collated, and packaged for public use by private hands. The dissemination of this information would help plunge America into the McCarthy era, a rabid, populist movement dedicated to wiping out Communism—and liberalism—in the United States at all costs. This frightening inquisition would invade American institutions private and public, and have dire personal and professional consequences for an entire generation of left-leaning artists, writers, politicians, and businessmen. Aline MacMahon would soon find herself circling the dark center of this indelible stain on twentieth-century history.

14

AH, WILDERNESS

In June 1950, a chill settled over the American entertainment industry when a small, privately printed booklet began turning up in the offices of film, radio, and television producers in New York and Hollywood. Published by a company known as American Business Consultants, *Red Channels* was the brainchild of three former agents of the Federal Bureau of Investigation and financed by millionaire textile importer Alfred Kohlberg. Listed inside were the names of 151 actors, writers, and directors who were denounced as Communists or Communist sympathizers. Among them was Aline MacMahon, and as a result of her appearance in the self-published book of a private citizen, producers and casting directors were afraid to employ her—and the others named—for fear of financial and political pressure from right-wing demagogues within the American power structure. Following *Red Channels*' release, Aline did not work on television or in film for two years. Soon she and her husband were also under increased scrutiny of FBI agents tasked with rooting out subversive behavior. It was like putting around-the-clock surveillance on your matronly aunt because she didn't like Eisenhower.

Red Channels and the Red Scare did not happen suddenly. It was an outgrowth of the friction between Communism and anti-Communism in America that had begun with the Bolshevik revolution of 1917 and continued on through the Second World War. HUAC nurtured the fight, and in 1950 a series of genuine Soviet espionage cases bolstered the fear. Then, during a speech in February, Senator Joseph McCarthy produced a fraudulent list of Communists he claimed were working in high levels of the State Department. The speech and his reckless demagoguery cynically lit the fuse of a national witch hunt that forever shattered America's ideal of moral integrity. For a decade the pervasive fear of Communists, or of being *branded* a Communist, would fester in the American psyche. The blacklist was underway.

Ah, Wilderness

As we know, Aline MacMahon did not appear in *Red Channels* by accident. She was not a radical, only someone who had thoughts and ideas favorable to the tenets of Communism. But her inclusion is a case study of what a runaway political ideology can do to citizens who merely wish to think for themselves. The proof is in the wide-ranging assignment of guilt found in the introduction to *Red Channels*: "It is the Party's boast that for every Party member there are at least ten 'reliables,' dupes or innocents," it said, "who will support its fronts. These 'colonists' need not be Party members or even deliberate cooperators. It is sufficient if they advance Communist objectives with complete unconsciousness."[1] Aline MacMahon was not unconscious, but neither was she dangerous or subversive. Yet the actress who had worked almost constantly since 1922 now managed only two film appearances and five television credits between 1950 and 1960.

Looking back from 1977, Aline was dismayed by what she thought of as a blurred cultural memory of what had happened almost thirty years earlier. "People keep saying, 'was there a blacklist'? Well, there jolly well *was* a blacklist! I was in the book [*Red Channels*] and the book was in the producer's desk, and if you came up for a part he ran his finger [down the list looking for your name]. I was blacklisted on television, in the movies and on Broadway. Playwrights would call me and say, 'I have a play coming up and there's an awfully good part for you,' and then I wouldn't hear from them. Later, they would tell me, 'Well, I suggested you, but the producers said . . .'[2] Everybody suspected of being in Communist front organizations was in that book. I was enraged at the idea."[3]

It was a fortunate happenstance that Aline avoided taking card-carrying membership in the Communist Party during her years in Hollywood. "The only thing that saved me from going—if that's the limit—to join the Party, was my contract," she reasoned. "Every time the people I was with were getting ready to do something active about it, I had to come home and be Mrs. Stein, so I missed that chapter."[4] It was only this incidental detail that allowed Aline MacMahon to circumvent questioning by HUAC. If there had been a Party card in her wallet she would almost certainly have been called to testify, where she would have had to inform, or refuse to name names and likely spend time in prison. She had already witnessed members of the so-called Hollywood Ten—a group of directors and writers suspected of Communist ties—jailed for keeping silent. "It worried me terribly watching [the HUAC hearings]. When the Hollywood Ten were called to testify I was not too active at that time for their defense. I think they were noble, I admire everything they did—simply extraordinary people, but gee, that's big stuff. Perhaps I gave some money, but it was not a time that I felt moved to carry any flags or do any protesting. I was probably scared. I thought when I was blacklisted that I just couldn't fight it.[5] I had my fighting period, like Picasso had a 'Blue Period' and I had a wonderful time doing it. Now I fight quietly."[6]

Aline was correct; during the early 1950s no one could escape the grasp of McCarthyism's long, bony fingers. As early as the autumn of 1949—before *Red Channels* had even been published—Aline was confused by the lack of work being offered through her new agent, Bert Allenberg. "I am needling my agent," she wrote. "I simply *can't* believe there isn't another job for me to follow this one [*The Flame and the Arrow*]. They make all the right answers to my pointed questions, but something is *wrong*—and it may or may not be me."[7] What Aline could not know—and of what even Bert Allenberg was possibly unaware—was that Red Scare innuendo was almost certainly at the heart of her inability to obtain work. Ignorant of the silent anti-Red campaign winding through the industry, Aline became convinced that she was simply no longer wanted ("my career is at the vanishing point," she feared) or that her agent was not doing all he could on her behalf. Working under these misapprehensions, Aline now asked Allenberg for a release from her contract. It would not be until *Red Channels* was issued the following summer that she would fully understand what was happening behind the scenes.

Later that year the Red Scare roughly insinuated itself into Aline's life when a pair of FBI agents appeared on an unannounced visit to the Steins' apartment at 1 West 64th Street. The bureau was then investigating Aline's friend Anna Rosenberg, the newly confirmed assistant secretary of defense in the Truman administration, looking for evidence of Rosenberg's connections to Communist organizations, including the John Reed Club. Aline MacMahon had known Mrs. Rosenberg for many years, and the agents queried her about Rosenberg's possible associations with the Party. The FBI report of the interview reveals that Aline divulged nothing incriminating—if there were, indeed, anything to divulge. When asked about Rosenberg's supposed connection to the JRC, Aline exclaimed, "Why, John Reed was a *radical!*" and insisted that her friend's loyalty and trustworthiness were above question.[8] The record of this meeting also confirms that the agents were not simply there to gather information about Anna Rosenberg—they were also training their lens on Aline, questioning her liberal politics in a way that she found a frightening invasion of privacy. Having now endured FBI intimidation, unwanted press scrutiny, and inclusion in *Red Channels*, Aline grew somewhat quieter in her

Ah, Wilderness

public advocacy, but without abandoning her liberal ideology. Even so, the FBI would not disappear; over the following decade their surveillance would include secret interviews with friends and coworkers, as well as recruiting willing informants even inside her own apartment building.

While *Red Channels* was first appearing on the desks of Manhattan producers and sponsors, the Method style that Aline MacMahon pioneered was still a relatively obscure discipline, largely unknown by mainstream audiences except for its connection to John Garfield and Monty Clift. In New York and Los Angeles teachers (including Aline herself) had been quietly producing Method acolytes until the slow burning fuse she lit decades earlier at last reached a ferocious powder keg. Marlon Brando's feral performance in Elia Kazan's *A Streetcar Named Desire* (1951) was the explosion that smashed the Method into popular consciousness and forever branded him as the unforgettable face of this "new" sensibility in acting. Brando's impact was so profound that the Russian technique almost immediately became the favored style for aspiring acting students the world over. This was the culmination of the transmigration of Stanislavski's original teachings—filtered through Boleslavsky, seeded at Pleasantville, and refined by Aline MacMahon and her successors. Interestingly, this revolution in acting—created and imported by Russians, and largely refined, taught and practiced by Red and Pink liberals—achieved its greatest prominence in American culture just as anti-Communist hysteria was reaching its zenith. In Brando, the Method baton that had passed from Aline, to Garfield, and then to Monty Clift was now perhaps in its final resting place. The following decades saw hundreds of others added to the honor roll of its practitioners, but in the public mind the Method has remained firmly associated with Marlon Brando—perhaps never to be relinquished.

To American conservatives and anti-Communists, the cultural liberalism that followed World War II, like that which also followed the Great War, was unruly and disconcerting. The Beat writers, the explosion of Abstract Expressionism, and the rise of film noir were responses to the tension, stress, and anxiety engendered by the carnage of war and the angst of living in a world which now had the atomic bomb. It is not surprising that in this atmosphere, Brando's torrent of primal emotions found resonance with postwar audiences. The Method encouraged—even demanded—that its practitioners express their love, anger, or frustration honestly and openly. The war-era toughness of John Garfield was more self-assurance than anger, but the inner rage that Marlon Brando unleashed in *Streetcar* found an audience that was both startled and energized by its unconscious connection to their own primal fears. Not every

Method actor may be capable of dredging that kind of charged emotional performance, but *only* the Method—and such a moment of cultural angst—could combine to produce a voice that dared touch this raw, open wound with the scream of pain, guilt, and incredulity that so many soldiers and citizens had locked inside. Exactly as the repressed Russians had found catharsis though the Method, so did we in the West. In the Method was a pathway to healing.

Even as the original American devotee of the Method, it is doubtful that Aline would have been capable of exposing herself so completely. She seems primarily to have used the Method to tap the quieter side of her emotions. Dejection, sorrow, and sadness came easily to Aline, perhaps an underground response to her long-established sublimation of self-pity, but not so anger or rage. The Method then, appears to be at its most successful when the combination of artist and role is properly married, since each actor is also a person who responds to emotions in a different way, manufactured or not. Even among the great practitioners of the Method we do not expect the same style from Al Pacino as we do from Daniel Day-Lewis or Eva Marie Saint. What we do expect is an expression of honesty and truthfulness, and that is the key to what the Method has brought to the art of performing.

As 1951 dragged on the Steins found themselves in a swale from which the horizon was obscured. That year Clarence had taken on the planning and building of an entire town, Kitimat, British Columbia, for the Aluminum Company of Canada, and the enormous workload he shouldered during those years mired him in yet another depressive episode.[9] Meanwhile, as the result of what was now a public blacklist, quality film work was being kept well outside Aline's grasp. Although she had never joined the Communist Party and was privately forthcoming in disavowing Communism, it mattered little—the taint was pervasive and few producers gave her a chance. Then, in early February 1952, with the Steins on the verge of a spring trip to Europe, word came that the State Department had suddenly refused to renew Aline's passport. On the Refusal Form in the files of the Passport Office is a handwritten note outlining the reason Aline's government did not want her traveling outside the country: "Alleged Communist," it says.[10] "There was some question from Washington about my passport renewal," Aline said in 1977. "I went down [to the passport office] on that case, but I had it out quietly, with no publicity because I was not interested in that kind of publicity, because I rather fear personally that kind of publicity."[11] Within days of the meeting, Aline was in the office of a Manhattan notary who witnessed her signature on a terse document requested by the director of the Passport Office. "The listing of my name in 'Red Channels' is inaccurate," the letter said. "I herewith state under oath that I am not and never have been a Communist."[12] The passport was renewed, but Aline's disillusion was rapidly growing.

It was 1953 before Aline at last had a breakthrough when Warner Brothers hired her for a small part in *The Eddie Cantor Story*. ("If I am very unlucky I will have to do this one," she said.) Sadly, her first film in nearly four years is a painful conglomeration of biopic clichés and exaggerated performances. Aline's is the sole realistic portrayal in the film (Cantor himself is reduced to a cartoon); she plays Eddie's grandmother with a warmth and tenderness that makes you wish that *you* had such a grandmother—and that any other character in the film were half as endearing. It was heartening that Warner Brothers took the risk in hiring Aline, but even at the studio where she had been long admired as a decorous, mannered artist, the taint of *Red Channels* pervaded. Aline would be welcomed back to Warners, but only if the errant daughter signed a statement for the studio lawyers saying that she was not, and had never been, a Communist. Irked, but still in need of funds to help pay for Clarence's treatments, Aline put her name to the statement, and the studio that made her momentarily a star momentarily brought her home. Describing the dark suspicions of the entertainment industry in early 1953, Aline did not mince words: "It is a witch hunt in progress," she mused.[13]

This was not the final time that Aline MacMahon would be required to deny ever having been a Red. In August 1954, as she was being considered for a role in Anthony Mann's *The Man from Laramie*, a Columbia Pictures producer ran *his* finger down the list of the Communist subversives provided by *Red Channels*. On seeing her name there, the executive lit a fire under the Columbia legal department to provide cover for the studio. Here, Columbia wanted more than a blanket statement of denial, instead sending a detailed list of the associations and "fronts" from Aline's past for her to disavow. On holiday in London, Aline responded with an outward calm that belied the turmoil inside.

Dear Sirs—
In response to a request from your organization, I hereby state:

1. I am not and never have been a Communist.
2. I have not—do not and never will engage in any activities deemed by my government as subversive.
3. As for the list Mr. Graf has offered for my perusal, I can only say that until I check on the items I have no way of

being sure they are correct, except for items: A member of the National Wallace for President Committee, which I definitely was, and I was a *member* of the League of Women Shoppers, though not an Honorary Vice-President.

And, in addition, if I was actually involved in any of the other items as described in this list I can swear it was only in the same way I gave my name and help to other causes for doing good and in no way was my participation inspired by any Communist connection.[14]

Unfortunately, Columbia was not entirely satisfied with this response. In early September yet another anonymous studio drudge called Aline with invasive questions about her political ideas. The letter Aline wrote to Clarence that afternoon had the look of a hastily scrawled death row confession and bristled with the chill of righteous indignation.

Someone with Columbia Pictures called to say he would like to go into certain details of my activities as listed in "Red Channels." He said that some folks at Columbia are not satisfied with the affidavit I gave—they think my past life has been "unfortunate" in some respects and they'd like to help me out of my "troubles." I answered that I do not consider anything I have done unfortunate—that I have no troubles—that the whole matter bores me—that I gave Warner's the same affidavit when I played in "The Eddie Cantor Story" and as far as I know there have been no complications of any kind. So what is Columbia worried about? Then I rang down the receiver in some haste. I don't like to be treated like I'm a damned soul because along with countless other people I tried to be useful in matters of public betterment.[15]

Before the telephone could even cool from her anger, Aline immediately contacted the head of Columbia's legal department in search of the unfortunate soul who had rang her with such importune questions. A few minutes later the offending (and apologetic) public relations man, Raymond Bell, was located and ordered to smooth things over with Aline. And although she was not mollified ("I still don't like Mr. Bell or his public relations technique.") Aline's personal character carried the day—a contract was presented by Columbia with no other contrition or confession required.[16]

Ah, Wilderness

During the greater part of the early 1950s, when Aline was persona non grata on Broadway and in films and television, it was regional theater that kept her working, however modestly. In 1951 she returned to Stockbridge as the mother in a well-received production of *The Glass Menagerie*.[17] Also in 1951 she had enormous critical success in *The Madwoman of Chaillot* at the Ivar Theatre in Los Angeles. Part social satire, part *Arsenic and Old Lace*, *Madwoman* concerns a middle-aged Parisian spinster who plots to murder greedy oil company executives who want to sink wells directly under the City of Lights. The title role was a magnificent canvas for Aline's mastery of farce, and she played it to the hilt. "Aline MacMahon, an actress of splendid resourcefulness, stirred an audience to long applause with her performance as Countess Aurelia last night," Edwin Schallert said in his opening-night review. "The production is the most interesting and significant given this year, and it yielded a special triumph to its leading feminine player. It is Miss MacMahon's play, because the role she acts, a veritable tour de force, demands great versatility and assurance, and she brought both to her unique interpretation."[18]

A highlight of her McCarthy-era exile, *Madwoman* also became a bitter reminder of the dire professional circumstances in which Aline now found herself. After the high-profile success as Countess Aurelia, she was immediately invited to bring *The Madwoman of Chaillot* to Catholic University of America in Washington, DC. "They must have thought that because my name was MacMahon, I must be a Catholic," Aline said. "So I found myself living among the nuns in a quiet, lovely place, rehearsing with Alan Schneider—when they fired me! They asked me to leave. It was a blow—somebody must have told them that I was a Communist. In any case I was asked to leave, and that was a crushing experience." When asked what she did when the university confronted her, Aline was typically direct and dismissive of her feelings. "I left," she said. "I didn't say a word. I packed my suitcase, and the Father drove me to the train station, and I said to him that I thought people would probably get the world they deserved. And I came home and luckily Clarence wasn't there, it was pouring rain, and I opened the door, put my suitcase down, nobody was in the apartment and I thought 'I'll have hysterics.' but there was nobody to watch, and I was hungry. So I went down and had the best steak that I could buy and forgot it."[19]

As much as she liked to dismiss it, this incident scarred Aline's faith in American ideals. But gradually came countervailing winds. Following some minor television work, producer Robert Whitehead (whom Aline had worked with in the 1947 production of *Medea*) refused to bow to anti-Communist pressure and returned Aline to Broadway with a solid part in T.S. Eliot's *The Confidential Clerk*, alongside Claude Rains. It was a noble gesture by an old friend, but it didn't convince others to take similar risks.

The year 1956 brought another small but heartening opportunity when Aline began a rewarding professional relationship with the autobiographical writings of Irish author Sean O'Casey. O'Casey, an Irish nationalist and avowed Socialist who had been blacklisted following the Dublin Lockout, appealed to the rebel in Aline MacMahon, but it was his skill as a memoirist that appeared to elicit emotions connected to her beloved Irish father. "If I cry when I'm reading it, if its sad, I'll do it. Irregardless of money or anything, if I'm moved. That's what happened with Sean O'Casey. When I read the script based on his books I started to cry. I was so touched."[20] Director Stuart Vaughn presented O'Casey's first coming-of-age memoir *I Knock at the Door* as a staged reading, with six actors sitting at concert desks in front of a cyclorama, more a radio play—or even an elderly cousin to the minimalist film movement *Dogme 95*—than theater. With little overhead and almost no money to pay actors, the producers worried little about the possibilities of an anti-Red boycott. "We all rehearsed for nothing in Rae Allen's kitchen and she made us breakfast every day, and for that first performance we each got, I think it was five dollars, but it led to wonderful, lifelong friendships." The results were so loved by the critics that the readings were first extended, then revived a few years later. "The two glowing performances of *I Knock at the Door* yesterday evening were of such high quality that there was no maladjustment between material and performance, nothing omitted, nothing left over—and so deeply laden with truth that they represent universal beauty."[21]

The same company of writer, director, and cast later mounted O'Casey's second memoir, *Pictures in the Hallway*, both on Broadway and in a road company with similar results. "'Pictures in the Hallway' has sounds as lyrical as an Irish harp and as wild as the Irish bagpipes. It is a sharp, ironical muddle of Irish politics and Irish reasoning, and stirs the tale of a boy's first job and his first girl with an Irish stick."[22] When O'Casey died in 1964 there was another revival, and later still, when Aline was seventy and part of the Repertory Company of Lincoln Center, director Jules Irving mounted yet another O'Casey memoir, *The Plough and the Stars* (which she had missed playing in Hollywood). Irving called Aline while she was in Lenox Hill Hospital recovering from a fall and promised that there would be a part waiting for her when she was released—even if she had to play it in a wheelchair.[23] For ten weeks in the little theater at Lincoln Center Aline again put on her

While Aline was blacklisted in the 1950s she participated in a series of staged readings based on the writings of Irish memoirist Sean O'Casey. There was almost no overhead and little money for the performers, but also nothing to lose from the potential backlash of anti-Communist crusaders. Studio publicity material.

impeccable Irish brogue and connected to the simple, honest emotions of family life in Dublin—and memories of William Marcus MacMahon.

The mid-1950s continued to be professionally thin for Aline; with only two small television appearances between 1955 and 1959, she was still largely exiled to regional theater, where audiences might be enthusiastic, but pay was morose. This was the fate endured by hundreds of highly successful liberal actors, writers, and directors of the era, unable to find producers who would employ them for high-profile mainstream work. After years of taking a philosophical view of the various troubles she and Clarence had endured, Aline was now exhausted from the fight. "I feel we have suffered enough for our term in Hell," she wrote. "Can we possibly have died and are sentenced to it forever? My God, the world is for laughing too."[24]

Disillusioned at the continuing influence of McCarthyism, Aline soon devised an ingenious way to leverage her professional credentials while neatly sidestepping the stigma of *Red Channels*. In 1958 she applied for and received a very rare Fulbright Scholarship from the United States Cultural Exchange Program. Devised for postwar intercultural outreach, the program provides grants for students, teachers, artists, and professionals to conduct research, study, or teach abroad. The grant request that Aline submitted was to undertake a study of France's numerous summer drama festivals, then collate and present what she had learned to American Festival organizers. Having long been irked at her parents' insistence that she get her university degree, Aline at last appreciated the value of her schooling. "When I applied for the Fulbright, the first question they asked was 'are you a college graduate?' I got the scholarship only because I had reluctantly obeyed my parents so many years ago."[25] In the summer of 1958 the Steins could be found tramping through the arrondissements of France, visiting festival after festival, and taking in every other sight in their view. "The Chateau country, with its legends and its architectural remains, is especially suited to historical drama," Aline told an interviewer. "In Avignon we saw Jean Vilar's Teatro Nationale Populaire in the courtyard of the Palace of the Popes. We even attended a performance in a marketplace. We arrived during the day when the local merchants were selling their wares in the same square which, later that night, was cleared and transformed into a stage." When she was finished, Aline had gathered so much research and reference that she hoped to produce a guidebook of the festival circuit for tourists. "Unfortunately, I've been so busy telling people about my Festival rounds and compiling presentations that I haven't had time to produce the handbook!" she said.[26] When Aline appeared in *Romeo and Juliet* at the Stratford Shakespeare Festival the following summer, she was able to bring some flavor of the French style to Connecticut. And while the Stratford Repertory was uneven and the salary modest, Aline MacMahon's performances became the undisputed hit of the 1959 season. At sixty, she had matured into the perfect embodiment of Shakespeare's beloved nurse and surrogate mother to Juliet. "Highest honors in the season go to Aline MacMahon, who played the best Nurse seen in many a year," the *Stratford Shakespeare Quarterly* reported.

"She was loving and lovable, possessive, and plainspoken enough, yet without the unnecessary coarse touches that some interpreters of this part add. Here was a seasoned actress, completely at home in a great play."[27] In summing up the Gotham press reviews, The *New York Herald Tribune* remarked: "'Romeo and Juliet' received mixed notices from the New York critics yesterday, with only two of the six endorsing the Stratford production. The other criticism was directed mainly at the performances. An outstanding exception was Aline MacMahon, whose portrayal of the Nurse was praised in all the reviews." And of her work in *All's Well That Ends Well*, there was this about the Queen of Stratford, 1959: "How fortunate the company has been to have Aline MacMahon in two of the four plays! Her Countess of Rousillon was satisfying in every particular. Voice, gesture, mood—all were as they should be. She was the titled lady in every inch of her bearing, in full command of her great household, yet sympathetic, understanding and warm-hearted."[28] That first year at Stratford scratched every one of Aline's professional itches. "It was Nirvana," she said. "The most wonderful season any performer could have."[29]

The following year Aline had another success when Judith Anderson was called on to recreate her performance from the legendary 1947 production of *Medea* for the inaugural episode of the syndicated TV series *The Play of the Week*. Aline was engaged to play the nurse, the role she had left before *Medea* reached Broadway twelve years earlier. It mattered little to her that the budget was paltry and the salary minuscule—it was a chance to continue the kind of deep, meaningful work she so craved. Aline's performance was impeccable; from the opening sequence where she appears alone from the shadows to review the dire circumstances of Medea's predicament, she is fraught with fear and apprehension, both trying to protect her mistress and herself. It is a rare opportunity to see Aline's stage presence, and watch her conjure the darker side of the Method technique, bringing genuine horror and despair from a seldom-visited place in her psyche. But *Medea* is nothing if not a showcase for the title character, and Aline was overshadowed by the focus pulled, tightly and deservedly, on Judith Anderson's operatic turn as the murderous Princess of Colchis. The production is helped by its elegant direction, with a simple set outside Medea's home and a camera that prowls the space sparingly while the actors create tight groupings or populate the foreground as Anderson emotes behind them, allowing her occasionally extreme theatricality to be reduced to an appropriate size. Although rare, this recording has helped enshrine Robert Whitehead's production of *Medea* as perhaps the greatest of all modern versions of the Euripides classic.

Aline (left), with Judith Anderson and Morris Carnovsky, in the 1959 television film of Euripides' Greek tragedy *Medea*. Produced by David Susskind, this was a re-creation of the widely praised 1947–48 stage production that Aline left after tryouts. Studio publicity material.

Fortunately, by the end of the decade the fog of political fear and oppression that was obscuring happiness for the Steins at last appeared to be lifting. Beginning in 1956 the Supreme Court had issued rulings that emasculated certain aspects of the blacklist, and the following year a radio host named John Henry Faulk sued the private company that had named him as a Communist, eventually winning a 3.5-million-dollar court settlement. Soon, even Hollywood power brokers would find that it was more advantageous to break the blacklist than cower under it.

Aline's final, retrospective look back at the era was perhaps emblematic of her attitude toward life. Even when painful events were out of her control—her husband's illness, the blacklist, or the loss of important work—Aline refused to be the victim of her own story. Typically, her anger at McCarthyism was almost entirely focused on the injustices visited on others rather than herself. "At the beginning there was a group of us, we hoped we were the intellectuals in Hollywood, who thought perhaps the Russian system was the solution and we met and we talked about it," Aline recalled. "I am a liberal and I was then and I suppose I always will be if socialism is liberal and to the left. I was of the generation who listened to Mrs. Roosevelt. She said if you believe in something go out and fight for it. So we were *all* belonging to societies, and then we found ourselves smacked in the bellies with wet fishes, because a lot of people lost their livelihoods on account of that, and many of them innocent. Some of my very good friends were destroyed by it—*very* good friends: Phil Loeb.[30] Yes, I was blacklisted. But I have never spent a sleepless night, I have never missed a meal with no appetite, I've never had a day when there wasn't money in my pocket. I was lucky enough to live 46 years with a remarkable man. I've had very good health and I've always worked somewhere. I mean, life is filled with tragedies and sorrows—but by and large I've had most of the breaks," she concluded. "I didn't suffer."

As McCarthyism's grip on America gradually released, the professional exile Aline and others had been living under was largely broken. Unfortunately, now in her sixties and having previously endured a gradual professional decline and years on the blacklist, she found her choices mostly relegated to the middle-aged character parts that she had learned so well as a young woman. Typical of these were *The Young Doctors* (1961) and *Diamond Head* (1962) in which she played an indomitable old sage counseling youngsters with the gentle wisdom of maturity. In the tear-jerker *I Could Go on Singing*, she was the sly, trusted confidante of singer Judy Garland, while *Cimarron* (1960), found her in a small but memorable role as a tough Western homesteader who loses her husband to foul play during the Oklahoma land rush of 1889. ("So much chagrin at being in stuff I dislike. Damn. Damn. Damn.")[31] Around 1960 she commissioned a proposal and shot a pilot film for a television series based on Conrad Richter's Pulitzer Prize–winning book trilogy, *The Trees*, *The Fields*, and *The Town*. The series was to star Aline as the matriarch of Richter's pioneer family, Sayward Wheeler, in a kind of gritty, violent *Little House on the Prairie*.[32] Sponsors and networks were entirely disinterested. But it was another role as a wise elder that would return her to the

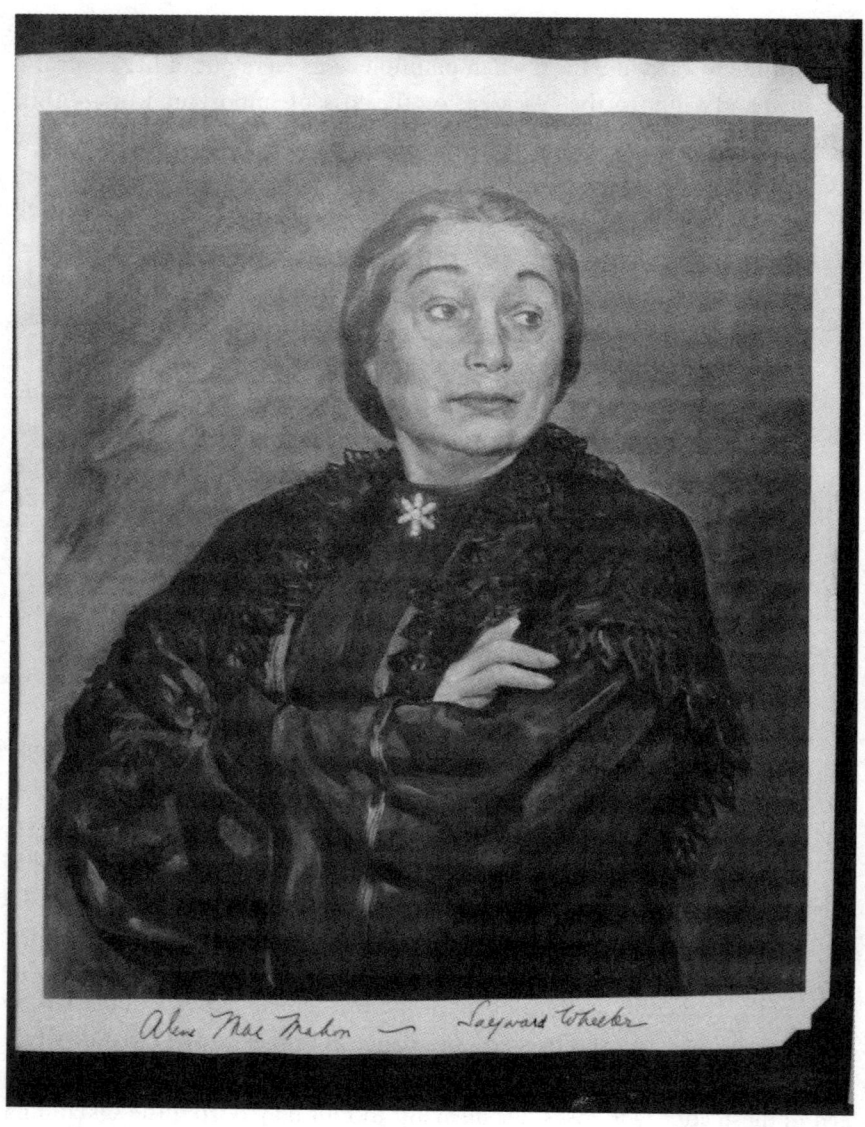

Aline MacMahon — Sayward Wheeler

In the early 1960s Aline paid to create an outline and pilot episode for a proposed television series based on *The Awakening Land* trilogy by Pulitzer Prize–winning writer Conrad Richter. Even this painted portrait of Aline as Richter's heroine Sayward Wheeler failed to interest sponsors. Donated to Cornell University by Aline MacMahon without copyright.

Ah, Wilderness

Manhattan stage in one of the great, unexpected success stories of Broadway in the 1960s, *All the Way Home*.

Based on James Agee's novel *A Death in the Family*, *All the Way Home* was originally commissioned as an episode of *Playhouse 90*, but circumstances instead sent this quiet, heart-wrenching story of family tragedy to scrimp for box office dollars against frothy Manhattan heavyweights such as *Camelot*, *Irma La Douce*, and *West Side Story*. Even *ATWH*'s producer Fred Coe anticipated doom, and when the opening-night performance resulted in only $340 in receipts, his prophecy was fulfilled. They next day, a Friday, the company posted an announcement that *ATWH* would close on Monday. "But on Sunday, Ed Sullivan praised the show on television," Coe said, "and on Monday we took in $3000. And took down the closing notices."[33] From there, the production endured a series of Sisyphean rises and falls, being forced to cut ticket prices, reinvest royalties, and ask the cast to add performances. "Things kept coming to keep us alive," said Coe. "A new notice. An award. First it was the Critic's Circle. That kept us going."[34] More and more plaudits rolled in, continuing to extend the show that nearly closed after its fourth performance. By the following September audiences had attended over 300 performances, and *All the Way Home* became the longest-running stage production of Aline MacMahon's career.

The framework of *All the Way Home* is as spare and congruous as can be: when a man with a young son and pregnant wife dies unexpectedly, the trauma tests the emotional and spiritual make-up of the survivors. Essential to the success of a play that is so decidedly lacking in incident is the quality of the playwright's words and the people delivering them. The sensitivity of Tad Mosel's script was so genuine that it captured the Pulitzer Prize for Drama in 1961, and the four principals upon which the burden of emotional truth rested (Aline, Lillian Gish, Colleen Dewhurst, and Arthur Hill) could not have been more keenly chosen. "'All the Way Home' is a dedication to the strength of the human spirit etched in heart-wrenching portraits," the *Los Angeles Times* wrote. "The wife telling her son that 'accident' means injury when she knows it means death; a grandmother prattling about 'everything will be alright' then talking of what undertaker to choose; the boy proud of the status death gives him in the neighborhood, then terrified of the loss of his father." Director Arthur Penn gave *ATWH* a compassionate, sure-handed treatment of such dangerously heavy fare, tempered by gentle humor and wise observations of people enduring grief. "'All the Way Home' is not the escapist play for those seeking fluffy, feathery and facile entertainment. It is for those souls strong enough to sit through a widow's lamentations, a dirgeful collection of bereaved relatives and a virtual funeral wake. Yet within the unconventional and not wholly satisfying structure—up a long hill to a magnificent view, then down again—were dozens of breath-catching insights."[35] For those who were attuned to such wan sentiments, *ATWH* was both emotionally draining and spiritually uplifting. Indeed, there were sermons built around its message (although the play itself questions the idea of religious faith), and groups of regular playgoers who took out newspaper ads at their own expense imploring audiences to see *All the Way Home*.

Unfortunately, by the time the play was transferred to the big screen in 1963, the changes made to *All the Way Home* robbed it of some essential element. Of the principal actors, only Aline returned as Aunt Hannah and Thomas Chalmers as the son. More importantly, Arthur Penn was replaced by fellow live television director Alex Segal, and the knowledge and experience Penn had gleaned while crafting the stage production was lost. Finally, with little incident to drive the story, *ATWH* lived almost entirely on the emotional resonance of its characters, and without the intimacy of the live performance, the film found a difficult time recapturing them.[36]

As the early 1960s produced increased cultural and political upheaval, Aline became further dedicated to her desire for a simpler, quieter life. Hollywood was changing, and although she still spent time in Los Angeles with the ageless Jennie Mac, it was television that now provided her most interesting opportunities, including two wonderful appearances on Reginald Rose's law series, *The Defenders*. In *Old Lady Ironsides* (1963) she is an aging suffragette who raises hell with the local school board after they expel her young neighbor-cum-surrogate-granddaughter for being pregnant out of wedlock. The script is surprisingly smart and bold for the era, expressly discussing abortion and challenging the convention of young women being forced to submit to unwanted marriages to avoid the single-mother stigma that the culture itself had installed. "I have such a wonderful part," she enthused, "that I wish she were in a series. She is the only character I've ever played that I can say that about. She's so healthy!" When asked if she was serious about taking on series television, Aline could not tell a lie. "If it came down to it, probably not," she said.[37]

The producers of *The Defenders* were so pleased with Aline's performance that they hired her for another fine part in *King of the Hill* (1964) as the wife of an old-time mob boss who is under investigation by the local district attorney. For years Mrs. Vronis (Aline) has pretended not to know about her husband's criminal ways, a forlorn, defeated woman trapped inside a false

All the Way Home won the Pulitzer Prize for Drama in 1961 and became Aline's longest-running show on Broadway. It was transferred to the screen in 1963, but did not quite capture the emotional resonance of the original stage production. Studio publicity material.

narrative that she refuses to acknowledge. But when her husband engineers the murder of the lone witness against him—a young man she loved like a son—Mrs. Vronis can no longer pretend that he is innocent, or that she is not complicit in his crimes. In a devastatingly emotional scene Aline focuses decades of anger at her husband, admitting that she had always known of his crimes and daring him to swear in front of God that he did not kill the boy. This highly charged scene and the denouement that follows are worthy of Aline's work at any time in her career. The performance also provides a rare look at what Aline's Method training could do in service of emotions not usually called upon. Mrs. Vronis's nervous energy, her anger tempered by her fear of losing control all ring true, perhaps because of Aline's own worry of letting loose her emotions. TV critics noticed her performances and gave her due plaudits. "'The Defenders' isn't like television at all," Aline observed. "It really is like the equivalent of a short feature movie every week."

Aline's appearances on *The Defenders* are very nearly the end of her career on film and television. From 1964 until her retirement in 1975, she has only three television credits, each a filmed record of a play; two Greek classics (*Antigone* and *The Prodigal*, based on *Orestes*), and *For the Use of the Hall*, a modern comedy/drama where Aline serves more as Greek chorus than a true character in the story. Beginning in 1966 however, she will concentrate on the longest sustained stage work of her career, spending seven years as a member of New York's Repertory Theatre of Lincoln Center.

15

SET MY FEET ON THE WAY

In spite of the jarring social and political changes of the decade, the 1960s proved to be kinder to Aline and Clarence than the 1950s had been. Like anyone who lives long enough to see younger generations supplant them as the dominant force driving cultural development, the Steins watched these changes with apprehension and bemusement. But neither ever became quite old enough to miss the value in the voices and ideas of the new decade. "The old order changeth," Aline said, "or perhaps it is I who have changed."[1]

By the time John Kennedy became president in January 1961, the Steins thoughts about Communism as a force for political change had soured. Russia's actions in the east proved that the Socialists were not living up to their purported interest in peace and equity, and the discovery of nuclear missile bases in Cuba during the autumn of 1962 bared Soviet expansionist designs for all to see. On location in Tennessee for the filming of *All the Way Home* at the height of the tension surrounding a possible missile exchange with Russia, Aline watched as the nuclear clock ticked ever nearer to midnight, and reacted as she often did to fear or worry, by minimizing it. "Such grim news," she wrote. "I think we will continue to say war is impossible and we will go inevitably to war. And if we all blow up—whazza diffrence? What a woild!"[2]

As a result of these incidents and others, the tide of Red-tinged ideology in America now dropped to its lowest levels since WWI. In the new decade it was John Kennedy's youthful vigor that captured the hope for change in the far left. "These are exciting days," Clarence wrote to a friend in Sweden. "It is like the first hundred days of Franklin Roosevelt. Things are happening. A forward-looking President is trying to see the hard facts of this changing world and do something about them. Kennedy has the enthusiasm of youth and astounding wisdom. We have great hopes for the future."[3] Although neither Clarence or Aline regretted their lifelong liberalism, or the work they had done on behalf of what they considered righteous causes, both were disheartened to realize that the seductive lure of the Communist movement had been only an illusion—a projection of their desires for "a more equal world." They were gravely disappointed that their ideal had not been achieved, but could not quite condemn themselves for having embraced hope, only for naivete. It was 1964 when the FBI at last closed the investigation and surveillance of the Steins, stating, with a strange, institutional sympathy, that the couple were in no way a danger to the country, and perhaps need never have been monitored at all. Their files—more than 400 pages of secret notes, documents, and memoranda, representing thousands of government work hours—were quietly filed away and forgotten.

By 1965, Aline MacMahon had been off the New York stage for four years. Since McCarthyism's demise, she had accepted television and film work only on her own terms, refusing anything stressful or cheap, or anything that would take her too long away from her husband. That year, however, an offer came from her friend Robert Whitehead to join the prestigious Repertory Theater of Lincoln Center, in residence at Manhattan's newly opened Vivian Beaumont Theater. After decades of attempting to instigate a National Repertory Theater to no avail, Aline was excited by the opportunity. Unfortunately, that summer she was again scheduled to perform at the Stratford Shakespeare Festival and could not accept Whitehead's offer. Aline had not planned to appear in the 1965 Stratford festival until she saw an announcement that *Coriolanus*—Shakespeare's tragedy of a mother (Volumina) and her soldier son (Coriolanus)—would be among that year's offerings. "Every actor has a dream part they'd like most to play," she admitted. "Volumina in *Coriolanus* is one of mine. When I heard that it was on the schedule I picked up the phone and called Allen Fletcher [Stratford's artistic director] and told him that I *dreamed* of doing it."[4] Fletcher, who knew full well Aline's talents, signed her on and was richly rewarded. "Miss MacMahon's Volumina was magnificent," critic Cecil Smith said, "majestic in her robes and commanding in the scenes with the son she'd raised to be a warrior and leader."[5] Not forgetting the political turmoil of the decade recently ended, Aline reflected on this story of the mother whose ambitious political maneuvering first elevates, then destroys, her son. "The play is pertinent today," she said. "It holds significance for the leaders of the world, and displays the effect of mob rule and public sway on issues of government."[6] Like much of Shakespeare's writings, the resonance remains, even now.

When planning of the 1966 season began, Robert Whitehead was no longer involved with the Repertory Theater of Lincoln Center. Fortunately the new directors, Herbert Blau and Jules Irving, understood Aline's great versatility and reiterated Whitehead's offer for her to join the company. Now at liberty to accept, Aline signed on and for the next six years could regularly be seen walking the quarter-mile stretch of West 64th Street that runs like an arrow from the Steins apartment to the Vivian Beaumont Theater on Columbus Avenue. At Lincoln Center Aline returned to the type of community that she had discovered again and again: in high school, within the Halls of Barnard, and at the Neighborhood Playhouse. Even among the contract players and technical crews of the Warner Brothers factory, Aline felt the comfort of familiarity—something that she may not have even realized was missing during those years without a contract or a long-lasting professional family.

Aline's tenure with the Repertory Company of Lincoln Center was a happy one. At last she was with a theater devoted to the kind of challenging, dramatic roles to which she constantly aspired. But there was a problem; except for a few members of the regular cast, the Repertory Company of Lincoln Center was often deemed by Manhattan critics to be a feeble, ordinary assemblage of talent from executives to directors and actors. With a financial endowment from the city of New York, and a lucrative subscription base of well-heeled cultural dilettantes, the Beaumont Company was regularly denounced as creatively complacent. "The Beaumont is, if I smell aright, beginning to be quite comfortable with itself," Walter Kerr wrote, "with its virtuous but unearned subscription base, with its mediocrity. It has an undistinguished company—always saving Aline MacMahon and Philip Bosco—but it isn't trying harder. Why should it? It has an automatic, unfair advantage."[7] Kerr's appreciation of Aline notwithstanding, his reviews and those of his fellow critics were often scathing. Among the eight productions in which Aline appeared, most were dismissed as "a bore," "a bomb," "a dry hole," "dull," or "gloomy." Of the Beaumont's 1968 production of *Tiger at the Gates*, a drama set during the Trojan War, *Women's Wear Daily* railed, "The Repertory Theatre of Lincoln Center has been recently managing to win the praise that painfully eluded it for so long by presenting warhorse plays with institutional craft. The praise has never been deserved. Although the craft has been welcome after so many years of ineptitude, the institutionalism is dull and the warhorsism cynical. But even that was preferable to the industrial show slickness of 'Tiger at the Gates,' which demonstrated the impressive finesse of business art while insulting the very nature of the theatre. It is plastic personified."[8]

Even as the Vivian Beaumont productions regularly infuriated the critics, Aline MacMahon remained an exception to their ire. Within even the direst reviews could be found kind words for the woman who had now become one of the undisputed treasures of New York theater. Even Walter Kerr, the acid-tongued writer who famously gave the fewest favorable theater reviews of any critic in New York, could not help but praise her. After seeing Aline in *Walking with Waldheim* in 1967, Kerr wrote what is among the finest reviews of her career:

> At The Forum Theater beneath the Vivian Beaumont in Lincoln Center, there is nothing in the airy lift of the small structure to suggest that you are under anything.[9] The house expands from a pinpoint and seems to breathe, as opposed to houses that dwindle to a lighted pinpoint—that faraway stage up there—and seem stifling.
>
> "I have been seeing Aline MacMahon for more years than I'm going to be honest enough, or ungentlemanly enough, to count. Always she has pleased me, sometimes more, sometimes less, nevertheless always. But as I watched her at work in the opening at the Lincoln Center Forum I realized that hitherto I'd only seen her sideways. Under a proscenium arch, she could—if she wished—do what actors are always doing; whisper to the other actors, become her private self, even make out of context jokes.
>
> "At the Forum, no one can do that. And for the first time I felt I had Miss MacMahon where I wanted her, surrounded, all visible, all there. As it turns out, she is an actress who can stand being bathed in eyes, forced to perform in every dimension. Miss MacMahon is wholly present, complete, committed.[10]

During Aline's tenure at the Vivian Beaumont, Clarence was gradually approaching his ninetieth birthday. Slowly, as the 1960s drew closer to the 1970s, all his ceaseless curiosity and indefatigable energy began to evaporate wisp by wisp. This mental decline was apparent in Aline's correspondence to her husband; once brimming with complex thoughts and ideas, her letters were now whittled to a few simple sentences about family or the weather, and insistent, underlined reminders of previous notes, conversations, and events. By decades' end the man who had courted Aline MacMahon from nearly the moment they met—who, in the 1920s had stood at the stage door of *Artists and Models* waiting for her to accompany him to a late-night Manhattan dinner and sacrificed a significant portion of his happiness to honor her work as an artist—was barely visible in the dwindling, increasingly forgetful figure at 1 West 64th Street.[11]

Set My Feet On the Way

In 1972, just weeks before his 90th birthday, Clarence's declining health forced Aline to resign from the Repertory Company of Lincoln Center to oversee his home care, where a rotation of nurses came and went, as even the memory of his wife of forty-four years quickly decayed. In the final years of his life Aline would sit with him on their balcony, looking east across Central Park to Temple Emanu-El, which Clarence had a hand in designing in 1929. On Fridays at 5:30 they would rest in silence, listening to the Shabbat ceremony on the Congregation's weekly radio broadcast. By the time Clarence curled under his blankets to sleep, even that would be forgotten.

On February 7, 1975, there was three inches of snow covering Central Park. It was beautiful and clear and only a few degrees below freezing. And Aline MacMahon's husband of forty-seven years passed out of her life. In many ways Clarence's death was merciful for both of them. Even during the decades of his periodic breakdowns, the Steins could always look forward to recovery, and a return to the warmth and love of earlier days. But new tomorrows were now impossible. "The sad, last years," is how Aline described her final time with Clarence, when she wished for him to be liberated, and to forget the degraded version of the utopian visionary she so loved. When it was over Aline was reminded of a verse by poet Harriet Lowenhjelm:

> May we be happy and rejoice
> On this green earth, oh my son!
> But tired and smiling we leave our toys
> When it's over, and life is done.

Aline MacMahon's devotion to her husband was perhaps the nearest thing to a religion in her life. It was passionate, unwavering, and deeply felt. Immediately after he was gone, she set about protecting and enhancing the legacy of the man who described his profession of architecture as "the art of making the Earth man's home, rather than man's prey."[12] Instead of arranging a conventional memorial service, Aline sent requests to architects and planners connected to Clarence's career and vision, asking them to give a series of talks to university students in order to "spread the ideas for which he lived."[13] Over the following years she helped curate a magnificent exhibition of his work, "Clarence Stein: America's Environmental Architect," even seeking a grant to send it on a national tour. "I'm searching for enough money to send it touring all the Universities," Aline said. "I am trying to find out where and how to accomplish that. It's something I *have* to do."[14] During the 1970s and '80s she badgered Clarence's New York publisher to keep his book *Toward New Towns for America* in print, and began a correspondence with Cornell University to establish an endowment that would eventually create the Clarence S. Stein Institute "for advance research, scholarship, and critical and creative practices to build a more sustainable, just, and resilient world." For the better part of a decade following his death, Aline's primary area of interest was in ensuring that the memory of Clarence Stein stayed alive.

After the emotional tumult and the enervating responsibilities of funeral arrangements, legal matters, and voluminous correspondence, Aline craved familiarity and care. She returned to California, to the house in Beverly Hills that she shared with Jennie Mac—herself now ninety-seven—and stayed through the summer. But Aline could only pine for so long. "While I was in California, Gordon Davidson in Los Angeles wanted me for a part in the play 'The Shadow Box,'" she recalled.[15] "I didn't like the play, and anyway I was homesick for the apartment where Clarence and I had lived for forty-plus years. So, although it was a good part, I turned it down and came home to mourn in the place I wanted to be. And instead of that, [theatrical producer] Joe Papp called up and said, 'There's a part, would you like to do it?' and I did it and I had the best time and I didn't have a minute to weep, I was so nice and busy with a lot of lovely people."[16]

The part Aline took on was both a beginning and an end. The play was *Trelawny of the Wells*, in which she had played the vivacious actress Rose Trelawny at Barnard in 1920, near the dawn of her career. Now instead, Aline was the elderly Lady Trafalgar, the patriarch of Rose's husband's family who is so dull and pompous that Rose is driven to abandon her marriage and return to the stage. "Aline MacMahon and Walter Abel had the proper measure and authority for the rich couple who make Rose's life a misery," the *Times* said of what would be Aline's final appearance on the Manhattan stage—her final appearance in front of a paying audience anywhere in the world.[17]

It was charming geometry that Aline should return to the production that marked the end of her amateur career to also call an end to her professional life after fifty-five years on stage and screen. The 1975 production of *Trelawny* was a kind of nexus between old and new. Also retiring was Aline's old friend and Lincoln Repertory cast mate Walter Abel, who had debuted on Broadway in 1919. Fortunately, the company was also brimming with a new generation of talented performers; among those making their debut or just beginning their careers were Mandy Patinkin, Jeffrey Jones, John Lithgow, and Mary Beth Hurt (as Rose). And in a small part was a fresh-faced, newly minted Yale graduate in her professional acting debut, Meryl Streep. Aline adored working with this youthful new generation of actors, and instead of hiding her long-obscured emotional side, age and tragedy allowed her to embrace it. "We're all so sentimental about the play," she said, "even if it is a sentimental picture."[18]

Now idle, Aline settled into a rich, quiet life of entertaining and recreation, periodically visiting the ageless Jennie Mac and traveling overseas in an ongoing effort to recapture the magical exoticism of those grade-school stereopticon slides that inspired her love of exploration. She took up painting ("What a joy it is," Aline enthused) and reveled in maintaining a connection to New York's theater world, where she encouraged the young careers of her former castmates in the Lincoln Repertory Company, and continued her crusade to keep Clarence's work alive in the mind of his professional descendants.

In the 1970s and '80s Aline's phone rang often with pleas of producers and directors who wanted her to come out of retirement, or simply loved her and wanted to assuage her perceived loneliness by giving her something to do. Although she was often tempted by the offers, none could remove the aging Rapunzel from her penthouse. Joseph Papp, the great impresario of the Public Theatre told Aline that any part he had that was age appropriate was hers for the asking. But at this stage Aline's appetite for work was quite specific. "I don't want to do something I don't want to do, that's all," she said. "So I make it tough for him. I only want to work around the corner [at the Vivian Beaumont]. I don't want to go way downtown. It's too far away."[19] Others tried different incentives. "I recently had a call from the Coast," she revealed in 1977. "They wanted me for a part in a picture called *Damien: Omen II*. Well, *unbelievably* badly written in my book, but for a vast sum of money—twenty thousand dollars for a minuscule part [eventually played by Sylvia Sidney]. Luckily I have a roof over my head and I've always had the problem of hating the material and loving doing the work, but this time I turned it down. Believe me, it wasn't worth doing."

Aline was also given the opportunity for a recurring role on one of the premiere TV series of the 1970s. "I was asked to play in 'All in the Family' as a foil to Carroll O'Connor," she explained. "Now, I love the show, but the part didn't appeal to me. You see, I have a friend who says that I have one attitude when I'm thin and another attitude when I'm fat. In this case, having no need for money, I was what you might call fat, and I turned it down. I guess what I really want now, at this stage of life, is to have everybody call up and to turn down everybody, because that's great fun."[20]

In 1984 Aline was in her sixth decade looking east over Central Park in the penthouse apartment of Harperley Hall at 1 West 64th Street. Also living in the building in 1984 were Madonna and Sean Penn. Donated to Cornell University by Aline MacMahon without copyright.

As the days and months of retirement assembled into years, Aline found herself searching for meaning in the repetition of a daily life without work. "The real problem in the Golden Years is the minute-to-minute problem," she confessed. "If you're alone and you have no duties, that makes a very special world. So what do you do? Well, I haven't solved that problem, I'm still finding out. There are half-hours and sometimes hours when I would rather be alone with no pressures of any kind—when that becomes most of the day, I'll feel I'm there. But I'm not there yet." Even when old friends passed away and her life shrank to fit, Aline still kept her humor and discarded her self-pity. "You know, a young friend asked me recently," she began, "'What do you do when all your thoughts go wrong—when everything is negative, what do you do?' and I said, 'You wash out your stockings.' You better just keep on."[21] This was Aline MacMahon. Just keep on.

On December 29, 1984, even the indomitable Jennie Mac finally passed on, just weeks shy of her 107th birthday. After visiting her mother eleven months earlier, Aline reported wistfully to a friend, "There was a birthday party for my little mother, and the cake said 'Jennie Mac is 106'—her mind is clear, her appetite excellent and she sleeps through the night—but, but, but—don't ever be 106."[22] Decades earlier—when Aline had first made her way to Hollywood, she pondered her parents' influence on her life. "Bless them," she said, thinking back over her youth. "They gave me all they are, and will until the end of the story, I expect."[23]

The end of the story had now arrived, and for the daughter who once declared her mother "perfect"—even without truly believing it—Jennie MacMahon's death was a seismic shock to her world. It severed the line to her heritage in Russia, and left her truly, finally alone in the sky parlor overlooking Central Park. Now eighty-five years old, often forlorn, sometimes depressed, Aline spoke to her neighbor—who also happened to be a psychiatrist—about her continually narrowing life. "The problem with living alone, and especially up in this beautiful apartment," she told him, "is that I'm in a kind of tower, and that I seem to be existing—I'm floating—I don't seem to be connected much. There's something the matter, I don't know what it is." A look of earnest understanding crossed her neighbor's face. "There is no echo," he said. At this Aline was deeply touched. "Is that not a fine thing to say?" she asked. "Things like that count very much for me—not because Eugene O'Neill said it, or somebody famous. Just if you say something sincere. Words count a lot."[24]

Aline had now outlived most of her close friends and contemporaries: Aline Bernstein had passed in 1955; in December 1961 Moss Hart died suddenly of a heart attack at fifty-seven; Ken MacGowan lasted until 1963, and Mervyn LeRoy succumbed in 1988, riddled with heart disease and suffering from Alzheimer's. In her final years Aline MacMahon's companions and correspondents were mostly younger people; sons and daughters of those friends long gone, or the producers and directors with whom she had worked at the end of her career. As she neared her nineties various accidents and illnesses slowed her physically, but her mind remained acute. Following a long series of negotiations, Aline secured an agreement with Cornell University; she would provide a large endowment—constituting the bulk of her $1,300,000 estate—to create the Clarence Stein Institute for Architecture. Perpetuating her husband's ideals was the final act of devotion to a man she loved and admired so deeply, and she took great pride in the accomplishment. When the arrangement was finalized and signed, Aline closed the meeting by remarking, "I only hope I won't linger too long, so you can get on with it."[25] In her mind—and in the lives of students who passed through the Stein Institute—Clarence Samuel Stein's ethos would live on.

By the fall of 1991 Aline's life had slowed to a crawl. From her penthouse apartment she could still watch the westerly shadows that lengthen and retreat across Central Park with the autumn's orange sunrise. In September she took ill with pneumonia. The woman who once counted the whole world her domain—who gathered speed at a moment's notice to visit Iran, or India, or Bali—was now confined to her bed and no more. As a nonreligious person, Aline likely did not ponder a reunion with her husband, but as the days shortened with the approach of winter she had lived well enough to gather few regrets. Divided between the Victorian propriety of her mother Jennie and the proto-feminism of her aunt Sophie, Aline MacMahon had managed an artful balance between career and marriage, duty and self-interest, personal reserve and professional exhibitionism. She had helped many and harmed none, achieved creative satisfaction, experienced the diversity of foreign cultures, stood her moral ground, found a true love, and never—or almost never—betrayed herself. Nothing was left but for the waiting.

Once upon a time, when there were still many sunrises left, Aline was at a dinner party seated next to the writer Bernard Drew. When Drew was a young boy in the 1930s, his mother counted Aline MacMahon as one of her favorite actresses, a preference he inherited. Excited to express his admiration, he told Aline that he felt the current films were not as interesting as the ones she and her Warner Brothers family had made forty years earlier. "Which ones do you mean?" she inquired. "Oh, 'Five Star Final,' 'Life Begins,' 'Gold Diggers of 1933,' 'Silver Dollar,'" he said, listing the films he and his mother loved. Her eyes twinkling, Aline asked, "How old were you when you saw them?" "Oh, five or six," Drew replied. Aline smiled at him with the wisdom of maturity. "At five or six, my dear, you were wonderful and beautiful," she said. "You should see them again."[26]

Aline Laveen MacMahon died on October 12, 1991, with a setting sun now casting lengthening shadows slowly eastward across Central Park. To her amiable chagrin Aline left behind no children except professional ones—generations of actors and actresses who, knowingly or unknowingly, followed the example of honesty and naturalism she first pioneered before Marlon Brando was born and before the movies had even become the Talkies. None of the many obituaries which appeared in newspapers and magazines that autumn mentioned Aline MacMahon's primacy as the American pioneer of the Method. When she began practicing it in 1923 the technique was merely an obscure professional discipline; by the time it became widely known by the general public Aline's part in its transmigration had long been forgotten and placed neatly out of sight, huddled with other secrets of history.

Aline's feeling about the Method was, like the devotion to her husband, lifelong and deeply felt. She thought of it as not just a key to her success and fame, but an essential building block in the pleasures and responsibilities of living. Its discipline of observation gave her keen insight into the feelings of others and from this, compassion; imagining the complex inner lives of her many diverse characters made it impossible for Aline to judge friends and colleagues too harshly. On another front, the Method helped create a psychological framework to resolve her inner battle between propriety and ego. By giving her the ability to imagine herself *as someone else*, the technique allowed Aline to disappear into character while drinking the joys of admiration without abashment. Bigger still, the Method led to, as she called it, "a life"—a long, unique journey as a student, teacher, artist, mentor, friend, daughter, and wife.

Aline MacMahon's life was fulfilling, but hardly perfect. There were disappointments and disillusion—but everything was seen in its proper perspective and measured against countervailing fortune. The years of Clarence's Dickensian illnesses were always contrasted with the greater joys of their sixty-year courtship. Disappointment at the gradual dissolve of her career was deemed petty after decades of free rein harvesting in the gold mine. To Aline even the failure of her political ideals, and being deemed a danger to her country, was little compared to others who lost their lives, careers, and families in the same cause. None of these things could challenge Aline's self-possession. She refused to be a victim, but felt deep compassion for the victimized.

Even with all her fine, humane qualities, a biography of Aline MacMahon would not exist but for her intimate connection to the beguiling nostalgia of classic Hollywood. Cinema looms large in the lives of its devotees, but we must never forget that the movies are a construct, a fantasy. They exist largely to help us cope with the real world we inhabit *between* movies. This goes for their makers as well as those of us who merely watch. Aline MacMahon understood this simple fact better than most. Throughout her life she sought approval through performing, and could easily have gotten lost in the daydream. But the world outside Hollywood never let her forget which was real and which was the chimera. There, even the things Aline loved most could not escape the gaze of her uncompromising introspection. "There was a time when I looked up to 'people who write'—'people who paint'—'people who'— 'people . . .'" she began. "Now I accept everything—and am interested not in how or wherein a King is kingly, but in what respects a King is only human after all. It's desolate game," she lamented. "Sometimes I think I never want to understand anything as long as I live—only enjoy or suffer. But the conscious revolt against understanding indicates that it is my fate always to try to understand." Even at this Aline MacMahon could not resist her penchant to dispel sadness with hope. "In the end all that matters is living fully, deeply and profoundly; enjoying every moment there is to enjoy, being appreciative of what life has to offer, establishing a sense of values, and putting first things first," she said. "Once, I thought books and art were bigger than life—bigger than anything. But I've learned that life is bigger than art. Personal satisfaction is more important."

ACKNOWLEDGMENTS

No book like this could be compiled and written without the dedication and knowledge of the archivists, research librarians, and historians whose job it is to husband the past for future generations.

My deep thanks go out to these incredibly kind people, and all the others I may have forgotten: Sylvia Wang of the Shubert Archive (who also introduced me to my favorite restaurant in the world); Mary Huelsbeck at the Wisconsin Center for Film and Theater Research; Martha Tenney, director of Barnard's Archives and Special Collections; Doug Reside, who went above and beyond the call of duty on my visits at the New York Public Library for the Performing Arts; Hilary Dorsch Wong, Reference Coordinator at the Division of Rare and Manuscript Collection of Cornell University; Janine Biunno, archivist at the Isamu Noguchi Foundation, and most of all to my friend and personal Reference Librarian Supreme, John McInnes, always willing and able to make my toughest requests possible.

I am also in debt to my close friends and editorial consultants Carlos Alverio and Greg Pierson. Their notes and suggestions invariably improved this book, and it would not be the same without them.

NOTES

1. Till the First Star Shook in the Air

1. Jennie MacMahon, *Oral history interview conducted by Irene Atkins.* New York Public Library, Dorot Division, 1978.
2. Ibid.
3. Aline MacMahon, *Oral history interview conducted by Leonard Probst,* NYPL, Dorot Division, 1977.
4. MacMahon, 1978.
5. Sophie Irene Loeb, *Everyman's Child.* Curtis Publishing Co., dedication, 1920.
6. The Nickname "The World's Greatest Mother" was coined by Florida Senator W. H. Hodges in Sophie's *New York Times* obituary, January 19, 1929. Sophie herself was childless.
7. *Jewish Tribune,* May 29, 1925.
8. MacMahon, 1977.
9. Ibid.
10. Ibid.
11. MacMahon, 1978.
12. Jeanne Stein, "Aline MacMahon," *Films in Review,* December, 1965.
13. Ibid.
14. MacMahon, 1978.
15. MacMahon, 1977.
16. MacMahon, 1978.
17. "Children Give Concert," *Brooklyn Daily Eagle,* 11/9/1915.
18. Noyes's poem is about a Huron Indian girl whose lover is killed by Mohawk braves as he is meeting her for a midnight rendezvous. Cornered by the Mohawks, the heartbroken girl feigns thanks to the men for ridding her of an unfaithful lover, and promises to lead them down the inky blackness of the Niagara River to pillage the Huron camp. On the river, the braves are too late in realizing that she is leading them towards the inescapable edge of Niagara Falls. Try as they might, they cannot escape the river's current, and the girl and her lover's killers are all swept over the edge.
19. Milton V. O'Connell, *The New Playbill.* 1924.
20. *Brooklyn Daily Eagle,* April 20, 1911.

21. Ibid.
22. MacMahon, 1977.
23. Ibid.
24. Aline MacMahon, "The Stereopticon," *Brooklyn Daily Eagle.* 1912.
25. "Erasmus Hall Celebration Brings Reminiscences from Former Student," *Brooklyn Daily Eagle.* 1937.
26. MacMahon, 1977.
27. Vera Mason, "I Don't Want to be Funny, says Aline MacMahon," *Shadowplay* magazine, Vol. 2–5.

2. Life Begins

1. Barnard was founded in 1883 and moved to its current location in 1892.
2. MacMahon, 1978.
3. Stein, 1965.
4. Letter from Aline to her husband Clarence, 12/28/1945. [Unless otherwise noted, all correspondence between the Steins is from the Clarence Stein papers in the Rare and Manuscript Division of Cornell University.]
5. "An Open Letter to the Younger Students in the Women's Residence Halls, 1917–1918'" Barnard orientation literature, 1917. The "dangerous" Morningside Park is directly across the street from where the upper-class MacMahon family was then living, 70 Morningside Drive.
6. "Projections," Barnard College *Alumnae Bulletin,* 1932.
7. "Curtain Calls," Shubert Organization press release, purportedly written by Aline herself, 1925.
8. Ibid.
9. "Projections," 1932.
10. *Columbia Spectator,* 12/11/1916.
11. *Not* the famous author of *The Autobiography of Alice B. Toklas.*
12. *Barnard Bulletin,* 12/19/1919.
13. "Don't Call Stars—Let 'Em Call You," *Hartford Times,* 3/30/1965.
14. "Curtain Calls," 1924.
15. *Columbia Spectator,* 4/26/1920.
16. *Barnard Bulletin,* 4/30/1920.
17. MacMahon, 1977.
18. *Barnard Bulletin,* 6/11/1920.
19. In another version of the story, Mrs. Morgenthau (or an assistant) dropped the letter down the elevator shaft of her own building and it was later delivered by a Samaritan who discovered it while cleaning the shaft. If Mrs. Morgenthau had lost her own letter, we must assume she would have composed and mailed new one.
20. *Barnard Bulletin,* report on commencement, 6/11/1920. Among the other honorees at the ceremony were future president Herbert Hoover, Naval Admiral William Sims, and Henry Davidson, Chairman of the War Council of the Red Cross.
21. "Projections," 1932.
22. MacMahon, 1977.

23. According to the Fitchberg, Massachusetts *Sentinel* (9/15/1934), Sophie had arranged a job with a NYC newspaper for Aline, but her part in *The Mirage* was offered the day before she was to start.
24. Ibid.
25. K. C. Parsons, *The Writings of Clarence Stein,* John's Hopkins Press, 1998, p. 140.
26. MacMahon, 1977.
27. The Neighborhood Playhouse was created as an oasis for the poor residents of the neighborhood, featuring plays (and films) congruent with their lives. Tickets were typically low-priced, often as little as 25 or 35 cents. As the popularity of the Playhouse grew, the uptown element of New York's theater scene often threatened to overwhelm the local flavor of the venue.
28. John P. Harrington, *The Life of the Neighborhood Playhouse on Grand Street,* Syracuse University Press, 2007, undated letter from Alice Lewisohn to Lillian Wald, circa 1914.
29. Carroll had two credits with the Playhouse prior to the 1921 season, one in 1916, and another in 1919. From 1921 on he appeared in almost every production until the Playhouse closed in 1927, as well as the revived *Grand Street Follies* of 1928 and '29.
30. Among the few within the orbit of the Playhouse who were not so charitable was Thomas Wolfe, who met Albert Carroll through Aline Bernstein and reportedly disliked his "flamboyant personality."
31. Extra-Curricular Activities card kept by Barnard College to track alumni career paths, Barnard archives.
32. Alice Lewisohn Crowley, *The Neighborhood Playhouse,* Theatre Arts Books, 1959.
33. Parsons, p. xxvii.
34. Clarence was there as an associate with the primary planner, Benton MacKaye, and Charles Whitaker. Talks began in July 1921 and planning was solidified over the weekend of November 24, 1922. See https://hudsonfarmnj.com/history.
35. Harrington, 2007.
36. John P. Harrington, *The Life of the Neighborhood Playhouse,* Syracuse University Press, 2007. p. 156.
37. Although she is not in the opening night cast list, Aline appears to have had a small part in A. A. Milne's successful play *Dover Road* in early 1922.

3. Teach Me, and Set My Feet On the Way

1. Mel Gordon, *Stanislavsky in America,* Routledge, 2010, p. xii.
2. A. L. Fovitzky, "Moscow Art Theatre and Its Distinguishing Characteristics," 1922.
3. The Moscow Art Theatre first toured America in 1906.
4. According to *Theatre Magazine,* the 1923 MAT Russian language production of *Lower Depths* outsold its English-speaking counterpart (staged by Arthur Hopkins in 1922) by more than 2,500%.
5. *Vanity Fair,* March 1923.
6. *New York Herald,* 11/23/1923.

7. Alice Lewisohn Crowley, *The Neighborhood Playhouse*, Theatre Arts Books, 1959, pp. 167–68.

8. In addition to the six Playhouse regulars, there were four others in the first group who studied with Boleslavsky in 1923. With Aline MacMahon, the nine were: Pamela Gaythorne, Ernita Lascelles, Esther Mitchell, Sophie Treadwell, Rhy Derby, Douglas Garden, Ralf Belmont, Albert Carroll and John Taylor. Among these nine are only a handful of minor film credits and little stage experience besides Neighborhood Playhouse productions. Aline maintained a long friendship with Sophie Treadwell, who went on to a successful career as a playwright and author.

9. MacMahon, 1977.

10. MacMahon, 1959.

11. The early days of Boleslavsky's school in the country were quite secret. On Aline's Occupation Card kept by Barnard College to track and facilitate students' career placement is a note dated May 25, 1923: "*Confidential!* [Miss MacMahon] is to begin June 15 with Boleslavsky of Moscow Art Theatre as summer student preparing three plays for fall." Boly's need for publicity quickly trumped any desire to have privacy for the program.

12. Percy Hammond, "Oddments and Remainders," *New York Herald-Tribune*, 6/14/1923.

13. Program, American Laboratory Theatre, 1924. (No record exists of a program from the inaugural class in 1923.)

14. H. I. Brock, "Grand Street Art Theatre," *New York Times*, 10/28/1923—the frequency of visitors to Pleasantville indicates that Boleslavsky and his backers were not entirely relying on chance to bring newspaper reporters to their country retreat.

15. MacMahon, 1959.

16. Hammond, 6/14/23.

17. Richard Boleslavsky, *Theatre Arts Magazine*, 1923.

18. Brock, 10/28/1923.

19. Ibid.

20. Crowley, 1959.

21. Burton Rascoe, "Bookman's Day Book," *New York Tribune*, 10/21/1923.

22. Ibid.

23. MacMahon, 1977.

24. Crowley, 1959.

25. Boleslavsky, 1923.

26. Ibid.

27. Program for *The Player Queen* and *The Shewing Up of Blanco Posnet*, Neighborhood Playhouse, 1923.

28. Crowley, 1959.

29. Margaret M. Knapp, "Theatrical Parody in the 20th Century American Theatre: 'The Grand Street Follies,'" *Educational Theatre Journal*, November 1975.

30. Charles Belmont Davis, "The Show Window," *New York Herald*, 6/22/1924.

31. "Grand Street Follies and the Grand Old Vogues," *New York Herald*, 7/6/1924.

32. *New York Times*, clipping file of the University of Wisconsin, 10/10/1924.

33. *New York Herald*, 7/6/1924.

4. The River of Stars is Rolling

1. *New York Herald*, 6/6/1924.
2. Press release announcing *Collusion*, Aline's maiden outing with the Shubert company, Shubert Archive Collection, 12/1925.
3. Letter to Lee Shubert, Shubert archive collection.
4. MacMahon, 1977.
5. Paragraph five of Aline's Shubert contract states: "It is understood that you shall be called to appear in a musical play the first season of 1924–25 . . in all subsequent seasons you are to play only in legitimate plays . ."
6. MacMahon, 1977.
7. Letters to the Shubert company from Aline MacMahon, Shubert archive collection.
8. Letter to Lee Shubert from Aline MacMahon, Shubert archive collection.
9. MacMahon, 1977.
10. MacMahon, 1959.
11. Jeanne Stein, *Films in Review*, December 1965.
12. Letter from Aline MacMahon to Lee Shubert, June 22, 1925, Shubert archive collection.
13. Letter from Aline MacMahon to J. J. Shubert, undated, circa late October 1925, Shubert archive collection.
14. MacMahon, 1977.
15. Stein, 1965.
16. Letters from Aline to Clarence, 4/12&13/1944. Evidence that Morehouse and Cummings were legally married is slim, but all of Aline's correspondence, including letters written when Morehouse was seriously ill in the spring of 1944, refer to her as "Marion Cummings." And when Aline sent checks to help with Morehouse's medical expenses, they were made out to "Marion Morehouse Cummings."
17. "Beyond the Horizon," *Brooklyn Daily Eagle*, 12/2/1926.
18. Stein, 1965.
19. MacMahon, 1977.
20. Ibid. (There is unspoken reason to think that Aline's antipathy for Jed Harris might have been as a result of unwanted sexual advances, but Aline kept any idea of the source of it to herself.)
21. Interview of Aline MacMahon by Kermit Parsons, Cornell University Department of Rare and Manuscript Collections, 9/28/1984.
22. Stein, 1965.

5. No One Has Ever Known Her Alive

1. "The Rise of Aline MacMahon," *Brooklyn Daily Eagle*, 2/18/1928.
2. *Maya* was also performed at the Studio Champs-Elysee sometime during late 1927 / early 1928.
3. Undated capsule autobiography (circa 1928) by Simon Gantillon, Shubert archives clipping file of the New York production of *Maya*.

4. "Why we are Producing *Maya*," press release from Actor-Managers, spring, 1928, Shubert Archives files on *Maya*.
5. "The Rise of Aline MacMahon."
6. Gantillon capsule autobiography.
7. Harry B. Witham, "The Play Jury," *Educational Theatre Journal*, December 1972.
8. Ibid.
9. Now known as Roosevelt Island.
10. Excerpt from the Wales Padlock Act, 1928.
11. Contract between Actor-Managers Corporation and Simon Gantillon, dated August 23, 1927, Shubert Archives files on *Maya*. The contract also called for a $500 payment to follow the symbolic dollar investment.
12. Ibid.
13. The Shubert booking agreement is dated November 29, 1927.
14. The contract between Actor-Managers and the Shubert Corporation calls for a $2,500 investment in return for 1/8th of the gross receipts of *Maya*.
15. Helen Arthur, letter to Joseph Gates of the Shubert Agency, 2/10/1928.
16. Helen Arthur, letter to Perrington Maxwell, editor of *Theatre Magazine*, 4/3/1928.
17. Aline MacMahon, interview with Leonard Probst, 12/8/1977.
18. "Actor-Managers to give 'Maya,'" *New York Times*, 1/11/1928.
19. MacMahon, 1977.
20. Letter from Helen Arthur to Joseph Gates, 2/10/1928.
21. Ibid.
22. Melville Cane, letter to Helen Arthur, Shubert Archives, 2/9/1928.
23. Helen Arthur, letter to Joseph Gates 2/10/28.
24. Unknown New York newspaper clipping, 2/23/1928, Shubert Archives clipping file. Less than two weeks earlier, Helen Arthur warned Lee Shubert that she might have to "give away" the boxes at the Comedy Theater in order to have the first night house appear sold out. If the boxes were indeed gifts to lucky theatergoers, it is unrecorded.
25. *New York Evening World*, date unknown, Shubert Archives clipping file on *Maya*.
26. J. Brooks Atkinson, "The Play," *New York Times*, 2/22/1928.
27. Gilbert Gabriel, New York Sun review of Maya, 2/22/1928.
28. Leonard Hall, "'Maya' by Gantillon, Starts at the Comedy," *New York Telegram*, 2/23/1928.
29. Brooks Atkinson, "One of the Flowers of Evil," *New York Times*, 2/23/1928.
30. John Anderson, "Mystical French Play Done by Actor-Managers," *New York Journal*, 2/23/1928.
31. Gilbert Gabriel, "Last Night's First Night," *New York Sun*, 2/23/1928.
32. Alexander Woolcott, "The Stage," *New York World*, 2/22/1928.
33. "Banton Denies Move to Padlock 'Maya,'" *New York Times* 2/26/1928.
34. Language from the Wales Padlock Act.
35. Letter from Helen Arthur to the editor of the *New York City Drama Calendar*, 3/16/1928.

36. "Theatre Padlock Invoked First Time," *New York Times*, 2/25/1928.
37. Helen Arthur, from a detailed letter she wrote documenting the meeting, including her exchanges with Sinnott and Wallace, 3/16/1928.
38. "'Maya' Ordered Closed," *New York Times*, 3/1/1928.
39. Before he moved to the Police Commissioner's office, James Sinnott wrote sports and theater reviews for the *Morning Telegraph*. Most of the leaks from the authorities were published in Sinnott's former paper, presumably delivered by their former reporter.
40. "'Maya' Will Wash Up or Off in 10 Days," *New York News*, 2/26/1928.
41. Four of the first five shows were sellouts, with standing room tickets reaching sixty-nine patrons during the Saturday matinee.
42. Letter to Helen Arthur from the Shubert company, 2/23/1928.
43. "Police Locks to Snap on Too-Naughty Plays," *New York News*, 2/25/1928.
44. "May Lock Up Theater," *New York Sun*, 2/25/1928.
45. Helen Arthur, 3/16/1928.
46. "Theatre Padlock Invoked First Time," *New York Times*, 2/25/1928.
47. "Tells of Proposal to 'Fix' Banned Play," *New York Times*, 10/10/1930.
48. Ibid.
49. Among those signing a petition sent to Mayor Jimmy Walker were many artists and society swells, including Mrs. William Vanderbuilt, Anne Morgan (social activist and daughter of J. P. Morgan), Lewis Mumford (noted architect and close friend of Aline and Clarence), George Jean Nathan, Eva LaGallienne, Stark Young, and producers David Belasco, Lawrence Langer, and Jed Harris.
50. "Banned 'Maya' Beautiful Play, Shubert Finds," *New York Herald Tribune*, 2/28/1928.
51. "Lee Shubert Sees No Wrong in 'Maya,'" *New York Sun*, 2/28/1928.
52. Ibid.
53. Letter to Joab Banton from Helen Arthur / Actor-Managers Inc, Shubert Archives on *Maya*, 2/29/1928.
54. Twenty members voted to continue *Maya*, and seven declined.
55. MacMahon, 1977.
56. "'Maya' Actors Reject Offer of Road Tour," *New York Herald Tribune*, 3/2/1928.
57. Ibid.
58. Interview with Aline MacMahon by Kermit Parsons, 9/28/1984.
59. *Variety*, 1/16/1929.
60. Letter from Aline to Clarence, 11/5/1936.
61. Letter from Aline to Clarence, 8/9/1941.
62. "Thunder in the Air," *Berkshire Eagle*, 7/20/1929.
63. Ibid.
64. *Brooklyn Daily Express*, 5/6/1934.
65. MacMahon, 1977.
66. "Plays Reviewed," *Brooklyn Life*, 11/30/1929.
67. "Sappho in Overalls," *Bay Area Reporter*, 10/29/1987.
68. Ibid.
69. "Another Captive," *Brooklyn Daily Eagle*, 11/13/1929.

70. Ibid.
71. "The Theatre," *Wall Street Journal*, 3/6/1928.
72. "Sappho in Overalls," 1987.

6. Once in a Lifetime

1. Moss Hart, *Act One*, Random House, 1959, p. 308.
2. Interview with Aline MacMahon, Oral history research program, Columbia University, 1959.
3. Miriam Gibson, "What is the secret of Aline MacMahon?" *Modern Screen*, June 1935.
4. Hart, *Act One*, 1959, p. 310.
5. Ibid, p. 313.
6. Moss Hart, "Men at Work," essay from *Three Plays by Kaufman and Hart*, Grove Press, 1980.
7. *Variety*, 5/28/1930.
8. MacMahon, 1959.
9. Hart, *Act One*, p. 333.
10. Ibid, p. 339.
11. Hart, *Act One*, p. 347.
12. *Brooklyn Daily Eagle*, 6/3/1930.
13. Hart, *Act One*, p. 357.
14. "To Play in Stockbridge," *New York Times*, 6/13/1930.
15. Hart, *Act One*, p. 365.
16. Interview with Aline MacMahon, Oral History Research Program, Columbia University, 12/8/77.
17. MacMahon, 1978.
18. Stories vary as to when Ouspenskaya immigrated to the United States. Some accounts say she stayed behind following the first MAT tour, while others believe that she accompanied them back to Europe and remained in New York only after their return tour in the United States ended in late 1923.
19. Also remaining behind with Madame Ouspenskaya in (likely) late 1923 was Akim Tamiroff, who developed a successful Hollywood career during the 1930s and '40s.
20. News Syndicate Co. article, 1933, University of Wisconsin clipping file.
21. Letter from Clarence to his friend Benton MacKaye 3/5/1931; the letter details Aline's last-minute remove from New York for the West Coast.
22. Letter from Sam Harris to Aline MacMahon, 1/1/31.
23. In Clarence's letter of January 2, 1931, he remarks that Aline's decision to go to Los Angeles or stay in New York was needed so quickly that friends had been "laying bets on it all afternoon."
24. Ibid.
25. Harmon Station (now known as Croton-Harmon Station) services the town of Croton-on-Hudson, New York. According to railroad timetables, Aline cried for a full hour after she left Manhattan.

26. Letter from Aline to Clarence, 1/1/1931
27. Letter from Clarence to Aline, 1/4/1931.
28. Letter from Aline to Clarence, 1/1/1931.
29. Letter from Clarence to Aline, 1/5/1931.
30. Letter from Aline to Clarence, 1/14/1931.
31. MacMahon, 1977.
32. Letter from Aline to Clarence, 1/27/1931.
33. "Hollywood Proves It Can Take the Drama's Joke," *New York Times*, 2/1/1931.
34. Ibid.
35. "Mirror Turned on Hollywood," *Los Angeles Times*, 1/29/1931.
36. Ibid.
37. MacMahon, 1959.
38. Letter from Clarence to Aline, 1/29/1931.
39. Letter from Aline to Clarence, 2/8/1931.
40. Letter from Aline to Clarence, 2/11/1931.
41. Aline was making $400 a week in the West Coast production of *Once in a Lifetime*
42. Letter from Aline to Clarence, 3/18/1931.
43. Letter from Aline to Clarence, 3/21/1931.
44. Letter from Clarence to Aline, 4/1/1931; Henry Klaber and his wife were close friends of the Steins' in New York.
45. Letter from Aline to Clarence, 4/2/1931—this letter details the initial contract negotiations for *Five Star Final*.
46. Letter from Aline to Clarence, afternoon of 4/8/1931.
47. Letter from Aline to Clarence, evening of 4/8/1931.
48. MacMahon, 1977.
49. Letter from Clarence to Aline, 3/30/1931.
50. Clarence's letter to Aline of January 4, 1931, says he heard about Dixon's jealous desire from Ethyl Bernstein, the Broadway costume designer and sister of Aline MacMahon's close friend Aline Bernstein.

7. At Once They Circled Her Round

1. Marlon Brando, from the Showtime documentary film *Listen to Me Marlon*, 2016.
2. MacMahon, 1977.
3. MacMahon, 1977.
4. Letter from Aline to Clarence, 4/7/1931.
5. "'Five Star Final' Out," *Los Angeles Times*, 10/29/1931.
6. Undated review clippings from Warner Brothers Archives file on *Five Star Final*.
7. Clarence's mother died on April 14, 1931.
8. Letter from Aline to Clarence, 4/15/1931.
9. Letter from Clarence to Aline, 4/15/1931.

10. Letter from Clarence to Aline, 5/3/1931.
11. Letter from Clarence to his friend Benton McKay, 5/15/31.
12. MacMahon, 1977.
13. Letter from Aline to Clarence, 7/20/1934.
14. Letter from Aline to Clarence, 9/11/1931.
15. Ibid.
16. Telegram from Clarence to Aline, 9/12/1931.
17. Letter from Clarence to Aline, 6/13/1944.
18. "Gotham Plays Invade Circle of the Family," *Chicago Tribune*, 11/22/1931.
19. *Silver Screen* magazine, February 1935.
20. *Los Angeles Times*, 3/23/1932.
21. Letter to Clarence from Aline, 12/29/1931.
22. "Aline MacMahon is wasted in 'The Heart of New York.'" *International Photographer* said. A number of her scenes were left in a cutting room scrap bin.
23. Letter from Aline to Clarence, 1/7/1932.
24. Letter from Aline to Clarence, April, 1932 (exact date unknown).
25. "'Mouthpiece' New Score for Mr. William," *Chicago Tribune*, 4/30/1932.
26. *Silver Screen* magazine, August 1932.
27. MacMahon, 1959.
28. "Signature on Dotted Line Denied," *Los Angeles Times*, 4/24/1932.
29. MacMahon, 1977.
30. *Brooklyn Daily Eagle*, 6/6/1932.
31. *Chicago Daily Tribune*, 7/12/1932.
32. *Hollywood Reporter* review of *Life Begins*, 1932 (exact date unknown).
33. Letter to Aline from Clarence 4/13/1932.
34. Hubbard Keavy, *Screen Life in Hollywood*, 5/1/1932.
35. The director of *Skyscraper Souls* was Edgar Selwyn, the man who had given Aline her first role on Broadway in 1920. Unfortunately for history, Aline was working on *Life Begins* at Warner's and could not make the MGM start date. Seeing the film upon its release, Aline called it "wretched and revolting" (letter of May 16, 1932).
36. Letter from Aline to Clarence, 5/17/1932.
37. Letter from Aline of Clarence, 7/30/1932.
38. Letter from Aline of Clarence, 2/10/1932.

8. Reward Unlimited

1. Letter from Aline to Clarence 5/17/1932 Aline's proprietary feeling about May Daniels comes across in the letter's wording ("... will not give me *my* part...").
2. Letter from Aline to Clarence 5/16/1932.
3. MacMahon, 1977.
4. Letter from Aline to Clarence 6/15/1932.
5. Letter from Aline to Clarence 5/24/1932.
6. Letter from Aline to Clarence 5/31/1932.
7. Letter from Aline to Clarence, 5/28/1932.
8. Frederick Lewis Allen, *Since Yesterday*, Perennial Library, 1940.

9. Letter from Aline to Clarence 6/7/1932.
10. Letter from Aline to Clarence 7/3/1932.
11. Letter from Aline to Clarence 6/21/1932.
12. Letter from Aline to Clarence 6/27/1932.
13. *Silver Screen* magazine, August, 1932.
14. Ruth Morris, "Uncommon Chatter," *Variety*, 11/1/1932.
15. "What the Picture Did for Me," *Motion Picture Herald*, 3/25/1933.
16. Letter from Aline to Clarence, 6/25/1932.
17. Letter from Clarence to Aline 8/20/1932.
18. Letter from Clarence to Aline, 7/3/1932.
19. Letter from Aline to Clarence, 7/6/1932.
20. A. MacMahon, 1959.
21. Ibid. (Aline did not quite remember the conditions of her first contract perfectly. It called for seven months on and five months off, with periods of two and three months vacation. Her six months on and six months off did not begin until her first option was taken up in 1933.)
22. Memo from Ralph Lewis to Roy Obringer, 9/1/1932, Warner Brothers archives.
23. Lewis to Obringer, 9/1932.
24. Memo from Roy Obringer to Ralph Lewis, 9/8/1932, Warner Brothers archives.
25. MacMahon, 1977.
26. Letter from Aline to Clarence, 7/6/1932.
27. "Projections," *Barnard Alumnae Monthly*, 11/1932.
28. "Signature on Dotted Line," *Los Angeles Times*, 4/24/1932.
29. Letter from Aline to Clarence, 6/26/1932.
30. Letter from Aline to Clarence, 7/13/1932.
31. *New York Sun*, 12/23/1932.
32. Letter from Aline to Clarence, 9/1/1932.
33. Letter from Aline to Clarence, 8/28/1932.
34. Letter from Clarence to Aline, 3/24/1931.
35. *The Life of Jimmy Dolan* was remade seven years later as *They Made Me a Criminal*, starring John Garfield and Claude Rains, and with the seventy-one-year-old May Robson filling Aline's role.
36. Letter from Clarence to Aline, 7/9/1932.

9. Gold Digging

1. Letter from Aline to Clarence, 12/1/1932.
2. Ibid.
3. Letter from Aline to Darryl Zanuck, 12/6/1932.
4. Letter from Aline to Clarence, 12/3/1932.
5. Warner Brothers lost $14,000,000 during 1932, the worst year of the Depression.
6. Letter from Aline to Clarence, 2/12/1933.

7. Letter from Aline to Clarence, undated, circa 2/25/1933.
8. Letter from Aline to Clarence, 2/9/1933.
9. Letter from Aline to Clarence, 2/22/1933.
10. Letter from Aline to Clarence, 2/28/1933.
11. Letter from Aline to Clarence, 2/2/1933.
12. Letter from Aline to Clarence, undated, circa 3/4/1933.
13. Kermit Parsons, *The Writings of Clarence Stein,* Johns Hopkins University Press, 1998, p. 272.
14. Ibid.
15. Letter from Aline to Clarence, 3/8/1933.
16. Handwritten note on studio waiver form, undated, circa 3/14/1933.
17. Letter from Aline to Clarence, 3/8/1933.
18. MacMahon, 1959.
19. Letter, circa 3/4/1933.
20. Ibid.
21. The so-called Bonus Army was a group of World War I veterans who congregated in Washington, D. C. to advocate for an early payment of the service bonus that had been granted by Congress. When Congress refused to move up the payout date, the Bonus Army clashed with U. S. Army regulars and were pushed out of their makeshift shantytown lodgings.
22. This was the last script of the prolific Wilson Mizner, who died just months after finishing *Heroes for Sale*. He was also a co-owner of the famous Brown Derby restaurant, where Aline was eating when the 1933 earthquake hit L.A.
23. Letter from Robert Lord chronicling the creation of *Heroes for Sale* held in Warner Brothers archives, 11/16/1933.
24. It is a shame that Aline came to Warners too late to be considered for the part of Selina in *So Big!* It is the exact type of role she aspired to, and would have fit her talent and demeanor perfectly.
25. MacMahon, 1959.
26. Letter from Aline to Clarence, 6/17/1933.
27. Letter from Aline to Clarence, 6/28/1933.
28. "Excellent Cast Can't Pull It Out," *Hollywood Reporter,* 5/17/1933.
29. Letter from Aline to Clarence, 3/26/1933.
30. Letter to Aline from WB legal department, 3/24/1933.
31. Letter from Aline to Clarence, 3/26/1933. And, yes, there were indeed three exclamation points!!!
32. The Steins apparently needed to take a loan on their paid-up stocks during the winter of 1932–33, and Aline did not want to go further into debt for fear of falling behind.
33. *Variety,* 4/4/1933.
34. *Hollywood Reporter,* 4/3/1933.
35. Excerpt from Aline's original Warner Brothers contract of 1932.
36. Hubbard Keavy, "Refusal of Movie Actors to Play Certain Roles Becoming Common," syndicated column, *Lubbock Avalanche-Journal,* 6/4/1933.

Notes to Pages 178–193

37. Frank Capra, *The Name Above the Title,* MacMillan, 1971, p. 146.
38. MacMahon, 1959.
39. Letter from Aline to Clarence, 6/12/1933.
40. Letter from Aline to Clarence, 6/25/1932.
41. MacMahon, 1977.
42. "Aline MacMahon Inherits Stardom," *Brooklyn Daily Eagle,* 12/10/1933.
43. MacMahon, 1959.
44. Ibid.
45. Even in this private letter to her husband, Aline's Victorian sensibilities obliged her to write "Hell" as "H—L."
46. MacMahon, 1959.
47. Letter from Aline to Clarence, 7/3/1933.
48. Letter from Aline to Clarence, 7/14/1933.
49. *New York Times,* 11/26/1933.
50. Letter from Aline to Clarence, 7/20/1933.
51. MacMahon, 1977.
52. Letter from Aline to Clarence, 7/27/1933.

10. Seeds Of Freedom

1. "Warners Starting to Build Aline MacMahon," Hollywood Reporter, 02/27/1933.
2. Pressbook for *Side Streets,* Warner Brothers Publicity Department.
3. *Silver Screen* magazine, August 1932.
4. Magazine article, publication unknown (c. 1933), University of Wisconsin clipping file.
5. Jennie MacMahon, 1959.
6. Abbott, who lived to be 107, was then in the midst of a legendary career on Broadway, which included such iconic productions as *Chicago, Coquette, Twentieth Century, Room Service, Pal Joey, A Tree Grows in Brooklyn, Pajama Game, Damn Yankees,* and many others.
7. Blind 1933 magazine article, University of Wisconsin files.
8. Contract of Aline MacMahon with Warner Brothers, Inc, executed 9/9/1932.
9. Letter from Aline to Clarence, undated, likely 11/24/1933.
10. Letter from Aline to Clarence, 11/21/1933.
11. Although critically panned, in 1936 *Anthony Adverse* brought in nearly $3,000,000 for Warner Brothers, their biggest film of the year.
12. Letter from Aline to Clarence, 11/25/1933.
13. Letter from Aline to Clarence, 12/6/1933.
14. Mervyn LeRoy's son from his marriage to Doris Warner, Warner LeRoy, became a well-known businessman and restauranteur in New York City, and was the longtime owner of Tavern on the Green. A portion of 67th Street at Central Park West is named for him, just blocks from Aline's 64th Street apartment.
15. *Brooklyn Daily Eagle,* 3/8/1934.
16. *Brooklyn Daily Eagle,* 3/22/1934.

17. *New Movie* Magazine, June 1934.
18. Letter from Aline to Clarence, 11/30/1933.
19. Letter from Aline to Clarence, 12/2/1933.
20. Davis was just then being loaned to RKO for *Of Human Bondage*.
21. After protesting to Jack Warner about *Heat Lightning* and seeing that they would not make a change in its release date, Aline gave up and said, simply, "I can't do any more."
22. Mordaunt Hall, *New York Times*, 8/15/1934.
23. Warner Brother Archive clipping file on *Side Streets*, *New York Post*, date unknown.
24. Letter from Aline to Clarence, 2/5/1934.
25. Ibid.
26. Letter from Aline to Clarence, 2/5/1934 (PM). In this letter Aline referred to Orson Welles, "alas" as "effeminate."
27. Letter from Aline to Clarence, 2/21/1934.
28. Letter from Aline to Clarence, 2/11/1934.
29. Stein, Films in Review, 1965.
30. Pressbook for *Babbitt*, WB Publicity Department, 1934.
31. "What the Picture Did for Me," *Motion Picture Herald*, 9/29/1934.
32. Letter from Aline to Clarence, 2/23/1934.
33. Letter from Aline to Clarence, 3/1/1934.
34. Letter from Aline to Clarence, 2/28/1934.
35. Telegram from Aline to Jack Warner, 5/5/1934.
36. *Chicago Tribune*, 12/9/1934.
37. "Aline MacMahon One Player with No Competition," *Los Angeles Times*, 11/17/1934.
38. *Los Angeles Times*, 6/23/1933.
39. *Variety*, 2/14/1933.
40. "I wish he weren't such an S.O.B.," Aline wrote. "I will not sign any contract with him, you can be sure."
41. Memo from Hal Wallis to William Koenig, 7/17/1934.
42. Among the proposed changes to *Heat Lightning* was this request to protect the morals of the movie going public: "As a matter of both Code and censorship, we suggest changing the dialogue of the blonde asking the direction so as to indicate that she wants to wash up, and avoid any inference that she wants to go to the toilet." Memo from the Association of Motion Picture Producers to Jack Warner, 11/21/1933.
43. Letter from Aline to Clarence, 6/24/1934.
44. Letter from Aline to Clarence, 6/27/1934.
45. *Brooklyn Daily Eagle*, 11/23/1934.
46. Frederick Lewis Allen, *Since Yesterday*, Perennial Library, 1972, p.150.
47. Letter from Aline to Clarence, 6/23/1934.
48. Letter from Aline to Clarence, 6/27/1934.
49. Letter from Aline to Clarence, 8/31/1934.
50. Letter from Aline to Clarence, 7/17/1934.
51. *Los Angeles Times*, August 1934.

52. Letter from Aline to Clarence, 8/19/1934.
53. Letter to Aline MacMahon from Warner Brothers legal department, 8/15/1934.
54. MacMahon, 1959.
55. Letter from Aline to Clarence, 8/20/1934.
56. MacMahon, 1959.
57. Letter from Aline to Clarence, 8/29/1934. The picture Aline discussed with Arno does not appear to have been made, at least not with Stanwyck as the star.

11. One Way Passage

1. Maria Ouspenskaya's School of Dramatic Arts was headquartered at 27 W. 67th Street, just blocks from Aline's home on Central Park West.
2. Mel Gordon, *Stanislavsky in America*, Routledge, 2010.
3. Letter from Warner Brother legal department to Aline MacMahon, 9/22/1934.
4. Edwin Schallert, *Los Angeles Times*, 10/1/1934.
5. Letter from Aline to Clarence, 1/12/1935.
6. In mid-November Aline happened to meet Bella Muni at the Brown Derby, where she informed Aline that Warners had refused her husband's loan-out to MGM for *The Good Earth*.
7. Letter from Aline to Clarence.
8. Letter from Aline to Clarence, 12/4/1934.
9. Letter from Aline to Clarence, 12/1/1934.
10. Letter from Aline to Clarence, 12/14/1934.
11. Letter from Aline to Clarence, 1/14/1935.
12. Letter from Aline to Clarence, 1/15/1935.
13. Letter from Aline to Clarence, 2/9/1935 (AM).
14. Letter from Aline to Clarence, 2/9/1935 (PM).
15. Aline was later told by *Good Earth* screenwriter Marc Connolly that Thalberg actually "did not like the first test at all."
16. Letter from Aline to Clarence, 5/20/1935.
17. Letter from Aline to Clarence, 5/16/1935.
18. "What the Picture Did for Me," *Motion Picture Herald*, 8/24/1935.
19. Edwin Schallert, *Los Angeles Times*, 4/6/1935.
20. Letter from Roy Obringer to Aline MacMahon, 4/1935.
21. Letter to Roy Obringer from Aline MacMahon, April 1935, Warner Brothers Archives.
22. Letter to Jack Warner from Aline MacMahon, April 1935, Warner Brothers Archives.
23. Letter from Aline to Clarence, 10/30/1935.
24. Stein, 1965.
25. Letter from Aline to Clarence, 5/18/1935.
26. Letter from Aline to Clarence, 6/3/1935.
27. Letter from Aline to Clarence, 6/4/1935.
28. *Los Angeles Times*, 6/16/1935.
29. Letter from Aline to Clarence, 6/5/1935.

30. As if in proof, MGM tested the theory. "The picture was too long and they chopped me out," Aline complained to Clarence.
31. Letter from Aline to Clarence, 6/17/1935.
32. Letter from Clarence to Aline, 7/20/1935.
33. Hillside Homes is still standing today, now known as Eastchester Heights.
34. Letter from Aline to Clarence, 6/20/1935.
35. Letter from Aline to Clarence, 9/26/1935.
36. According to an MGM press release, Aline cobbled together her own costuming for *Ah, Wilderness!* from secondhand stores in Manhattan. "I stopped in several small towns but I couldn't find anything there. The stores there are full of gowns patterned after Joan Crawford and Myrna Loy!"
37. Letter from Aline to Clarence, 10/08/1935.
38. Letter from Aline to Clarence, 11/11/1935.
39. Letter from Aline to Clarence, 11/23/1935.
40. Letter from Aline to Clarence, 10/11/1935.
41. Letter from Aline to Clarence, 9/28/1935.
42. Letter from Clarence to Aline, 10/2/1935.
43. Letter from Aline to Clarence, 11/2/1935.
44. Letter from Aline to Clarence, 11/9/1935.
45. Letter from Aline to Clarence, 11/21/1935.
46. Parsons, *The Writings of Clarence S. Stein*, 1998.

12. The World Changes

1. MacMahon, 1977.
2. Letter from Aline to Clarence, 10/4/1936.
3. Letter from Aline to her mother, Jennie Mac, 3/12/1936.
4. Letter from Aline to Clarence, 6/29/1945—here, Aline is reminiscing to Clarence about their adventures in Asia nine years earlier.
5. Chaplin's trip with Goddard was worldwide news at the time, and it was speculated that the pair would marry while in Shanghai. Although it has never been firmly established, they allegedly did marry while in China, but slightly later, in Canton Province. Lin Yutan soon emigrated to the United States and continued his friendship with the Steins.
6. "Visit to China Aids Actress in Portrayal," *Los Angeles Times*, 8/22/1944.
7. MacMahon, 1977.
8. Ibid.
9. Letter from Aline to Clarence, 9/24/1936.
10. Letter from Aline to Clarence, 10/10/1936.
11. Letter from Aline to Clarence, 10/8/1936.
12. Letter from Aline to Clarence, 10/18/1936.
13. Letter from Aline to Clarence, 10/19/1936.
14. Letter from Aline to Clarence, 10/21/1936—the meeting took place on October 20, 1936.

15. "What the Picture Did for Me," *Motion Picture Herald*, 4/24/1937.
16. Letter from Clarence to Aline, 10/11/1936.
17. The project was eventually realized and is now part of New York's Museum of Modern Art.
18. Letter from Clarence to Aline, 4/11/1937.
19. "What the Picture Did for Me," *Motion Picture Herald*, 6/24/1939.
20. The *Chicago Tribune* reported that Aline "withdrew" from *Years*, 1/11/1937.
21. MacMahon, 1977.
22. Letter from Aline to Clarence, February 1938.
23. Letter from Aline to Clarence, 2/2/1938.
24. *Columbia Daily Spectator*, 9/29/1937.
25. *Columbia Daily Spectator*, 3/17/1938.
26. Norman Lloyd, *Stages of Life in the Theatre*, Limelight, 2004, p. 52.
27. Vincent Price, interviewed by Lawrence French, on Wellesnet.com, posted 5/28/08.
28. Attributed to Welles in David Thompson's *Dictionary of Film*, 2010. Sources differ as to whether this outburst came after the scuttling of *Five Kings* or *The Duchess of Malfi*.
29. Barbara Leaming, *Orson Welles: A Biography*, Viking Adult, 1985.
30. Geraldine Fitzgerald took the part as Hesione Hushabye in the 1938 production.
31. Letter from Aline to Clarence, 2/18/1938. With Welles's production of *Malfi* still uncertain, Aline toured with *The Ghost of Yankee Doodle*, a play produced by Agnes Morgan and Helen Arthur, which ended its run at the University of Michigan. The tour was a modest success, but Aline was unhappy with the quality of the staging.
32. *Counselor at Law* was broadcast January 16, 1939.
33. Letter from Aline to Clarence, 9/1/1939.
34. Letter from Aline to Clarence, circa 9/4/1939.
35. Letter from Aline to Clarence, 1/4/1937.
36. Although sources claim Stella Adler worked as an associate producer at MGM for six years, her only credit appears to be *DuBarry Was a Lady* (1943).
37. Letter from Aline to Clarence, 4/9/1940.
38. Letter from Aline to Clarence, 4/1/1940.
39. *Washington Evening Star*, 4/28/1940.
40. Clifford Odets, *The Time is Ripe*, Grove Press, 1989.
41. Unidentified newspaper clipping, circa 5/1940, University of Wisconsin clipping file.
42. Aline was announced as the lead in *Dawn in Lyonesse*.
43. Undated letter from Aline to Clarence, likely 2/11/1941.
44. Letter from Aline to Clarence, 6/1/1941.
45. Letter from Aline to Clarence, 3/10/1941.
46. Letter from Arthur Stein to Aline, 3/17/1941.
47. Memo from Henry Blanke to Hal Wallis, 2/7/1941, Warner Brothers Archives, USC.

48. Letter from Aline to Clarence, 2/13/1941.
49. *Film Daily,* undated clipping.
50. Letter from Aline to Clarence, 6/14/1941.
51. Letter from Aline to Clarence, 5/6/1941.
52. Clarence appears to have vetoed Aline's suggestion, citing costs and liabilities associated with sponsorship. At the time Aline was still between assignments and at a low ebb in her earning power, while Clarence was waiting for architectural commissions that were tenuous at best.
53. Letter from Clarence to Aline, 4/21/1942.
54. Letter from Clarence to Aline, 5/20/1941.
55. During WWII the American Theatre Wing opened Manhattan's Stage Door Canteen servicemen's club. In 1947 they also created, and still operate, the Tony Awards.
56. Letter from Aline to Clarence, 4/21/1942.
57. Letter from Aline to Clarence, 4/23/1942.
58. Letter from Aline to Clarence, 4/27/1942.
59. Letter from Aline to Clarence, 5/6/1942—Corregidor, an island guarding Manila Bay was taken from US forces by Japanese troops that day.
60. Letter from Aline to Clarence, 12/9/1943.
61. *The Writings of Clarence S. Stein,* John's Hopkins University Press, 1998, p. 400.
62. Douglas Gilbert, "Aline MacMahon Joins Stage to War Industries," *New York World Telegram,* 10/20/1942.
63. Helen Ormsbee, "Long Absent, Back to Stage Comes Aline MacMahon," University of Wisconsin clipping file, newspaper unknown, circa 10/1942.
64. Gilbert, 1942.
65. "She Hopes for Bard Roles," unidentified newspaper article, circa 10/1942, University of Wisconsin clipping file.
66. Burns Mantle, "Eve of St. Mark Broadway's Best to Date," *Chicago Tribune,* 10/18/1942.
67. "'Lunch Time Follies' Entertains War Workers," *New York Herald,* 1/17/1943.
68. Mantle, 1942.
69. Lawrence Greene, "Versatile Aline MacMahon," *Silhouette Magazine,* circa November 1942.
70. Letter from Aline to Clarence, 2/20/1943.
71. Unlike most Broadway shows, which produce no road companies until after a long run in New York, *The Eve of St. Mark* opened nearly simultaneously in twenty theaters across the country.
72. Greene, 1942.

13. We Fight It Round By Round

1. Not the Robert Reed of *The Brady Bunch* and *The Defenders.*
2. Federal Bureau of Investigation declassified file on Aline MacMahon, FOIPA #1321270-0.

3. Letter from Aline to Clarence, 6/4/1941. Among Aline's other political advocacy was a suggestion that her young cousin Jimmie read a book called *The Soviet Power*. A trained pilot about to be drafted into the war, Jimmie took one look at the title and exclaimed: "Oh no! I'm just at the impressionable age!"

4. FBI file of Aline MacMahon, p. 11. When the Dies Committee seized files of the Communist Party in Philadelphia, they found records indicating that the LWS was sponsored by the Soviets. Although the FBI claimed that Aline had organized the League with Aline Hays Davis, there appears to be no corroborating evidence to support the idea.

5. Other signers included Groucho Marx, Myrna Loy, Joan Crawford, Rosalind Russell, and Henry Fonda.

6. "To All Active Supporters of Democracy and Peace," text of open letter appearing in *Soviet Russia Today*, September 1939.

7. After the war many signers of this letter were investigated, blacklisted, or imprisoned by the US Government, including Langston Hughes, Lionel Stander, Sam Jaffee, and Dashiell Hammett.

8. Although the official name of the Congressional investigating body was The House Committee on Un-American Activities, it soon became popularly known by the unofficial but easier to remember acronym HUAC (House Un-American Activities Committee).

9. "Jaffee Seeking to Drive Equity into Red Ranks," *Chicago Tribune*, 10/30/1945.

10. *Los Angeles Times*, 8/22/1944.

11. Letter from Aline to Clarence, 11/8/1943.

12. Letter from Aline to Clarence, 12/8/1943.

13. Letter from Aline to Clarence, 1/9/1944.

14. Letter from Aline to Clarence, 7/10/1944.

15. Letter from Aline to Clarence, 4/17/1944.

16. Letter from Aline to Clarence, 5/21/1944.

17. Letter from Aline to Clarence, 6/1/1944.

18. Letter from Aline to Clarence, 6/26/1944—Aline was making $2,000 a week on *Guest in the House*, which limped on through August.

19. Letter from Clarence to Aline, 7/29/1945.

20. Letter from Aline to Clarence, 7/7/1945 During the era of his periodic breakdowns, Clarence had a total of seven years of nursing care, which was largely paid for by the Steins themselves.

21. Letter from Aline to Clarence, 8/9/1945.

22. Letter from Aline to Clarence, 5/21/1945.

23. *My Indian Family* was successfully tested at Stanford in the summer of 1945 with Aline in a lead role. Unfortunately, she did not find backers for a full-scale Broadway production. The Stanford production did result in one other memorable event. A young actor named Jack Palance read for Aline and was given his first significant stage role. "After the play she wrote several letters to people about me," Palance recalled. "That started my career."

24. Telegram from Aline to Equity Council, 12/12/1945—Fay, widely known as an anti-Semite, was also brought up on changes for vulgar language directed at Philip Loeb, who was later blacklisted and committed suicide as a result.

25. Margo was the stage name of Mexican actress Maria Maguerita Guadalupe Teresa Estela Bolado Castilla y O'Donnell. She and her husband Eddie Albert were both blacklisted during the Red Scare era.

26. Letter from Aline to Clarence, 2/3/1946. "It's a good play—and a good part—and a good cause," she said of *On Whitman Avenue*, lamenting the necessity to opt out.

27. Letter from Aline to Clarence, 1/8/1946. Aline was teaching classes at the Lab while preparing her directorial debut, a production of *The Shewing Up of Blanco Posnet*, which she knew from the 1923 Neighborhood Playhouse production.

28. Smith was a right-wing clergyman and demagogue who made three independent runs for President under his own America First Party. In his 1956 campaign Smith received a grand total of eight (yes, *eight*) votes.

29. Aline was confused about the correspondence. Schweizer was the *writer* of *The Search*, not its producer.

30. Letter from Aline to Clarence, 5/10/1947.

31. Aline had recently been paid $3,250 a week by David O. Selznick to NOT appear as Mrs. Spinney in *Portrait of Jennie*, after he changed his mind and instead cast Ethyl Barrymore in the role. Letter of 5/10/1947.

32. MacMahon, 1977.

33. Aline MacMahon, "On Location," *The Christian Science Monitor*, 7/26/1948.

34. Letter from Aline to Clarence, 7/5/1947 written en route to Europe on the *M. S. Gripsholm*

35. Letter from Aline to Clarence, 7/25/1947.

36. Letter from Aline to Clarence, 7/30/1947.

37. Letter from Aline to Clarence, 8/17/1947.

38. Letter from Aline to Clarence, 7/30/1947.

39. Letter from Aline to Clarence, 8/29/1947.

40. Letter from Aline to Clarence, 8/19/1947.

41. Letter from Aline to Clarence, 8/24/1947.

42. Telegram to producer Robert Whitehead, 08/29/1947.

43. In 1959 Aline and Judith Anderson recreated their performances from the 1947–48 production of *Medea* for the syndicated TV series *Play of the Week*.

44. Letter from Aline to Clarence, 12/28/1948.

45. MacMahon, 1977.

46. At Stanford that summer she appeared in *L'Arlesienne* and *The Rivals* with Whitford Kane and Theo Marcuse. She tried to interest Fred Zinneman in taking *L'Arlesienne* to Broadway, to no avail.

47. Ben Hecht was brought in to salvage the second half of *Roseanna McCoy's* embattled script. Hecht promptly wrote Sarie McCoy out of the story, and Aline was suddenly no longer needed.

48. Letter from Aline to Clarence, 9/7/1948.

49. A. Scott Berg, *Goldwyn: A Biography*, Knopf, 1989.

50. Aline had apparently forgotten about playing Titania in Boleslavsky's 1930 version of *A Midsummer Night's Dream*.
51. *Kingsport News*, 8/2/1949.
52. Charlotte M. Canning, *On the Performance Front: US Theatre and Internationalism*, Palgrave MacMillan, 2015, p. 149. Quote attributed to Richard Coe.
53. MacMahon, 1977. In the *Hamlet* company (as Guildenstern) was a young actor just beginning his career, Ernest Borgnine.
54. Letter from Aline to Clarence, 10/12/1949.
55. Letter from Aline to Clarence, 10/21/1949.
56. Letter from Aline to Clarence, 1/18/1949.

14. Ah, Wilderness

1. *Red Channels,* American Business Consultants, June 1950.
2. Among the jobs Aline missed out on as the result of the blacklist were *The Story of Ruth* and *The Madwoman of Chaillot* [in Washington, D.C.].
3. MacMahon, 1977.
4. Ibid.
5. Ibid.
6. Joan Crosby, "Actress Would Rather have Live Atmosphere," *Fort Lauderdale News*, 12/21/1963.
7. Letter from Aline to Clarence, 11/17/1949.
8. Declassified FBI file of Aline MacMahon, report dated 6/11/1956, p. 3.
9. Clarence's work on Kitimat, which wore on through the mid-1950s, was a constant source of anxiety for both he and Aline.
10. FBI file, 11/29/1955.
11. MacMahon, 1977.
12. Letter dated 3/8/1952, files of the Passport Office, Department of State.
13. Letter from Aline to Clarence, 2/10/1953.
14. Letter from Aline to Columbia Pictures Corp., 8/25/1954.
15. Letter from Aline to Clarence, 9/7/1954.
16. Mr. J. Raymond Bell soon became a vice president in the Columbia Pictures Corporation.
17. *North Adams Transcript*, 7/21/1951.
18. Edwin Schallert, *Los Angeles Times*, 3/29/1951.
19. MacMahon, 1977.
20. MacMahon, 1977.
21. Brooks Atkinson, *New York Times*, circa 9/30/1957.
22. Claudia Cassidy, "On the Aisle," *Chicago Tribune*, 6/18/1957.
23. Aline spent fourteen weeks in Lenox Hill Hospital during the spring of 1971 with a fractured leg.
24. Letter from Aline to Clarence, 1/27/1953.
25. Harvey Pack, "Aline MacMahon Selects Roles," White Plains *Reporter-Dispatch*, 12/20/1963.

26. "Festival Activity Familiar Assignment," *The Hartford Times*, 6/24/1959.
27. *Stratford Shakespeare quarterly*, Fall 1959, p. 573.
28. Ibid.
29. Allen M. Widem, "Don't Call Stars—Let 'Em Call You," *The Hartford Times*, 3/30/1965.
30. Aline met Philip Loeb at the Theatre Guild in the 1920's and they served together on the board of Actor's Equity. In 1955, depressed over his inability to get work, Loeb committed suicide.
31. Letter from Aline to Clarence, 11/23/1959.
32. *This is America*, series proposal, circa 1960, Cornell Division of Rare and Manuscript Collections.
33. CBS executives reprimanded Sullivan for plugging *All the Way Home* on the air. Sullivan was unapologetic and repeated his praise the following night.
34. Cecil Smith, "The Doomed Play That Wouldn't Die," *Los Angeles Times*, 5/21/1961.
35. Thomas R. Dash, "'All the Way Home,' Trip of Sad and Somber Beauty," unidentified newspaper clipping, N. Y. Public Library.
36. After two weeks of rehearsals, producer David Susskind took the company on location to Tennessee, spending fourteen weeks deconstructing and reinterpreting what had been reliably delivered to audiences in just two hours every night. The overwork seemed to have sapped *ATWH* of the spontaneous charm of the stage.
37. Crosby, 1963.

15. Set My Feet On the Way

1. Letter from Aline to Clarence, 6/23/1969.
2. Letter from Aline to Clarence, 10/22/1962
3. Letter from Clarence Stein to Yngve Larsson, 2/3/1961.
4. Allen M. Widem, "Don't Call Stars—Let 'Em Call you," *Hartford Times*, 3/30/1965.
5. Cecil Smith, "All the Land's a Stage for Shakespearean Summer," *Los Angeles Times*, 6/13/1965.
6. Widem, 1965.
7. Walter Kerr, "A Theater That's Unfair," *Chicago Tribune*, 5/5/1968.
8. *Woman's Wear Daily*, 3/1/1968.
9. The Forum is now known as the Mitzi Newhouse Theatre.
10. Walter Kerr, "Unreal Hippies: A Real Actress," *Chicago Tribune*, 11/19/1967.
11. In a FBI memo of 9/18/1964, John Dwyer, doorman of the Steins' building on Central Park West and "confidential informant" for the bureau, reported that Clarence "does not have complete control of his mental faculties."
12. Wolf Von Eckardt, "Architect Left Humanist Monuments," *Los Angeles Times*, 12/9/1976.
13. Douglas Haskell, Undated letter, circa 3/1975, Archives of Clarence Stein, Cornell University.
14. MacMahon, 1977.

15. Ibid. *The Shadow Box* opened on Broadway in 1977 and won the Tony Award for Best Play and the Pulitzer Prize for drama.
16. MacMahon, 1977.
17. Clive Barnes, *New York Times,* 10/16/1975.
18. Sylviane Gold, "At 76, Acting is Still Aline's Passion," *New York Post,* 10/14/1975.
19. MacMahon, 1977.
20. Ibid.
21. Ibid.
22. Letter from Aline to members of the Little Theater, 1/31/1984.
23. Letter from Aline to Clarence, 1/19/1931.
24. Ibid.
25. Carol Cooke, Memorandum to file, held in the Clarence Stein Papers, Cornell University, 2/28/1984.
26. Bernard Drew, "You Can't Go Home Again, But You Can Glance Back," *The Herald Statesman,* 8/14/1973.

SELECTED BIBLIOGRAPHY

Allen, Frederick L. *Since Yesterday: The 1930's in America*. New York, Evanston, San Francisco, London: Perennial Library, 1972.

Churchill, Allen. *The Theatrical 20's*. New York, St. Louis, San Francisco: McGraw-Hill, 1975.

Crowley, Alice L. *The Neighborhood Playhouse: Leaves from a Theatre Scrapbook*. New York: Theatre Arts Books, 2018.

Curtain, Kaier. "Sappho in Overalls: 'Winter Bound,' Compared to 'The Captive' and 'The Well of Loneliness,' Opened and Closed in 1929." San Francisco: *Bay Area Reporter*, 10/29/1987.

Gordon, Mel. *Stanislavsky in America: An Actor's Workbook*. London, New York: Routledge/ Taylor and Francis Group, 2010.

Harrington, John P. *The Life of the Neighborhood Playhouse*. Syracuse: Syracuse University Press, 2007.

Hart, Moss. *Act One: An Autobiography*. New York: Random House, 1959.

Larsen, Kristin E. *Community Architect: The Life and Vision of Clarence S. Stein*. Ithaca: Cornell University Press, 2016.

MacMahon, Aline L. Surveillance file assembled by the Federal Bureau of Investigation, c. 1949–1964. FOIPA: 1321270-0, Unclassified.

MacMahon, Aline L. Letters held in the Rare and Manuscript Collections of Cornell University, Ithaca, NY. 1931–1973.

MacMahon, Aline L. Interview for the American Jewish Committee Oral History Collection, New York Public Library, 1959.

MacMahon, Aline L. Interview for the American Jewish Committee Oral History Collection, New York Public Library, 1977.

MacMahon, Jennie. Interview for the American Jewish Committee Oral History Collection, New York Public Library, 1978.

Stein, Clarence S. Surveillance file assembled by the Federal Bureau of Investigation, c. 1949–1964. FOIPA: 1321279, Unclassified.

Stein, Clarence S. Letters held in the Rare and Manuscript Collections of Cornell University, Ithaca, NY. 1931–1973.

Selected Bibliography

Stein, Clarence S. *The Writings of Clarence Stein*. Edited by Kermit Parsons. Baltimore: Johns Hopkins University Press, 1998.

Stein, Jeanne. "Aline MacMahon: Had the Wit to Sense What Audiences Liked Her to Project." Phillipsburg: *Films in Review,* December 1965.

INDEX

Page numbers in italics *refer to photographs.*

Actor's Laboratory Theatre, 267
Adler, Stella, 52, 116, 133, 211, 245
Ah Wilderness! (film), 223–24
All in the Family (TV series), 303
All the Way Home (film), 294, 297
All the Way Home (play), 293–95
American Laboratory Theatre, 50, 52–58, 60, 115–17
Arthur, Helen, 44–45, 48, 53–55, 57, 66, 77–79, 81–82, 84–85, 88–97, 103, 168
Artists and Models (revue), 67–68, *69*, 71, 167, 300
Astor, Mary, 123, 180, 181

Babbitt (film), 208–10, 214, 226
Baclanova, Olga, 133–34
Bainter, Faye, 219
Barrymore, Lionel, 223
Beery, Wallace, 224, 266
Berkeley, Busby, 164
Bernstein, Aline, 4, 44, 66, 83, 212–13, 220–21, 239, 305
Beyond the Horizon (play), 70–71, *72*, 73, 103, 121, 159, 173
Big Hearted Herbert (film), 203, 205–8
Blondell, Joan, 1, 164, *165*, 174
Boleslavsky, Richard, 52–57, 59–62, 65–66, 74, 115–17, 134, 211, 244, 273, 276, 281
Brando, Marlon, 3–4, 54, 133, 135, 281, 306
Breen, Robert, 247, 274
Brown, Clarence, 223–24
Buck, Pearl S., 212, 261, 262, 265

Cagney, James, 1, 132, 159, 179, 207, 218
Carroll, Albert, 45, 48
Chaplin, Charlie, 233
Clift, Montgomery, 3, 135, 267, 271–73, 281
Clurman, Harold, 52, 116, 211
Cobb, Lee J., 244, 260
Communism, 4, 50, 157, 159, 226, 266, 274–75, 277–78, 297
Cornell, Katherine, 197–98, 241
Coward, Noel, 73
Crawford, Joan, 126, 146, 219–20, 228
Cummings, E.E., 4, 70
Curtiz, Michael, 162–63, 209, 222

Davis, Bette, 52, 162, 195, 203, 218–19
Daylight Saving (play), 99, 115
Defenders, The (TV series), 294, 296
Dickinson, Thomas, 103–5
Dixon, Jean, 115, 120–21, 130, 137, 139, 149, 159, 188
Dodsworth (film), 114, 181, 211, 218
Dragon Seed (film), 261–62
Dressler, Marie, 153, 186–88, 219
Duchess of Malfi, The (play), 241–42
Dvorak, Ann, 191

Erasmus Hall (school), 23, 25–27
Ethical Culture movement, 47, 117
Eve of St. Mark, The (play), 255–57, 261

Fazenda, Louise, 152
Federal Bureau of Investigation (FBI): surveillance of Aline MacMahon and Clarence Stein, 4, 258–60, 278, 280, 297

Index

Five Star Final (film), 1, 3, 127, 130–32, 134–37, 243, 306
Flame and the Arrow, The (film), 275–77, 280–81
Foster, Preston, 191
Fox, Sydney, 151–53

Garfield, John, 3–4, 54, 245–48, 250, 267, 281
Gold Diggers of 1933 (film), 2, 163–68, 169, 174–78, 180, 189, 199, 219
Good Earth, The (film), 212, 215–16, 223, 225, 229, 231, 235, 261–62, 306
Grand Street Follies, 47–48, 62–67, 71, 73
Grapes of Wrath, The (film), 243–44
Grauman, Sid, 117, 119–21, 123, 125–26
Green, Alfred, 172, 195, 209
Group Theatre, 211, 244, 276

Hampden, Walter, 34
Harris, Jed, 74
Harris, Sam, 108–13, 115, 119
Hart, Moss, 4, 108–15, 119–21, 123, 126, 151, 194–95, 199, 202, 222–23, 252–54, 265, 305
Hayes Code (censorship), 98
Heart of New York, The (film), 148–49
Heat Lightning (film), 188–93, 195–96, 205
Heavenly Express (play), 245–48
Henry Street Settlement (the Settlement), 43
Heroes for Sale (film), 170–74, 185
House Committee on Un-American Activities (HUAC), 260, 266–67, 279
Huston, Walter, 126, 211, 261, 262

Kaufman, George, 4, 74, 101, 108–15, 119–20, 151, 195, 199, 202, 254
Keeler, Ruby, 164
Kibbee, Guy, *165*, 167–68, 179, 184, 199, 201, 203–4, 206–8, 212, 214–15, 217–18, 237, 252
Kind Lady (film), 99, 222, 224–25, 227–29

Lancaster, Burt, 275–77
Latham, Minor, 29–30, 34, *36*, 37
Laveen, Rose (Aline's paternal grandmother), 11–12

LeMaire, Rufus, 128–29, 148, 204
LeRoy, Mervyn, 122, 125, 127–28, 140, 146, 163, 167–68, 170, 172, 175, 178, 182, 189–92, 209, 305
Lewis, Sinclair, 208, 211, 226, 311
Lewisohn, Alice, 42–44, 46–48, 53–54, 57, 60, 61, 66
Lewisohn, Irene, 43–44, 48, 54, 57, 66, 239
Life of Jimmy Dolan, The (film), 159–62, 182
Light, James, 34, 36, 40, 44, 70–71, 104–5
Little Theatre movement, 43–44, 48, 54, 62, 96
Loeb, Philip, 260
Loeb, Sophie Irene (nee Simon), 4, 8–12, 22, 26–27, 38, 40, 100–101, 306

MacGowan, Kenneth, 70–71, 159, 199, 216, 222, 225–26, 305
MacKaye, Benton, 47, 157, 168
MacMahon, Aline: on children, 145, 153–54, 166–67, 183; college education, 28–39, 288, 299; Communism and, 4, 27, 45, 100, 103, 106–8, 170, 181, 207, 226–27, 237, 247–48, 252, 258–61, 265–67, 278–87, 291; death of, 306–7; elocution career, 15, 16–17, *18*; 19–23, 24; Method acting and, 105, 112, 115, 133–35, 137, 144, 157–58, 282, 289, 296, 306–7;; performing Shakespeare; 26, 34, 74, 115, 273–75, 288–89, 298
MacMahon, Jenny (Aline's mother), 6, 7, 8–11, *13*, 14, 16, 19, 27, 100, 138–39, 142, 166, 188, 194–95, 253, 266, 294, 302–5
MacMahon, John (Aline's paternal grandfather), 11
MacMahon, William Marcus (Aline's father), 12, *13*, 14–17, 19, 27–28; death, 137–38, 194
Madras House, The (play), 45–47, 83
Madwoman of Chaillot, The (play), 285
Mary Jane's Pa (film), 214–15, 217
Maya (play), 77–98, 104–5, 121, 173
McCarthyism (political movement), 277–78, 280, 285, 288, 290–91, 297
McKeesport, PA, 8, *10*, 11–12, 14, 148, 194, 246

338

Index

Medea (play), 271, 289, *290*
Merry Frinks, The (film), 201–3
Method, the (the Stanislavsky Method), 2–4, 27, 50–52, 54, 115–17, 133–34, 211; 245–46, 267, 276, 281–82; American debut of, 57–61
Metro-Goldwyn-Mayer (MGM), 117, 126, 130, 146, 164, 186, 190–91, 204, 212, 214–16, 219–20, 222–29, 252, 268
Mizner, Wilson, 171–72
Moore, Grace, 235–37
Morgan, Agnes, 44, 48, 53, 57, 66, 77, 83, 103, 158, 216
Morgenthau, Rita, 36, 42–43
Moscow Art Theatre, 50–54, 116, 133–34
Mourning Becomes Electra (play), 137–38, 140, 149, 204, 244
Mouthpiece, The (film), 140–43, 146–47, 152, 243
Mumford, Lewis, 46
Muni, Paul, 179–81, 204, 212, 262

Neighborhood Playhouse, 36, 42–49, 53, 57–66, 68, 83, 96, 103, 115, 162, 212–13, 246, 299
Noguchi, Isamu, 4, 200

Obringer, Roy, 155, 217
O'Casey, Sean, 222, 286–87
Once in a Lifetime (film), 2, 146–47, 148–54, 156, 211, 219, 252, 254
Once in a Lifetime (play), 1, 3, 108–15, 117, 119–30, 137, 159
O'Neill, Eugene, 4, 34, 70–73, 103, 137, 139, 153, 188, 223, 305
One Way Passage (film), 147–50, 162
Orsatti, Frank (Orsatti Talent Agency), 154–56, 205, 212, 235, 240, 244, 250, 253
Ouspenskaya, Maria, 3, 5, 54, 116–17, 179, 211, 218, 276
Out of the Fog (film), 247–50

Pitts, Zasu, 111, 152, 185, 218–19, 252, 253
Player Queen, The (play), 58, 59–61, 63
pre-Code era, 2, 131, 142, 144, 146, 171–72, 174, 191, 193, 206

Provincetown Players (theatrical troupe), 34, 40, 44, 70, 96–97, 103, 106

Rathbone, Basil, 80, 197, 225–26, 228
Red Channels (book), 278–81, 283–84, 288
Repertory Theatre of Lincoln Center, 296, 298–301, 303
Robinson, Edward G., 1, 3, 127, 131, 135, 154, 157–58, 262
Rogers, Ginger, 1, 175, 190
Romeo and Juliet (play), 288–89

Search, The (film), 267–74
Selwyn, Edgar, 40, 48
Shubert Theatrical Agency (brothers Lee and J.J.), 55, 65–71, 73, 81–82, 84, 88, 90, 93–95, 97, 208
Side Streets (film), 195–98
Silver Dollar (film), 157–58, 306
Simon, Sam (a.k.a Sam Shimon, Aline's maternal grandfather), 6–9
Simon, Sylvan, 195, 252
Stanislavski, Konstantin, 2–3, 50–56, 59, 116, 133–34
Stein, Clarence Samuel, 1–2, 33, 40, *41*, 42, 46–47, 49, 68, 70, 74, 83–84, 96, 98–99, 105–8, 117, 119–20, 124–25, 127–28, 135–36, 138, 147, 149, 163, 166–69, 174, 183, 207, 213, 220–22, 284, 302; Communism/politics and, 150, 157, 159, 227, 248; 253, 258, 288, 297–98, 305; death of, 300–302; health troubles, 122, 153, 221, 237–40, 250, 254, 263–65; professional career, 145, 154, 161, 193–94, 237–38, 250
Stein, Gertrude (Clarence's sister), 33, 40, 42, 46
Strasberg, Lee, 3, 52, 54, 116, 179, 211
Streep, Meryl, 5, 303
Streetcar Named Desire, A, 3, 281
Strickland, Cowles, 102, 114, 265

Talbot, Lyle, 192
Thalberg, Irving, 212, 216, 223, 231, 261
Theatre Guild, 44, 137, 204, 211
This Fine-Pretty World (play), 61–62, 66
Tone, Franchot, 52, 211, 244
Tracy, Spencer, 52, 132

Index

travel (Aline and Clarence Stein): around the world, 229-30; in China, 4, 23, 229-35, 261-62; in Europe, 99, 136, 288; in India, 23, 105-7; in post-war Europe (Aline), 268-70, 272-74; in Switzerland, 23

Trelawny of the Wells (play), 32, 35, 302-3

Wald, Lillian, 43-45, 103
Wales Padlock Act, 80, 84, 90, 94, 97-98, 106
Wallis, Hal, 180, 205, 208, 209
Warner Brothers, 1, 121-22, 126-29, 134-35, 140, 143-50, 152, 154-71, 172-83, 185, 187-92, 195-99, 200-205, 207-9, 212-14, 216-20, 225-26, 228, 237, 243, 245, 247-50, 252, 275, 283-84, 299, 306

Warner Brothers v. MacMahon (lawsuit), 176-78
Welles, Orson, 197, 241-43
Wellman, William, 171-73, 209-10
While the Patient Slept (film), 212-14, 217
William, Warren, 128, 141-42, 146, 152, 165, 174, 176, 178
Winter Bound (play), 103-6
Wolfe, Thomas, 44, 83, 213, 220
World Changes, The (film), 179-83, 188, 190

Young, Loretta, 144, 161, 173, 236

Zanuck, Daryl, 123, 163, 170-71, 174, 177-78, 222, 226, 244
Zinneman, Fred, 268, 271-73

Screen Classics

Screen Classics is a series of critical biographies, film histories, and analytical studies focusing on neglected filmmakers and important screen artists and subjects, from the era of silent cinema through the golden age of Hollywood to the international generation of today. Books in the Screen Classics series are intended for scholars and general readers alike. The contributing authors are established figures in their respective fields. This series also serves the purpose of advancing scholarship on film personalities and themes with ties to Kentucky.

Series Editor
Patrick McGilligan

Books in the Series

Olivia de Havilland: Lady Triumphant
    Victoria Amador
Mae Murray: The Girl with the Bee-Stung Lips
    Michael G. Ankerich
Harry Dean Stanton: Hollywood's Zen Rebel
    Joseph B. Atkins
Hedy Lamarr: The Most Beautiful Woman in Film
    Ruth Barton
Rex Ingram: Visionary Director of the Silent Screen
    Ruth Barton
Conversations with Classic Film Stars: Interviews from Hollywood's Golden Era
    James Bawden and Ron Miller
Conversations with Legendary Television Stars: Interviews from the First Fifty Years
    James Bawden and Ron Miller
You Ain't Heard Nothin' Yet: Interviews with Stars from Hollywood's Golden Era
    James Bawden and Ron Miller
Charles Boyer: The French Lover
    John Baxter
Von Sternberg
    John Baxter
Hitchcock's Partner in Suspense: The Life of Screenwriter Charles Bennett
    Charles Bennett, edited by John Charles Bennett
Hitchcock and the Censors
    John Billheimer
A Uniquely American Epic: Intimacy and Action, Tenderness and Violence in Sam Peckinpah's The Wild Bunch
    Edited by Michael Bliss

My Life in Focus: A Photographer's Journey with Elizabeth Taylor and the Hollywood Jet Set
    Gianni Bozzacchi with Joey Tayler
Hollywood Divided: The 1950 Screen Directors Guild Meeting and the Impact of the Blacklist
    Kevin Brianton
He's Got Rhythm: The Life and Career of Gene Kelly
    Cynthia Brideson and Sara Brideson
Ziegfeld and His Follies: A Biography of Broadway's Greatest Producer
    Cynthia Brideson and Sara Brideson
The Marxist and the Movies: A Biography of Paul Jarrico
    Larry Ceplair
Dalton Trumbo: Blacklisted Hollywood Radical
    Larry Ceplair and Christopher Trumbo
Warren Oates: A Wild Life
    Susan Compo
Improvising Out Loud: My Life Teaching Hollywood How to Act
    Jeff Corey with Emily Corey
Crane: Sex, Celebrity, and My Father's Unsolved Murder
    Robert Crane and Christopher Fryer
Jack Nicholson: The Early Years
    Robert Crane and Christopher Fryer
Anne Bancroft: A Life
    Douglass K. Daniel
Being Hal Ashby: Life of a Hollywood Rebel
    Nick Dawson
Bruce Dern: A Memoir
    Bruce Dern with Christopher Fryer and Robert Crane
Intrepid Laughter: Preston Sturges and the Movies
    Andrew Dickos
Miriam Hopkins: Life and Films of a Hollywood Rebel
    Allan R. Ellenberger
Vitagraph: America's First Great Motion Picture Studio
    Andrew A. Erish
Jayne Mansfield: The Girl Couldn't Help It
    Eve Golden
John Gilbert: The Last of the Silent Film Stars
    Eve Golden
Stuntwomen: The Untold Hollywood Story
    Mollie Gregory
Jean Gabin: The Actor Who Was France
    Joseph Harriss
Otto Preminger: The Man Who Would Be King, updated edition
    Foster Hirsch
Saul Bass: Anatomy of Film Design
    Jan-Christopher Horak
Lawrence Tierney: Hollywood's Real-Life Tough Guy
    Burt Kearns
Hitchcock Lost and Found: The Forgotten Films
    Alain Kerzoncuf and Charles Barr
Pola Negri: Hollywood's First Femme Fatale
    Mariusz Kotowski
Ernest Lehman: The Sweet Smell of Success
    Jon Krampner

Sidney J. Furie: Life and Films
    Daniel Kremer
Albert Capellani: Pioneer of the Silent Screen
    Christine Leteux
A Front Row Seat
    Nancy Olson Livingston
Ridley Scott: A Biography
    Vincent LoBrutto
Mamoulian: Life on Stage and Screen
    David Luhrssen
Maureen O'Hara: The Biography
    Aubrey Malone
My Life as a Mankiewicz: An Insider's Journey through Hollywood
    Tom Mankiewicz and Robert Crane
Hawks on Hawks
    Joseph McBride
Showman of the Screen: Joseph E. Levine and His Revolutions in Film Promotion
    A. T. McKenna
William Wyler: The Life and Films of Hollywood's Most Celebrated Director
    Gabriel Miller
Raoul Walsh: The True Adventures of Hollywood's Legendary Director
    Marilyn Ann Moss
Veit Harlan: The Life and Work of a Nazi Filmmaker
    Frank Noack
Harry Langdon: King of Silent Comedy
    Gabriella Oldham and Mabel Langdon
Charles Walters: The Director Who Made Hollywood Dance
    Brent Phillips
Some Like It Wilder: The Life and Controversial Films of Billy Wilder
    Gene D. Phillips
Ann Dvorak: Hollywood's Forgotten Rebel
    Christina Rice
Mean . . . Moody . . . Magnificent! Jane Russell and the Marketing of a Hollywood Legend
    Christina Rice
Fay Wray and Robert Riskin: A Hollywood Memoir
    Victoria Riskin
Lewis Milestone: Life and Films
    Harlow Robinson
Michael Curtiz: A Life in Film
    Alan K. Rode
Ryan's Daughter: The Making of an Irish Epic
    Paul Benedict Rowan
Arthur Penn: American Director
    Nat Segaloff
Film's First Family: The Untold Story of the Costellos
    Terry Chester Shulman
Claude Rains: An Actor's Voice
    David J. Skal with Jessica Rains
Barbara La Marr: The Girl Who Was Too Beautiful for Hollywood
    Sherri Snyder
Buzz: The Life and Art of Busby Berkeley
    Jeffrey Spivak

Victor Fleming: An American Movie Master
    Michael Sragow
Aline MacMahon: Hollywood, the Blacklist, and the Birth of Method Acting
    John Stangeland
My Place in the Sun: Life in the Golden Age of Hollywood and Washington
    George Stevens, Jr.
Hollywood Presents Jules Verne: The Father of Science Fiction on Screen
    Brian Taves
Thomas Ince: Hollywood's Independent Pioneer
    Brian Taves
Picturing Peter Bogdanovich: My Conversations with the New Hollywood Director
    Peter Tonguette
Carl Theodor Dreyer and Ordet: *My Summer with the Danish Filmmaker*
    Jan Wahl
Wild Bill Wellman: Hollywood Rebel
    William Wellman Jr.
Clarence Brown: Hollywood's Forgotten Master
    Gwenda Young
The Queen of Technicolor: Maria Montez in Hollywood
    Tom Zimmerman